MW01493757

THE COLLEGE PRESS NIV COMMENTARY

JOHN

THE
COLLEGE
PRESS
NIV
COMMENTARY

JOHN

BEAUFORD H. BRYANT
&
MARK S. KRAUSE

New Testament Series Co-Editors:

Jack Cottrell, Ph.D.
Cincinnati Bible Seminary

Tony Ash, Ph.D.
Abilene Christian University

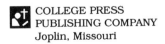
COLLEGE PRESS
PUBLISHING COMPANY
Joplin, Missouri

Library of Congress Cataloging-in-Publication Data
Bryant, Beauford H. (Beauford Harding), 1923–1997.
    John / Beauford H. Bryant & Mark S. Krause.
      p.   cm. — (The College Press NIV commentary)
    Includes bibliographical references (p.   ).
    ISBN 0-89900-631-0 (hard cover: alk. paper).
    1. Bible. N.T. John—Commentaries. I. Krause, Mark S. (Mark
Stephen), 1955–   . II. Series.
BS2615.3.B76 1998
226.5'077—dc21

                                                        98-33931
                                                          CIP

A WORD
FROM THE PUBLISHER

Years ago a movement was begun with the dream of uniting all Christians on the basis of a common purpose (world evangelism) under a common authority (the Word of God). The College Press NIV Commentary Series is a serious effort to join the scholarship of two branches of this unity movement so as to speak with one voice concerning the Word of God. Our desire is to provide a resource for your study of the New Testament that will benefit you whether you are preparing a Bible School lesson, a sermon, a college course, or your own personal devotions. Today as we survey the wreckage of a broken world, we must turn again to the Lord and his Word, unite under his banner and communicate the life-giving message to those who are in desperate need. This is our purpose.

DEDICATION

To Dorothy Bryant and Susan Krause, two strong women whom God provided for two men who would have been lost without their support and encouragement.

Λέγει Ἰησοῦς ἐὰν μὴ νηστεύσητε τὸν κόσμον,
οὐ μὴ εὕρητε τὴν βασιλείαν τοῦ θεοῦ.

[Jesus said, "If you do not fast from the world,
you will never, ever find the kingdom of God."]
P Oxy I.1

PREFACE

This commentary is the result of the work of a number of individuals. Several years ago, College Press engaged the services of Dr. Beauford Bryant to write the John commentary for a new series based on the New International Version. Dr. Bryant was a well-known scholar and preacher in the Christian Churches and the Churches of Christ. He taught for many years at Milligan College and was one of the founding professors of Emmanuel School of Religion. In these roles he taught the New Testament to thousands of men and women who now have ministries all over the world.

Dr. Bryant was a remarkable man. He had one of the finest educations of any person I have ever known. He had degrees from Johnson Bible College, Phillips University, Princeton Theological Seminary, and the University of Edinburgh. He traveled to Germany to hear Rudolf Bultmann lecture. In the period after World War II he was one of the very few teaching in our colleges with an earned doctorate, a legitimate Ph.D. He had obtained this degree in Scotland at great personal sacrifice. He told me of being so cold while there that he would put on every piece of clothing he owned and crawl into bed in order to be warm enough to study. He also taught me the trick of standing up to read late into the night so that you do not fall asleep.

Dr. Bryant's career at Emmanuel was legendary. There are probably still underground editions floating around of the class notes from his famous "New Testament Introduction," a year-long course from which many of his students have borrowed in their own teaching careers (including me). The amazing collection of books he assembled for the "New Testament Seminar Library" has astounded learned visitors to Emmanuel and is a source of great pride for the institution. His chapel messages surprised those who had grown used to this gentle man with his soft Virginian accent, for his voice would rise as he thundered home his passion for the lost and his love for his Savior.

One of the last times I saw Dr. Bryant was at a Society of Biblical Literature convention in Kansas City. I was reading a paper at this convention, and he made a special effort to attend the session. His simple pride in this modest accomplishment of his student both gave me joy and humbled me. At that meeting Dr. Bryant spoke eagerly of his last big project: this commentary on John. But alas, death took him home to be with the Lord on September 27, 1997 before he finished it.

I have attempted to complete this book in the spirit of Dr. Bryant. In some ways that is not difficult, for he probably influenced me more than any other teacher, and a great deal of him is in me. He finished through chapter 5 of John and did some work on chapter 6. I had access to transcribed sermon notes and other material from Dr. Bryant, but from chapter 6 on don't blame him for what you find; the responsibility falls on my head. I would be remiss if I did not also acknowledge the influence of Dr. D.A. Carson, my Ph.D. dissertation mentor at Trinity Evangelical Divinity School. I have tried not to steal too much from his own marvelous commentary on John.

Credit should be given to Mrs. Dorothy Bryant, who would not give up on this project, to Dr. Bryant's son, John, and daughter, Susan, who took notes from his bedside, to Eric Thomason, who helped compile Dr. Bryant's notes, and to John Hunter of College Press, who gave important and timely editorial assistance. A final thanks to my faithful Sunday School class at Shoreline Christian Church in Seattle, who have patiently allowed me to bounce my interpretive ideas around with them for the last six months.

To God be the glory!
Mark S. Krause
Puget Sound Christian College, Edmonds, Washington
July 1998

ABBREVIATIONS

BAGD . . . . . . *A Greek-English Lexicon of the New Testament by Bauer,
Arndt, Gingrich, and Danker*

BDB . . . . *A Hebrew and English Lexicon of the Old Testament by
Brown, Driver and Briggs*

BDF . . . . *A Greek Grammar of the New Testament by Blass,
Debrunner and Funk*

BJRL . . . . . . *Bulletin of the John Rylands University Library of
Manchester*

CBQ . . . . *Catholic Biblical Quarterly*

DNT . . . . *Dictionary of the New Testament*

HTR . . . . *Harvard Theological Review*

ICC . . . . *International Critical Commentary*

IDB . . . . *Interpreter's Dictionary of the Bible*

JAMA . . . . . . *Journal of the American Medical Association*

JBL . . . . *Journal of Biblical Literature*

JETS . . . . *Journal of the Evangelical Theological Society*

KJV . . . . *King James Version*

LSJ . . . . *Greek-English Lexicon by Liddell, Scott and Jones*

NASB . . . . . . *New American Standard Bible*

LXX . . . . *Septuagint*

NIV . . . . *New International Version*

NLT . . . . *New Living Translation*

NovT . . . . . . *Novum Testamentum*

NRSV . . . . . . *New Revised Standard Version*

NT . . . . *New Testament*

OT . . . . *Old Testament*

TDNT . . . . . . *Theological Dictionary of the New Testament by Kittel and
Friedrich*

ZNW . . . . . . *Zeitschrift für die neutestamentliche Wissenschaft*

INTRODUCTION

Even the casual reader of the New Testament will notice that the first three accounts of Jesus' life are generally similar in their overall story line, whereas the fourth Gospel (John) is quite different. Scholars refer to Matthew, Mark, and Luke as the Synoptic Gospels (Synoptic = "seen together" or "as parallel") because of their similarities, but John is called, well . . . John (no special name). It is part of the New Testament collection known as the Johannine Writings (John, 1, 2, 3 John, and Revelation).

The differences between the Synoptic Gospels and the Gospel of John are readily apparent to the alert reader. For example the Synoptics all present one major trip of Jesus from Galilee to Jerusalem, whereas John portrays Jesus as being in Judea and Jerusalem often. Indeed, for John the primary ministry of Jesus seems to be in Judea rather than the Galilean setting of the Synoptics. Another difference is seen in John's lack of true parables in his recorded teachings of Jesus. In the Synoptics, parables are the characteristic form of Jesus' teaching, with the often repeated introduction, "Jesus told them a parable, saying, 'the kingdom of God is like this . . . .'" John is also loaded with characters we do not find in the Synoptics: Nicodemus, the Samaritan woman at the well, and Lazarus, just to name a few. Furthermore, some of our most memorable Gospel phrases are not found in the Synoptics, but only in John: "In the beginning was the Word." "Behold the Lamb of God!" "God so loved the world that he gave his only Son." "I am the way, the truth, and the life." "I am the vine." "What is truth?" "It is finished!" "So send I you." By some estimates about 90% of the material found in John is not found in the Synoptic Gospels.[1]

---

[1] Compare this to the Gospel of Mark. About 90% of the material in Mark is also found in Matthew in some form.

Christian scholars have noticed these differences from ancient times. Clement of Alexandria, writing approximately AD 185, called John the "spiritual Gospel." By this, Clement did not mean that John was nonhistorical, but that John was more concerned with internal, spiritual matters. In the more recent past overly critical scholars have pronounced the differences between John and the Synoptics to be irreconcilable and concluded that John is, in effect, the first commentary on the Gospels. This assumption (that John is historical fiction) exists in many commentaries of previous generations and is still held by some today. In general, though, current scholarship is much less certain about the nonhistorical character of John. In this commentary we assume that John relates a historically reliable version of the life, death, and resurrection of Jesus, albeit quite different from that of the Synoptic Gospels. These differences are part of what makes the study of this book so fascinating and will be discussed at the appropriate places through the commentary.

WHO IS THE AUTHOR?

We have been writing as if we knew for sure that John was the author of this Gospel. But this begs the question, how do we know for sure that John wrote it, and if so, which John was this? To answer the first question in complete honesty, we do not know for sure who wrote this book, for it was published anonymously in line with the publishing standards of the ancient world. We do have some very early witnesses to John as the author, however. The so-called "Muratorian Canon" (date disputed, but probably AD 150-200) says, "John, one of the disciples, wrote the fourth book of the Gospel." An early church leader by the name of Irenaeus (AD 185) is also an important witness. Tradition claims that Irenaeus was a student of Polycarp of Smyrna, and that Polycarp was a student of John himself. This means that Irenaeus is only one generation of believers removed from John, which gives added weight to what he writes. Irenaeus states in no uncertain terms that John was the author of the Fourth Gospel (in his book *Against Heresies* 3.1.1).

Some scholars have suggested, however, that the author of the Fourth Gospel was indeed a man named John, but not John the

Apostle. It is true that there were other early Christian leaders named John, and it is possible that one of them is the true author of the Fourth Gospel. This issue may be addressed by determining the identity of the so-called "beloved disciple" within the book of John.

In John 21:20-24 the "disciple whom Jesus loved" is said to be the author of the book. If we work backwards through the book, we encounter the beloved disciple in other places. He is the one who recognizes Jesus after the resurrection during the miraculous catch of fish (21:7). Jesus entrusts the care for his mother, Mary, to this disciple while hanging on the cross (19:26-27). This disciple reclines next to Jesus at the Last Supper (13:23, 25). The beloved disciple is intended to be seen in some places where he is simply called the "other disciple." He is the one who races Peter to the tomb on Easter morning, and arrives first (20:3-5, probably indicating that he was younger than Peter). It is the "other disciple" who gains entrance for Peter and himself into the high priest's courtyard during the interrogation of Jesus (18:15-16). The "other disciple" may also be the unnamed disciple of John the Baptist who, along with Andrew, is pointed to Jesus by the Baptist himself (1:35-40).

The intimacy the beloved disciple has with Jesus points to one of the inner circle of disciples. In the Synoptic Gospels, this "inner circle" is pictured as Peter, James, and John. Peter is clearly not the author of the Fourth Gospel, because he is often portrayed as being with the "beloved disciple." James is an unlikely candidate, because he suffers early martyrdom at the hands of Herod Agrippa I (Acts 12:2). This leaves only John the Apostle, the son of Zebedee, the brother of James. This case is somewhat strengthened by the fact that the Apostle John is named nowhere in the Fourth Gospel (nor is James, the only reference being to the "sons of Zebedee" at 21:2). It is not easy to understand why any other early Christian writer would have omitted the name of such a prominent Apostle. The solution to the mystery is that we are intended to see John himself as the author, and that he does not mention himself except as the "beloved disciple" or the "other disciple." We should also note that this is not an expression of pride (he "loved me best"). It is an expression of deep humility, wonderment, and thankfulness on the part of the author: Jesus loved me, even me?!

WHEN AND WHERE WAS IT WRITTEN?

Many locations have been suggested as the place of composition for the Gospel of John, but the traditional site is the city of Ephesus. The ruins of Ephesus are in southwestern Turkey, near the modern city of Kusadasi. Ephesus was one of the largest and most important cities of the Roman Empire in the first century. Ephesus was the site of the Temple of Artemis (sometimes incorrectly called the Temple of Diana, see Acts 19:28). This temple was recognized as one of the seven wonders of the ancient world according to the Greek geographer, Strabo. This large city (perhaps as many as 500,000 inhabitants) had a very mixed population. There was a strong Christian community in Ephesus, for Paul had a three-year ministry there in the AD 50s. The presence of the Temple of Artemis shows that there was also a strong pagan community, dedicated to the worship of the ancient Greek gods. Overall it was a large, cosmopolitan city, with a well-developed Greek culture. The common language of the city would have been Greek, the language of the New Testament.

Although it cannot be proven, there is strong tradition that the Apostle John, along with Mary the mother of Jesus, made his way to Ephesus sometime after the destruction of Jerusalem in AD 70. John, at least, was probably in Ephesus during the reign of Emperor Domitian (AD 81-96). After a few years, Domitian seems to have actively persecuted the Christian community, and this atmosphere of persecution probably forms the background for the Fourth Gospel, written sometime between AD 85-95. Also, by this time, the Jewish synagogue community had solidified in its opposition to the Christians, and Jews had to make a choice between the two. Jews who chose to believe in Jesus were "thrown out of the synagogue," a circumstance mentioned by John (9:22; 16:2).

This makes John one of the last books of the New Testament to be written, and certainly the last of the Gospels. If we theorize that John was about 20 when Jesus was crucified (AD 30), then he would have been 75-85 years old when this book was written, a very old man in the ancient world. For this and other reasons, it is likely that John had quite a bit of help in writing this book. Some scholars want to speak of the "Johannine community" or the "community of the beloved disciple" as the author, and there is some merit to this (cf. 21:24, "we know his testimony in true"). For our purposes, however, we will assume that the Apostle John, an eyewitness to many of the Gospel events, is the primary author of this book.

WHAT ARE THE CHARACTERISTICS OF JOHN?

First, we would say that the style of John's writing is simple, but its thought is profound. John is written in some of the simplest Greek in the New Testament, although this does not mean it is "bad" Greek. It uses many common words, many monosyllabic words, and relatively short sentences. Yet the message of the book is profound. Fred Craddock notes that this is a Gospel in which "a child can wade and an elephant can swim."[2]

A second characteristic of John is that he has laid out the bulk of the book as a series of lengthy accounts of works followed by words. We can characterize these combinations as miraculous signs followed by discourses or sermons of Jesus. John has only seven miracles, five of which are not found in the Synoptic Gospels. The story of each of these miracles is told at some length, and the material of the sermon that follows is primarily material not found in the Synoptics.

A third characteristic of the Fourth Gospel is the emphasis upon the personal ministry of Jesus. John relates several one-on-one situations (e.g., Jesus with Nicodemus, chapter 3), which teach us that Jesus had an active private ministry. It was not all public preaching, although this was important, too. In John we see a Jesus who cares for people and has time for them. This has another side, however. Sometimes it emphasizes the aloneness of Jesus. He often seems to be by himself without the support of the disciples or anyone else, a solitary figure.

Fourthly, John has a highly developed theological interest. He is particularly concerned with the matter of Christology, explaining who Jesus is in relation to God. John lays stress on the divinity of Jesus, often referring to him as the Son or the Son of God. He also stresses the humanity of Jesus: he is thirsty at Sychar and weeps at the tomb of Lazarus. John develops the theme of Jesus as the Jewish Messiah, the one God sent to his people.

---

[2]Fred B. Craddock, *John*, Knox Preaching Guides (Atlanta: John Knox, 1982), p. 3.

John also explores the nature of God the Father, particularly through the Father-Son relationship between Jesus and God. John emphasizes that faith for the Christian must be in both the Father and in the Son. And John also has a great deal of discussion about the Holy Spirit. This is found throughout the book, but particularly in the Farewell Discourses of chapters 13-17. Here the Holy Spirit is portrayed as the coming Paraclete or Advocate for the community of believers.

A fifth characteristic might also be called the purpose of John. This purpose is strongly evangelistic, to bring the readers to faith. There is a constant contrast in the Fourth Gospel between believers and unbelievers, between faith and unfaith. Toward the end of the book John lays out his purpose in very straightforward language, "These [things] are written that you may *believe* that Jesus is the Christ, the Son of God, and that by believing you may have life in his name" (20:31).

HOW WILL THE STUDY OF JOHN BE APPROACHED?

There are many possible ways to study John, but it is helpful to know what the primary emphasis will be in this commentary. Our main focus will be to listen carefully to what John is saying to us, to understand his intended message. This is not as easy as it may seem at first glance, for John is far removed from twentieth century English speakers. We want to know the general story, to pick up on the nuances, to be sensitive to the theological implications John is drawing out. For the most part we will not be concerned with evaluating the historical nature of John's account. When we bring historical data into the mix, it will be to help the reader understand the background of John's story, not to judge his accuracy. This is a modified narrative approach, an attempt to understand John's story as it is intended to be understood. While some may find this intolerably naïve, it is certainly the first and necessary step to a full appreciation of this marvelous book. If we can get you to listen to John carefully and hear his message, we will have succeeded in what we set out to do.

OUTLINE

A good outline is more than half the battle in one's understanding and remembering the contents of any book. There is more than one way to break up and organize the materials in the Gospel according to John. Most students have observed two large divisions in its structure: (1) chapters 1-12 and (2) chapters 13-21. These larger units include a prologue (1:1-18) and an epilogue (chapter 21). Perhaps the easiest way to organize the materials of the book for commentary purposes might be to number the larger units of thought in the book (over fifty such units) and comment successively on these from the beginning of the book to the end. One may endeavor, however, to organize the materials of the Fourth Gospel in some kind of elaborate outline, structured under the two large divisions noted above. We follow this latter procedure below:

I. **JESUS MANIFESTS HIMSELF TO THE WORLD** — 1:1–12:50
   A. **The Prologue** — 1:1-18
      1. The Logos before Time — 1:1-4
         a. His Relationship to Deity — 1:1-2
         b. His Relationship to the World — 1:3-4
      2. The Logos Manifested in History — 1:5-18
         a. John the Baptist's Initial Testimony to the Logos — 1:5-13
         b. The Logos in Flesh — 1:14-18
   B. **The Testimony of John the Baptist and of Jesus' First Disciples** — 1:19-51
      1. The Testimony of John the Baptist — 1:19-34
         a. The Testimony of John to the Jewish Leaders — 1:19-28
         b. The Testimony of John to the Jewish People — 1:29-34
      2. Jesus' Calling and the Testifying of His First Disciples — 1:35-51

a. The Background — 6:1-4

b. Jesus' Feeding of the Five Thousand — 6:5-13

c. Jesus, Not That Kind of King — 6:14-15

d. Jesus' Walking on the Sea of Galilee — 6:16-21

e. The Crowds' Search for Jesus — 6:22-25

f. Two Discourses on the Bread of Life — 6:26-34, 35-40

g. Conflict Concerning Bread from Heaven and Flesh and Blood — 6:41-59

h. Rejection and Acceptance of Jesus — 6:60-71

3. Jesus at Tabernacles — 7:1-52

   a. Introduction: Question If Jesus Would Go to This Feast — 7:1-13

   b. Jesus' Discourses Spoken during the Feast — 7:14-36

   c. Jesus' Discourses Spoken on the Last Day of the Feast and the Audience's Response to it — 7:37-52

   d. *Textual Parenthesis:* The Woman Taken in Adultery — 7:53–8:11

4. The Light of Tabernacles and Jesus' Great Confrontation with the Jews — 8:12-59

   a. Jesus Discourse at the Temple Treasury: Jesus the Light of the World and the Authority of His Testimony to Himself — 8:12-20

   b. Jesus' Attack on the Jews Who Disbelieved and the Origin of His Testimony and the Problem of Who He Is — 8:21-30

   c. Truth, Sin, Freedom, and the Children of Abraham — 8:31-59

5. Healing of the Man Born Blind — 9:1-41

   a. The Setting — 9:1-5

   b. The Healing — 9:6-7

   c. Interrogations of the Man — 9:8-34

     (1) Questions Posed by the Neighbors and Friends — 9:8-12

     (2) Preliminary Quizzing by Some Pharisees — 9:13-17

     (3) The Man's Parents Questioned by the Jews — 9:18-23

     (4) The Man Questioned a Second Time by the Jews, and Excommunicated — 9:24-34

BIBLIOGRAPHY

Note: There are many, many commentaries and other books related to the study of John. Dr. Bryant's favorites were the ones by Rudolf Bultmann, Barnabas Lindars, and Raymond Brown (even though he had sharp disagreements with all of them). Bultmann has a great deal of excellent material, although his theological bent makes him difficult for less advanced students. Lindars is excellent in technical discussion, but spiritually dry. Brown is wordy, but often gives great insights. I think the finest commentary on John is that of D.A. Carson. While Carson may be too conservative for some, he never avoids the hard questions and takes the time necessary to do thorough exegesis. Other outstanding choices for the more advanced student include the commentary of C.K. Barrett and George Beasley-Murray's commentary in the Word Biblical Commentary series. For the less advanced student the commentary by Paul Butler contains a wealth of accessible material, although written for an earlier generation.

Abbot, Ezra, Andrew P. Peabody, and J.B. Lightfoot. *The Fourth Gospel: Evidences External and Internal of Its Johannean Authorship*. London: Hodder & Stoughton, 1892.

Ashton, John. *Understanding the Fourth Gospel*. Oxford: Clarendon, 1991.

Bacon, Benjamin W. *The Fourth Gospel in Research and Debate: A Series of Essays on Problems Concerning the Origin and Value of the Anonymous Writings Attributed to the Apostle John*. New York: Moffatt, 1910.

_____. *The Gospel of the Hellenists*. New York: Holt, n.d., c.1933.

Barclay, William. *The Gospel of John*. The Daily Study Bible Series. Philadelphia: Westminster, 1956.

Barrett, C.K. *The Gospel according to St. John.* Second Edition. Philadelphia: Westminster, 1978.

_____. *The Gospel of John and Judaism.* Philadelphia: Fortress, 1975.

Bauer, Walter. *Das Johannesevangelium.* Tübingen: Mohr, 1925.

Beasley-Murray, George R. *John.* Word Biblical Commentary 36. Waco: Word, 1987.

Bernard, John H. *A Critical and Exegetical Commentary on the Gospel According to St. John.* 2 volumes. International Critical Commentary. Edinburgh: T&T Clark, 1928.

Blomberg, Craig L. *Jesus and the Gospels.* Nashville: Broadman & Holman, 1997.

Boice, James M. *Witness and Revelation in the Gospel of John.* Grand Rapids: Eerdmans, 1978.

Borchert, Gerald L. *John 1-11.* The New American Commentary 25A. Nashville: Broadman & Holman, 1996.

Bowman, John. *The Fourth Gospel and the Jews: A Study in R. Akiba, Esther, and the Gospel of John.* Pittsburgh: Pickwick, 1975.

Brown, Raymond E. *The Community of the Beloved Disciple.* New York: Paulist, 1979.

_____. *The Death of the Messiah: From Gethsemane to the Grave.* 2 volumes. New York: Doubleday, 1994.

_____. *The Gospel according to John.* 2 volumes. The Anchor Bible 29A-B. Garden City, NY: Doubleday, 1966-70.

Bruce, F.F. *The Gospel of John.* Grand Rapids: Eerdmans, 1983.

Bultmann, Rudolf. *The Gospel of John.* Philadelphia: Westminster, 1971.

Burney, Charles F. *The Aramaic Origin of the Fourth Gospel.* Oxford: Clarendon, 1922.

Butler, Paul. *The Gospel of John.* 2 volumes in 1. Bible Study Textbook Series. Joplin, MO: College Press, 1961.

Carpenter, Joseph E. *The Johannine Writings: A Study of the Apocalypse and the Fourth Gospel.* London: Constable, 1927.

Carson, D.A. *The Gospel According to John.* Grand Rapids: Eerdmans, 1991.

Charlesworth, James H., editor. *John and Qumran.* London: Geoffrey Chapman, 1972.

Colwell, Ernest C., *The Greek of the Fourth Gospel: A Study of Its Aramaisms in the Light of Hellenistic Greek.* Chicago: University of Chicago Press, n.d., c. 1931.

Craddock, Fred B. *John.* Knox Preaching Guides. Atlanta: John Knox Press, 1982.

Cullmann, Oscar. *The Johannine Circle.* Philadelphia: Westminster, 1975.

Culpepper, R. Alan. *The Anatomy of the Fourth Gospel: A Study in Literary Design.* Philadelphia: Fortress, 1983.

_____. *The Gospel and Letters of John.* Interpreting Biblical Texts Series. Nashville: Abingdon, 1998.

Dodd, C.H. *Historical Tradition in the Fourth Gospel.* Cambridge: Cambridge University Press, 1963.

_____. *The Interpretation of the Fourth Gospel.* Cambridge: Cambridge University Press, 1953.

Drummond, James. *An Inquiry into the Character and Authorship of the Fourth Gospel.* New York: Scribner, 1904.

Eisler, Robert. *The Enigma of the Fourth Gospel.* London: Methuen, 1938.

Erdman, Charles R. *The Gospel of John.* Philadelphia: Westminster, 1917.

Fortna, Robert T. *The Gospel of Signs: A Reconstruction of the Narrative Source Underlying the Fourth Gospel.* Cambridge: Cambridge University Press, 1970.

Foster, R.C. *Studies in the Life of Christ.* Grand Rapids: Baker, 1985. Reprint, Joplin, MO: College Press, 1996.

Gardner-Smith, Percival. *St. John and the Synoptic Gospels.* Cambridge: Cambridge University Press, 1938.

Gnilka, J. *Johannesevangelium.* Neue Echter Bibel. Würzburg: Echter, 1983.

Godet, Frederic. *Commentary on the Gospel of John.* Translated by Timothy Dwight. 2 volumes. New York: Funk & Wagnall, 1886.

Haenchen, Ernst. *A Commentary on the Gospel of John.* Hermeneia Series. 2 volumes. Philadelphia: Fortress, 1984. (German ed., 1980.)

Hendriksen, William. *Exposition of the Gospel according to John.* 2 volumes. New Testament Commentary Series. Grand Rapids: Baker, 1954.

Hengel, Martin. *The Johannine Question.* Philadelphia: Trinity Press International, 1989.

Higgins, A.J.B. *The Historicity of the Fourth Gospel.* London: Lutterworth, 1960.

Hoskyns, Edwyn C. *The Fourth Gospel.* 2 volumes. London: Faber, 1940. Revised. ed. in one vol., 1947.

Howard, Wilbert F. *Christianity According to St. John.* Philadelphia: Westminster, 1946.

_____. *The Fourth Gospel in Recent Criticism and Interpretation.* London: Epworth, 1931.

Howard, Wilbert F., and Arthur J. Gossip. "The Gospel According to St. John." In *Interpreter's Bible* 7:437-811. Nashville: Abingdon/Cokesbury, 1952.

Hunter, Archibald M. *According to John*. The Cambridge Bible Commentary. London: SCM Press, 1968.

_____. *The Gospel According to John*. Cambridge: Cambridge University Press, 1965.

Jauncey, James H. *The Compelling Indwelling* [Studies on John 15]. Chicago: Moody, 1972.

Jeremias, Joachim. *New Testament Theology*. Old Tappan, NJ: Scribners Reference, 1977.

Jervell, Jacob. *Jesus in the Gospel of John*. Minneapolis: Augsburg, 1984.

Kysar, Robert. *The Fourth Evangelist and His Gospel*. Minneapolis: Augsburg, 1975.

_____. *John*. Augsburg Commentary on the New Testament. Minneapolis: Augsburg, 1986.

_____. *John's Story of Jesus*. Philadelphia: Fortress, 1984.

_____. *John, the Maverick Gospel*. Atlanta: John Knox, 1976. Reprinted Louisville, KY: Westminster/John Knox, 1993.

Lee, Edwin Kenneth. *The Religious Thought of St. John*. London: S.P.C.K., 1950.

Lenski, R.C.H. *Interpretation of John's Gospel*. Columbus: Lutheran Book Concern, 1936.

Leon-Dufour, Xavier. *Dictionary of the New Testament*. New York: Harper & Row, 1980.

Lightfoot, Robert H. *St. John's Gospel*. Edited by C.F. Evans. Oxford: Clarendon, 1956.

Lindars, Barnabas. *The Gospel of John*. New Century Bible Commentary. Grand Rapids: Eerdmans, 1972.

MacGregor, George H.C. *The Gospel of John*. The Moffatt New Testament Commentary. London: Hodder & Stoughton, 1928.

MacGregor, George H.C., and A.Q. Morton. *The Structure of the Fourth Gospel*. Edinburgh: Oliver & Boyd, 1961.

Maier G. *Johannes-Evangelium*. BKNT 6. Neuhausen-Stuttgart: Hänssler, 1984.

Marsh, John. *The Gospel of St. John*. Westminster Pelican Commentaries. Philadelphia: Westminster, 1968.

Martyn, J. Louis. *History and Theology in the Fourth Gospel*. New York: Harper & Row, 1968.

_____. *The Gospel of John in Christian History: Essays for Interpreters*. New York: Paulist, 1979.

McGarvey, J.W., and P.Y. Pendleton. *The Fourfold Gospel or a Harmony of the Four Gospels*. Cincinnati: Standard, 1914.

Michaels, J.R. *John*. San Francisco: Harper, 1984.

Moloney, Francis J. *The Gospel of John*. Sacra Pagina. Collegeville, MN: Liturgical Press, 1998.

Montefiore, C.G., and H. Loewe. *A Rabbinic Anthology*. New York: Schocken Books, 1974.

Morris, Leon. *The Gospel according to St. John*. The New International Commentary on the New Testament. Grand Rapids: Eerdmans, 1971.

_____. *Reflections on the Gospel of John*. 4 volumes. Grand Rapids: Baker, 1986.

_____. *Studies in the Fourth Gospel*. Grand Rapids, Eerdmans, 1969.

Murray, John O.F. *Jesus according to St. John*. London: Longmans, 1936.

Nicol, W. *Semeia in the Fourth Gospel*. Leiden: Brill, 1972.

Nolloth, Charles F. *The Fourth Evangelist: His Place in the Development of Religious Thought*. London: J. Murray, 1925.

O'Neill, J.C. *Who Did Jesus Think He Was?* Leiden: Brill, 1995.

Odeberg, Hugo. *The Fourth Gospel: Interpreted in Its Relation to Contemporaneous Religious Currents in Palestine and the Hellenistic-Oriental World.* Amsterdam: B.R. Grüner, 1968.

Pack, Frank. *The Gospel according to John.* Living Word Commentaries. Austin: Sweet, 1975.

Palmer, Earl F. *The Intimate Gospel.* Waco: Word, 1978.

Plummer, Alfred. *The Gospel according to St. John.* Cambridge Greek Testament. Cambridge: Cambridge University Press, 1890.

Rainsford, Marcus. *Our Lord Prays: Thoughts on John XVII.* London: 1873; reprint Chicago: Moody, 1950.

Redlich, Edwin B. *An Introduction to the Fourth Gospel.* London: Longmans, 1939.

Ridderbos, Herman N. *The Gospel of John: A Theological Commentary.* Grand Rapids: Eerdmans, 1997.

Rigg, William Harrison. *The Fourth Gospel and Its Message for Today.* London: Lutterworth, 1952.

Robinson, John A.T. *The Priority of John.* London: SCM Press, 1985.

Sanday, William. *The Authorship and Historical Character of the Fourth Gospel.* London: Macmillan, 1872.

_____. *The Criticism of the Fourth Gospel.* New York: Scribner, 1905.

Sanders, J.N. *The Fourth Gospel in the Early Church.* Cambridge: Cambridge University Press, 1943.

Sanders, J.N., and B.A. Mastin. *The Gospel according to St. John.* Black's New Testament Commentaries. London: A.& C. Black, 1968.

Schlatter, Adolf. *Der Evangelist Johannes.* Stuttgart: Calwer, 1948.

Schnackenburg, Rudolf. *The Gospel according to St John.* 3 volumes. Translated by Cecily Hastings, et al. New York: Crossroad, 1982.

Sidebottom, E.M. *The Christ of the Fourth Gospel.* London: SPCK, 1961.

Sloyan, Gerard S. *John.* Interpretation Commentary Series. Atlanta: John Knox, 1988.

Smith, D. Moody. *The Composition and Order of the Fourth Gospel.* New Haven, CT: Yale University Press, 1965.

_____. *John.* Proclamation Commentaries. Philadelphia: Fortress Press, 1976.

Smith, D. Moody, C. Clifton Black, and R. Alan Culpepper, eds. *Exploring the Gospel of John: In Honor of D. Moody Smith.* Louisville: Westminster/John Knox, 1996.

Smith, Jonathan R. *The Teaching of the Gospel of John.* New York: Revell, 1903.

Stevens, George B. *The Johannine Theology: A Study of the Doctrinal Contents of the Gospel and Epistles of the Apostle John.* New York: Scribner, 1894.

Strachan, Robert H. *The Fourth Evangelist: Dramatist or Historian?* London: Hodder & Stoughton, 1925.

_____. *The Fourth Gospel: Its Significance and Environment.* 3rd Revised Edition. London, S.C.M. Press, 1941.

Tasker, Randolph V.G. *The Gospel according to St. John.* Tyndale New Testament Commentaries. London: Tyndale, 1960.

Temple, William. *Readings in St. John's Gospel.* 2 volumes. London: Macmillan, 1939-40; one volume edition, New York: St. Martin's Press, 1955.

Tenney, Merrill C. "The Gospel of John." In *The Expositor's Bible Commentary*, 93-203. Grand Rapids: Zondervan, 1981.

_____. *John: the Gospel of Belief.* Grand Rapids: Eerdmans (1948), 1954.

Turner, George A., and Julius R. Mantey. *The Gospel according to John.* The Evangelical Commentary on the Bible. Grand Rapids: Eerdmans, 1964.

Wead, David. *The Literary Devices in John's Gospel.* Basel: Komm. Friedrich Reinhardt, 1970.

Weber, Gerard P. and Robert Miller. *Breaking Open the Gospel of John.* Cincinnati: St. Anthony Messenger Press, 1995.

Westcott, Brooke F. *The Gospel according to St John.* London: John Murray, 1882.

_____. *The Gospel according to St. John; the Greek Text with Introduction and Notes.* 2 volumes. London: John Murray, 1908. Reprinted in 1 volume, Grand Rapids: Baker, 1980.

Wiles, Maurice F. *The Spiritual Gospel: The Interpretation of the Fourth Gospel in the Early Church.* Cambridge: Cambridge University Press, 1960.

Witherington, Ben, III. *John's Wisdom: A Commentary on the Fourth Gospel.* Louisville, KY: Westminster/John Knox, 1995.

JOHN 1

I. JESUS MANIFESTS HIMSELF (HIS GLORY) TO THE WORLD (1:1–12:50)

A. THE PROLOGUE (1:1-18)

For an inscription or title manuscripts ℵ and B read "According to John"; older manuscripts ($\mathfrak{P}^{66,75}$) read "(The) Gospel according to John." The former may be more primitive here and the likely original title of the book.

1. The Logos before Time (1:1-4)

His Relationship to Deity (1:1-2)

[1]**In the beginning was the Word, and the Word was with God, and the Word was God. [2]He was with God in the beginning.**

1:1. The words "In the beginning" echo Genesis 1:1, especially to Jewish Christians; however, these words in John 1:1 do not refer to the act of creating but to the one who existed and who was present when creation took place, that is, the Word. One might expect to read "In the beginning . . . God," but instead is surprised to read **In the beginning was the Word,**[1] and this title is more fitting here than the titles "the Christ," "the Son of Man," "the Son of God," etc. John's prologue seems specially composed to *introduce* and to *summarize* the person and work of Jesus who is the Christian gospel. It is possible also that the words "In the beginning" are

---

[1]E. Haenchen, *A Commentary on the Gospel of John.* Hermeneia, German edition, 1980 (Philadelphia: Fortress, 1984), p. 116.

meant to recall the opening of the Gospel according to Mark.[2] Each of the four evangelists opens his Gospel by pushing the activity of Jesus back to the beginning (ἀρχή, *archē*): Mark to the ministry of John with its baptism of Jesus, the descent of the Spirit, and God's acknowledgment of Jesus' sonship; Matthew and Luke to the virginal conception and birth of Jesus; and John to the creation and to the time before it. John may refer to the opening events recorded by Mark (see 1:6-8,13) and by Matthew and Luke (1:13); his opening is surely a stunning one, for the writer begins with God in eternity. Not many books so begin!

The background to the title "Word" is claimed by the scholarly world to be varied and diverse. (1) Some students have seen the ideas that John associated with the term "Word" as deriving from Grecian philosophy, specifically from Heraclitus and the Stoics; i.e., both Heraclitus and the Stoics described the Word as the omnipresent force used by God to create the world. Philo, a Jewish philosopher and Old Testament commentator, followed the Greeks, which meant that none of these people conceived the Word as a genuinely *personal being*[3] but mostly as an *impersonal force* much like gravitation or the fusion of catenae (chains of atoms). (2) Others derived the meaning of "Word" from (a) the Old Testament (Prov 7:22–8:1, where God's wisdom attended the world's creation; but again, wisdom was here less personal and more of an impersonal force) and/or (b) from extracanonical Jewish literature (e.g., Wisdom 24). (3) More than likely the term "Word" derived from *Jesus* and *his preaching and ministering*. He preached the Word with his mouth, enacted the Word with his actions, and embodied the Word with his birth and person. In the New Testament the gospel of Jesus is often referred to as "the Word of God." The title for Jesus, "the Word," may, therefore, derive entirely from the Christians, and from neither the pagans nor the Jews, though some students contend that the emphases of both paganism and the Old Testament cling here to the term "Word."[4]

---

[2]C.K. Barrett, *The Gospel According to St. John* (New York: Macmillan, 1955), p. 131.

[3]Cf. Haenchen, *The Gospel of John*, 1:137a.

[4]George R. Beasley-Murray, *John*, Word Biblical Commentary (Waco, TX: Word, 1987), pp. 9-10.

The following may have been the meaning (and reason for the usage) of the title Word as applied to Jesus: (1) Jesus was the major revelation of God's will to humankind,[5] and revelation usually takes the form of words. This explanation has to do primarily with God's relationships to human beings which are described in 1:3ff, not with relationships within the deity himself. John, however, never used the terms ἀποκαλύπτω (apokalyptō) and ἀποκάλυψις (apokalyp-sis), but instead employed such words as λέγω (legō, "I say"), λαλέω (laleō, "I speak"), and φανερόω (phaneroō, "I manifest"). (2) Jesus not only spoke God's word or message to humankind, but he is God's word or message.[6] There may be a further truth concealed in the use of Logos as the title for Jesus in John 1:1ff; it is simply this: (3) as any word is intimately bound to its idea (or vice versa), so that one cannot have a word without its accompanying idea (in speech or in writing), so close are the Father and Jesus the Son — to have one is to have the other. This observation may help to understand such difficult verses as 10:30; 14:9, 28; etc.

The title "Word" for Jesus has been compared to the relation of the term "name (שֵׁם, shēm) of God" in the Old Testament, in which the name of God sometimes stands alongside of God as a separate power, and yet in fact is not anything separate. It describes God in so far as he acts, and especially as he reveals himself (Exod 23:21; Isa 30:27; Ps 8:2,10; 20:2; etc.).[7]

[A]nd the Word was with God, and the Word was God. Πρὸς τὸν θεόν (pros ton theon, "with God") can mean "in the presence of God" (cf. Mark 6:3), or in "fellowship with God."[8] In the phrase "the Word was God," θεός (theos), without the article, is predicative; that is, theos is somewhat like a predicative adjective. One should not, however, translate theos as "divine," nor should one translate it as "the God" (with the definite article) as though Jesus were the only being of whom this could be asserted. "The Word was God" (or deity) is the best way to render the short sentence. The words

---

[5]Rudolf Bultmann, *The Gospel of John, A Commentary* (Philadelphia: Westminster, 1971), p. 21.

[6]Edwyn C. Hoskyns, *The Fourth Gospel*, Francis Noel Davey, ed., 2 vols (London: Faber, 1940); rev. ed. 1 vol. (London: Faber, 1947), p. 139.

[7]Bultmann, *The Gospel of John*, p. 34, n. 2.

[8]See Beasley-Murray, *John*, p. 10.

"with God" describe the nature and environment of the Word in eternity prior to his coming to earth. The verse also says that Jesus, who was the one in whom the Word came to earth, was not a mere man (and Jesus' mission was not performed by a mere human being), but was the Word of God who was God. These opening words of the Fourth Gospel ground things aright from the very beginning. The story that is to follow in this book centers on one who is a human being, but who also is God himself. There are no polytheistic notions nor concepts of imagination in this text;[9] thus, John warns the reader that the words and works ascribed to Jesus in this book are the words and works of God himself.[10]

1:2. In 1:2 John reaffirms what he has already said of Jesus in verse 1, as οὗτος (*houtos*, "this one") shows.

His Relationship to the World (1:3-4)

[3]Through him all things were made; without him nothing was made that has been made. [4]In him was life, and that life was the light of men.

1:3. In 1:3, the Word is described as the agent (δι' αὐτοῦ, *di' autou*, "through him") of all creation, and the description is stated both positively (**all things**) and negatively ("nothing without him").[11] This creating definitely makes the Word deity, because who or what else can make a universe except God? "All things" (πάντα, *panta*) means the universe (ὁ κόσμος, *ho kosmos*, cf. 1:10). Note that the Word **was** appears four times in verses one and two, the imperfect of duration, but 1:3 ἐγένετο (*egeneto*, a second person aorist form) connotes "came into being" as over against the Word who, on his divine side, did not begin, evolve, or maturate.

The Hellenistic Greeks, especially the Stoics, called the universe (τὰ) πάντα ([*ta*] *panta*) or τὸ πᾶν (*to pan*, "all"), e.g., Heraclitus: ἐκ πάντων ἓν καὶ ἐξ ἑνὸς πάντα (*ek pantōn hen kai ex henos panta*), "out of all things (is) one and out of one (are) all things."[12] The

---

[9]Bultmann, *The Gospel of John*, p. 33.

[10]Barrett, *The Gospel According to St. John*, p. 156.

[11]Bultmann, *The Gospel of John*, p. 37.

[12]Wilhelm Kraus, *Index zu den Vorsokratikern*, p. 642. Cf. the line in the

Jews likewise used the same expression to refer to the world or uni-verse.[13]

Some Christian students understand the words "all things" to refer to the world of human beings,[14] while most take the words to refer to the creation in its entirety and not simply to mankind.[15]

Though the Gnostics made early use of the Fourth Gospel,[16] these words in the first half of 1:3 eliminate the possibility of the author's being a Gnostic. According to Gnostics, the created world could not have come into being by God or by the Logos.[17] Verse 3, however, bluntly declares that everything in creation, which must include all forms of matter, came into being by the direct agency of the Word (δι' αὐτοῦ ἐγένετο, di' autou egeneto).

Since punctuation is not used in the oldest manuscripts of the New Testament, the place of the period at the close of 1:3 has been debated: should ὃ γέγονεν (ho gegonen) be joined to the preceding or succeeding words; that is, should the text read ". . . nothing was made that has been made" (so NIV) or "That which has been made in him was life"?[18] The former reading seems more Johannine.[19]

1:4. The two words ἐν αὐτῷ (en autō, "in him") remind the reader of Paul's much used formula "in Christ." **In him was life and that life was the light of men.** Life and light are two of the

---

Corpus Hermeticum (edited by A.D. Nock and A.J. Festugiere) 11:1: ὡς ἔχει ὁ θεος καὶ τὸ πᾶν (hōs echei ho theos kai to pan); and see L. Delatte, S. Govaerte, and J. Denooz's *Index du Corpus Hermeticum*, pp. 148-149.

[13]See Genesis 1:26,28; 2:2 — Massoretes & LXX; Berakoth VI 38b, Soncino English edition, p. 241, lines 10-13, also pp. 223, 227, 239, 249; cf. IQS 11:11.

[14]Bultmann, *The Gospel of John*, pp. 36-38.

[15]Haenchen, *The Gospel of John*, 1:112.

[16]The earliest extant commentary on the Gospel was by Heracleon about A.D. 150, a Valentinian Gnostic.

[17]The surviving fragments of Heracleon's *Commentary on John* (at least on the first eight chapters of John) are collected (mostly from Origen, a church father about A.D. 200) and translated in Robert M. Grant's *Gnosticism: A Sourcebook of Heretical Writings from the Early Christian Period.* (New York: Harper, 1961), pp. 195-208.

[18]So Nestle-Aland 27 ed. of Greek New Testament; ZNW 59 (1968): 104-209.

[19]Cf. 5:26, 39; 6:53, and, further, the latter puts a strain on the Greek that follows. See Bruce M. Metzger, *A Textual Commentary on the Greek New Testament* (London: United Bible Society, 1971), pp. 195-196.

most frequent terms in this Gospel. The terms had a long and broad background. Both words are used in (1) *the Old Testament* of creation and salvation (Gen 1). God supplies life (Ezek 37:1-14; Dan 12:2) and also light (Ps 119:130; cf. Ps 36:10). Torah, for the Jews, became the source of life (cf. Aboth 2:7, "The more study of the law the more life") and light (see *Deuteronomy Rabbah* 7:3 ". . . as oil is light for the world, so also words of Torah are light for the world"). Life and light were terms also extensively used in (2) *Hellenism*.[20] Gnosticism, whether pagan, Jewish, or heretical-Christian, used the same two words repeatedly, though extant Gnostic literature is probably post-Christian.[21] The same was true of these terms in Zoroastrianism and other pagan religious thought. (3) More important for John is the *Christian* background of life and light: Jesus' works and words showed him to be the life and light of his followers (cf. Matt 5:14; Mark 4:21-22; Luke 17:24). That Jesus was the life of human beings meant that he was and is the basic energy that makes possible the entire world, not only the existence and activity of human individuals. He is the light of the world in that he reveals such life which is inherent in God (5:26) and can be shared by God with humankind, in spite of the prevalence of death and darkness in this world. The Word's life made the world and the human race possible; the Word's light will make that life (not sin and death) dominant in the world and its race. In other words, "In him was life" meant that life was *inherent* in Jesus so that he could make the physical world and its habitants, and "the life was the light of man" meant that he was the *revealer* of this truth to humankind. Both statements meant also, in the light of the rest of this Gospel, that Jesus came to make *a new creation* (the church), and to *reveal* this new order to the human race.

How was Jesus' life the light of human beings? It was light in that he supplied the standards or patterns, principles, power, and purpose by which the human race might live; otherwise, the race

---

[20]Cf. the Hermetic literature, especially tractates 1 and 13.

[21]Cf. the Odes of Solomon 54. For more information on the Odes of Solomon see R.J. Bauckham, "Apocryphal and Pseudepigraphal Writings," and J.L. Wu and S.C. Pearson, "Hymns, Songs," *Dictionary of the Later New Testament and Its Developments*, Ralph P. Martin and Peter H. Davids, eds. (Downers Grove, IL: InterVarsity, 1997), pp. 72, 525.

would perish — and this perishing includes both Jews and Gentiles. He showed humanity how to live, die, and live again; nobody else could do this. We live in and by his life. (Cf. Rom 6:4; Phil 1:20-21; Col 2:20-3:4. Note Col 3:4, "Christ our life.") The *power* supplied by his *life* and the selfless ethical examples supplied by his *living* seem to be alluded to here. "Jesus' light" shines in the physical world, (human intellect and understanding), in the spirit world (the church), and in the eschatological or heavenly world (heaven).

2. The Logos Manifested in History (1:5-18)

John the Baptist's Initial Testimony to the Logos (1:5-13)

⁵The light shines in the darkness, but the darkness has not understood[a] it.

⁶There came a man who was sent from God; his name was John. ⁷He came as a witness to testify concerning that light, so that through him all men might believe. ⁸He himself was not the light; he came only as a witness to the light. ⁹The true light that gives light to every man was coming into the world.[b]

¹⁰He was in the world, and though the world was made through him, the world did not recognize him. ¹¹He came to that which was his own, but his own did not receive him. ¹²Yet to all who received him, to those who believed in his name, he gave the right to become children of God — ¹³children born not of natural descent,[c] nor of human decision or a husband's will, but born of God.

[a]5 Or *darkness, and the darkness has not overcome*   [b]9 Or *This was the true light that gives light to every man who comes into the world*   [c]13 Greek *of bloods*

1:5. The light shines in the darkness of an ignorant and sinning race. The verb "shines" (φάινει, *phainei*) is present active indicative which means (1) that it is the nature of light to continue to shine, or (2) that Jesus' light continues to shine or goes on shining — probably as over against numerous efforts to extinguish it, as the rest of the verse may imply. "The darkness did not κατέλαβεν (*katelaben*)." The Greek word may mean either (1) *grasp/understand* or (2) *conquer/suppress*. Some have suggested that perhaps John intended to include both meanings here and have proposed that some such translations as "master" might suggest this.[22] Verses 10-12 seem to suggest that receiving or rejecting the truth that Jesus made manifest in this world is what the verb means.

1:6. There came a man who was sent from God; his name was John. History within earthly time is now reached with John the Baptist. He was sent from God (ἀπεσταλμένος, *apestalmenos*), his message was repentance, and his action was immersion in water, so that his audience could publicly certify their repentance.

1:7. John's real purpose was not (1) to save the world (he never died or rose for anyone), nor (2) to seek recognition as the Messiah of Old Testament prophecy (he acknowledged that he was not the Messiah), nor (3) to found the Kingdom and/or the church (he was not even a part of or in the kingdom/church [Matt. 11:11]). John's purpose was (4) *to testify* or *to bear witness* to the Light, who was Jesus.

Witness bearing or testifying in the New Testament is of supreme importance. One bears testimony to facts. The noun "testimony" or "witness" and the verb "to testify" or "to bear witness to" are courtroom terms — in paganism, Judaism, and Christianity. One bears witness to the truth of what one has seen and/or heard — to the facts as facts. This testimony is preserved to this day — usually in writing in books. John's testimony to Jesus as the Light was preserved in a book, our present Gospel according to John. Testimony is preserved that people may believe the facts which are being testified to[23] — **that through him all men might believe.** These words refer to John, because people do not believe *through* Jesus but *in* Jesus.

1:8. Verse 8 continues with the purpose for the Testimony: in order that (ἵνα, *hina*) all might believe what they have heard or read. There are two purpose clauses here in verses 7 and 8 and the second is dependent on the former. John came in order that he might testify to the Light, and that testimony is produced in order that all persons might believe. Here in verse 8 is the Bible's clear

---

[22]BAGD, p. 413.
[23]Barrett, *The Gospel According to St. John,* p. 160.

statement of what faith is: *faith is the acceptance of testimony (recorded in the Scriptures) to Jesus the Light – the Messiah, the Son of God.* That is why the Fourth Gospel is so full of testimony and testifying to Christ — by the Baptist (1:7-13,15,32-34; 3:26; 5:33), by the woman of Samaria (4:39), by Jesus' works (5:36; 10:25), by the Old Testament (5:39), by the crowds of people (12:17), by the Father (5:37; 8:18), by Jesus himself (8:18), by the Holy Spirit (15:26) and by the apostles (15:27).

"Faith" has been defined as "the acceptance of testimony";[24] such a definition certainly fits the four Gospels, and especially the Fourth Gospel. If one accepts the data in any biblical book, then one believes; but if one rejects or refuses to accept the data, one disbelieves. What John's book seeks to realize in each of its readers is one's acceptance of Jesus as the Christ the Son of God, so that one might have everlasting life as a result (20:31). John the Baptist's testimony was both negative and positive: he was not the Light but merely bore witness to the Light; that is, he told people that Jesus is the Christ. John, therefore, by means of testimony evoked their acceptance or belief in Jesus as Messiah.

1:9. In the expression **was coming into the world** (ἐρχόμενον εἰς τὸν κόσμον, *erchomenon eis ton kosmon*), *erchomenon* may be (1) *nominative*, neuter, singular, agreeing with φῶς (*phōs*), or (2) *accusative*, masculine, singular, agreeing with ἄνθρωπον (*anthrōpon*). Number (2) contains a formula that is used in Hebrew for "every person." The line may be read "gives light to every person who comes into the world" (so KJV). Number (1) may be translated "the true light . . . was coming into the world." Number (1) seems to be the intended sense, and thus refers to the incarnation. Reasons for so thinking are as follows: (a) Number (1) has an imperfect periphrastic participle: "the light was coming," which is in harmony with Johannine literary style; and, (b) number (1), further, agrees with 12:46, which says, ἐγὼ φῶς εἰς τὸν κόσμον ἐλήλυθα (*egō phōs eis ton kosmon elēlytha*, "I have come into the world as a light") (NIV). Number (1), therefore, seems preferable: the "coming" refers to Jesus' incarnation and not to each person's natural birth.[25]

---

[24]Alexander Campbell, *The Christian System* (Cincinnati: Christian Publishing, 1836), p. 94.

[25]See Barrett, *The Gospel According to St. John*, pp. 160-161.

C.H. Dodd[26] sought to hold both positions together: light came when Jesus came, but light (ultimately from Jesus) came also when each person came into the world.

Κόσμος (*kosmos*) appears here for the first time in this Gospel. The term means in this context the physical creation or universe.

1:10. The same word *kosmos* appears in this verse three times. In John *kosmos* rarely means simply the physical world or the totality of creation (exceptions are 11:9; 17:5,24; 21:25) (so 10a) and often means the world inhabited by and including human beings and human affairs (so 10b). Sometimes it means simply humanity,[27] as here in 10c.

Though the Logos made the inhabitants of the world, none of them recognized or accepted (believed) him when he made his appearance among his creatures, though they should have known him (Rom 1:18-21; Acts 10:16-17). John uses γινώσκειν (*ginōskein*) here; sometimes he uses ἐιδέναι (*eidenai*) synonymously with *ginōskein*.

1:11. In the phrase **He came to that which was his own**, "his own" (τὰ ἴδια, *ta idia*) is literally "his own things" or possessions/ property,[28] his own home. What constituted *ta idia*? (1) Possibly Israel,[29] or (2) human beings (not those confined to Israel).[30] The NIV seems to understand the plural *idia* as a singular collective noun (nation, race, etc.).

1:12. Notice that in this verse believing and receiving are equated: **Who received him . . . who believed in his name.** This may help solve the dilemma created by the doctrine which asserts that nothing but faith saves, which is understood to mean that Christ is *received* by faith alone; however, repentance from sin, confession of Jesus as Messiah, and baptism into Christ are also, in the New Testament, related to salvation for every person. These are the means of one's receiving Christ or of one's being saved (Acts 2:38; 22:16; Rom 10:10;

---

[26]C.H. Dodd, *The Interpretation of the Fourth Gospel* (Cambridge: University Press, 1953), p. 284.

[27]Beasley-Murray, *John*, p. 12; Barrett, *The Gospel According to St. John*, p. 161.

[28]Barrett cites Thucydides 1, 141 as a parallel.

[29]Barrett, *The Gospel According to St. John*, p. 163.

[30]So Bultmann, *The Gospel of John*, p. 56; Beasley-Murray, *John*, p. 12.

Gal 3:27; 1 Pet 3:21). The broader or more inclusive term is "receive," yet in John 1:12 the word is equated with "believe." This would imply that "believe" can be used to embrace more than simple "believing"; "believe" may also include the entire process that is called "conversion." This would still preserve the doctrine that one is saved by divine grace or mercy rather than human merits. Many theologians have yet to wrestle seriously with this problem posed by the biblical and traditional views of conversion and salvation.

For those who receive and believe **he gave the right to become children of God.** Note that becoming children of God is not a human but a divine arrangement. Note also that if one tries to extend the concept (of becoming a child of God) to human infants (as is often attempted), becoming a child of God involves actions that an infant cannot perform, and that these words were intended to be applied to adults, not to babies. By receiving Christ, through faith, repentance, confession, and baptism, one attains the *right* (ἐξουσία, *exousia*) to become a child of God.

1:13. Verse thirteen contrasts birth from God with human begetting and birth (cf. 3:3,5). "Not of bloods" — the Greek is plural and probably is due to (1) the common use of דמים (*damim*) in the plural in Hebrew, and also to (2) the blood of the two parents who beget and bear.[31] The NIV translates **children born not of natural descent.** The clause could refer to one's godly ancestors (e.g., Abraham) who cannot confer divine sonship on human beings.[32] Οὐδὲ ἐκ θελήματος σαρκός (*oude ek thelēmatos sarkos*) is translated (by NIV) **nor of human decision;** οὐδὲ ἐκ θελήματος ἀνδρός (*oude ek thelēmatos andros*) is rendered **nor of a husband's will,** and may refer to the initiative in sexual relations usually ascribed to the husband.[33] In short, the children of God are those who have not been begotten "of bloods."[34]

Several textual scribes and theologians have sought to change the opening word of verse 13, οἵ (*hoi,* "who," a plural form) into a singular (ὅς, *hos*), "[he] who was born, not of blood nor of the will

---

[31]Barrett, *The Gospel According to St. John,* p. 164.

[32]J.W. McGarvey and P.Y. Pendleton, *The Fourfold Gospel or a Harmony of the Four Gospels* (Cincinnati: Standard, 1914), p. 3.

[33]So Beasley-Murray, *John,* p. 13.

[34]Robert F. Hull, Jr., "'Lucanisms' in the Western Text of Acts? A reappraisal," *JBL* 107:702.

of the flesh nor of the will of man, but of God." They thus make
the verse apply to Jesus and, ultimately, to his virgin birth. This
would be a tremendously important allusion in the Fourth Gospel
to a very important doctrine (which is not elsewhere clearly
referred to in the Gospel), and a number of learned commentators
adopt the singular reading.[35] The fact, however, that *all* the *Greek*
manuscripts, as well as nearly all of the versions and patristic citations of the verse, read the plural calls for caution. (The ancient witnesses for the singular are mostly Latin). The singular *hos* may also
have been influenced by the singular number of the immediately
preceding αὐτοῦ (*autou*), "of *him*."

The Logos in Flesh (1:14-18)

[14]**The Word became flesh and made his dwelling among us.
We have seen his glory, the glory of the One and Only,[a] who came
from the Father, full of grace and truth.**

[15]**John testifies concerning him. He cries out, saying, "This
was he of whom I said, 'He who comes after me has surpassed me
because he was before me.'"** [16]**From the fullness of his grace we
have all received one blessing after another.** [17]**For the law was
given through Moses; grace and truth came through Jesus Christ.**
[18]**No one has ever seen God, but God the One and Only,[a,b] who is
at the Father's side, has made him known.**

[a]*14,18 Or the Only Begotten*   [b]*18 Some manuscripts but the only* (or *only
begotten*) *Son*

1:14. This is one of the most profound and meaningful verses in
the Bible: the Logos who was God **became flesh** (a human being)
and "lived for a while" among us (so the 1978 edition NIV), so that
people could see **his glory**, glory of the only son of God. Jesus is
therefore God and God's highest revelation, not merely in spoken
words or writings, but in his human person and actions. The verse
does not say merely that God took up residence in Jesus in a

---

[35]Such as Zahn, Resch, Loisy, R. Seeburg, Barney, Buechsel, Boismard,
Dupont, F.M. Vraun; see Metzger, *Textual Commentary,* p. 197.

manner or degree not realized in anyone else. Rather, the verse says that God turned into a human, masculine being who was made of plain human flesh and resided for a while among plain human beings. In fact, it was through the flesh of the human Jesus that God's glory and truth would be revealed in the fullest way.[36] The truth of this verse concerning Jesus is startling and exciting. Once this is grasped, a reader can never be the same again, because the impact of the incarnation of Jesus upon us changes all of our thoughts, philosophy, life, and influence. The rest of this Gospel shows what this verse means.

The Word became . . . (ἐγένετο, *egeneto*) is a more graphic statement than 1 Tim 3:16: Ὃς ἐφανερώθη ἐν σαρκί (*hos ephanerōthē en sarki*), "who was manifested in the flesh." When used with a noun in the predicative position, the verb γίνομαι (*ginomai*, "to become") signifies that something changed its features or began a new situation by becoming what it was not beforehand.

"The word . . . made his dwelling among us." The Greek verb **made his dwelling** (σκηνόω, *skēnoō*) means "to live in a tent," "to take up one's residence." Some take the verb to be an echo of the Hebrew שָׁכַן (*shakan*) meaning "to dwell," and a noun derived from this Hebrew root (שְׁכִינָה, *shekinah*) meaning "presence," which sounds a bit like the Greek "tent" (σκηνή, *skēnē*), and so in John 1:14 the verb points to the Word's incarnation. The Greek Old Testament (the Septuagint), however, did not usually translate שָׁכַן by *skēnoō*,[37] but this does not prove that John could not have made the association for himself.

From the statement **We have seen** (ἐθεασόμεθα, *etheasometha*), it should be concluded that this Gospel was written by an eyewitness. Many modern exegetes discount such a view, but they certainly are unable to demonstrate that it cannot be so understood.[38] Who is the "us" and the "we" of 1:14? Are they (1) Humanity;[39] (2) John

---

[36]Bultmann, *The Gospel of John*, p. 63.

[37]Barrett, *The Gospel According to St. John*, p. 165.

[38]See Bultmann, *The Gospel of John*, p. 69, who says that Johannine "seeing" is not concerned with eye-witnessing in a historical or legal sense, which is surely false. Cf. Barrett, *The Gospel According to St. John*, p. 166.

[40]Haenchen, *The Gospel of John*, p. 119b.

and the prophets;[40] (3) or most likely, the apostle John and the early Christians?[41]

The author also says **We beheld his glory** (δόξαν, *doxan*). Like his holiness God's glory may be defined as (1) "the sum of all God's attributes."[42] (2) In classical and Hellenistic Greek *doxa* normally meant (a) opinion or (b) honor.[43] It came to mean (3) *dynamis* or might. The term in the Old Testament and Rabbinic literature is (4) כָּבוֹד (*kavod*), which came to be associated with "lights."[44] In the Septuagint, the New Testament, and Hellenistic literature the word can refer to (5) an *epiphany* or *manifestation of the Godhead*.

Doxa here seems to point to Jesus' greatness, (as seen, for example, in his miracles),[45] which lies not only in his deity, wisdom, and power, but all through this Gospel to his humiliating death by crucifixion and to his resurrection from the dead. His "glory" is thus seen in his dying and rising; in these acts the "perfection" of the incarnate Logos is witnessed by many Jews and Gentiles. The Gospel according to John is, then, a book of testimony to Jesus' glory (cf. 20:30-31a; 21:24). Jesus' glory is *seen*, not primarily in his attributes (even "grace and truth"), but in his actions, or works as John calls them, especially in his culminating works of dying and rising. For John, Christ's highest moment of glory is his crucifixion (and rising again). At first, it is indeed difficult to see that a blood-letting death of a criminal on a cross could have anything at all to do with "glory," but this book will go on to show how this very horror became the occasion of revealing the divine "glory."

The words **The glory of the one and only Son** translate δόξαν ὡς μονογενοῦς παρὰ πατρός (*doxan hōs monogenous para patros*). Μονογενοῦς (*monogenous*) means "only one of its category"[46] — μόνος "only" and γένος "race," "kind," and when used in relation to

---

[40]Barrett, *The Gospel According to St. John,* p. 168.

[41]Ibid., p. 167.

[42]A.B. Davidson, *The Theology of the Old Testament* (Edinburgh: T&T Clark, 1904), p. 155.

[43]See Dodd, *Interpretation,* 206-208; TDNT 2:233-234, 255.

[44]Philo, *On the special laws.* 1:45.

[45]Haenchen, *The Gospel of John,* p. 119b.

[46]BAGD, p. 527a.

the "father" it means "only begotten son."[47] Bultmann cites instances
of the term's being applied to pagan divinities with the meaning
"begotten by one alone," that is, by one father without the aid of a
mother (as in the case of Athena who sprang fully grown from the
brain of Zeus),[48] but the LXX's translation of יָחִיד (*yaḥid*) as μονο–
γενής (*monogenēs*) favors "only son," not "only father" (or mother),[49]
or as Bultmann translates: "unique."[50] Jesus is for the first time
called "Son" here.

"Full of grace and truth." "Grace" is not a favorite term in the
Fourth Gospel — in fact, it appears only in 1:14, 16, and 17 —
though its threefold appearance here shows the importance of the
term for the author. Grace is God's undeserved favor.[51] The term
"truth" is a real Johannine term. Sometimes "truth" retains (1) its
ordinary Greek meaning: that which pertains to fact and so is not
false. The Greek ἀλήθεια, "truth," derives from *a-*, "not," and *lan-
thanō*, "to be hidden;" hence "truth" (for the Greek) was "that
which is not hidden," or "what is made manifest."[52] This applies to
what is "uncovered" by human science as well as by divine revelation. (2) The Hebrew for "truth," אֱמֶת, *emeth* (from *amath*, "to be
solid or stable") applies more to personal relationships, and its
opposite was "to break the tie between two or more persons."
These two emphases in truth flow together in Jesus in John's
Gospel. It was suggested by Hoskyns that χάρις (*charis*) referred to
Jesus' miracles, while ἀλήθεια (*alētheia*) referred to his teachings,[53]
but some students have thought this an impossible idea.[54]

1:15. The words **This was he of whom I spoke** are awkward in
Greek (οὗτος ἦν ὃν εἶπον, *houtos ēn hon eipon*), and as one would
expect, several attempts were made by copyists through the earlier
centuries to smooth out the text.[55]

---

[47]Barrett, *The Gospel According to St. John,* p. 166.
[48]Bultmann, *The Gospel of John,* p. 71, n. 2 — the note continues onto
pp. 72 & 73.
[49]So Beasley-Murray, *John,* p. 14.
[50]Bultmann, *The Gospel of John,* p. 72, footnote, line 17.
[51]BAGD, p. 97; *TDNT* 9:392; Leon-Dufour, *DNT,* 215-216.
[52]Leon-Dufour, *DNT,* p. 412.
[53]Hoskyns, *The Fourth Gospel.*
[54]E.g., Bultmann, *The Gospel of John,* p. 74, n. 1.
[55]Another reading, therefore, appears in 𝔓[66] 𝔓[75] א[b] B[3] D Q: οὗτος ἦν ὁ

Notice that John the Baptist's words still witnessed to unbelieving Jews and Gentiles. These words in 1:15 also refer to 1:30.

He who comes after me has surpassed me, because he was before me. Jesus was before John (1) in chronology and (2) in significance. John the Baptist had preached about Jesus before Jesus appeared to begin his ministry. John was by six months Jesus' chronological antecedent; Jesus, however, as Logos, existed long before John and also surpassed John in nature, mission, rank, and importance. Jesus, as the Word, existed from eternity, while John was simply a human prophet whose identity would probably have been extinguished and would have remained unknown to posterity except for the renown of Jesus. The expression "before me" (πρῶτός μου, *prōtos mou*) refers to Jesus' preexistence (as the Logos).[56] (On John's understanding of Jesus' preexistence see 1:30; 6:62; 8:58; 17:5,24.) John's testimony (1) affirms the truth of the incarnation in 1:14 and also (2) rejects any attempt by John or his followers to assert that John was greater than the Messiah due to (1) John's appearing first in history, and (2) John's baptizing Jesus. There were later Baptist sects in the early history of the church who held just such positions.[57]

1:16. The words in verses 16-18 are sometimes ascribed to the writer of the Gospel,[58] while others trace them to the Baptist.[59] The Greek begins, "From his fulness we all have received." Jesus was full of grace and truth (1:14) (and all the other features of deity). **We** here surely means Christians, who by union with Christ, receive many of his qualities, especially grace (cf. Phil 1:9-11; 1 Cor 1:30).

The words **one blessing after another** (χάρις ἀντὶ χάριτος, *charis anti charitos*). have stimulated a mass of interpretations, some of which are: (1) the grace of Jesus takes the place of an earlier Old

---

εἰπών (*houtos ēn ho eipōn*), but the former reading, supported only by the original scribe of the Aleph manuscript, should probably be adopted as in B[5] and Nestle 27 and as given above. The reading ὃν εἰπών is Johannine. See Barrett, *The Gospel According to St. John*, p. 167.

[56]Bultmann, *The Gospel of John*, p. 76.

[57]Cf. Acts 18:25; 19:1-7; Eusebius, *Historia Ecclesiastica* 4:22; Justin Martyr, *Dialogue with Trypho* 80.

[58]See McGarvey and Pendleton, *The Fourfold Gospel*, p. 4.

[59]Cf. Barrett, *The Gospel According to St. John*, p. 168.

Testament grace (ἀντί often means "instead of;" so Chrysostom, but 1:17 says that law, not grace, came through Moses); (2) the phrase describes grace as inexhaustible, in that fresh grace replaces grace that is used up or consumed and will go on doing so perpetually;[60] (3) behind the Greek lies an Aramaic wordplay that eluded the translator: hisda (grace) instead of hisuda or hisda (shame), that is, "shame" (the law) came through Moses, but grace and truth come through Jesus Christ. To this last interpretation it may be objected that (a) an Aramaic prologue remains unproven, and (b) so does a translation error, and further, (c) the Old Testament is never referred to by John as a matter of shame.[61] Number (2) above makes good sense.

1:17. For the law was given (ἐδόθη, edothe). The law was not of human origin,[62] though much of it can be paralleled in human/pagan law codes of the old civilizations of the Near East and Greece and Rome. Such laws, however, as reveal and pertain to Monotheism are largely absent from pagan law collections, though note the law of Hammurabi as a gift of the deity and the view of some Greeks that presupposed one, single God as creator and sustainer of the universe. These, however, were the decidedly minority views of most ancient peoples.

Note that the law was given from God to Moses by angels on Mt. Sinai (Heb. 2:2) and that the law is set in contrast to grace very early in this Gospel; that is, the heart of the Old Testament is seen as less than the New Testament early on in John. Indeed, law and grace or law and gospel are here sharply contrasted. Through Jesus came God's grace and truth (see Heb. 1:1-2; 2:3). This verse excludes Judaism, mystery religions, Gnosticism and all other false "isms" (old and new) as means of salvation.[63]

The law of Moses was intended to bear witness to Jesus (John 5:39), but Moses was more often an accuser (5:45). Note that Jesus is here called Jesus Christ.

---

[60]Somewhat as in Philo, de posteritatis Caini 145; so Barrett, The Gospel According to St. John, p. 169 and Beasley-Murray, John, p. 15.

[61]Barrett, The Gospel According to St. John, citing Matthew Black.

[62]Cf. Pirage Aboth 1:1; Josephus, Antiquities 7, 338.

[63]Bultmann, The Gospel of John, p. 169, n. 5.

1:18. The phrase **No one has ever seen God** shows that just as invisibility is a basic feature of God in the Old Testament (cf. Exod 34:18-20), so it is in the New (1 John 4:12-20; 1 Tim. 6:10). This is why God must reveal himself; he is nondiscoverable until he takes initiative to make himself known. The Bible is a repository of God's disclosure(s) of himself to human witnesses and recipients. Little can be learned of God (except his existence, his power, and possibly that he is a high God morally) without his special revelation to us (Rom 1:20). His *will*, like the will of a stranger, has to be disclosed by revelation from God (1 Cor. 2:11). Once God has revealed his will, he does not need to repeat this revelational information to every human being individually, or to groups, or to special leaders. And John insists here that such revelation of God comes at its highest and clearest form only in Jesus Christ.[64]

The center of this revelation is Jesus Christ because he is the one who **has made him** [the Father] **known.** The term "make known" is ἐξεγήσατο (*exegēsato*), and related to it is the English "exegete." Ἐξηγέομαι (*exēgeomai*) seems to have been more of a Hellenistic than a biblical term. The word meant (1) to recount facts or relate a narrative. This was the main Greek use of the term.[65] The word also meant (2) to make known or explain divine secrets. This latter is its meaning here, and has to do with Hellenistic notions of revelation as well as biblical. It seems important that the prologue closes with such a term. To Jew and Hellenist, Jesus is the revelation of God's glory, grace, and truth.[66]

Should **God the One and Only . . . has made him known** or "the only Son . . . has made him known" be read; that is, should we read "God" or "Son?" The oldest manuscript evidence is heavy for the former reading "God the One and Only."[67] Some students object on the ground that the rest of this verse calls for "son" (υἱός,

---

[64]Bultmann, *The Gospel of John*, p. 169.

[65]See LSJ, sec. III under *exēgeomai*.

[66]Barrett, *The Gospel According to St. John*, p. 170.

[67]This evidence includes the two oldest manuscripts of John, found in the last few decades, 𝔓[66 & 75], as well as the best of the Greek manuscripts (ℵ, B, 33) and most of the Coptic and Syriac translations. Cf. Rudolf Schnackenburg, *The Gospel according to St John* (New York: Herder, 1964), 1:279-280.

huios), that is, the *Son* is the "one who is in the *Father's* bosom" (or with NIV, "at the Father's side"); Jesus (as the Logos), however, has already been described in 1:1 as God and, further, John may be intentionally coming back, at the end of his preface, to this very revelation made in 1:1, namely, that Jesus is God (in flesh).

Some commentators of the twentieth century[68] construe μονο–γενής (*monogenes*) as a noun and so take *monogenes*, θεός (*theos*), and ὁ ὢν εἰς τὸν κόλπον τοῦ πατρός (*ho ōn eis ton kolpon tou patros*) as three titles of the one who makes God known: "the only (begotten)," "God," and "the one being in the bosom of the father." This is a real possibility.[69]

B. THE TESTIMONY OF JOHN THE BAPTIST
AND OF JESUS' FIRST DISCIPLES (1:19-51)

1. The Testimony of John the Baptist (1:19-34)

The Testimony of John to the Jewish Leaders (1:19-28)

[19]Now this was John's testimony when the Jews of Jerusalem sent priests and Levites to ask him who he was. [20]He did not fail to confess, but confessed freely, "I am not the Christ.ᵃ"

[21]They asked him, "Then who are you? Are you Elijah?"

He said, "I am not."

"Are you the Prophet?"

He answered, "No."

[22]Finally they said, "Who are you? Give us an answer to take back to those who sent us. What do you say about yourself?"

[23]John replied in the words of Isaiah the prophet, "I am the voice of one calling in the desert, 'Make straight the way for the Lord.'"ᵇ

---

[68]Edwin A. Abbott, *Johannine grammar.* (London: A. & C. Black, 1906), p. 42; J.H. Bernard, *A Critical and Exegetical Commentary on the Gospel According to St. John*, ICC (Edinburgh: T. & T. Clark, 1929), 1:31; and others more recently.

[69]See John Marsh, *The Gospel According to St. John* (Baltimore: Penguin Books, 1969), p. 112; also Bruce M. Metzger, *A Textual Commentary*, p. 198.

²⁴Now some Pharisees who had been sent ²⁵questioned him, "Why then do you baptize if you are not the Christ, nor Elijah, nor the Prophet?"

²⁶"I baptize with[c] water," John replied, "but among you stands one you do not know. ²⁷He is the one who comes after me, the thongs of whose sandals I am not worthy to untie."

²⁸This all happened at Bethany on the other side of the Jordan, where John was baptizing.

[a]20 Or Messiah. "The Christ" (Greek) and "the Messiah" (Hebrew) both mean "the Anointed One"; also in verse 25.   [b]23 Isaiah 40:3   [c]26 Or in; also in verses 31 and 33

Many think that 1:19-51 is the second and subsidiary introduction to the Gospel. The first, the Prologue, is more theological; the second more practical in that it is centered in the beginning of the ministry of John and Jesus.[70] All four Gospels view John the Baptist as the introducer of Jesus' ministry. In 1:19-34 the Jewish leaders sent a delegation to examine John's own claims and purposes (19-28). John identified himself with no model known to the delegation, though finally in 1:26-27 John enlarged his testimony about the one who was to come after him. In 1:19 he said that that one is the Lamb of God, and in 1:32, 34 John testified that Jesus both received the Holy Spirit and will baptize with the same.

Verses 19-34 seem to echo the Synoptic accounts of the coming one (Mark 1:7-8) and the baptism of Jesus (Mark 1:9-11). Verse 19 is the heading that announced the theme of 1:19-34, namely, "witness" or "testimony" of John.[71] John was the first of a line of witnesses to Jesus in this Gospel. This is because "faith" is "the acceptance of testimony," and here begins the testimony concerning Jesus so that people can accept or reject him (believe or disbelieve) (cf. John 5:32-33).

1:19. In the expression **the Jews of Jerusalem,** "Jews" (in the plural) is the designation usually ascribed by John to Judaism and its leaders (some 70 times). They opposed Jesus and the church, which is presupposed by the writer of this Gospel, even though he

---

[70]Beasley-Murray, *John,* p. 18-19.
[71]Bultmann, *The Gospel of John,* p. 85.

never uses the term "church." The Jews represent the unbelieving world; John the Baptist is a forerunner, not only of Christ, but also of the believing Christians. The Baptist witnessed to a struggle between belief and unbelief that continues and intensifies throughout the life of Jesus.

The **priests** were the main worship functionaries in the temple in Jerusalem and the **Levites** assisted them, especially in music and as temple police. They were also teachers of the law (2 Chr 5:4-14; Neh 8:7-9). John's success in attracting crowds and public excitement probably prompted the investigation by the Jewish leaders. This is the only time that the priests and Levites are mentioned in this Gospel.

1:20. The Baptist was asked to give testimony concerning himself and to answer the Jewish leaders' enquiry as to his own identity. He answered first by a negative piece of testimony concerning who he is *not*: he is not the Messiah. This is the first of a series of denial testimonies from the Baptist, and it concerned the greatest person and title in the series. In verses 19-20, the Baptist testified with the solemnity of a trial; that is, John did *not deny* but *confessed*. These verbs suggest confession and denial of Christ, both of which occur in John (9:22; 12:42; 13:38; 18:25,27). Some suppose that these very words were included in this Gospel in order to refute the false belief of followers of the Baptist towards the end of the first century that the Baptist was the Christ.[72]

1:21. The delegation then asked if he were Elijah. Among Jews it was a well established piece of apocalyptic expectation that Elijah would return before the Messiah's coming[73] and indeed would introduce the Messiah by anointing him.[74] Such expectations rested on Malachi 4:5.[75] See verse 31 below. John denied that he was Elijah.

They then asked if he were **the Prophet** (ὁ προφήτης, *ho prophētēs*). This was not simply a title for the Messiah, but for some old or new prophet who would surpass the great prophet Moses (Deut. 18:15-18), as well as all the other prophets of the Old

---

[72]See, e.g. the *Pseudo-Clementine Recognitions* 1:54,60.
[73]See Barrett, *The Gospel According to St. John*, pp. 173, 177.
[74]Justin, *Apology* 35:1.
[75]Cf. Sirach (or Ecclesiasticus) 48:10.

Testament.[76] John's preaching of repentance reminds one of many
Old Testament prophets, but his real greatness lay in his relation to
Jesus, not to the Old Testament.

1:22. Who are you? The emissaries from Jerusalem were back
where they started. The Baptist fit no known person within the
spectrum of Jewish history and religion.

1:23. For identification of himself and his work, John resorted
to the Scriptures, to the line in Isaiah 40:3 that did not point to him
even as a full person much less as a famous person: **I am [a]** *voice*
of one calling [βοῶντος, *boōntos*, "call," "shout," "cry out"] **in the
desert. Make straight the way for** [τοῦ, *tou*, "of"] **the Lord.** John
was God's word spoken, not God's word incarnate;[77] indeed, he was
like a nameless voicebox that announced God's call for people to
prepare themselves by repentance and immersion in water for the
appearance of the Lord. These were the techniques or methods
used "to make the way straight": people's living was straightened by
repentance and baptism. By stressing the fact that John was a mere
voice, he laid stress, not on his person but on his message. John was
not the literal Elijah but the spiritual Elijah because he performed
the work of Elijah.

The quotation from Isaiah 40:3 agrees with the Septuagint text,
except for εὐθύνατε (*euthynate*, "make straight"); the LXX has
ἑτοιμάσατε (*hetoimasate*, "prepare"). It is possible that the Baptist
made his own translation from the Hebrew פנו (*pannu*), "prepare."

1:24. Some students[78] contend that this parenthetical verse containing the phrase **Some Pharisees who had been sent** casts doubt
on the author's acquaintance with Judaism before A.D. 70, because
the priests and Pharisees were enemies prior to A.D. 70. However,
it should be noted that (1) at least some priests were Pharisees, and
(2) of all the Jewish sects, the Pharisees gave most attention to
rituals, such as baptism, and so were eager to learn why John was
practicing such a ritual.

1:25. Since John denied being the Messiah, Elijah, or the
Prophet, why did he dare to introduce immersion in water as a new

---

[76]Cf. Dead Sea Scrolls 1QS 9:11 ". . . until the coming of the prophet
and the Messiahs of Aaron and Israel."

[77]Barrett, *The Gospel According to St. John,* p. 174.

[78]Ibid., p. 174.

ritual beyond anything contained in Mosaic law? The answer points to John's baptism as a new rite. Even if Jewish proselyte baptism existed in the first century (and this is not certain), it differed from John's practice in at least two ways: (1) John baptized his own converts while proselytes to Judaism practiced self-immersion, (2) John baptized Jews but no non-Jews.[79] This is the first mention of baptism in the Fourth Gospel.

1:26-27. John replied that he baptized with water, but among the present company stood one whom they did not know. Why not introduce here and now the fact that this one who stood among them would baptize with Spirit? (cf. 1:33). It was because that truth was not revealed to the Baptist until he beheld the Spirit's coming down on Jesus at Jesus' own baptism.

Not even John knew Jesus for what he really was, namely, the Messiah of Israel. Jesus stood in their midst as the hidden Messiah. **He is the one who comes after me**, i.e., after the Baptist had prepared the way for Jesus.[80]

1:28. This all happened at Bethany beyond **the Jordan.** There are several variant forms for Bethany in the manuscripts but they all boil down to only two: "Bethany" and "Betharbara." Origen could find no Bethany beyond Jordan, so he adopted Betharbara as the reading, because the name's meaning, he said, was "House of Preparation," which fit the meaning of the Baptist's work there — calling for baptism and repentance *to prepare* Israel for the Messiah. The meaning of the names, however, are probably Bethany = House of the poor man and Betharbara = House of the ford or ferry (of the Jordan).[81] "Bethany" is surely the best reading here.[82]

The Testimony of John to the Jewish People (1:29-34)

[29]**The next day John saw Jesus coming toward him and said, "Look, the Lamb of God, who takes away the sin of the world!**

---

[79]McGarvey and Pendleton, *The Fourfold Gospel*, p. 104.

[80]The manuscripts in v. 26 read four different tenses for "he stands," of which the perfect, ἔστηκεν (*hestēken*), seems most likely to preserve the original reading. See Metzger, *A Textual Commentary*, p. 199.

[81]Cf. ibid., p. 199, n. 5.

[82]See Barrett's discussion, *The Gospel According to St. John*, p. 175.

³⁰**This is the one I meant when I said, 'A man who comes after me has surpassed me because he was before me.'** ³¹**I myself did not know him, but the reason I came baptizing with water was that he might be revealed to Israel."**

³²**Then John gave this testimony: "I saw the Spirit come down from heaven as a dove and remain on him.** ³³**I would not have known him, except that the one who sent me to baptize with water told me, 'The man on whom you see the Spirit come down and remain is he who will baptize with the Holy Spirit.'** ³⁴**I have seen and I testify that this is the Son of God."**

1:29. Note the phrase **The next day.** Many commentators make little of the chronological notes in the Fourth Gospel, but in 1:29, 35, 43; 2:1 the writer clusters a group of events in days. The earthly Jesus actually appears here for the first time in the Gospel. He was approaching John, and John **said, "Look, the Lamb of God, who takes away the sin of the world!"** Jesus was not coming to John for baptism; this had already occurred. The scene has changed from the day before because the delegation has departed, and Jesus is now center stage. It is possible that verses 19ff refer to verses 6-8, and now verses 29f refer to verse 15.

Why did John call Jesus **the Lamb of God**?" In the Old Testament, lambs were used for sin-offerings (Lev 4:32), in the cleansing of a leper (Lev 14:10), in the daily morning and afternoon sacrifices in the temple (Exod 19:38), and at the Passover supper (Exod 12:3-4). There is also the lamb (ἀμνός, *amnos*) of Isaiah 53:7. The death of none of these lambs, however, was said to be an expiatory or atoning sacrifice, unless Leviticus 4:32 be so construed. The lambs of the Testament of Joseph 19:8 and of the Testament of Benjamin 3:8 also were not treated as offerings for forgiveness of sin; the same is true of the lamb mentioned in the Dead Sea Scrolls, 1 QH 3:10; 8:10f, because the Essenes of Qumran rejected animal sacrifice.

This Lamb of God "takes away the sin of the world." The death of this Lamb will remove the power and penalty of sin from individual human beings. Jesus is the Lamb who, by his death and resurrection, died and rose out from under sin's power and penalty and is now able to share his victory over sin, death, hell, and Satan by our becoming one with him in his death and resurrection.

Notice that "sin" is (a collective) singular, though no great weight should probably be placed on this fact (as does, e.g., Brown).[83] Jesus as God's Lamb that "takes away" sin is a fulfillment of the imagery of the Passover lamb. Note that it is not Jesus' teaching that removed sin, nor his miracles. Lambs do not teach or perform signs; they each die as a sacrifice, so especially a paschal lamb. Sin is removed by sacrifice (Heb 9:22; Rev 5:9). The Jews who first heard these words from the Baptist must have had difficulty understanding them because they had thought little of the Old Testament sacrifices as being fulfilled in a human being. Jesus is God's only adequate sin offering (Heb 10:4-18; 1 Pet 1:19). If the Passover lamb was the background of this "Lamb of God" figure in verses 29 and 36, there was a difference between the paschal lamb and God's lamb: the Passover dealt only with *Israel's* sins, while the Lamb of God took away the *world's* sins.

Commentators shy away from the grammatical relationship of "God" and "the Lamb." Is "God's" (τοῦ θεοῦ, *tou theou*) a genitive of possession ("God's lamb") or a genitive of description ("a divine lamb") or an ablative of source ("the lamb from God"), or some other possibility?

1:30. The greater does not *precede* but *succeeds*. See verses 15 and 27 for John's testimony.[84]

1:31. I myself did not know him. It should not be concluded that John did not know Jesus at all (the two were kinsmen only six months apart in age), but only that John did not know Jesus as the Coming One or the Messiah. The Fourth Gospel goes on to say that the reason for John's baptism was not only to prepare the people for the Messiah, but to manifest (φανερωθῇ, *phanerōthē*) Jesus as the Messiah to Israel. Jesus was revealed at his baptism as Messiah — to John and to the rest of Israel. Elijah was to do this "manifesting," though this Gospel does not concur that the Baptist was identical to Elijah. Many Jews believed that the Messiah would be an obscure person until revealed to Israel (by Elijah).[85] "Israel" is

---

[83]Raymond E. Brown, *The Gospel According to John*, The Anchor Bible (Garden City, NY: Doubleday, 1966-70), 1:56.

[84]Ibid., p. 64.

[85]See Justin Martyr, *Trypho* 8:49 and the *Mishnah, Sotah* 9:15; *Eduyoth* 8:7; cf. Barrett, *The Gospel According to St. John*, p. 177.

used four times in the Fourth Gospel and does not convey the bad connotations associated with the term "the Jews."

1:32-33. These verses repeat and elaborate the essence of 1:31; they are also the heart and climax of John's testimony about Jesus: John saw the Spirit come down as a dove from heaven and remain on Jesus. John then testified (ἐμαρτύρησεν, *emartyrēsen*) in verse 33 that he would not have recognized the Messiah had not God, who had sent John to baptize, told him that the man on whom he would see the Spirit come down and remain would be the one who was to baptize with the Holy Spirit. The Baptist added in 1:34, **I have seen and I testify that this is the Son of God.** This Jesus thus both takes away sin and gives the Spirit — because he is God's Son (cf. Mark 1:10 and parallels).

1:34. The Fourth Gospel assumes knowledge of the story of the baptism of Jesus in the Synoptic gospels. John himself did not actually report the baptism of Jesus. It is possible, so some say, that this Gospel omitted the Baptist's baptizing of Jesus because the early church was embarrassed by the Baptist's followers who saw in this act a denigration of Jesus and an exaltation of the Baptist.[86] This Gospel, however, stressed two things: (1) Jesus was the one who baptized in Spirit, not the Baptist, and (2) the Synoptics portray Jesus as the one primarily to see the Spirit descend as a dove, but John portrayed *the Baptist* (also) as seeing the Spirit's descent, and this prevents one's viewing the event as simply a private, subjective experience of Jesus with no external reality to it.

It has been observed that the Fourth Gospel never called John "the Baptist," as Mark 1:4 and Matthew 3:1 do.[87] To whom is John speaking in verses 29-34? Probably (1) not the emissaries of verses 19-27, but possibly (2) John's own disciples, (3) possibly the readers of this Gospel, or most likely (4) a mixed audience of all kinds of persons who had come out to hear him in the wilderness.[88]

These first paragraphs, devoted to John's ministry and witness, close with the straightforward testimony of John to Jesus: **I have seen and I testify that this [one] is the Son of God** (v. 34). This

---

[86]See Luke Timothy Johnson, *The Real Jesus* (San Francisco: Harper, 1996), p. 124.

[87]Cf. Haenchen *The Gospel of John*, 1:149a.

[88]Haenchen disagrees; ibid., 1:152.

testimony was the main purpose and product of the Baptist's mission: to bear witness to Christ as more than a prophet or teacher; Jesus is the Son of God. Faith is the acceptance of testimony. People can now begin to believe — or disbelieve — as they begin to accept or reject — the testimony to Jesus in this Gospel. Both Jesus and John were prophets, but only Jesus was God's Son.

Alfred Plummer, in his commentary on Luke 3:21,[89] insists, on the basis of the Greek, that Jesus was baptized after all the multitudes had been baptized and gone from the site; that is, Jesus' baptism was *private* and not *public*. This accounts, Plummer says, for the voice and dove's appearance not being experienced by the multitudes: the crowds were not present. The words in Luke 3:21 more likely mean that Jesus was baptized after the crowds on a particular day had dispersed, or more likely it means that Jesus came after the climax of John's ministry had been attained and hence not as many people were on hand. None of the Gospels presents Jesus' baptism as a private affair. Jesus was not ashamed of the humble moments of his career; he did not hide his incarnation at such times, as the coming of the Spirit upon him and the voice that spoke concerning him show.[90] Jesus' baptism was quite like our own (and at the same time vastly different): it marked the close of one part of his life and career and the beginning of a greatly different part.

The title "Son of God" was encountered more often in Judaism than has sometimes been admitted. (1) The *nation* of Israel was called God's first-born son (Exod 4:22-23; cf. Hosea 11:1); (2) David's promised male descendant, who would sit on David's throne, would be acknowledged as God's son according to 2 Samuel 7:14, a passage that by the first century A.D. had come to be understood messianically. This means that *the king* had come to be spoken of as "God's Son" (cf. Ps 1:7; 89:26-27). In the Daniel Apocryphon of the Qumran Cave 4, therefore, reference is made to the king as the "Son of God."[91] (3) In Sirach 4:10; Wisdom of Solomon 2:18; and

---

[89]Alfred Plummer, *A Critical and Exegetical Commentary on the Gospel According to St. Luke* (New York: Scribners, 1896), p. 98.

[90]See R.C. Foster, *Studies in the Life of Christ* (Grand Rapids: Baker, 1938-68; reprint, Joplin, MO: College Press, 1996), pp. 225-226.

[91]Cf. also in Qumran literature the references to "Son of God" in 4Q Flor 1:61; IQ Sa 2:11ff.

Jubilees 1:24-25, *"the righteous"* were called God's sons. (4) Even so-called *"miracle workers"* were sometimes called "Sons of God."[92] (5) Also the *angels* were called "God's sons" in the Septuagint Greek of Deut. 32:43.[93]

It was, therefore, inevitable that (6) *the Messiah* should be called "the Son of God" (on the basis of Ps 2:7 and 2 Sam 7:14). The unbelieving Jews, of course, sought to reinterpret any application of the title "Son of God" to these passages, and to the Messiah at all. It is surprising to find Psalm 2:7 still interpreted of God's Son, the Messiah, in *Midrashim on the Psalms* (2:9) and in an even older passage in a Baraitha (an addition) to the Babylonian Talmudic tract called *Sukka* (52a), which relates Psalm 2:7 to the Messiah ben David.[94]

2. Jesus' Calling and the Testifying of His First Disciples (1:35-51)

John the Baptist's Disciples Follow Jesus. (1:35-42)

[35]The next day John was there again with two of his disciples. [36]When he saw Jesus passing by, he said, "Look, the Lamb of God!"

[37]When the two disciples heard him say this, they followed Jesus. [38]Turning around, Jesus saw them following and asked, "What do you want?"

They said, "Rabbi" (which means Teacher), "where are you staying?"

[39]"Come," he replied, "and you will see."

So they went and saw where he was staying, and spent that day with him. It was about the tenth hour.

[40]Andrew, Simon Peter's brother, was one of the two who heard what John had said and who had followed Jesus. [41]The first

---

[92]See Martin Hengel, *The Son of God* (Philadelphia: Fortress, 1976), pp. 42-43.

[93]See Eduard Lohse, "υἱός" in OT, Josephus, Philo, Palestinian Judaism, *TDNT* 8:354-363, especially 355.

[94]See Hermann Strack and Paul Billerbeck, *Kommentar des neuen Testament aus Talmud und Midrasch* (Munich: C.H. Beck, 1923), 3:19; Lohse, "υἱός," *TDNT* 8:361-362.

thing Andrew did was to find his brother Simon and tell him, "We have found the Messiah" (that is, the Christ). **⁴²And he brought him to Jesus.**

Jesus looked at him and said, "You are Simon son of John. You will be called Cephas" (which, when translated, is Peter).ª

ª*42 Both Cephas (Aramaic) and Peter (Greek) mean rock.*

1:35-36. On the morrow John the Baptist was standing with two of his disciples and Jesus passed by; again, John **said, "Look, the Lamb of God!"** These two disciples of John are left unnamed, but the Synoptics name James and John as Jesus' first disciples; so, the second of these two was probably the writer of this Gospel.[95]

1:37. Then these two began to follow Jesus (ἠκολούθησαν (*ēkolouthēsan*) is probably an ingressive aorist, i.e., the use of a verb form that describes the beginning of an action). "To follow" (ἀκολουθέω, *akoloutheō*) is a technical term in Hebrew and Greek for the reactions and relationships of a disciple to his teacher/model/guide. This scene is more the *call* of the disciples than their actual *following a leader*. The text means primarily that the two disciples simply followed Jesus to the place where he was temporarily lodging because they wanted to talk with him. At the same time, they did begin to follow Jesus as disciples. The essence of Christianity lies in those words: to follow Jesus. Following is the expected result of the Baptist's testimony (μαρτυρία, *martyria*).

1:38. When Jesus saw the two disciples following, he turned and asked what they wanted. They replied that they wished to know **where he was staying**. The word for "staying" is μένεις (*meneis*), which has a rich meaning in this Gospel, but here it probably was meant to be taken literally and with no profound theological implications, such as the suggestion of Bultmann[96] that the question "What do you seek?" is always Jesus' question to every potential disciple.

Rabbi means literally "my great one," and John's translation of it as **teacher** (διδάσκαλος, *didaskalos*) is not literal but done according to usage.[97] The absence of evidence for the title "Rabbi" before

---

[95]Brown, *John*, 1:73.
[96]Bultmann, *The Gospel of John*, p. 100.
[97]Brown, *John*, 1:74.

A.D. 70 has raised the question of the Gospels' possible anachronistic usage of the term. E.L. Sukenik, in a work published in 1931,[98] reported his discovery of an ossuary (a jar for keeping the bones of a dead person) on the Mount of Olives, which bore the word *didaskalos*, the very word that John used for "Rabbi." The New Testament's usage of the title "Rabbi," therefore, is not anachronistic after all.[99]

1:39. The two disciples visited with Jesus — and possibly spent the night with him, because John says it was the tenth hour; that is, it was about 4:00 P.M. when they left with Jesus.[100] All of the Gospels use this method of reckoning time — the day of twelve hours from roughly 6:00 A.M. to 6:00 P.M.[101]

1:40-41. Andrew was the name of the disciple of the Baptist who heard John's testimony to Jesus and came and visited Jesus. The identity of the unnamed disciple here is unknown, though Brown thinks that he is to be identified with the one whom this Gospel calls "the beloved disciple;"[102] Boismard thinks that the unnamed disciple was Philip, since Philip and Andrew go together in this Gospel (6:5-9; 12:21-22) and came from the same village (1:44).[103] Andrew "first, before he did anything else," or, "before the other unnamed disciple could find his brother,"[104] found Simon Peter, his very own (ἴδιον, *idion*) brother (not simply a relative). Andrew then brought Simon to Jesus, and thus, in a sense, became the first Christian evangelist.[105]

John explains here the Hebrew or Aramaic title used of Jesus (Messiah) and translates it as the Christ, i.e., "the one anointed" by God — anointed as a prophet, priest, and king (the persons usually anointed in the Old Testament) — who was intended to fulfill the Old Testament prophecies and to inaugurate a new covenant.

---

[98]E.L. Sukenik, *Juedische Graeber Jerusalems um Christi Geburt* (1931).

[99]Cf. Brown, *John*, 1:74.

[100]Beasley-Murray, *John*, p. 26.

[101]Barrett, *The Gospel According to St. John*, p. 181.

[102]Brown, *John*, 1:73-74.

[103]M.E. Boismard, *Du baptême à Cana* (Jean 1:19–2:11) (Paris: Cerf, 1956), pp. 72-73.

[104]See Barrett, *The Gospel According to St. John*, pp. 181-182.

[105]McGarvey and Pendleton, *The Fourfold Gospel*, p. 110.

1:42. When Jesus first saw Peter, he said, **"You are Simon son of John. You will be called Cephas" (which, when translated, is Peter).** The other Gospels locate this change of Simon's name about midway through each of the Synoptics. The fact that the future tense is used "You will be called" points to a later time of fulfillment at least of the meaning if not the giving of the new name. As Beasley-Murray writes, ". . . v. 42 (is) recording the *source* of Simon's new name, not the *time* when it was given."[106]

What did Jesus intend here (v. 42) by changing Simon's name to Peter? He probably intended to point to Simon's character and stability: as Simon was now constituted, he was immature and unreliable, but in time, by sufferings and even defeats, he would become a stable Christian disciple, and even eventually a pioneer and leader in the church.

Jesus' Calling of Philip and Nathanael (1:43-51)

[43]The next day Jesus decided to leave for Galilee. Finding Philip, he said to him, "Follow me."

[44]Philip, like Andrew and Peter, was from the town of Bethsaida. [45]Philip found Nathanael and told him, "We have found the one Moses wrote about in the Law, and about whom the prophets also wrote — Jesus of Nazareth, the son of Joseph."

[46]"Nazareth! Can anything good come from there?" Nathanael asked.

"Come and see," said Philip.

[47]When Jesus saw Nathanael approaching, he said of him, "Here is a true Israelite, in whom there is nothing false."

[48]"How do you know me?" Nathanael asked.

Jesus answered, "I saw you while you were still under the fig tree before Philip called you."

[49]Then Nathanael declared, "Rabbi, you are the Son of God; you are the King of Israel."

[50]Jesus said, "You believe[a] because I told you I saw you under the fig tree. You shall see greater things than that." [51]He then

---

[106]Beasley-Murray, *John*, p. 27.

added, "I tell you[b] the truth, you[b] shall see heaven open, and the
angles of God ascending and descending on the Son of Man."

[a]*50* Or *Do you believe . . . ?*   [b]*51* The Greek is plural

1:43. On the next day, Philip was called by Jesus. Only in John's
Gospel is much said of him (6:5-8; 12:21-22; 14:8-10). He is simply
alluded to in the list of apostles in the other Gospels. His name is
Greek (it means "Lover of horses") and was borne by Alexander
the Great's father. This may not prove, however, that Philip was of
Greek ancestry because the same name was worn by one of the
Jewish Amora (famous rabbis of the late first and second centuries
A.D.).[107] It may point to some of the family's education in things
Grecian as well as Jewish — somewhat like the apostle Paul's cul-
tural situation. Philip was from the city of Bethsaida in Galilee, an
area whose culture was quite mixed, and it was also the region of
Andrew and Peter. Philip is the first one to be called personally by
Jesus to discipleship.

1:44. The city of Bethsaida actually lay in Gaulanitis on the east
side of the Jordan where the river empties into the Sea of Galilee.
The city, however, (1) may have had a Jewish community or (2) it
may have had a smaller part of its locale situated also on the western
bank of the Jordan. At any rate, evidence exists that the common
folk used "Galilee" to refer to some of the area east of the Jordan;
for example, Josephus speaks of "Judas the Galilean" as from
Gamala, which lay east of the lake.[108] Moreover, Capernaum (the
home of Peter and Andrew) was only a few miles west of Bethsaida.
Edwin A. Abbott[109] says that Philip, Andrew, and Peter were *out of*
(*ek*) Bethsaida because they had been born there, but they were also
from (*apo*) Capernaum, because they currently lived there.

1:45. Philip found Nathanael, who is not mentioned even in the
lists of the apostles. His name does appear a second time in John
21:2, so commentators have been eager to supply him with a name

---

[107]Barrett, *The Gospel According to St. John,* p. 183.

[108]D.A. Carson, *The Gospel According to John* (Grand Rapids: Eerdmans,
1991), p. 158.

[109]Edwin A. Abbott, *Johannine Grammar* (London: A & C Black, 1905),
section 2289.

from the apostolic lists. Bartholomew is the favorite choice. Unlike the NIV, there is no definite article with "son" (*huios*) in the oldest manuscripts: **Jesus . . . son of Joseph.** This is naturally the way that one who was uninformed would look upon Jesus — as Joseph's son.

1:46. Nathanael responded that nothing good could come from Nazareth. Why? Because it was a *No place*: it is never mentioned in the Old Testament, the Jewish Talmud and Midrash, nor in any extant pagan writing. Jesus' residence in Nazareth is like his birth in a stable, his crucifixion, or his burial in a borrowed tomb: aspects of the offense of the incarnation.[110] In the long run, the best thing in the universe came out of Nazareth.

Philip requested that Nathanael come and see — the same request that Jesus made of the two disciples of the Baptist in verse 39.

1:47. Jesus greeted Nathanael as **a true** [the Greek uses an adverb "truly"] **Israelite in whom there is nothing false.** The Greek says δόλος οὐκ ἔστιν (*dolos ouk estin,* "there is not deceit"). Why the expression "not deceit"? (1) The words were possibly drawn from Psalm 32:2, "And in whose spirit is no deceit" (NIV). More likely (2) Nathanael is thought of as being in the lineage of Jacob/Israel but who does not partake of the deceit of his forebearers; cf. Genesis 27:35, "your brother came and *with deceit* took your blessing."[111]

1:48. Jesus' statement about Nathanael prompted Nathanael to ask how Jesus knew him. Jesus responded that he had seen Nathanael as the latter sat under a fig tree some distance away from Jesus. Many modern commentators associate such uncanny knowledge with what they call a "divine man" among pagans and even some Jews. Such knowledge was part of the divine man's magical powers.[112] Jesus, however, never seems to have been viewed as such a "magician" in the Gospels. The Old Testament knew something of such a power among some of the prophets (cf. 2 Kgs 6:8-12; Ezek 8:1-18; 21:21-23). Jesus, however, was more than the Old Testament prophets, because he knew both the mind of God and the mind of mankind.

1:49. Nathanael sensed this truth and so exclaimed, "**. . . you are the Son of God; you are the king of Israel.**" In this context the

---

[110]Beasley-Murray, *John,* p. 27.

[111]Masoretic and Septuagint texts.

[112]Cf. Haenchen, *The Gospel of John,* 1:166a.

titles may have been roughly synonymous for Nathanael.[113] They
are surely Messianic titles (cf. 1:34).

1:50. Jesus paused to note both the maturity and immaturity of
Nathanael's faith, exhibited by the titles that he gave to Jesus (Son
of God, King of Israel). Here was the beginnings of faith in Jesus by
another new disciple, but Jesus pointed out that it is faith based on
the supernatural (Jesus' knowledge of Nathanael's character and
location at a distance). Jesus seemed to hint that the greater kind of
faith rests on a less physical base, though the rest of the verse says
that Nathanael will see greater things than this rather mild display
of the supernatural in Jesus: **You shall see greater things than that.**
What greater things? (1) Jesus' revelations; (2) Jesus' miracles;
(3) Jesus' perfect life; (4) Jesus' death and resurrection; and (5) the
gospel of Jesus and its winning of the world; (6) the Parousia and
End — that is, the greatness of the Son of Man[114] from the incarnation to the parousia.[115]

1:51. I tell you the truth translates the "Truly, truly I say to
you," which was much used (25 times) in this Gospel to introduce
an important saying of Jesus. Jesus then proceeded to say that the
disciples (the number is plural, so more than simply Nathanael
seem to be addressed) would **see heaven open and the angels of
God ascending and descending on the Son of Man.** Commentators struggle with this saying. It is difficult! The saying surely has
Jacob's dream in Genesis 28:12 in mind with the angels' ascending
and descending, though notice that in this verse John reversed the
order of these angelic actions, and also in John both Jacob and the
ladder faded away and the angels ascend and descend on or to (ἐπί,
epi) the Son of Man. The saying seems to tell us that Jesus keeps in
touch with both heaven and earth, that the highest creatures in all
creation serve him, that he stands as the junction point that holds
heaven and earth together, and that it is no longer patriarchs,
angels, or anything else in all creation and beyond it that count but
only the God who is in Jesus.

Jesus sees the angels in relation to "the Son of Man." This is the
first occurrence in John of this title. In all instances (except one,

---

[113]Beasley-Murray, *John*, p. 27.

[114]Carson, *The Gospel According to John*, p. 162.

[115]See Beasley-Murray, *John*, p. 28.

Acts 7:56) the title was used by Jesus only, so it is the title that he preferred. Why? It referred only to him. It was an imprecise designation, unlike King of Israel or Son of God, which could be politically or theologically explosive among the Jews of the first century A.D. Jesus, therefore, could more easily pack new meaning into the title Son of Man than into probably any other. The expression appears 13 times in John. Other reasons why Jesus preferred to use the title "Son of Man" were: (1) it appeared in the Old Testament (cf. Dan 7:13-14) (2) often meant simply "I" on the lips of Jesus (John 6:20, 27), (3) held a prominent place with Jesus' several predictions of his death and resurrection (John 3:14; 8:28), (4) quite often was associated with the future end of the world and Jesus' parousia (5:27; 9:39), and (5) in John especially, was allied with divine revelation in and through Jesus (6:27, 53). While the title Son of Man surely pointed to Jesus' human nature, it also carried strong messianic overtones, uniting the divine and the human in Jesus.[116]

In the first chapter of John, titles carry much of the testimony presented here to Jesus. In John chapter one, Jesus is called Word, teacher (Rabbi, 1:34), Lamb of God, Messiah, Son of God, King of Israel, and Son of Man. These epithets really say that Jesus is unique. John the Baptist was at most only a witness — important, but only as a servant, not as the Master.

---

[116]Clay Ham, "The Title 'Son of Man' in the Gospel of John," *Stone-Campbell Journal* 1 (Spring, 1998): 67-84.

JOHN 2

C. JESUS' FIRST SIGNS (2:1-25)

1. Jesus Changes Water into Wine (2:1-12)

¹On the third day a wedding took place at Cana in Galilee. Jesus' mother was there, ²and Jesus and his disciples had also been invited to the wedding. ³When the wine was gone, Jesus' mother said to him, "They have no more wine."

⁴"Dear woman, why do you involve me?" Jesus replied. "My time has not yet come."

⁵His mother said to the servants, "Do whatever he tells you."

⁶Nearby stood six stone water jars, the kind used by the Jews for ceremonial washing, each holding from twenty to thirty gallons.ᵃ

⁷Jesus said to the servants, "Fill the jars with water"; so they filled them to the brim.

⁸Then he told them, "Now draw some out and take it to the master of the banquet."

They did so, ⁹and the master of the banquet tasted the water that had been turned into wine. He did not realize where it had come from, though the servants who had drawn the water knew. Then he called the bridegroom aside ¹⁰and said, "Everyone brings out the choice wine first and then the cheaper wine after the guests have had too much to drink; but you have saved the best till now."

¹¹This, the first of his miraculous signs, Jesus performed at Cana in Galilee. He thus revealed his glory, and his disciples put their faith in him.

¹²After this he went down to Capernaum with his mother and brothers and his disciples. There they stayed for a few days.

ᵃ6 Greek *two to three metretes* (probably about 75 to 115 liters)

A wedding feast that is attended by Jesus, his disciples, and his mother became the site of Jesus' first miracle. The miracle consisted of turning the water that filled six stone water pots, just filled by servants of the feast, into wine. This miracle has no parallel in the Synoptics, but some students have sought parallels in Philo the Jew (*Legum Allegoriae* 3:82) and in Dionysiac worship of the pagans (Euripides, *Bacchae* 704-707); Pausanias 6:26:1f).[1] No one has demonstrated that this miracle was not performed by Jesus just as it is related, though it is possible that John may have written the story with Jewish and Hellenistic customs and parallels in mind so as all the more to appeal to both groups.

2:1-2. These verses are tied to chapter one by reference to the third day, though the content of the first and second chapters of John is very different. The "third day" is from the calling of Philip in 1:43.[2]

Cana in Galilee was probably not far from Nazareth. There are at least three sites that bear some form of this name in modern Palestine, but which is the correct site is not certain. It is significant that the first miracle of Jesus was performed in Galilee and not in Judea.

Jesus' mother was there. John never uses the name Mary, but always relates her to Jesus. She derives her identity from Jesus, not Jesus from her. (She is mentioned in 2:12; 6:42; 19:25ff).

2:3-4. Wine, as a refreshment, ran out at the feast. Mary told Jesus about this embarrassment for the host. Jesus asked her, **"Why do you involve me?"** Literally, he asked her "What (is it) to me and to you, woman? Not yet has my hour come." These words have troubled many exegetes. There is no disrespect here by Jesus to his mother, nor is there any sign of adoring her.[3] Jesus seems to be saying that his decisions are his own and that they depend only on him and his Father.[4] The "coming of Jesus' hour" in John refers to the time of his being glorified — not to the glory of a miracle like changing water to wine but to the glory of his death on the cross.

2:5. His mother then asked the servants to **do whatever he tells you** — possibly the wisest request that Mary ever made, though the

---

[1]Barrett, *The Gospel According to St. John*, p. 188.
[2]McGarvey and Pendleton, *The Fourfold Gospel*, p. 114.
[3]Carson, *The Gospel According to John*, p. 170.
[4]Barrett, *The Gospel According to St. John*, p. 191.

application of these words in this setting was restricted to a rather mundane performance. Mary was probably well known to the family that hosted the wedding. At any rate, she made herself at home by proceeding to remedy the short supply of the wedding refreshment.[5]

Just why the wine at the wedding ran out was not stated, so Zahn's guess that it was due to the unexpected arrival of Jesus and his disciples is groundless[6]; and, even if it were true, Jesus became the *solution,* as well as cause, of the dilemma.

2:6-7. Nearby stood six stone water jars, the kind that the Jews used for ceremonial washings, each holding from twenty to thirty gallons. Their total content was thus from 120 to 180 gallons. Jesus had the servants of the feast fill them completely with water. No one could therefore say that Jesus' power was limited so that he could perform on only one or two of the jars. Likewise, he had each jar filled to its brim, so no one could assert that some magic potion was added by him to the water. When God performs a special work he does an adequate job of it!

2:8-10. The servants brought the wine to the master of the banquet (v. 9), who tasted the water-made-wine and told the bridegroom that usually the best wine was served first and then the lesser or cheaper, but in this case, the bridegroom had saved the best until last.

Some problems remain with this story: (1) Did Jesus create fermented wine (οἶνος, *oinos*)? (2) What was/were his purpose or purposes in performing this activity? (3) Why stone jars, not, say, ceramic jars?

(1) The wine may not have been intoxicating. *Oinos* may also mean unfermented grape juice, though the usual word for grape juice is τρύξ, *tryx*.[7] Among most Jews in Palestine there is evidence that wine was mixed with water for drinking purposes — from 70% to 90% water was usual.[8] However, we cannot ignore the possibility that the steward had intoxication in mind when he said the guests

---

[5]Cf. Bultmann, *The Gospel of John*, p. 116, n. 2.

[6]T. Zahn, *Das Evangelium des Johannes ausgelegt* (Leipzig: Deichert, 1921), p. 152.

[7]BAGD, p. 562a.

[8]Cf. Carson, *The Gospel According to John*, p. 169.

could no longer tell the difference between wines after they had drunk freely (NIV: "have had too much to drink"). (2) The purpose of this story was to arouse in the disciples faith in Jesus. True, it is faith in what is seen rather than in what is unseen; but, it *is* faith! (3) Stoneware, unlike earthenware, did not contract Jewish uncleanness; thus, stone utensils were more fitting for holding water that was to be used for ceremonial purifications. There was probably little symbolic significance in the number six. There is great significance in transforming the ordinary ceremonial water into delicious wine.

2:11. This was **the first of his miraculous signs, Jesus performed at Cana in Galilee**. John calls them "signs," while other New Testament writers call them "signs, powers, and wonders" (NIV "miraculous signs"). What Jesus performed was a miracle. It usually takes soil, sunshine, showers, and time to make wine or grape juice — and Jesus created wine instantly from nothing but water. **He thus revealed his glory, and his disciples put their faith** [trust] (an ingressive aorist, "began to believe,") **in him**. Notice that they accepted the testimony which this miracle offered concerning Jesus — to his humanness and to his power. The first testimony to Jesus in this Gospel is that of John the Baptist in (1:19, 20, 27, 29 34, 35), a testimony that was based on the miraculous manifestation of the Spirit as a dove at Jesus' baptism. Next, Andrew and Peter come to Jesus, whose faith seems to have been strengthened, if not created, by Jesus' prophecy that Simon's name would become Peter, the Stone. Then, Philip and Nathanael's faith is incited by their response to Jesus' miraculous knowledge (both present and future) of Nathanael's name and character. All of these have one thing in common: a positive response to Jesus' power to work miracles. These earlier instances are quite privately done (even the Spirit's coming as a dove at Jesus' baptism was primarily for Jesus' and John's sake); the work performed at the wedding feast was more public. The aim and result, however, are all the same — to create faith in Jesus; that is, to encourage people to accept the testimony to Jesus provided by these signs, shown to John the Baptist and to the earliest disciples.[9]

---

[9]Bultmann, *The Gospel of John*, pp. 118-119, esp. 119, n. 1. Bultmann, therefore, misses totally the point of the water-to-wine event at the

2:12. Jesus, his mother, brothers, and disciples then traveled from Cana to Capernaum for a few days. Peter had a home in Capernaum which became a kind of headquarters for Jesus and his disciples.

2. Jesus Cleanses the Temple (2:13-22)

[13]When it was almost time for the Jewish Passover, Jesus went up to Jerusalem. [14]In the temple courts he found men selling cattle, sheep and doves, and others sitting at tables exchanging money. [15]So he made a whip out of cords, and drove all from the temple area, both sheep and cattle; he scattered the coins of the money changers and overturned their tables. [16]To those who sold doves he said, "Get these out of here! How dare you turn my Father's house into a market!"

[17]His disciples remembered that it is written: "Zeal for your house will consume me."[a]

[18]Then the Jews demanded of him, "What miraculous sign can you show us to prove your authority to do all this?"

[19]Jesus answered them, "Destroy this temple, and I will raise it again in three days."

---

wedding feast. He says that the story was taken over from the heathen legend of Dionysius (Greek -os) in Greece that wine poured from a temple spring in Andros and also at Teos. These legends, however, did not say that the water was turned to wine, but that water ceased to flow and then wine flowed briefly. Bultmann also cites that three *empty* jars were set up in the temple at Elis in Greece on the eve of Dionysius' feast, and that they were found full of wine the next morning. Note that nothing (water, oil, blood, etc.) *turned into* wine, but that wine was said to *fill* three *empty* jars. Anyone could effect such a "miracle" — even this writer could fill three empty jars with wine! Bultmann says that John applied this heathen legend to Jesus. Bultmann possessed a brilliant mind, but it surely went astray in treating John 2:1-12! Dionysius' feast was on the fifth of January. Bultmann thought that the Eastern churches celebrated Jesus' birth on January 6, because of the story in John 2:1ff. If so, why did the Eastern Christians put Jesus' birth on the wrong day — the sixth, not the fifth (the fifth was one of Dionysius' days)? See the thorough-going rejection of Bultmann's theory by Haenchen, *The Gospel of John*, p. 178.

20The Jews replied, "It has taken forty-six years to build this temple, and you are going to raise it in three days?" 21But the temple he had spoken of was his body. 22After he was raised from the dead, his disciples recalled what he had said. Then they believed the Scripture and the words that Jesus had spoken.

ª*17* Psalm 69:9

It was Passover time, and so Jesus went up to Jerusalem. Every male, who had become a *bar Mitzvah* (son of the commandment) at about thirteen years of age, was obligated to keep the feasts of Passover, Pentecost, and Booths or Tents. Passover was vital to the existence of Israel as a nation because it commemorated God's death angel who "passed over" and thus spared the first born sons of Israel from death, while the first born sons of the Egyptians were slain. Egypt, the master of Israel, the enslaved, thus let Israel go free into the desert of Sinai to worship Israel's God, Jehovah. As a consequence, Israel became not simply a collection of tribes, but a nation who went on to receive God's law through Moses and to live in covenant relationship with God as his people (Exod 12).

The Synoptic Gospels mentioned clearly only two Passover feasts (Mark mentioned only one, Mark 11:15-18), from which some have concluded that Jesus' ministry lasted only one and one half years. John, on the other hand, mentioned three (or perhaps four Passovers, 2:13; 6:4; 11:55; cf. 18:28 and see 5:1), from which is deduced the usual view of Jesus' ministry as having lasted some three or three and one half years.[10] John called the Passover "the Passover of the Jews," possibly as over against a "Passover of the *Christian* Jews."

The question of how many times Jesus cleansed the temple is still debated. Many plump for a single cleansing and they usually side with the presentation by the Synoptics as the really historical one (Barrett). The Synoptics place the cleansing at the close of Jesus' ministry and see this bold act as Jesus' major challenge to the Jewish authorities that led to his death. Such students often see this account in John as deliberately misplaced (as contrasted with the

---

[10]Barrett, *The Gospel According to St. John*, p. 197.

position of the incident in the Synoptics). Others see both John's and the Synoptists' accounts as historically valid, and therefore, conclude that there were two cleansings, not one: one at the beginning and the other at the close of Jesus' public ministry (so Carson, Morris, Foster, and others). If there were two cleansings, why are they not both recorded by all of the Gospels? The answer is because the Synoptics omitted completely this early ministry in Judea and so lacked room for this first cleansing, while John, on the contrary, omitted many of the happenings of the last week, such as the cursing of the fig tree, the cleansing of the temple, and the institution of the Lord's Supper, which had already been recorded by the Synoptics (assuming that John wrote *after* the Synoptics).[11]

It has been observed that the primary objection to a double cleansing of the temple are two: (1) there is a deeply ingrained bias of modern scholarship against doublets of any kind in the Bible, probably because of efforts to squeeze out trajectories of developments or evolutions from the text. One event, described in two reports that are a bit different from each other is said to provide evidence of the direction in which the tradition changed or evolved. Such trajectories are highly speculative and without firm evidence. If there were two cleansings, there would be similarities and differences — such a similarity as their taking place at Passover (but note that only at one of the major feasts would Jesus likely be found in Jerusalem), or such differences as one cleansing's occurring at the beginning and the other at the end of Jesus' ministry (but Jesus surely would not have cleansed the temple twice within a week, a month, or probably a year). (2) It is frequently contended that if Jesus had cleansed the temple once, the Jewish (and Roman?) authorities would not have allowed him to do so a second time. This is a very difficult assertion to prove, especially since at least two or three years intervened between the cleansings, which was time enough for the authorities to let down their guard concerning Jesus. Furthermore, the saying of Jesus about destroying and raising the temple in three days appears later in Jesus' trial in the synoptic records, but the saying is alone given here in John's and not in the Synoptists' accounts of the cleansing. Finally, the Jewish

---

[11]Foster, *Studies*, pp. 370-371.

reaction to the cleansing in John is rather mild (Jesus had not yet established his reputation at the opening of his ministry), while the reaction in the Synoptic accounts at the close of his ministry led directly to a conspiracy of the Jewish authorities against him that eventuated in his arrest and crucifixion; that is, the aftermath of the cleansing account sounds as though there were not merely one, but two cleansings.

2:13. Jesus went up to Jerusalem. The expression "going up to Jerusalem" throughout the history books of the New Testament reflects the city's elevation (2600 feet above sea level) which was above most of the territory of Palestine (Bethlehem and Hebron were higher by some three to five hundred feet). "To go up" (ἀν–αβαίνω, *anabaino*) had become a quasi-technical expression for pilgrimage to Jerusalem.[12]

2:14. In the outer courtyard of the temple Jesus **found men selling cattle, sheep and doves, and others sitting at tables exchanging money.** Israel Abrahams surveys some of the trade that transpired in the temple.[13] He seeks to soft-pedal the nature and unruliness of the business transactions there, and it is true that the animals sold in the temple's precincts for sacrifice were convenient for worshipers who came from some distance and needed to purchase animals that met the ceremonial requirements of the Mosaic (and oral) laws. Nevertheless, such trafficking made the priests in control of the system fabulously rich; it desecrated the temple and derailed its purpose as *the* national *worship* center; it surely turned off numbers of people from prayer and praise in the midst of such a raucous county-fair setting in God's own house. Jesus, thus, drove out the animals and their sellers.

The temple consisted of two parts, and our English word "temple" is used for both of them. (1) The ναός (*naos*) or sanctuary or shrine was the smaller part, the house that contained the Holy Place and the Most Holy Place, and was based on the plan of the old tabernacle that was first built and used under Moses in the wilderness. (2) The ἱερόν (*hieron*) included the *naos* and the court areas, some of which were covered against hot sun and rain and

---

[12]Barrett, *The Gospel According to St. John*, p. 197.

[13]Israel Abrahams, *Studies in Pharisaism and the Gospels* (Cambridge: University Press, 1917-1918), 1:80-89.

snow. In fact, in the New Testament, the *naos* and *hieron* are often not distinguished. The large court area in the temple in Jerusalem included some thirteen to nineteen acres, and was divided into four smaller areas: the court of the Gentiles, of the women, of Israel (or Jewish men), and of the priests. It was in the court of the Gentiles (by far the largest of the four courts) that the selling of livestock and the exchanging of money took place. This may reflect (simply) that the court of the Gentiles was the most usable area because of its greater size. It may also show a condescending attitude of Jews towards the Gentiles; that is, trade in God's house was too reprehensible for Jews but not for Gentiles.

2:15. Jesus also **scattered the coins of the money changers and overturned their tables**. Temple taxes had to be paid in the Phoenician coinage of Tyre. Usually a modest fee was charged for this service (2%-4%, so Barrett[14]), but at festival times, when crowds increased and money changing was more in demand, the fee for money changing was usually noticeably increased. It has been observed, though, that Jesus was not charging the merchants and money changers with thievery so much as taking over what belonged solely to God).[15] Jesus made a whip or scourge (φραγέλ–λιον, *fragellion*, derived from Latin flagellum, a very severe instrument of torture which could be used on human beings and also cattle). The whip which Jesus used, however, was made out of cords or ropes (σχοινίον, *schoinion*), not leather or other heavy materials, probably so it would not have harmed a human being very badly. Furthermore, the oldest manuscripts add ὡς (*hos*): "he made a kind of whip of cords."[16] Verse 15 seems to say that he drove out the animals (not the men), but both men and animals may have been expelled. The tractate in the Babylonian Talmud called *Berakoth* (1:5) forbade one's carrying a staff in the temple, and for that reason Jesus may have made a whip of cords or ropes; however, this prohibition may not have applied to those who herded animals.[17] At any rate, Jesus was forceful but not cruel.[18]

---

[14]Barrett, *The Gospel According to St. John*, p. 197.
[15]Carson, *The Gospel According to John*, p. 179, n. 1.
[16]Metzger, *Textual Commentary*, pp. 202-203.
[17]See Barrett, *The Gospel According to St. John*, p. 197.
[18]Carson, *The Gospel According to John*, p. 179.

2:16. Jesus did not destroy the animals or confiscate the coinage; he was not an annihilator of other's property. Trading in God's temple is viewed by Jesus as an act of desecration, so he commands, **"Get these out of here! How dare you turn my Father's house into a market!"** Jesus probably alluded here to Zechariah 14:21, "And on that day there will no longer be a Canaanite [or trader] in the house of the LORD Almighty." Did Jesus intend to teach here that worship and commerce cannot be mixed? Probably not, but the rush and noise of industry and trade often do make worship more difficult.

2:17. Jesus' cleansing the temple prompted his disciples to remember a passage in Psalm 69:9, **"Zeal for your house will consume me."** As the Psalmist was devoured by zeal for God's house, so Jesus will be destroyed by the same. When did Jesus' disciples recall this line and understand its fulfillment: (1) *immediately*[19] or (2) as in 2:22, *after Jesus' resurrection*[20] or *both now and later* with even greater understanding and appreciation at the later date?[21] For all Jesus' zeal for the temple as a house of prayer (Matt 21:13 and Luke 19:46, quoting Isa 56:7), however, he is never portrayed as praying in the temple, but in the desert, sea, and mountain.[22]

The words **will consume me** probably refer to Jesus' death (by crucifixion), brought about by his zeal for God and God's house.

2:18-19. The Jews (here the traders and not only the Jewish leaders may be intended) asked him for a sign to prove that he had authority to cleanse the temple! He gave them an instant but enigmatic answer: **"Destroy this temple, and I will raise it again in three days."** Even his disciples did not grasp the meaning of the saying until after the resurrection (v. 22). "Destroy" (λύσατε, *lysate*) and "raise it again" (ἐγερῶ, *egerō*) were used of *tearing down* and *building up* a building .[23]

2:20. The Jews completely misunderstood and thought only of the physical temple in Jerusalem. They did not consider that Jesus may have had another application of his words about "destroying

---

[19]Barrett, *The Gospel According to St. John*, p. 198.

[20]Carson, *The Gospel According to John*, p. 180.

[21]Raymond E. Brown, *The Community of the Beloved Disciple* (New York: Paulist, 1979), p. 115.

[22]Foster, *Studies*, p. 373.

[23]See Homer, *Iliad* 16:100; Josephus, *Antiquities of the Jews* 8:96.

and building up the temple" (*naos*); they asked, therefore, how he could raise up the temple in three days (if torn down) when it took forty-six years to build up to that point (and it really was not finished until A.D. 63). It also required tons of rocks and a considerable army of masons and carpenters to erect it.

2:21-22. John furnished Jesus' reply. Jesus was not talking about simply the physical temple in Jerusalem but about his own human body. If the Jews should destroy his body (by death), he would raise it up again after three days. This was Jesus' sign that he has authority to cleanse a physical temple: if he could raise up a dead "temple" (a dead human body, namely, his own), he certainly had authority or power to clean up a physical temple. The death and resurrection of Jesus are introduced here into the Gospel for the first time in a subtle way. They explain much of the rest of the Gospel and are one of the chief themes of the book.

It may be noted that Jesus here equated his body with the temple, and showed that his body was the real temple. Origen had the temple stand for the church, but that is more Pauline than Johannine. As we have said already in John, that is allegory; yet, Carson, Beasley-Murray and others take this approach.[24] Lohmeyer thinks that John, or an early congregation influenced by John, or much of the whole early church simply created this pericope and placed it early in Jesus' ministry in order to have Jesus assert his power and authority over the temple, the center of Judaism, and thus over Judaism as such. Haenchen accepts Lohmeyer's verdict that the story is hardly to be labeled a historical report.[25]

Haenchen's reasoning is that Jesus by himself could not have driven so many animals out of such a large temple area and done so without the intervention of the temple guard or the Roman police in the Tower of Antonia. This is a bit ludicrous. Haenchen was probably never in Texas (nor in many other American states) where a single cowboy, even on foot, can corral hundreds of cattle (and sheep) and force them to go many miles over land without a

---

[24]See Carson, *The Gospel According to John*, p. 180; Beasley-Murray, *John*, p. 41.

[25]Haenchen, *The Gospel of John*, 1: 188a, on Lohmeyer, *Das Evangelium des Markus, übersezt und erklärt*, 16th ed. (Göttingen: Vandenhoeck und Ruprecht), pp. 235-237.

fence or rows of buildings to help guide the herds. After all, the temple was near the eastern and northern outer walls of Jerusalem; once the cattle started moving towards one of the outer gates, say, in the eastern wall, people would have to step quickly out of the way and let them move outside the city as the animals rushed rapidly into and down the terrain towards the Valley of Hinnom. No temple police nor Roman soldiers could easily have stopped the animals once they started their rushing forward movement. Such a treatment of this passage by an otherwise gifted exegete is absurd. Haenchen seems to wind up his discussion of this passage by accepting it, like Origen (Book 10:25), as allegory.

Two small but important matters, related to this account, remain. First, the Synoptists recorded that during Jesus' trial before the Sanhedrin false witnesses alleged that Jesus said, "I will destroy this man-made temple and in three days will build another, not made by man" (Mark 14:58 and parallels; cf. also Mark 15:29). The only record of such a statement on Jesus' lips is in John 2:19; thus, John here provides a trifle that supplements and corroborates the Synoptic accounts. Second, if John 2:19 records Jesus' actual words, he at no time ever said, "*I will* destroy, " but instead, "(You) destroy . . . and I will raise it up again." The words recorded in the Synoptics are from false witnesses, who plainly misunderstood or deliberately twisted his utterances.

3. Summary of Response to Jesus (2:23-25)

[23]Now while he was in Jerusalem at the Passover Feast, many people saw the miraculous signs he was doing and believed in his name.[a] [24]But Jesus would not entrust himself to them, for he knew all men. [25]He did not need man's testimony about man, for he knew what was in a man.

[a]*23 Or and believed in him*

2:23. The summary of some of the reaction to Jesus given here is typical of such summaries scattered throughout the four Gospels and the Acts of the Apostles. Karl Ludwig Schmidt, Martin Dibelius, and Rudolf Bultmann, in the name of Form

Criticism, all declared most of these summaries to be nonhistorical productions of the final edition(s) of these books of stories.[26] There is no reason, however, not to accept this summary as written by John himself.

Many people saw the miraculous signs he was doing. John did not mention any specific signs in Jerusalem. People saw whatever miracles Jesus performed and, like the disciples in verse 11, **believed in his name.**

2:24. Jesus, however, could not really "believe in or entrust himself" to them because "he knew all beings [men]"; that is, he had divine knowledge of each person (cf. 1:48). There is a play on the Greek word "to believe" or "trust" here: "many *trusted* in his name," but Jesus "did not *entrust* himself to them." The reason was that Jesus knew people to be "*un*faithful" to one another, and thus, dangerous.

2:25. Every human being needed to have testimony borne to Jesus so that each might accept or reject such testimony and thus believe or disbelieve in him. He, however, needed no testimony to be borne to other human beings so that he might believe or disbelieve them because he already knew human nature, apparently even concrete details of each person's nature and life. According to the Jewish commentary on Exodus called *Mekhilta*, "Seven things are hidden from man: the day of death, the day of consolation, the depths of judgement, one's reward, the time of restoration of the kingdom of David, the time when the guilty kingdom (Rome) will be destroyed, and what is within another."[27] Scriptural proof for the unknown is cited in *Genesis Rabbah* 65 (11b) namely, Jeremiah 17:10, "I the LORD search the heart." Jesus' knowledge of what is in mankind, therefore, proves him to be deity.[28] Chapter two of John painted a portrait of what was in mankind: temple desecraters, money lovers, miracle seekers, opponents of reform, immature believers, but no one worthy of Jesus' trust.

---

[26]Karl Ludwig Schmidt, *Der Rahmen der Geschichte Jesus* (Berlin: Trowitzsch, 1919); Martin Dibelius, *From Tradition to Gospel* (New York: Scribner, 1934); Rudolf Bultmann, *History of the Synoptic Tradition* (New York: Harper, 1963).

[27]*Mekhilta*, Exod 15:32.

[28]Strack and Billerbeck, *Kommentar*, 1: (2:412).

The singular of "the man" (ἐν τῷ ἀνθρώπῳ, *en tō anthrōpō*) in verse 25 does not point to Judas the betrayer, as some have supposed, but to all humanity. The summarizing statement in verses 23-25 may look backward to Chapters 1 and 2, and also forward to Chapter 3 of John. It is clear that the passage was meant to sum up the impact of the sign of changing Jewish ceremonial water to wine, of cleansing the Jewish temple, and of Jesus' other signs or miracles done while he was at the Passover in Jerusalem. In addition, some see verses 23-25 also as a prelude that prepares for the Nicodemus' story in chapter 3, which is said to examine the significance of Jesus' miracles as well as the nature, and perhaps the maturity, of Nicodemus' faith. All these stories clearly show the purpose of the Fourth Gospel was meant to elicit faith in Jesus, as the readers accept the testimony offered about him (20:31).

JOHN 3

D. 3:1-36 JESUS AND NICODEMUS (3:1-36)

1. The New Birth (3:1-10)

¹Now there was a man of the Pharisees named Nicodemus, a member of the Jewish ruling council. ²He came to Jesus at night and said, "Rabbi, we know you are a teacher who has come from God. For no one could perform the miraculous signs you are doing if God were not with him."

³In reply Jesus declared, "I tell you the truth, no one can see the kingdom of God unless he is born again.ª"

⁴"How can a man be born when he is old?" Nicodemus asked. "Surely he cannot enter a second time into his mother's womb to be born!"

⁵Jesus answered, "I tell you the truth, no one can enter the kingdom of God unless he is born of water and the Spirit. ⁶Flesh gives birth to flesh, but the Spiritᵇ gives birth to spirit. ⁷You should not be surprised at my saying, 'Youᶜ must be born again.' ⁸The wind blows wherever it pleases. You hear its sound, but you cannot tell where it comes from or where it is going. So it is with everyone born of the Spirit."

⁹"How can this be?" Nicodemus asked.

¹⁰"You are Israel's teacher," said Jesus, "and do you not understand these things?

ª3 Or *born from above*, also in verse 7   ᵇ6 Or *but spirit*   ᶜ7 The Greek is plural.

The narrative portion of this passage is very brief. Nicodemus appeared before Jesus from the shadows and did not actually state the purpose of his visit with Jesus. Jesus began at once a monologue that seemed to start with Nicodemus but quickly moved on to include a larger audience — at least the plural "you" is used almost immediately (3:7), "You must be born again," though Jesus had begun with the singular (3:3,5). From this, some have concluded that what we have here is not so much reliable, historical discourse as a snippet of early preaching on the beginnings of the Christian life and on the clash of the church and the synagogue. If so, however, such was not the section's main purpose; it proceeded like a genuine discourse or didactic session of a Jewish teacher with an older, but not as mature a student as might be expected. The reason that Jesus took up and ran with the speech in John 3 seems apparent: Jesus knew what needed to be said and done with Nicodemus's life, but Nicodemus knew nothing at all that could change his life or future — or ours also. A certain aura of mystery seems to interpenetrate the entire third chapter of John. The themes treated contribute to this atmosphere: the new birth, the Son of Man, and testimony that is borne without saying to whom it is directed. Further, Jesus speaks of the one who is being revealed in the third person, and he never used an ἐγώ εἰμι (*ego eimi*, "I am") saying, though he thrice introduced sayings with the solemn formula, "Amen, amen, I say" (3:3,5,11). He never forthrightly says in this chapter that he was speaking of himself. Even in the closing verses of the chapter, who the one is "who comes from above" remains obscure.[1]

3:1. How one translates the conjunction δέ (*de*) at the opening of the Nicodemus story may reflect how one understands the relation of this and the previous passage. If *de* is rendered simply "and" ("now" in the NIV), then the writer may be numbering Nicodemus with those just mentioned in verses 23-25, whose faith was more spurious than genuine and to whom Jesus could not entrust himself. On the other hand, if one translates this small part of speech as an adversative conjunction, that is, as "but," then the writer may be viewing Nicodemus as one whose faith is a little less flawed than the faith of those in verses 23-25, whose faith was more sight than faith. Nicodemus, indeed, valued Jesus' signs above the

---

[1]Bultmann, *The Gospel of John*, p. 133.

COLLEGE PRESS NIV COMMENTARY

truth that Jesus had to give; however, he eventually came to a more mature faith in Jesus (7:45-52; 19:38-42).[2]

Nicodemus was a common Greek name (Νικόδημος, *Nikodēmos*). A wealthy Jew who bore this name is said to have been in Jerusalem in A.D. 70 at the time of the city's fall to the Romans (Josephus, *Antiquities* 14:37) and C.G. Montefiore and Loewe suggest that he could have been the Nicodemus of John 3,[3] though Barrett[4] and Carson[5] think otherwise. Nicodemus has also been identified with a certain Buni alluded to in the Talmudic tractate *Sanhedrin* 43a as a disciple of Jesus, but Joseph Klausner thought that Buni is a corruption of the name of John, the brother of James.[6]

Nicodemus is called a **Pharisee**, which would make him an ardent student and serious practitioner not only of the Old Testament but of the Jewish oral legal tradition that had been emerging (and continued to grow) in the days before and after Jesus. He is also called "a ruler of the Jews" (ἄρχων τῶν Ἰουδαίων, *archōn tōn Ioudaiōn*) which probably meant (as the NIV interprets the phrase) that he was a member of the Sanhedrin, the Jewish governing body in Jerusalem. He is also given a third title, "teacher" (v. 10), which would make him a teacher and an expert of the law. Nicodemus is mentioned only by John.

3:2. At night in Greek is an adverbial genitive of time and described the *kind* of time involved; that is, night time, not day time. Why did he seek out Jesus "at night"? (1) It is the writer's reminiscence of a genuine, historical detail. (2) Most rabbis studied and debated far into the night.[7] (3) Nicodemus came rather secretively to Jesus in the darkness, hoping to be concealed from the public eye, and in fact, fearing at this time public disclosure of any relations with Jesus. (4) Some see the expression as akin to "darkness" in John, and so metaphorically the words "at night" hint at

---

[2]Carson, *The Gospel According to John*, pp. 185-186.
[3]C.G. Montefiore and H. Loewe, *A Rabbinic Anthology*. (New York: Schocken Books, 1974), p. 687, n. 90.
[4]Barrett, *The Gospel According to St. John*, p. 204.
[5]Carson, *The Gospel According to John*, pp. 185-186.
[6]See Klausner, *Jesus of Nazareth*. (New York: Macmillan, 1926), p. 30. Cf. the Babylonian Talmud, *Ta'anith* 19b, 20a; *Gottin* 56a; *Ketuboth* 66b.
[7]Strack and Billerbeck, *Kommentar*, 2:420.

what is spiritually dark or evil.[8] Indeed, some would say: Nicodemus's night was darker than he realized.[9]

Nicodemus began with the title **Rabbi** for Jesus and with a plural "we" (**we know you are a teacher**). The title "rabbi" was quite a compliment to Jesus because it came from a distinguished teacher. Who is represented by the "we"? The following answers have been suggested. (1) Nicodemus and his disciples (whether they came with Nicodemus that night or not; the text, however, does not mention any disciples). (2) Nicodemus here represents the many whose faith is meager in 2:23-25. (3) It was a sort of "editorial we" used by Nicodemus so as not to sound too individualistic or personal. (4) It served to introduce Jesus' "we" in verse 11. (5) It represented Nicodemus and several other members of the Sanhedrin who were his friends. (6) It reflected the general public assessment of Jesus among many Jews in Jerusalem.

Nicodemus opened the conversation with a compliment and a profound observation that Jesus' miracles (such as those mentioned in 2:23) affirmed that he, a teacher, had come from God. Jesus' reply quietly ignored Nicodemus' statement, and began with the thing that Nicodemus came to discuss, namely, the kingdom of God.

3:3. Jesus answered not so much the words as the thoughts and needs of Nicodemus. Jesus' reply was almost abrupt: "I tell you the truth, unless a man is born again, he cannot see the kingdom of God." Nicodemus (in v. 4) understood the words literally and physically, and asked, "Can a man be born when he is old? . . . Surely he cannot enter a second time into his mother's womb to be born!" In verse 5 Jesus repeated with amplification his words here: "I tell you the truth, unless a man is born of water and the Spirit, he cannot enter the kingdom of God." (See further comments at v. 5.)

3:4. Some understand Nicodemus' question **How can a man be born when he is old?** to refer to (1) Nicodemus's lack of astuteness or mental agility;[10] but since he was Israel's teacher (v. 10), this

---

[8]Robert H. Lightfoot, *St. John's Gospel*, C.F. Evans, ed. (Oxford: Clarendon, 1956), p. 116.

[9]Carson, *The Gospel According to John*, p. 186.

[10]Cf. H.A.W. Meyer, *Critical Exegetical Handbook on the Gospel of John* (New York: Funk & Wagnalls, 1884), 3:123.

could scarcely be true of him. (2) Others think that Nicodemus understood Jesus to be asking for the transformation of Nicodemus's lifestyle that was too demanding for an old man, so deeply set in his ways by heritage, education, and age.[11] (3) Very likely Nicodemus did not understand at all what Jesus was talking about. It was a case of unbelief prompted by a lack of knowledge, or at least by a gross misunderstanding of what Jesus was saying.

3:5. This verse differs little from verse 3, which says that unless one is born again from above, he cannot see the kingdom of God. Verse 5 states that generation from above is birth by water and the Spirit, and that those who do so *see* and *enter* the kingdom of God.

These words seem to be debated endlessly, and always the answer given is so vague and mystical that Christians across nearly two thousand years cannot know with certainty what the so-called "new birth" is or whether they have been born again or not. Consider a few of the explanations of what this regeneration is said to be or to mean. (1) Since verse 6 speaks of two births, one of the flesh and the other of the Spirit, being "born of water and the Spirit" (v. 5) refers to *two births, one natural and the other super-natural.* The first birth of water refers to the amniotic fluid that surrounds the unborn infant in the womb and breaks from the womb soon before childbirth. No ancient sources, however, describe natural birth as "from water," and further, the birth "of water" here is a part of the new birth or birth from above, not a natural birth.[12] (2) "Being born of water and Spirit" refers to *John's baptism (in water) and to Jesus' baptism (in Spirit);*[13] but the birth of water and Spirit both refer to the same, one, new birth, and Jesus' baptism was performed in water *and* Spirit. This text does not support this view. (3) Jesus argued here *against the ritual of washing of the Essenes or against Jewish ceremonies altogether;* that is, what is required by Jesus is Spirit-birth not simply water-cleansing. "Spirit" and "water," however, are not opposed in verses 3 and 5. (4) The *passage cannot refer in any way to Christian baptism,* because the words "water and"

---

[11]Cf. Carson, *The Gospel According to John,* p. 190.

[12]Barrett, *The Gospel According to St. John,* p. 208.

[13]Cf. Frederic Godet, *Commentary on the Gospel of John,* Timothy Dwight, trans. (New York: Funk & Wagnalls, 1886), 2:49-52.

(ὕδατος καὶ, *hydatos kai*) must not have been part of the original text but were added later by an editor or early copyist.[14] There is no textual evidence of such an omission. (5) Water in the Old Testament was said in some passages to be a figure or picture of Spirit, but no one seems effectively to have related water and Spirit from these passages in the Old Testament to John 3:3,5. (6) Passages have been cited from Qumran that were supposed to connect Spirit and water in cleansing (1QS 3:7; 4:20ff; 1QH 7:21f; 9:32; CD 19:9) but these Qumran citations made no connection of the terms Spirit and water with regeneration, and none of them was very close to John 3:3,5.[15] (7) Being born of *Spirit* is said to be the really important item in the passage, not water, and the whole process belongs to the Spirit, who alone can perform a new birth. Such treatment leaves the passage so mystical and mystifying that the most astute and erudite scholar cannot make sense of Jesus' words here.

There is another explanation of the passage, however, that makes sense and is not so mysterious or mystical. Most explanations see the Spirit as arbitrarily and directly making persons into believers or unbelievers without any regard to their personal say in the matter. Jesus said that to see, much less to enter, the kingdom of God (the only times that the expression appears in the Gospel, an expression that usually means "the sovereignty of God") one **must be born again** (δεῖ ὑμᾶς γεννηθῆναι ἄνωθεν, *dei hymas gennēthēnai anōthen*) **of water and the Spirit.** These words ("born of water and Spirit") in verse 5 surely clarify what is meant by being "born again" or "from above" or "from the beginning" (*anōthen*).[16] The birth "of water" surely refers to baptism — to which Nicodemus and all Jerusalem had been introduced by John the Baptist. The birth is further said to be "of the Spirit," surely referring to the begetting of new life through the gospel message (cf. 1 Cor 4:15 and 1 Pet 1:23).

---

[14]So Hans H. Wendt, *The Gospel According to St. John.* (Edinburgh: T&T Clark, 1902), p. 102; Nestle-Aland (27 ed.) mentioned this conjectured reading in the apparatus to 3:5, and Bultmann adopted the position (*The Gospel of John*, pp. 138-139, n. 3), as did also more recently M. Vellanichal, *The Divine Sonship of Christians in the Johannine Writings.* (Rome: Biblical Institute Press, 1977), pp. 170ff.

[15]Barrett, *The Gospel According to St. John*, 209.

[16]BAGD, p. 77.

"Rebirth" is an idea probably not drawn (1) from the Old Testament, nor (2) from Hellenism. Instead, the idea of "the kingdom of God" (Jewish) and the idea of "rebirth" (or "from above") are joined by Jesus to create that which is different but *Christian*.[17] What John records in chapter 3 is not initiation into the small, earthly Palestinian kingdom of the Jews nor into the empty and powerless rites of the pagan mysteries, but the way of entry into God's kingdom, a kingdom that will cover the earth and last beyond time.

3:6. Flesh gives birth to flesh, but the Spirit gives birth to spirit. Like gives birth to like. Some students say that "Flesh" (σάρξ, *sarx*) here probably does not refer to a part of human nature (the *material* as opposed to the *spiritual* portion of an individual person), i.e., not to a contrast between the lower and higher parts or aspects of human nature, but to the distinction between human beings and God. *Sarx* in Paul and John often meant a human life lived without God. In verse 6 the contrast is (1) between flesh and spirit within an individual, not (2) between two spirits (as in Qumran, 1QS 3:10), and not (3) between transitory and permanent beings or the temporal and eternal sides of an individual (as in Platonic dualism[18]). The contrast is not, further, (4) between God and mankind though this last contrast may be slightly echoed here, and certainly not (5) between John the Baptist and Jesus.[19]

3:7. Jesus repeats the necessity of the new birth, and the plural of **you** (ὑμᾶς, *hymas*) emphasizes that Nicodemus and the rest of humanity have the same need of rebirth. It may be also that Nicodemus was addressed as a kind of representative of those whose faith is weak and nearly nonexistent.[20]

3:8. The wind blows wherever it pleases. You hear its sound, but you cannot tell where it comes from or where it is going. So it is with everyone born of the Spirit."

The point of this much debated verse seems to have been an illustration of the mystery and yet the comprehensibility of the

---

[17]See Barrett, *The Gospel According to St. John*, p. 207.
[18]So Schnackenburg, *The Gospel according to St John*.
[19]Hugo Odeberg, *The Fourth Gospel* (Amsterdam: BRG, 1974), pp. 65-66.
[20]Barrett, *The Gospel According to St. John*, p. 210.

second birth. Πνεῦμα (*pneuma*) in Greek may mean both "spirit" and "wind"; here it probably is to be understood as "wind." One can know that the wind is present and blowing by what it does, but one cannot know its place of origin or site of its destiny; so one born of water and the Spirit may be certain of the event (i.e., the rebirth) by its results, though one may not be able to know the place of origin or final location of the Spirit.

3:9. Nicodemus asked how such things could happen (γένεσθαι, *genesthai*), a question that he should have been able, at least partially, to answer, because (1) he was *the* great, learned, widely recognized teacher of Israel, and (2) he ought to have been adequately informed from the Old Testament (of which he was an expert student and exegete) on the subject of renewal (Deut 10:16; 1 Sam 10:9; 16:14; Ps 2:10; Ezek 18:31; Jer 4:4); and to have been informed on the need for a definite change by John the Baptist's attack on Jewish reliance on their physical descent from Abraham (Matt 3:9; Luke 3:8).

3:10. "You are Israel's teacher," said Jesus, "and do you not understand these things?" Why is the definite article so prominently used in verse 10, "You are *the* [ὁ, *ho*] teacher of Israel"? (1) It may have pointed to Nicodemus's widespread fame as a Jewish teacher,[21] or (2) it may have made him the representative of Israel's teachers whom Jesus here encountered,[22] or (3) it simply may have been used to contrast the ignorance of the learned teacher of Jewry with the as yet unknown teacher from Nazareth — the teachers of Israel have no answer to the questions of the nature of the Kingdom and of the requirements for entry into it, while Jesus has the answer (the truth) to those and other important questions.[23]

2. The Son of Man (3:11-21)

[11]**I tell you the truth, we speak of what we know, and we testify to what we have seen, but still you people do not accept our testimony.**

---

[21]Carson, *The Gospel According to John*, p. 198.
[22]Bultmann, *The Gospel of John*, p. 144, n. 2.
[23]Ibid., p. 144.

[12]I have spoken to you of earthly things and you do not believe; how then will you believe if I speak of heavenly things? [13]No one has ever gone into heaven except the one who came from heaven — the Son of Man.[a] [14]Just as Moses lifted up the snake in the desert, so the Son of Man must be lifted up, [15]that everyone who believes in him may have eternal life.[b]

[16]"For God so loved the world that he gave his one and only Son,[c] that whoever believes in him shall not perish but have eternal life. [17]For God did not send his Son into the world to condemn the world, but to save the world through him. [18]Whoever believes in him is not condemned, but whoever does not believe stands condemned already because he has not believed in the name of God's one and only Son.[d] [19]This is the verdict: Light has come into the world, but men loved darkness instead of light because their deeds were evil. [20]Everyone who does evil hates the light, and will not come into the light for fear that his deeds will be exposed. [21]But whoever lives by the truth comes into the light, so that it may be seen plainly that what he has done has been done through God."[e]

[a]*13* Some manuscripts *Man, who is in heaven*   [b]*15* Or *believes may have eternal life in him*   [c]*16* Or *his only begotten Son*   [d]*18* Or *God's only begotten Son*   [e]*21* Some interpreters end the quotation after verse 15.

Verses 11-15 begin to uncover the mystery behind the new birth: regeneration is dependent on acceptance of (or belief in) testimony. Verses 11 and 12 tell what the testimony is, whose testimony it is, and why the testimony did not do what the witnesses who bore it intended it to do.

3:11. The NIV's **I tell you the truth**, which introduces verse 11, represents the double *amen, amen* of Jesus, and affirms that the following words from Jesus are of great importance. Jesus asserted that he had told the truth and spoke of what he knew, and bore witness (testified) to what he had seen, but people did not accept his word (or testimony). These are the basic ingredients behind the purpose of the entire gospel — Jesus' (and others') testimony to the early Christian gospel, which many accepted and many others rejected.

The plurals (**we** and **you**) in verses 11-12 may be (1) rhetorical, as in Mark 4:30;[24] or (2) some think that John envisioned Jesus as addressing these words to all his audiences or at least to the twelve, not just to Nicodemus; or (3) John practiced anachronism here, i.e., John let Jesus speak to John's own congregations and their needs in this speech. F.F. Bruce sees number (3) as likely happening here,[25] but (a) the content of verse 11 (**we speak of what we know, and we testify to what we have seen**) cannot apply to early Christians at this point in their lives but to Jesus; that is, the disciples could not be depicted as speaking of what they knew and testifying to what they had seen, namely, heavenly things (v. 12), and (b) John is very careful to distinguish between what the disciples understood *during* Jesus' ministry and that which they understood only *after* it (cf. John 2:22).[26] Another explanation (4) sees Jesus as picking up on and aping the plural with which Nicodemus began this scene: "Rabbi, *we* know" in verse 2. Bultmann[27] suggests (5) that Jesus no longer addressed the Jews (represented by Nicodemus), but by the plural "you" he now addressed the whole κόσμος (*kosmos*, vv. 16-17,19). (6) Surely the "we" did not include Jesus with the OT prophets, the Baptist, and even the Christian prophets.[28] Possibilities 1, 2, or 4 make the best sense. Nicodemus had not simply misunderstood Jesus and who he was, but he failed to accept Jesus' testimony to himself; that is, Nicodemus did not believe, or if he did, it was such weak faith that he could scarcely understand Jesus' teaching, particularly on the new birth.

3:12. What did Jesus know and speak, and see and testify to (v. 11)? He testified to the truth and necessity of the new birth. It seems likely that verse 12 gives part, if not all, of the answer to this question: **I have spoken to you of earthly things and you do not believe; how then will you believe if I speak of heavenly things?** Here Jesus separated religious phenomena into two parts or divisions: earthly and heavenly. Earthly phenomena have their locale in

---

[24]Cf. Brooke F. Westcott, *The Gospel According to St. John: The Authorized Versiom with Introduction and Notes* (London: John Murray, 1882), 1:113.

[25]F.F. Bruce, *The Gospel of John* (Grand Rapids: Eerdmans, 1983), pp. 86-87.

[26]Carson, *The Gospel According to John*, p. 198.

[27]Bultmann, *The Gospel of John*, pp. 144f.

[28]So Ernst von Dobschütz, *ZNW* 28 (1929): 162; Zahn, *Das Evangelium*.

this world; heavenly items belong to the sphere of heaven. Regeneration may have its roots in heaven, but its daily occurrence belongs to our life on earth. Heavenly phenomena, such as the daily and ultimate functioning of the universe, the changes wrought in God's relation to his creation by the Messiah's death, the impact and limitations of Messiah's priestly intercession, the future rule of God,[29] etc. transcend the earth and Nicodemus's (and our) understanding. The contrast here is that if Nicodemus would not accept Jesus' testimony (i.e., believe) when Jesus told him about things that he could partially understand, how could he believe if Jesus should go on to tell him of things completely unknown to him?[30] "Earthly things," then, are the new birth (its nature and necessity) — this is what Jesus in verse 11 knew and spoke of, and what he had seen and testified to — and in verse 12 the new birth was central in the "earthly things" which Jesus had spoken to Nicodemus. This means that Jesus in this discourse really had, as his topic, the true way of salvation (a truth that is recognized by even such negative commentators as Bultmann[31] and Haenchen[32]), and this means that the teachers of Israel can give no answer to Jesus but must necessarily fail when they are faced with decisive questions, issues, and solutions that pertain to the problem of how one is to be saved.[33]

3:13. Verses 12 and 13 go together. The "heavenly things" of which Jesus spoke in verse 12 were not humankind's nature (evil) or the angelic hierarchies,[34] nor does verse 13 say that Jesus first ascended to heaven and then descended, but rather that he descended from heaven (at his incarnation) and then at his death and resurrection ascended into heaven. This language of verse 13 went on beyond anything that Jesus had said in 1-12, so Nicodemus would not easily understand the verse. In verse 13 Jesus spoke of his own descent from heaven and returning ascent to the same, under the title of Son of Man, a title which he applied to himself. This title in John, as in the Synoptics, was certainly a Messianic title,

---

[29]Cf. Carson, *The Gospel According to John*, p. 190.
[30]McGarvey and Pendleton, *The Fourfold Gospel*, p. 130.
[31]Bultmann, *The Gospel of John*, p. 145.
[32]Haenchen, *The Gospel of John*, 1:204a.
[33]Bultmann, *The Gospel of John*, p. 144.
[34]See Odeberg, *The Fourth Gospel*, pp. 46-47.

the title used most frequently by Jesus, because (as seen already in 1:51) it was a title more neutral and less loaded with political and theological associations in the Jewish public mind than many other titles that might have been used by Jesus. Verse 13 also notes the impossibility for all other human beings' ascent into heaven (Deut 30:12; Prov 30:4; Baruch 3:29; 2 Esdras 4:8). Verse 13 does not contain an anachronism in which the writer was looking back from the end of the first century on Jesus' ascension decades earlier (as Bauer and Brown hold[35]), but rather Jesus is here said to have been in heaven and so knew what no one else on earth knew, namely, the things of heaven. When Jesus, therefore, came to earth and talked of heaven, he knew from firsthand experience what he was talking about.[36] It may be, however, that the author primarily referred, by the going up of Jesus, to his lifting up on the cross,[37] though some think it more likely that the ascent of Jesus in verse 13 refers to his ascension into heaven.[38] If the words apply to Jesus' death, notice that Jesus here not only predicted his death but *the manner* of that death, and thus he predicted also that he would die at the hands of the Romans and not merely by the Jews (cf. John 18:31-32).[39]

3:14. Verses 14 and 15 shift the chronology of the Son of Man from the past to the future by means of an illustration from the history of Israel and Moses in Numbers 21:4-9. In the wilderness the people murmured against God and Moses. As punishment, God sent poisonous serpents among the Israelites. Many persons were bitten and died. Some Israelites came to Moses for help. God instructed him to make a bronze serpent, place it on a pole in the camp, and all who were bitten by the serpents but looked at the serpent on the pole would live. In somewhat similar way, the Son of

---

[35]Walter Bauer, *Das Johannesevangelium* (Tübingen: Mohr, 1925), p. 56; Brown, *John*, 1:145

[36]See Carson, *The Gospel According to John*, p. 200.

[37]So Hoskyns, *The Fourth Gospel*, pp. 217-218.

[38]Cf. Ben Witherington, *John's Wisdom.* (Louisville: Westminster/John Knox, 1995), p. 100.

[39]Westcott, *The Gospel According to St. John*, 1:114; see also the discussion of Jesus' ascent and descent in John Ashton, *Understanding the Fourth Gospel* (Oxford: Clarendon, 1991), pp. 248-256.

Man is to **be lifted up** on a pole or cross and all persons who look to him in faith will live. The parallels between the Mosaic serpent on the pole and Jesus on the cross ought not to be overly extended: the snake was "lifted up" on a pole and gave physical life to those who looked at it; so Jesus would be "lifted up" (on a cross) and give spiritual life to everyone who believes in him. Notice the divine impulsion behind the "lifting up" of the **Son of Man**: (he *must* [δεῖ, *dei*] be lifted up). There was no other way for God and human beings to alter the human situation except that Jesus be "lifted up." He *must* die. There were no alternatives even for God. This *dei* played a prominent role in all four of the Gospels in the New Testament (cf. Mark 8:31; 9:31; 10:33-34 with John 3:14). Brown thinks that John's statement of Jesus' forthcoming death is briefer and so earlier than Mark's.[40]

3:15. Note that Jesus' death is tied from the start to **eternal life** for "the one who goes on believing in him" (ὁ πιστεύων, *ho pisteuōn*). This is the first appearance of the expression "eternal life" (ζωὴν αἰώνιον, *zōēn aiōnion*) in this Gospel. The words **in him** may go with "has life in him," not as in the NIV, "everyone who believes in him may have eternal life," because in John, the verb "believe" is not followed by "in" and the dative case, as here (ἐν αὐτῷ, *en autō*), but by εἰς (*eis*) and the accusative case. This is probably why several manuscripts read εἰς αὐτόν (*eis auton*).

3:16. The writer cannot mention and then quickly abandon the death of Jesus. That death's importance must be stressed, so he added verse 16. It is the most cited biblical verse in Christendom in the twentieth century, and perhaps since the sixteenth century.[41] The sentence elucidates the importance of Christ's being "lifted up" on a pole or cross (in order to die there). This death of Jesus demonstrated the reality, enormity, and salvific power of the love of God for a sinful world and this human race which lives in that world of sin.

Verses 16-18 contain one of the best doctrinal summaries pertaining to salvation in early Christian literature. Verse 16 has been said to describe Jesus as the *agent* of salvation, verse 17 states God's

---

[40]Brown, *John*, 1:146.
[41]Cf. Witherington, *John's Wisdom*, p. 100.

purpose in sending his Son, and verse 18 depicts the divine *judgment* that can be averted by believing, that is, accepting Jesus as God's only Son who came to earth to provide "salvation," which is here equated to "eternal life."[42] John repeats these truths more than once (12:47).

 Οὕτως (*houtōs*), translated "so" (**God *so* loved the world**), may be rendered "in this way" or "in this manner"; that is, "In this way (by means of Jesus' being lifted up on the cross) God loved the world, that God gave his one and only Son." "The world" here means the entire human race (not just the elect). The world hates Jesus' followers (15:19); therefore, they are asked not to love the world or anything in it (1 John 2:15-17). There is no contradiction here, because God can love the world without danger; the disciples, being finite and weak, cannot do so without loss and destruction.[43]

John 3:16 states the extent and consequences of God's love, especially when the verse is linked to verses 14-15. God loved the world by means of Jesus' being lifted up on the cross, and the result is that all who believe in Jesus will not perish but have everlasting life. Verses 14b-15 and verse 16 have been described as two different ways of saying the same thing.[44] John 3:16 is a succinct summary of the gospel (God gave his one and only Son), the way of appropriating it ("believing," cf. John 1:11-12), and the consequence of accepting or rejecting it ("have eternal life"/"perish"). "God gave his one and only Son" means that God gave his Son over to die (to be lifted up); cf. Rom 8:32; Gal 2:20.

In the fourth Gospel the comments of the author are sometimes difficult to distinguish from those of Jesus. In Greek, there were no quotation marks or other devices to separate the writer's comments from Jesus' words. Some students, therefore, have accepted (1) 3:1-10 as containing activities and words from Jesus and Nicodemus,[45] and 3:11-21 as John's comments; (2) others see the words of the writer as having started after verse 12 or 13 or

---

[42]See Gerald L. Borchert, *John 1-11*, The New American Commentary (Nashville: Broadman & Holman, 1996), p. 183.

[43]See Carson, *The Gospel According to John*, p. 200.

[44]Witherington, *John's Wisdom*, pp. 101-102.

[45]G.C. Nicholson, *Death as Departure: The Johannine Descent/Ascent Schema.* (Missoula, MT: Scholars Press, 1983), p. 89

even 15, and continued down to verse 21. One of the chief reasons why 3:1-15 must be from Jesus himself is the title "Son of Man," which elsewhere in Scripture (with one exception) always appeared on the lips of Jesus.[46]

John 3:16 has been read from different theological stances, e.g., from that of Augustine and Calvin with stress on *God*, who loved the world and gave the Son, or from that of Arminius, with stress on the *whoever*, a term that may point to human freedom and human decision in the process of appropriating salvation. The balanced view of salvation, however, which runs all through the Bible, sees God as the originator and primary performer in salvation, and human beings as appropriators (or "believers") of God's saving actions. John 3:16 involves both the divine and the human roles.[47]

3:17. In verse 17 the purpose of the Son's mission is stated both negatively and positively: *not* **to condemn** (that is surely what κρίνῃ [*krinē*] means here) the world — John often explains his ideas by stating what they do not mean[48] — *but to save it*. By the Son's incarnation, death and resurrection, Jesus can save the world if it believes, but that means that part of the world may and will reject the Son's accomplishments and thus will be condemned.

3:18. In this verse, notice that the present tense verbs (πιστεύων, κρίνεται; *pisteuōn, krinetai*) connected with believing, give way to perfect tense verb forms (κέκριται, πεπίστευκεν, *kekritai, pepisteuken*) connected with nonbelievers. The idea expressed here is that the one who chooses to disbelieve Jesus has already been judged and received the sentence of condemnation. Jesus thus divided humanity into two groups when he came (or was sent) into the world in accord with their response to him; those who are being saved and those who have been condemned. This probably is John's way of confronting unbelievers with the harsh realities that face them — not only *will* they be condemned, they *already* have been condemned.[49] This, however, does not mean that, like the Mandoeans

---

[46]Carson, *The Gospel According to John*, p. 203. A third option, adopted by the NIV editors, would continue Jesus' words through verse 21.

[47]Borchert, *John 1–11*, p. 184.

[48]Bultmann, *The Gospel of John*, p. 154, n. 1.

[49]See Beasley-Murray, *John*, p. 51; Borchert, *John 1–11*, p. 185.

in *Ginza* 323, 13ff; 512, 22ff, the believers and unbelievers thereby will have escaped from appearing in a final judgment, as Zahn seems to suggest.[50]

There is in John a present and a future condemnation, as well as a present and a future element or aspect of salvation. Bultmann's stress on existentialism and the present led him to minimize, if not eliminate altogether, the futuristic nature of belief and unbelief, condemnation and salvation in John's Gospel. Bultmann, therefore, failed to understand these verses (14-21), because he stressed the present at the expense of the future. Indeed, Bultmann is vague about the future in this Gospel, and created unnecessary problems for himself. Note that in verse 18 one is to **believe in the name of God's one and only Son.** His literal, earthly *name* was *Jesus*, which means "savior." Notice also that in 14-15 one is to believe in the Son of Man, while here in 18 one is to believe in him as the Son of God; thus, one is to believe in both Jesus' human and divine natures. Notice also that a rather high Christology is contained in these titles — titles that are in the Synoptic Gospels as well as in John, and titles that apparently go back to Jesus in his earthly ministry.[51]

3:19. Verses 14-21 remind one of the structure of the New Testament epistles: the first part of the letter usually contained doctrine, the latter part of the letter followed with practical applications and exhortations. Verses 14-18 contain the "doctrinal" matters, 19-21 append the practical implications, warnings, and exhortations. In verses 19-21 the nature and reason for judgment are discussed. By the use of light and darkness (introduced earlier in 1:1-4), these verses expand the reader's understanding of both the condemned and the accepted. Verses 19-20 are negative (darkness, hatred, and doing evil); verse 21 is positive (light, doing the truth, and the works done through [διά, *dia*], "in," "by," "in accord with" God). Verse 19 states the cause or grounds of judgment: **the light has come into the world** — this light is Jesus (John 8:12) and the light came at his incarnation — but many persons **have loved**

---

[50]Zahn, *Das Evangelium.*, pp. 206,207; cf. Bultmann *The Gospel of John*, p. 155, n. 2.

[51]McGarvey and Pendleton, *The Fourfold Gospel*, p. 132.

darkness instead of light. One's faith produces one's personal actions. What one believes, one becomes and does.

3:20. Those who practice evil works love darkness, under the cover of which their evil deeds are done; they, therefore, reject the light because they do not wish their evil deeds to be exposed (ἐλεγχθῇ, *elenchthē*), Behind all of one's evil deeds stands one's disbelief in Christ and the rejection of Christ's light or revelation. The unbeliever stays as far from Christ as he/she can, because Christ's standards of truth, by contrast, will brand the unbeliever's deeds (τὰ ἔργα/φαῦλα, *ta erga/phaula*) for what they are.

3:21. On the other hand, the one who **lives by the truth** comes readily to the light. "To do the truth" or "to live by the truth" (ποιῶν τὴν ἀλήθειαν, *poiōn tēn alētheian*) reproduces the Old Testament's עשה אמת (*'emeth 'asah*) which originally meant "to demonstrate one's faithfulness," and then came to mean "to act faithfully"[52] or "to act uprightly."[53] Notice the close connection between doing and being: one's deeds spring from what one believes (3:21). This is expressed by Jesus in slightly different language, though the concepts are the same, in Matt 12:34, "Out of the overflow of the heart the mouth speaks"; cf. 15:11.

Many commentators handle verses 19-21 in such a way that believing and unbelieving appear to be divinely predetermined by God or by the nature that God has assigned to each of us at physical birth — that one belongs to the circle of light or darkness and does good or evil deeds accordingly. The third chapter, however, seems to say that one makes one's own decisions and produces good or evil works as one responds to Jesus with acceptance or rejection. How one comes into the light has been explained in the first eight verses of the chapter.

3. The Further Testimony of John the Baptist (3:22-30)

[22]**After this, Jesus and his disciples went out into the Judean countryside, where he spent some time with them, and baptized.**

---

[52]Carson, *The Gospel According to John*, p. 207.
[53]See *BDB*, p. 794a; Bultmann, "ἀλήθεια," *TDNT*, 1:242 (D,1,C). Cf. Gen 47:29; Neh 9:33.

[23]Now John also was baptizing at Aenon near Salim, because there was plenty of water, and people were constantly coming to be baptized. [24](This was before John was put in prison.) [25]An argument developed between some of John's disciples and a certain Jew[a] over the matter of ceremonial washing. [26]They came to John and said to him, "Rabbi, that man who was with you on the other side of the Jordan — the one you testified about — well, he is baptizing, and everyone is going to him."

[27]To this John replied, "A man can receive only what is given him from heaven. [28]You yourselves can testify that I said, 'I am not the Christ[b] but am sent ahead of him.' [29]The bride belongs to the bridegroom. The friend who attends the bridegroom waits and listens for him, and is full of joy when he hears the bridegroom's voice. That joy is mine, and it is now complete. [30]He must become greater; I must become less.

[a]25 Some manuscripts *and certain Jews*   [b]28 Or *Messiah*

3:22. A problem is raised by the geographical statement that Jesus and his disciples **went out into the Judean countryside**, literally "into the Judean land." The previous incident occurred in Jerusalem (2:23), which belongs to Judea; hence, Jesus could not have *entered* Judea here, since he was already there. Some have suggested a bad arrangement of sources to account for this problem. Possible displacement in John's texts have been discussed all through this century but the discussion never advanced beyond imaginative guesswork, and the new suggested arrangements never seem to improve the meaning of the texts.[54] The NIV above probably is the best way to translate the passage: "the Judean countryside"; that is, Jesus and his disciples merely traveled from the city of Jerusalem to the more rural areas of Judea.[55]

---

[54]See for example, F.R. Hoare, *The Original Order and Chapters of St. John's Gospel* (London: Barnes Oates and Washbourne, 1944); Bernard, *A Critical and Exegetical Commentary*, 1:26-30 and all through his commentary; also similarly Bultmann, *The Gospel of John*, pp. vii-xii, 167-168.

[55]So Carson, *The Gospel According to John*, p. 209; Borchert, *John 1-11*, p. 188; cf. W.D. Davies, *The Gospel and the Land: Early Christianity and*

The writer here introduced additional testimony of John the Baptist to Jesus, as though he wanted one last confirming bit of his witness to Jesus.[56] Jesus "was spending some time" (διέτριβεν, *dietriben*), the only time this word appears in the Fourth Gospel, though Luke employed the verb rather frequently (Acts 12:19; 14:3,28; 15:35). During this time Jesus "was baptizing" (ἐβάπτιζεν, *ebaptizen*). Both verbs are imperfect active, third person singular, and from the latter it could be concluded that Jesus himself was doing the baptizing. The writer clears up any possibility of one's so misunderstanding by noting in John 4:2 that not Jesus, but his disciples were doing the baptizing. We would like to know more here. Was this baptism simply like John's — done as a sign or even incentive to the recipient's repentance and looking towards something more significant in the future? Was this the occasion when Jesus' twelve disciples were baptized in water? If so, was this water baptism of the Twelve simply supplemented by the baptism of the Spirit on the day of Pentecost in Acts 2, since there is no other record of their being baptized in water? Were they baptized by John or Jesus — or by both (cf. John 1:35 and 40)?

This passage (vv. 22-30) also has raised the question of the chronology of Jesus' ministry in the Synoptics and in John. These verses, and indeed the chapters up to this point, have shown Jesus as very active in his ministry in Judea — and this emphasis will continue throughout John. On the other hand, the Synoptic Gospels portray Jesus' ministry as being located mostly in Galilee and the North. There is no contradiction in this geographical and chronological order, however, but an emphasis by John on the Judean ministry that was not stressed (though it seems alluded to) in the Synoptic writers.

3:23. Why did the author of the Fourth Gospel include at this point the statement of where John was baptizing? Surely he wished further to contrast Jesus with the Baptist, which he proceeded to do. John is the witness, Jesus is the light (1:7-8); he is the voice, Jesus is the word (1:14,23); he baptizes with water, Jesus with the

---

Jewish Territorial Doctrine (Berkeley: University of California, 1974), pp. 322-330.

[56]See Walter Wink, *John the Baptist in the Gospel Tradition* (London: Cambridge University Press, 1968), pp. 93-99.

Spirit (1:35).[57] John was **baptizing at Aenon near Salim**, Jesus in Judea. "Aenon" means "springs" (**plenty of water** was needed for John's and Jesus' immersions of many people, a passing phrase that supports their immersing [not sprinkling] many persons). Where were Aenon and Salim? Three traditions have come down as to the location: (1) at the northeastern end of the Dead Sea — and least likely; (2) in the Jordan valley south of Beth Shan (Scythopolis);[58] and (3) near Shechem in Samaria.[59] The contrast expressed here is that Jesus went south and John moved north — in opposite settings for their current ministries.[60]

3:24. The Synoptic record seemed to date the beginning of Jesus' ministry with the death of the Baptist, but John filled in the gaps for the readers — at least a little of Jesus' ministry commenced (preparationally?) before John the Baptist was imprisoned and his ministry brought to a close. It is sometimes asserted that the Fourth Gospel is here quietly correcting the Synoptic chronology, but this is not so. The events of John 1–3 took place early, before Mark began his account of Jesus' ministry (Mark 1:14).[61] Some have concluded from verse 24 that John had read one or more of the Synoptics. Perhaps so, but that is difficult to prove.[62]

The cause of John's imprisonment is told by the Synoptics: the animosity of Herodias, Philip's wife, now married to his brother Herod Antipas, and her daughter Salome (Matt 14:1-12; Mark 6:14-29; Luke 9:7-9); Salome is not mentioned by this name in the New Testament but is so called by Josephus.[63] Their animosity to John was because he rebuked Antipas and Herodias for marrying since she had been married formerly to Philip, Antipas's brother, and thus the union was forbidden during Philip's lifetime.[64]

---

[57]Brown, *John*, 1:154.

[58]This location is accepted by Schnackenburg (*The Gospel according to St John*, 1:412-413).

[59]This is the opinion of W.F. Albright ("Some Observations Favoring the Palestinian Origin of the Gospel of John" *HTR* 17 [1924]: 193-194).

[60]Borchert, *John 1–11*, pp. 189-190.

[61]Barrett, *The Gospel According to St. John*, p. 220.

[62]See Borchert, *John 1–11*, p. 190; Carson, *The Gospel According to John*, pp. 49ff, 210.

[63]Josephus, *Antiquities* 18:5:4.

[64]Some think that the Philip of Matt 14:3; Mark 6:17; Luke 3:19 is

3:25. A debate or argument (ζήτησις, *zētēsis*) developed between the Baptist's disciples and a Jew (some manuscripts read "Jews," but the singular is the more likely original reading[65]). The argument centered around purification or **ceremonial washing** (cf. 2:6). Likely the debate centered on forms of purifications used in the Old Testament and traditions that had risen since, such as groups who bathed daily in cold water, like those at Qumran.[66] The debate did not really pit John against Jesus, but Jesus against Judaism: John the Baptist is a great person, but he is part of the Judaism that Jesus will surpass. Neither John nor the Jew comes from above (v. 31), nor can either one give life (v. 36).[67] The writer simply wished at this point to introduce the Baptist again into his narrative in order that the Baptist might bear further witness to Jesus.

3:26. Presumably (1) the subject **they** is the disciples of the Baptist (2:25), but (2) the expression may be impersonal: "people came and told John."[68] Alternative (1) seems to be more accurate.

The Baptist is addressed as **Rabbi** (Master, Lord, teacher), the only time that the title is applied to anyone other than Jesus in the Fourth Gospel (cf. 1:38; 6:25; 9:22; 11:8; 20:16). The Baptist's disciples tell their teacher that the one to whom he bore testimony on the other side of the Jordan made and baptized more disciples than the Baptist. Their report seems to echo a note of jealousy or at least rivalry, concerning Jesus' numerical success in making more disciples than John their teacher. Their statement prompted John to repeat his testimony to Jesus in newer terms. **Everyone** is πάντες (*pantes*), an obvious "historical exaggeration," though cf. 11:48 and 12:19.[69] This was exactly what the Baptist desired.

3:27. John responded to the information that Jesus' following was outnumbering his own: A person (ἄνθρωπος, *anthrōpos*), or mankind, **can receive only what is given him from heaven.** God gave a greater following to Jesus and a lesser following to John.

---

another Philip than the tetrarch of northern Palestine. See H.H. Platz, "Philip," *IDB*, 2:785B.

[65]See Metzger, *A Textual Commentary*, p. 205.
[66]See Josephus, *Wars* 2:129; *Life* 11; see also Tosefta, *Jews* 2:20.
[67]Cf. Barrett, *The Gospel According to St. John*, p. 221.
[68]So Barrett, ibid.
[69]Ibid., p. 222.

Individuals (and groups) owe their success and/or failures ultimately to the sovereignty (or will) of God. Had John sought to be more than he was and did, he would have found himself at odds with God and trying to be God. The Baptist recognized and submitted to God's will regarding his and Jesus' ministry: if his dwindled and Jesus' grew, that was the way that God intended both to be.[70]

3:28. John's submissive attitude is repeated from 1:28, **"I am not the Christ, but am sent ahead of him."** Here John clearly recognized and publicized his mission and relation to Jesus: "I am . . . sent ahead of him [Jesus]" (ἔμπροσθεν ἐκείνου, *emprosthen ekeinou*). John is Jesus' forerunner, harbinger, preparer, not his competition or superior. John was satisfied with his status and role, and Jesus was also with his. The assessment of the Baptist by Jesus (Matt 11:7-11) and the Fourth Gospel (10:40-42) is, therefore, no startling surprise.

3:29. In verses 29 and 30 John used a parable in which he intended to draw a contrast between himself and Jesus. **The bride belongs to the bridegroom,** Jesus. The bride is the people of God (as in the Old Testament, cf. Isa 62:4-5; Jer 2:2; 3:20; Ezek 10:8; 23:4; Hos 2:21) — and later also as the church in the New Testament was the bride of Christ (2 Cor 11:2; Eph 5:25-27, 31-32; Rev 21:2; 22:17). The "friend" (φίλος, *philos*) of the bridegroom is the equivalent of the modern day "best man" who took care of many of the details of the wedding, including the order of service, coaching participants, preparing a banquet and refreshments (cf. John 2:8-10), invitations to guests, probably even presiding over the whole ceremony. Galilean weddings were said to be a little different from those in Judea[71] in that there may have been two "best men" at a wedding in Judea, one for each of the two families, but only one in Galilee.[72]

This friend "stands and listens" for the bridegroom; that is, the best man served the bridegroom and remained a servant and subordinate to him. Carson notes that ancient Sumerian and Babylonian law absolutely prohibited the best man from marrying the bride —

---

[70]Ibid., 222-223.

[71]See Israel Abrahams, *Studies*, 2:213. Strack and Billerbeck, *Kommentar*, 1:45-46, 502.

[72]On Jewish weddings see A.W. Argyle, "Wedding Customs at the Time of Jesus." *ExpTim* 86 (1974–75): 214-215.

the "friend" could be only a friend and servant to the bridegroom, but never himself a bridegroom to this bride.[73] The "friend" rejoiced in the bridegroom's happiness — a proverbial topic in the Old Testament relative to weddings (Isa 62:5; Jer 7:34; 16:9; 25:10).[74]

The expression **is *full of joy* [when he hears the bridegroom's voice]** is χαρᾷ χαίρει (*chara chairei*), a somewhat rare Greek expression, and seems to be an effort to reproduce the Hebrew infinitive absolute (as in Gen 2:17; 16:10), which intensifies the action of the verb one would translate literally "with joy he rejoices." This is the only occurrence of this Greek construction in John. This Greek expression cannot be used as evidence of an Aramaic original format of this Gospel; it is not a sign of translation, but more likely is an imitation of the Greek Septuagint of the Old Testament.[75] John's joy is complete because Jesus' surpassing of John's ministry means the end of John's work.

3:30. This verse is a summary of John's and Jesus' ministries, relationships, and futures: henceforth, John must decrease but Jesus must increase. The words "increase" (αὐξάνω, *auxanō*) and "decrease" (ἐλαττόω, *elattoō*) are words used in an astrological sense of a sinking old star and the rising of a new star, and too much was made of these ideas in the early commentators from Ambrose and Augustine onwards. Certainly the attempts to extract from these two words the date of the birth of the Baptist (summer solstice) and of Jesus (winter solstice) seem absurd.[76] Notice that Jesus *must* (δεῖ, *dei*) increase; it is nothing less than God's will that he do so.[77]

4. The Son's Testimony (3:31-36)

[31]"The one who comes from above is above all; the one who is from the earth belongs to the earth, and speaks as one from the earth. The one who comes from heaven is above all. [32]He testifies

---

[73]Carson, *The Gospel According to John*, p. 212.

[74]See Strack and Billerbeck, *Kommentar*, 1:504-517.

[75]Barrett, *The Gospel According to St. John*, p. 223.

[76]Bultmann, *The Gospel of John*, p. 175, n. 1; Borchert disagrees (*John 1-11*, 1:192, n. 134); and also Brown, *John*, 1:153.

[77]Carson, *The Gospel According to John*, p. 212.

to what he has seen and heard, but no one accepts his testimony. [33]The man who has accepted it has certified that God is truthful. [34]For the one whom God has sent speaks the words of God, for God[a] gives the Spirit without limit. [35]The Father loves the Son and has placed everything in his hands. [36]Whoever believes in the Son has eternal life, but whoever rejects the Son will not see life, for God's wrath remains on him."[b]

[a]34 Greek *he*   [b]36 Some interpreters end the quotation after verse 30.

Many suppose that 31-36 is a summary or a commentary on the Son by the writer of the Fourth Gospel and thus end the quotation after verse 30; or is 31-36 the continued testimony of the Baptist?[78] These verses may be the writer's own special *testimony* (μαρτυρία, *martyria*) to Jesus — and thus again, one of the major themes of the Gospel crops up: belief (or unbelief) of testimony borne to Jesus.

3:31. The testimony in verses 31-36 describes Jesus' person, status, activity, relationships, and accomplishments. Verse 31 continues the thought of verses 22-30, that is, the contrast between Jesus and John and not simply the contrast between those who live with Jesus and those who live without him. **The one who comes from above is above all** — this is surely Jesus. **The one who is from the earth belongs to the earth** — this is surely John. Verses 31 and 32 explain verse 30 — why Jesus must increase and John must decrease — because Jesus came from heaven, is above all, and testified to what he saw and heard in heaven, while earth limited John's origin, speech, and activity (cf. v. 13). The word for "earth" is γῆ (*gē*) not κόσμος (*kosmos*), and so does not point to sin but to limitation.[79]

The expression **The one who comes *from above*** is ἄνωθεν (*anōthen*), the same word that is used of the new birth in verses 3 and 7; there is "a birth from above" because there is "one who comes from above." John could call to repentance and to baptism in water, but he could not give new birth and the Spirit because he was not from above and could not speak from above. In short, he could not save to the uttermost; only Jesus could do that. As the

---

[78]Bernard, *A Critical and Exegetical Commentary*, 1:117,123; Carson, *The Gospel According to John*, p. 212; Borchert, *John 1-11*, p. 193.

[79]Carson, *The Gospel According to John*, p. 212.

one who is above all,[80] Jesus is the highest ruler over all things and persons.

3:32. Because Jesus is ultimately from heaven, he is able to testify to **what he has seen and heard** there (cf. vv. 11-12). **[B]ut no one accepts his testimony** means "no one believes what he says."[81] The expression "no one" (οὐδείς, *oudeis*) was probably not intended to be understood literally, but was a literary hyperbole and meant to emphasize the world's rejection of Jesus. At his death, however, few (if any) did believe in Jesus (cf. 1:11-12).[82]

3:33. This verse uses a metaphor derived from the sealing of a document: to set one's seal on anything is to approve or to accept its condition and the status of its contents. One might have expected the sentence to have read "he who has accepted [the testimony] has certified that *Jesus* is truthful," but the text reads **that God is truthful.** To accept Jesus is to accept God; to deny Jesus is to deny God and regard both as liars.

3:34. Jesus is the one sent by God and is the one who speaks God's words. Jesus says only what the Father says and does what the Father does. Jesus alone is the one **to whom God gives his Spirit without limit.** The Jewish teachers taught that the different prophets had received various measures of the Spirit according to the demands of their assigned tasks.[83] For example, Rabbi Aha said that the Spirit worked in each prophet according to the measure (*bemishqal*) of each prophet's task assigned by God (*Leviticus Rabbah* 15:2). This was true also of the Baptist, but not of Jesus, to whom God gave the Spirit in fullness or without limitations (cf. Col 1:19; 2:9).

3:35. The reason is here stated for the Father's giving of the Spirit to the Son without limits and for giving all things into his hand: it is because **the Father loves the Son.** This theme appears in all the Gospels. It is repeated often in John, and is one of the most majestic truths of the Bible, especially because God's love is extended

---

[80]The heart of the textual problem in verses 31-32 centers on the presence or absence of the words "is above all" (ἐπάνω πάντων ἐστίν, *epanō pantōn estin*). The words were retained by the editors of the Nestle and the United Bible Societies' text. See Metzger, *A Textual Commentary*, p. 205.

[81]Barrett, *The Gospel According to St. John*, p. 226.

[82]See Borchert, *John 1-11*, 1:193.

[83]See Strack and Billerbeck, *Kommentar*, 2:431.

outwards to all of his creation (v. 16). God has placed all power and all authority in the hands of Jesus, in order to bring about salvation for mankind (cf. 3:31; 5:19-47).

3:36. This chapter closes with a somber note: **Whoever believes in the Son has life, but whoever rejects the Son will not see life, but God's wrath remains on him.** The word translated "rejects" in the NIV is ἀπειθῶν (*apeithōn*) and means "to be unbelieving" or "to be disobedient." These words are the climax of this chapter. The person who believes that Jesus is the Son (of God, or Messiah, Matt 16:16) already has (ἔχει, *echei*, present tense) eternal life (at least eternity has *begun*), but the one who disobeys (or does not believe) the Son will not see (note the future tense) life, but the wrath (ὀργή, *orgē*) of God continues or remains (μένει, *menei*, present tense) on that one. The wrath of God is his intolerance of evil (cf. Rom 1:18). The lives of persons without Christ are always bent towards sin, so John's term *apeithō* is accurate: "they are disobedient" or "rebellious" towards God. To reverse this way of thinking and living, one must believe in Jesus, the Son of God. Not to do so is to continue under God's wrath or condemnation, not merely to become or begin to be condemned.[84]

---

[84]See Borchert, *John 1-11*, 1:195.

JOHN 4

E. JESUS AND THE SAMARITANS (4:1-42)

1. Introduction (4:1-4)

[1]The Pharisees heard that Jesus was gaining and baptizing more disciples than John, [2]although in fact it was not Jesus who baptized, but his disciples. [3]When the Lord learned of this, he left Judea and went back once more to Galilee.
[4]Now he had to go through Samaria.

The fourth chapter of John begins with a transition paragraph that ties together passages before and after, somewhat like 2:12 and 3:22-24. The passage contains geographical, chronological, and didactic information of considerable significance.

4:1. The Pharisees' attitude toward Jesus may have been one reason why Jesus moved *from Jerusalem* to the *Judean countryside* (2:23; 3:22) and now to *Samaria* (4:4) and later to *Galilee*, (4:3)[1] but it sounds as though here Jesus was already walking the mission road geographically that he called his disciples later to travel (compare the "mission geography" of Jesus in Acts 1:8).[2] These first several chapters of the Johannine Gospel have predominantly stressed *preaching* and *believing*, but with the Pharisees and perhaps Herod Antipas in 3:24, the clouds of *opposition* loom on the horizon, beginning in earnest in the next chapter.

A second reason why Jesus left Judea was the imprisonment of the Baptist by Herod (3:24; Matt 4:12; Mark 1:14; Luke 3:20). The

---

[1]Bultmann, *The Gospel of John*, p. 176; Carson, *The Gospel According to John*, p. 215.
[2]Borchert, *John 1–11*, 1:198.

closing of the Baptist's ministry left Jesus free to move northward and fill the silent gap.[3]

4:2. Some students see this verse as a later "editorial corrective," inserted to set straight a possible misunderstanding on the part of the reader of 3:26 that Jesus' disciples, but not he, baptized new disciples in greater numbers than the Baptist. There are, however, no genuine grounds for such a suggestion, textual, grammatical, theological or otherwise, and the so-called "corrective" would better have been inserted at 3:22, as Bultmann himself admits. A sort of parallel with Paul's assertion in 1 Corinthians 1:14-17 that he was not sent to baptize but to preach the gospel, has been drawn with John 4:2.[4] Neither passage, however, was intended to trivialize baptism but to set aright the proper relation of baptizer and baptized in both instances.

4:3. That Jesus left Judea because of the jealousy of the Pharisees, has been questioned on the grounds that there were also Pharisees in Galilee.[5] Their influence was apparently weaker in Galilee. Jesus was returning again (πάλιν, *palin*) to Galilee, the goal of his journey (note 1:43–2:12).

4:4. In saying that Jesus **had to go through Samaria**, does the "had to" (ἔδει, *edei*) imply God's providential leading (a real possibility)? The expression could alternatively be simply the result of Jesus' human decision to leave Judea, where trouble seemed to have been brewing, and to go immediately to Galilee — the shortest route to which lay through Samaria, as opposed to the route east of the Jordan river. Even Josephus acknowledges Samaria as the shortest way.[6] A third view would seek to harmonize and mesh divine leading and human volition in Jesus' decision. The reference to "Samaria" means the province, not the city from which the province derived its name; it lay between Judea to the south and Galilee to the north. Samaria was not a single political entity in New Testament times, but was governed along with Judea by the

---

[3]Bultmann, *The Gospel of John*, 1:176, n. 4; Dodd, *Interpretation* 311, n. 3; Joachim Jeremias, *New Testament Theology* (Old Tappan, NJ: Scribners Reference, 1977), 1:45.

[4]Borchert, *John 1–11*, 1:199.

[5]Haenchen, *The Gospel of John*, 1:218b.

[6]Josephus, *Life*, p. 269. See Haenchen, *The Gospel of John*, 1:218b.

Roman procurator from Caesarea on the shore of the Mediterranean Sea. Samaria had had a long history, however, by the days
of Jesus. Omri, king of the ten northern tribes, built his new capital
and called it Samaria (1 Kgs 16:24). The name was eventually
applied to the region surrounding the capital and sometimes to the
whole northern kingdom (Ezek 16:46). When the Assyrians captured the northern kingdom in 721 B.C., they deported the more
gifted and wealthier Israelites and imported foreign pagans and
settled them in the old kingdom of Israel. These foreigners brought
with them their pagan gods and intermarried with the Israelites
left in the land; thus, "Samaritan," came to mean a half-breed
Israelite whose religion lacked features of a purer Judaism.[7]
Around 400 B.C. the Samaritans built a large temple atop Mount
Gerizim, but near the end of the second century B.C. this structure was demolished by John Hyrcanus I, the Maccabean ruler
over Judea. This act heightened for centuries the animosity between
Jews and Samaritans.

2. Jesus and the Woman of Samaria (4:5-30)

The Setting (4:5-6)

**5So he came to a town in Samaria called Sychar, near the plot of
ground Jacob had given to his son Joseph. 6Jacob's well was there,
and Jesus, tired as he was from the journey, sat down by the well.
It was about the sixth hour.**

4:5. Sychar in this verse is called a **town** (πόλις, *polis*) — the term
is usually translated "city" but it can mean "village" or "town."[8]
Sychar appeared in neither the Old Testament nor rabbinic literature,[9] but was mentioned for the first time in the journal of the so-
called pilgrim of Bordeaux (France) who made a trip to Palestine
about A.D. 333 and saw all the villages named in the New

---

[7]2 Kings 17 and 18; Neh 13; Josephus, *Antiquities* 11:297-347, esp. 340-341.

[8]Zahn, *Das Evangelium*, p. 233

[9]So Haenchen, *The Gospel of John*, 1:218b, but Strack and Billerbeck
(*Kommentar*, 2:431) disagrees on the rabbinic evidence.

Testament.[10] Sychar often has been identified with the modern 'Askar on the shoulder of Mt. Ebal and opposite Mt. Gerizim.[11] Sychar was said to be **near the plot of ground Jacob had given to his son Joseph.** This refers to Genesis 48:22, where Jacob on his deathbed said to Joseph, "And to you, as one who is over your brothers, I give the ridge of land (*š^ekem*, shoulder of a mountain) I took from the Amorites with my sword and my bow." When Israel conquered Canaan, they brought with them from Egypt the bones of their forefather Joseph, and buried them near Shechem "in the tract of land that Jacob bought for a hundred pieces of silver from the sons of Hamor, the father of Shechem" (Josh 24:32). This tract became the heritage of Joseph's descendents at Shechem. If Sychar and 'Askar should be identified, then Sychar was about half a mile northeast of Jacob's well.[12]

4:6. The Old Testament did not record when and why Jacob dug this well (πηγή, *pēgē*), but the reason may have lain in his desire for space between himself and his pagan neighbors, based on the unpleasant experiences of his father Isaac with pagan neighbors concerning common watering places (Gen 26:15-33). The well is walled with masonry for some ten feet from the top, and below that for nearly a hundred more feet the well was cut through solid rock. The word that John used here to describe the well is *pēgē*, which was a spring or fountain, but that is the kind of well it was (and still is): the well shaft penetrated a spring of flowing water which bubbled upwards at the bottom of the well. In 4:11-12, the term used to describe the well is φρέαρ (*phrear*), which usually means a cistern or dug-out well. Jacob's well seemed to have been both: it was dug out of solid rock, but it also was fed by a bubbling underground spring that was unusually dependable year in and year out.[13] The shaft of the well was about seven and a half feet in diameter, and the opening at the top was covered over like a cistern.

---

[10]Cf. Haenchen, *The Gospel of John*, 1:218b.

[11]So Schnackenburg, *The Gospel according to St John*.

[12]Haenchen, *The Gospel of John*, 1:218-219; some, since the days of Jerome, identify the town with Shechem; see Gustaf Dalman, *His Sacred Sites and Ways* (New York: Macmillan, 1935), p. 214; Brown, *John*, 1:169; D. Biggs, "Sychar," *ISBE*, 4:674-675.

[13]Cf. Carson, *The Gospel According to John*, p. 217.

This covering had a round opening in it nearly two feet wide for lowering a vessel on a rope to draw water. It was on this thick covering that Jesus **tired as he was from the journey, sat down by the well.**

Suprisingly for such a "spiritual" gospel (as Origen called it) the writer recorded more unmistakable marks of Jesus' humanity and creatureliness than did the Synoptics: tiredness, thirst, sleep, groaning, weeping, hunger, etc. The reality of Jesus' human nature was early called in question by the Gnostics; today his humanity is usually accepted, and his nature as deity is much more often questioned. The truth of the incarnation involves not only an assertion about Jesus' deity but also in an equal way about his humanity.

It was about the sixth hour when Jesus waited at the well. If this time notation was reckoned with the Jews from sunrise, then it was about noon, the time of day when most people took a break from labor and high heat. Some think the hour was reckoned according to a supposed Roman manner of time from either midnight or noon, so that it was either six o'clock in the morning or evening, not strange times for carrying water, especially should the day be hot.[14] "About" (ὡς, *hōs*) appears before all descriptions of time in this Gospel.

Jesus' Request for Water (4:7-9)

7When a Samaritan woman came to draw water, Jesus said to her, "Will you give me a drink?" 8 (His disciples had gone into the town to buy food.)

9The Samaritan woman said to him, "You are a Jew and I am a Samaritan woman. How can you ask me for a drink?" (For Jews do not associate with Samaritans.ᵃ)

ᵃ9 Or do not use dishes Samaritans have used

4:7. A well or spring, like a town gate, was a site where people congregated, quite like the meeting places in the Old Testament of Abraham's servant and Rebekah (Gen 24:11,15-17), of Jacob and

---

[14]Borchert, *John 1-11*, p. 1:201.

Rachel (Gen 29:2-12). The Samaritan woman seems to have been alone. Since women more often came in groups to draw water, some have speculated that the public shame attached to her lifestyle (vv. 16-18) caused her to shun crowds and possibly endure noonday heat in order to do her work alone.[15]

There was no vessel at the well to hold water; each person brought her/his own water drawing paraphernalia — and Jesus had no bucket or other vessel. The bucket would have been a vessel made of leather, and such that it could be collapsed for convenience in carrying. A stone jar could not be substituted for a bucket, because it could be too easily damaged or destroyed by hitting against the well's inner stone walls.[16]

When **Jesus said to her, "Will you give me a drink?"** he took the initiative, as he usually did in all the Gospels. Jesus set up a crisis for Jewish legal procedures, because Jews avoided all social contact with Samaritans and women in public. A Jewish man did not talk with any women in public — even with his own wife.[17]

Some Jews could envision their eating with Samaritans[18] but most could not lest they be defiled; and so a Jewish legal statement soon was formulated that declared "all the daughters of the Samaritans are menstruants from their cradle,"[19] which made them continuously unclean.[20] The Samaritan woman naturally was shocked when Jesus spoke to her. Jesus' disciples, who had gone into the town to buy food, would have been shocked along with her. This explanatory aside in verse 8 is not an addition appended at a late date, but added from the first writing of the Gospel in order to make sense of why the disciples were not with Jesus when he first met the Samaritan woman. Jesus broke the taboo and asked her for a drink.

---

[15]Carson, *The Gospel According to John*, p. 217; Schnackenburg, *The Gospel according to St John*, 1:424.

[16]Haenchen, *The Gospel of John*, 1:219a.

[17]Cf. *Kiddushin* 49b; Mishnah, *Aboth* 1:5; *Shabbath* 152a; Philo, *On drunkenness* 58-59.

[18]Cf. Mishnah, *Berakoth* 7:1.

[19]Mishnah, *Niddah* 4:1.

[20]Cf. Carson, *The Gospel According to John*, pp. 217-218.

4:8. When Jesus' disciples went **into town to buy food** this would have been *kosher* food, and hard to find in Samaria. Perhaps the least ceremonially defiling food for them would have been bread and fruits. Just to have passed through Samaria would have contaminated a Jew ceremonially. Sometimes such a journey brought physical attack by Samaritans.[21]

4:9. The shocked woman spoke in surprise: **"You are a Jew and I am a Samaritan woman. How can you ask me for a drink?"** She recognized Jesus as a Jew probably by his dress and speech.[22] This is the only time in John's Gospel that Jesus is bluntly called a Jew.[23] This female Samaritan viewed him as a Jew; in 8:48 Jews will view him as a Samaritan!

Who spoke the line **For Jews do not associate with Samaritans?** Was it the woman, or more likely, the author of the Fourth Gospel?[24] The meaning of the explanatory statement in verse 9b is much debated; the meaning of the statement rests on the meaning of συγ-χράομαι (*synchraomai*). This verb may mean "to associate with" or "to have dealings with."[25] David Daube suggested that the word may mean "to use (vessels) in common with" the Samaritans.[26]

Living Water (4:10-15)

[10]Jesus answered her, "If you knew the gift of God and who it is that asks you for a drink, you would have asked him and he would have given you living water."

---

[21]Josephus, *Antiquities*, 20:118-136; *Wars*, 2:232-246.

[22]Bernard, *A Critical and Exegetical Commentary*, 1:137.

[23]Haenchen, *The Gospel of John*, 1:219b.

[24]Barrett, *The Gospel According to St. John*, p. 232; Borchert, *John 1–11*, 1:203.

[25]"χράομαι," *BAGD*, 2:775a; J.H. Moulton and G. Milligan, *The Vocabulary of the Greek New Testament Illustrated from the Papyri and Other Non-literary Sources* (Grand Rapids: Eerdmans, 1949), p. 616a, b).

[26]David Daube, "Jesus and the Samaritan Woman: The Meaning of συγχράομαι," *JBL* 69 (1950): 137-147. Cf. the marginal reading of the NIV. See D. Hall's article "The Meaning of *synchraomai* in John 4:9." in *Expository Times* 83 (1971): 56-57 and George Kilpatrick, "John 4:9," *JBL* 87 (1968): 327-328; Borchert, *John 1–11*, 1:203.

[11]"Sir," the woman said, "you have nothing to draw with and the well is deep. Where can you get this living water? [12]Are you greater than our father Jacob, who gave us the well and drank from it himself, as did also his sons and his flocks and herds?"

[13]Jesus answered, "Everyone who drinks this water will be thirsty again, [14]but whoever drinks the water I give him will never thirst. Indeed, the water I give him will become in him a spring of water welling up to eternal life."

[15]The woman said to him, "Sir, give me this water so that I won't get thirsty and have to keep coming here to draw water."

4:10. Jesus quickly directed the conversation in a new direction, to what he wished her to learn. He challenged her to know two things: (a) the gift (δωρεά, *dōrea*) **of God** and (b) who was really speaking to her. What was the gift of God? Numerous answers have been offered to this question: (1) For the Jews God's greatest gift was the Torah or law.[27] (2) In Gnostic thought the gift of God was the life-giving revelation, e.g., Corpus Hermeticum 4:5.[28] (3) The gift of God is Jesus himself and his ability to transmit eternal life to those who receive him (see 2 Cor. 9:15). This verse thus is identical with the thought of 3:16.[29] Some refer the gift to the Holy Spirit[30] but it is Jesus who gives the Spirit (Acts 2:33).

What did the woman not know about Jesus? That he was much more than a mere Jewish man; he was also the Son of God. Jesus said that if she had known the gift of God and who asked her for a drink, she would have asked him and **he would have given** her **living water**; that is, she would have been seeking the water that Jesus could give — their positions were reversed: he was the giver and she in need. She spoke of physical water; Jesus spoke (on a different plane) of "living water." She understood "living water" in the

---

[27]Midrash *Rabbah* to Genesis 6:7 — other gifts were the lights, the rain, peace, the land of Israel, mercy, the parting of the Red Sea, the future world; see Odeberg (*The Fourth Gospel*, pp. 149-152) for references to other gifts.

[28]*Corpus Hermeticum* 4:5; cf. Odeberg, *The Fourth Gospel*, p. 152; Bultmann, *The Gospel of John*, p. 181, n. 3.

[29]Odeberg, *The Fourth Gospel*, p. 152.

[30]Bernard, *A Critical and Exegetical Commentary*, 1:138.

ordinary sense: water that is running or springing as contrasted with cistern or still water (Gen 26:19; Lev 14:5). Jesus used "living water" in a spiritual sense (cf. John 7:37-39): "life-giving water."[31]

4:11. The woman took Jesus' words literally, as she continued the conversation, **"Sir . . . you have nothing to draw with and the well is deep. Where can you get this living water?"** The "sir" (κύριε, *kyrie*) probably meant "sir" here, not "Lord."[32] Jesus had no bucket, and the water was deep in the earth; where could he get water for her or for himself? "Where" (πόθεν, *pothen*) was used thirteen times in John and points to the source or origin of things; it is a key term here and throughout the Gospel. Most persons in John did not know from where Jesus came, as the woman here did not know from whence Jesus received this living water.

4:12. In order to obtain water at this place, Jacob, the ancestor of both Jesus and the Samaritans, had to dig a deep well and provide the means for lifting the water from it. If Jesus could provide living water without digging a well, he must be greater than Jacob[33] — or he was a pretender and deceiver. The form of the woman's question in Greek expected a negative answer, but it also gave Jesus the opportunity to present and press his message of good news. The woman failed to comprehend on two matters: (1) Jesus' type of living water did not come from an ordinary well, even one with a gushing spring in the bottom of it, and (2) Jesus was far greater than the ancestor Jacob. (Notice that in 8:53, a similar question contrasted Jesus and Abraham). That Jacob drank from the well showed its distinction, that his cattle drank from it shows the copiousness of its supply and that it could not satisfy man nor beast for long.

4:13-14. In these verses Jesus continued to disclose what he meant by his having living water to give, and to clear up the misunderstanding of verse 10. Notice the negativism of verse 13, but by contrast the positivism of verse 14. What Jesus said of water here cannot be said of natural water from a well: (1) after drinking it one

---

[31]See Bultmann, *The Gospel of John*, p. 186.

[32]Carson, *The Gospel According to John*, p. 219.

[33]Jacob was revered by Samaritans and Jews. See John MacDonald, *The Theology of the Samaritans* (London: SCM Press, 1964), pp. 234-248, 296-298.

will never thirst again; (2) the water within one, once drunk, will make that person a veritable spring; (3) such water will give **eternal life** to the one who drinks it. Jesus did not say that he was the living water (as he later said that he was the living bread [6:51]), but that *from him* the living water would proceed, just as later the Spirit was sent *from him* (7:39).[34]

4:15. The woman continued to think in physical terms of all that Jesus had said, as is evidenced by her expressed desire for the water that Jesus claimed to be able to give her which would quench thirst forever, so that she could abandon these trips to Jacob's well forever. She did seem to think that Jesus talked of something miraculous, so some understanding had begun to take place in her.

The woman revealed (4:16-19)

[16]He told her, "Go, call your husband and come back."
[17]"I have no husband," she replied.

Jesus said to her, "You are right when you say you have no husband. [18]The fact is, you have had five husbands, and the man you now have is not your husband. What you have just said is quite true."
[19]"Sir," the woman said, "I can see that you are a prophet.

4:16-18. The woman must have been shocked by the next happening. Jesus was about to show to her her need for living water and its relation to her need for changing her personal, marital behavior. These verses clearly display the close relation of religion and ethics in Jesus' thinking and living. In order to receive Jesus' living water she must deal with the flagrant misuse of her sexuality. Jesus asked her to fetch her husband. She replied that she had no husband. He responded that she was correct, because she had had five husbands, and the man with whom she was currently living was not her husband. She was amazed that a stranger knew so much about her personal life; so, she exclaimed, **"I can see that you are a prophet"** — another response that marked a change in her perception of who Jesus was.

---

[34]Bernard, *A Critical and Exegetical Commentary,* 1:139.

Any number of marriages was allowed by Jewish oral law[35] but the rabbis approved only three. She had married five different men, who had died or divorced her, and she had not bothered to marry her present partner. John surely did not mean to relate this story so as to show the Samaritans as morally worse than the Jews. One of John's aims was rather to demonstrate Jesus' supernatural knowledge (cf. 1:48; 4:29).[36] Another aim was to show Jesus' ability to salvage the worst of sinful persons, and to make something very much better of their lives.[37] In verse 18 the woman was learning what truth (ἀληθές, alēthes) was.

4:19. Jesus' recounting of the sordid truth about a person (the woman herself) whom he had never met led the Samaritan woman to the swift conclusion that he was a prophet, since prophets were thought by Jews and Samaritans to have access to divine knowledge and secrets not available to others. Such precise information about her past proved that Jesus was inspired.[38]

The Samaritans accepted only the Pentateuch as Scripture. Deuteronomy 18:15-19 contained the promise of a prophet to come who would be like Moses but greater than Moses. The Samaritans called their messianic-like figure *Taheb.* Many have speculated that the Samaritan woman had this "prophet" in mind when she called Jesus "Prophet," but the text says nothing further on what kind of prophetic person she may have had in mind — beyond his possessing supernatural knowledge.

---

[35]Cf. Strack and Billerbeck, *Kommentar,* 2:437.

[36]Barrett, *The Gospel According to St. John,* p. 235.

[37]Haenchen, *The Gospel of John,* 1:221b. This story has been allegorized ever since Heracleon's commentary in the second century: The woman represented Samaria; the husbands were five pagan deities (based on the fact that a husband is called a *ba'al* in Hebrew, a title also used of deity, and based also on Samaria's having been peopled by five foreign tribes each with its god; the sixth who was 'not a husband' was either a false god [perhaps Simon Magus? — Acts 8:9-24]) or the Samaritans' own false worship of the true God Jehovah (v. 22).

[38]Carson, *The Gospel According to John,* p. 221.

Jesus Reveals Himself (4:20-26)

[20]Our fathers worshiped on this mountain, but you Jews claim that the place where we must worship is in Jerusalem."

[21]Jesus declared, "Believe me, woman, a time is coming when you will worship the Father neither on this mountain nor in Jerusalem. [22]You Samaritans worship what you do not know; we worship what we do know, for salvation is from the Jews. [23]Yet a time is coming and has now come when the true worshipers will worship the Father in spirit and truth, for they are the kind of worshipers the Father seeks. [24]God is spirit, and his worshipers must worship in spirit and in truth."

[25]The woman said, "I know that Messiah" (called Christ) "is coming. When he comes, he will explain everything to us."

[26]Then Jesus declared, "I who speak to you am he."

4:20. This verse seems to mark an abrupt change of topic, but if Jesus could possibly be a genuine prophet (v. 19) with access to superhuman knowledge (vv. 17b-18), would one not naturally turn to him for answers to questions that had long puzzled everyone concerned, such as the validity and location of Jewish and/or Samaritan worship? The woman therefore lost little time in taking advantage of the new possibility and posed the problem of what constituted true worship. Such a position understands the woman as making a sort of confession that Jesus was *the* prophet or *Taheb* awaited by the Samaritans.[39]

Another understanding of verse 20 is that the Samaritan woman, embarrassed by Jesus' revelation of her sordid past, simply raised a thorny theological issue concerning the site of worship in order to avoid having to face up to and deal with her guilt. It is always easier to discuss theology than to face one's own sins and to repent.[40] This position, however, has been criticized as psychologizing the text.[41] It is, however, a very old approach to the meaning of the text.

---

[39]So John Bowman, "Samaritan Studies," *BJRL* 40 (1957): 298-329.

[40]Carson, *The Gospel According to John*, p. 221; Borchert, *John 1-11*, p. 206; and most modern commentators.

[41]Barrett (*The Gospel According to St. John*, p. 236) and others.

Whatever the reason she raised the issue, the woman touched on a vital subject (and she may have been ready to use Jesus' answer to help her evaluate him as a prophet and as a possible candidate for the Messiah [v. 25]). She wanted to know which place was the correct site for acceptable worship of God: Mount Gerizim of the Samaritans, or Mount Moriah **in Jerusalem** of the Jews? Samaria could have made quite a case for itself as the location of the nation's shrine: (1) At this site God first appeared to Abraham after entering Canaan (Gen 12:6-7). (2) Here Jacob first lived (Gen 33:18). (3) Here Joseph first sought for his brothers (Gen 37:12-13). (4) In this area was one of the cities of refuge (Josh 20:7-9). (5) Between Mt. Ebal and Mt. Gerizim Joshua read the blessings and cursings on those who keep or neglect the Mosaic law (Josh 8:33). (6) Here Joshua delivered his valedictory to Israel (Josh 24:1). (7) Here were interred the bones of Joseph (Josh 24:32). (8) Here (in the city of Samaria) was the capital of Israel, the northern nation of the ten divided tribes (1 Kgs 12:1, 25).

Further, if Samaritan traditions of later centuries existed in the time of Jesus, one might add even more to Samaria's record: (1) Paradise (that is, for the Samaritans) was situated on top of Mt. Gerizim. (2) Adam was formed from the dust of Mt. Gerizim. (3) On Gerizim Adam built his first altar. (4) Seth also here did the same. (5) Gerizim was the Mt. Ararat on which Noah's ark rested, and the only place that the flood did not inundate, and so was the only place not defiled after the flood by dead bodies. (6) On this mountain Noah reared his altar. (7) Here Abraham attempted to offer Isaac. (8) Here Abraham met Melchizedek. (9) Here was the Bethel, where Jacob had the ladder dream.[42]

Jerusalem had an equally brilliant record as a place of great importance in early and later biblical history and worship, including Abraham's presence there, and the first kings and priests of the united nation. Most important, however, was the fact that the Jews worshiped on Mt. Moriah in Jerusalem because God said he would select the spot for his worship (Deut 12:5-11; 1 Kgs 9:3; 2 Chr 3:12), and thus, God eliminated other locations as possible competing sites.[43]

---

[42]See McGarvey and Pendleton, *The Fourfold Gospel*, pp. 147-148.

[43]The Jews took "the place God will choose" (Deut 12:5) as pointing to the eventual worship in Jerusalem. The Samaritan text of Deut 12:5 read

4:21. Jesus did not rudely ignore the woman's challenge to debate, nor did he turn aside to discuss the merits of Jerusalem vs. Mt. Gerizim as the place for worship. What he did was to emphasize *not* the *place* but the *nature* of worship. Jesus said that the time was coming (apparently after the crucifixion and resurrection) when neither Jews nor Samaritans would seek to worship God at any exclusive site, as though the site or the worship conducted there were superior to any other site or sites (cf. 1 Tim. 2:8).

The Father is the most used Johannine designation for God and one of the most often used in Judaism. He is thought of as primarily the Father of the Son, but also of the Jews — and apparently of the Samaritans too, or at least potentially of some of the Samaritans (cf. vv. 39,42).

4:22. Jesus spoke now as a Jew, and presented a contrast between the intelligent worship of the Jews and the (at least in part) ignorant worship of the Samaritans. The latter rejected all the revelation in the Old Testament except that of the Pentateuch; the Jews accepted the entire Old Canon; thus, Jesus is able to say that we (Jews) worship what we know, while you Samaritans worship what you do not know (because you reject so much of the content of divine revelation in the Scriptures). Further, this rejection led to a dead end because salvation came from revelation and promises given to the Jews but not (directly) to the Samaritans. From the Jews came the Messiah, according to the flesh, and from them came also the prophets, apostles, and other inspired writers who gave the full knowledge of salvation accomplished by the Messiah in accord with God's eternal plan or will. This is a passage of tremendous significance. Worship without revelation may be spontaneous but it can never be informed or saving.[44] Samaria in the Old Testament became a center of Baal worship and in the Christian era became the home of magicians or sorcerers and theological errorists

---

"the place God has chosen," reasoned to be Mt. Gerizim (see Carson, *The Gospel According to John*, p. 222). For information on Samaritan worship see Robert J. Bull, "Archaeological Context for Understanding John 4:20," *Biblical Archaeologist* 38 (1975): 54-59, and Bull's "An Archaeological Footnote to 'our fathers worshiped on this mountain,' John 4:20," *NTS* 23 (1977): 400-462.

[44]Cf. Barrett, *The Gospel According to St. John*, p. 237.

(Gnostics), who prided themselves on their ignorance of the unknowable God.[45]

4:23. Jesus said that **a time is coming and has now come.** The time was already here, though its meaning and significance were not understood. As that "time" came to greater fulfillment, **the true worshipers** would **worship the Father in spirit and truth.** Spirit and truth are two of the characteristic, fundamental elements in God's nature and ours. Both terms set God apart, along with mankind and angels, from all the rest of his creation. When human beings worship, they use the part of their nature that is already nearest to God in construction and operation. To refuse to worship or to worship anything less than God is to deny that our and God's nature is spirit, and to worship what is false, not true.

4:24. God is not *a* spirit, but spirit. Because "spirit" here is a predicate adjective that modifies God, Spirit is the essence of God's nature. Apparently the expression meant (1) that God is not confined to space and time in temples (Acts 7:48), (2) that he is not made of material, as idolaters (even the Stoics) contended (Acts 17:29), and (3) that he is not an abstract, impersonal force but a personal being.

The nature of God dictates the nature of worship: **His worshipers must worship in spirit and in truth.** This verse is admittedly of great significance, but the meaning of these words seems to elude many commentators. Of the numerous interpretations that have been offered of these lines, the following four are a sampling: (1) the verses 23 and 24 show that acceptable worship is offered to the Trinity: the Father in 23b, the spirit in both verses as the Holy Spirit, and the truth as the Son.[46] (2) Ἐν πνεύματι (*en pneumati,* in spirit) points to "the supernatural life that Christians enjoy," while ἐν ἀληθείᾳ (*en alētheia,* in truth) points to "the single basis of this supernatural life in Christ, through whom God's will is faithfully fulfilled."[47] Apparently Barrett understood "spirit" to mean "Holy Spirit" and worship must occur in "a supernatural life," but what the latter is he does not say — perhaps it is equal to Paul's "life in

---

[45]Dodd, *Interpretation,* 314.

[46]See J.A. Bengel, *Gnomon of the New Testament* (Edinburgh: T&T Clark, 1858), 2:293-294.

[47]Barrett, *The Gospel According to St. John,* p. 239.

Christ." (3) Worship that is acceptable to God is not cultic worship but worship that takes place in the eschatological age.[48] Bultmann never really says, but apparently it is worship indebted entirely to the incarnation, death and resurrection, ascension and glorification of Jesus. If that is accurate, then verses 23-24 mean worship in the Christian age is true worship only if "the eschatological event is realized in it." (4) A different understanding of worship in spirit and truth arose from the fact that a *Jewish* man and a *Samaritan* woman met at Jacob's well and discussed worship acceptable to God. Judaism of the first century A.D. has been said to be a worship of the letter and not of the spirit; thus, as over against the Jew one is to worship God in spirit, not primarily in letter. Samaritanism was a worship dominated by falsehood (note their rejection of the truth in most of the Old Testament), and so, as over against the Samaritan, the time is coming when acceptable worshipers will employ all of God's truth that is available, especially the truth in the Scriptures.[49]

The first and third options for the meaning of "spirit and truth" are closer to one another than at first appears: acceptable worship must (δεῖ, *dei*) involve deity as its object (the Father) and be offered through the spirit (Holy Spirit?) because of the achievements (revelation, death-resurrection, and judging) by the Son.

4:25-26. Jesus' intuitive knowledge of the woman's personal life and his ability to answer a difficult question about the place of worship led the woman to think of him as a possible Samaritan Messiah, who, in her Samaritan thinking would be a prophet-teacher, called *Taheb* (probably meaning "the one who restores" or perhaps "the one who returns").[50] This Messiah would teach the people and explain all things. Jews did not seemingly think primarily of their Messiah as a teacher, unless it was as a teacher of the Gentiles.

The woman said that when Messiah came, he would **explain everything to us.** This statement is both revealing and concealing: it reveals that a modicum of belief in Jesus is in the woman, but it conceals her doubts and the immaturity of her faith. It does,

[48]Bultmann, *The Gospel of John*, pp. 189-192.

[49]Westcott, *The Gospel According to St. John*, 1:159.

[50]Barrett, *The Gospel According to St. John*, p. 239; Carson, *The Gospel According to John*, p. 226.

however, enable Jesus to reveal himself to her in verse 26, "I, the one speaking to you, am he (the Messiah)."[51]

This confession of Jesus' Messiahship may be the first such confession in the four Gospels. Why should Jesus confess himself as Messiah, and why first to a half-pagan? As to the latter question, (1) he needed to be more explicit with Samaritans than Jews; (2) he could speak more openly in Samaria than either Judea or Galilee because fewer Jews were present in Samaria (no one was about to make him a king there (as in 6:15), and (3) he intended to be in Samaria only a brief time (cf. v. 4). As to why he himself confessed his Messiahship, (a) the Twelve did not hear it, so they were the first *among his disciples* to confess him, and (b) non-Jews and half-Jews, from the start, were viewed by Jesus as of great importance and worth, even though Palestinian culture around him acted otherwise (cf. Mark 7:24-30, esp. 26-27).

Reactions to Jesus (4:27-30)

[27]**Just then his disciples returned and were surprised to find him talking with a woman. But no one asked, "What do you want?" or "Why are you talking with her?"**

[28]**Then, leaving her water jar, the woman went back to the town and said to the people,** [29]**"Come, see a man who told me everything I ever did. Could this be the Christ[a]?"** [30]**They came out of the town and made their way toward him.**

[a]**29 Or Messiah**

4:27. Jesus' **disciples returned** from Sychar where they had purchased food (v. 8), and were somewhat shocked to find him talking with a woman.[52] Shocked though they were, yet the disciples did

---

[51]For the usage of ἐγώ εἰμι, (*egō eimi*) see notes at 6:35.

[52]For Rabbinic views on men's conversations with women in public or private, see Strack and Billerbeck, *Kommentar*, 2:438; George F. Moore, *Judaism in the First Centuries of the Christian Era* (Cambridge, MA: Harvard University Press, 1927), 2:269ff. See also the prayer prayed daily by every male Jew in which he thanked God that God had not made him a heathen, a woman, or a slave (Menahoth 43b). Jewish masculine contempt for

not ask, **"What do you want?" or "Why are you talking to her?"** It seems unlikely that the first question is addressed to the woman and the second to Jesus.[53] They probably did not question Jesus for speaking with a strange woman in public (1) for fear of being rebuked by Jesus for their own male prejudices,[54] or (2) because they knew the character of Jesus well enough by now not to doubt his "personal moral standards and commitment" in every ethical situation.[55] Concerning Jesus' relations with women see 7:51–8:11; 11:5, and also Luke 7:36-50; 8:2-3; 10:38-42.

4:28. The Samaritan woman left **her water jar** at the well and **went back to the town.** Why did she leave the water jar behind? (1) She had just filled the jar, so she left it that Jesus could finally receive the drink which he had earlier requested;[56] (2) she simply forgot it in her excitement to tell her townsfolk what had happened;[57] (3) she had not yet filled the jar, so it was foolish to carry it back and forth empty, especially since it was a heavy jar;[58] (4) she was making a complete break with her past, and so she abandoned her jar as a sign of the complete abandonment of that past;[59] (5) she

---

women was displayed by the readiness with which Jewish husbands divorced their wives (Matt 5:31-32) or limited social contacts outside the home (Sotah 6:1; Yebamoth 76b-77a), or refused them the right to testify in courts (Mishrah *Shebuot* 4:1), and though Megilla 23a says that women were eligible to read Scripture in the synagogue, they were expected to decline, and merely listen (*Hagigah* 3a). For an excellent summary of the views on pagan women in the days of early Christianity, see Gregory E. Sterling, "Women in the Hellenistic and Roman Worlds (323 BCE to 138 CE)," *Essays on Women in Earliest Christianity*, Carroll D. Osburn, ed. (Joplin, MO: College Press, 1993), 1:41-92. For views about Jewish women in the same era, see Randall D. Chesnutt in the same volume: "Jewish Women in the Greco-Roman Era," 1:93-130.

[53]As with Bernard, *A Critical and Exegetical Commentary*, 1:152.

[54]Borchert, *John 1-11*, p. 210.

[55]Carson, *The Gospel According to John*, p. 227.

[56]Barrett, *The Gospel of John*, p. 240.

[57]Richard A. Edwards, *The Gospel According to John* (London: Eyre & Spottiswoode, 1954), p. 47; also Haenchen, *The Gospel of John*, 1:224a.

[58]Bernard, *A Critical and Exegetical Commentary*, 1:152; Schnackenburg, *The Gospel according to St John*, 1:443.

[59]Borchert, *John 1-11*, 1:210-211; but would she not have to drink water again?

abandoned the jar as a symbol of renunciation of the old worship ceremonies in favor of worship in spirit and truth.[60] Numbers (2) and (3) make the greatest sense; number (4) seems also a possibility.

4:29. The woman went back to invite the town to come and see a man who told her details about her life that only a prophet could know, and this ability probably meant for a Samaritan that such a one could certainly be *the* prophet of Deuteronomy 18:15-18, that is, the Samaritan Messiah. She expressed her conclusion about Jesus bluntly and yet somewhat cautiously, "Could this be the Christ?" Her question, which was introduced by the word μήτι (*mēti*), may denote a negative answer, or at least imply some sense of uncertainty.[61] At this point, Haenchen[62] noticed that the woman did not base her acknowledgement of Jesus' possible Messiahship on Jesus' own direct disclosure to her in verse 26 that he was the Christ or Messiah. Haenchen, however, seemed to misunderstand the situation: (1) This was a *Samaritan* whose expected Messiah was rather different from the Messiah of the Jews — a Samaritan *prophet/teacher* as over against a Jewish *king/warrior* (at least in the popular mind) — so she may have been slow to repeat the bold language of Jesus in verse 26, and instead she cautiously asked her fellow townsfolk if this might be the (Samaritan) Messiah. (2) Furthermore, Haenchen himself[63] suggested that the woman based her recognition of Jesus' Messiahship (in v. 29) on Jesus' miraculous knowledge of her life (in v. 18).[64]

4:30. At any rate the Samaritans left the city (the tense is aorist) and were heading (imperfect) toward Jesus. The call (**Come, see**) and testimony of the woman were already at work in their lives. While they were coming, Jesus spoke with his disciples at the well; and John recorded this conversation.

---

[60]Carson, *The Gospel According to John*, p. 227.
[61]See *BAGD*, p. 520 and *BDF* § 127.2.
[62]Haenchen, *The Gospel of John*, 1:227a.
[63]Ibid.
[64]Ibid., 1:230b.

3. Jesus and the Samaritans (4:31-42)

Jesus and the Testifying of His Disciples (4:31-38)

[31]Meanwhile his disciples urged him, "Rabbi, eat something."
[32]But he said to them, "I have food to eat that you know nothing about."
[33]Then his disciples said to each other, "Could someone have brought him food?"
[34]"My food," said Jesus, "is to do the will of him who sent me and to finish his work. [35]Do you not say, 'Four months more and then the harvest'? I tell you, open your eyes and look at the fields! They are ripe for harvest. [36]Even now the reaper draws his wages, even now he harvests the crop for eternal life, so that the sower and the reaper may be glad together. [37]Thus the saying 'One sows and another reaps' is true. [38]I sent you to reap what you have not worked for. Others have done the hard work, and you have reaped the benefits of their labor."

4:31-33. The disciples asked Jesus to eat some of the food that they had secured in Sychar, but he answered that he had food to eat that they knew nothing about. The disciples then proceeded to misunderstand about Jesus' food, just as the Samaritan woman had misunderstood earlier about Jesus' living water. They asked him if anyone had brought him food, to which Jesus began to explain what kind of food he was talking about.

4:34. Jesus described his food as "doing the will of God" and as "finishing (τελειόω, *teleioō*, "perfect" or "complete") God's work." He spoke of God as "the one who had sent him," a designation of God used often in this Gospel (e.g., 3:17; 5:23-24,30,37; 6:38-39; 7:16; etc.). His work with the Samaritan woman (and her fellow townspeople) was Jesus' "doing the will of God," and in this "doing" was greater nourishment and satisfaction than in any amount of food that the disciples could provide him.[65] He had rather "do God's will than to eat when he was hungry." Actually he did both, because the whole discussion was meant to distinguish

---

[65]So Carson, *The Gospel According to John*, p. 228.

the physical from the spiritual, and to stress the necessity of both. Some, therefore, see this passage as echoing Deuteronomy 8:3 ("man shall not live by bread alone but by every word that proceeds from the mouth of God") as quoted by Jesus in his first temptation in Matthew 4:4 and Luke 4:4.[66] "To do God's will" has been said to be within the reach of every person; "to accomplish God's work" was Jesus' lot alone, if by this latter should be meant the incarnational, atoning-by-dying, and resurrectional work of Jesus — and this latter, doubtless, was what Jesus had in mind.[67] Notice, however, that ministering to human needs by evoking faith in Jesus was as much "God's will" and "God's work" as the great miraculous acts of virginal birth and resurrection of Jesus. One, without the other, was incomplete and even futile.

4:35. This paragraph is a sort of sermonette based on two proverb-like sentences, both related to harvesting (vv. 35a and 37) and both with a comment (vv. 35b-36 and 38). The first proverbial saying was **"Four months more and then the harvest."** To what did the saying refer? (1) Jesus' disciples may have said that harvest time was four months away, but Jesus said the harvest was already ripe and needed reaping instantly. The word for "ripe" is λευκαί (*leukai*, "white") and may have been suggested by the approaching Samaritans dressed in white.[68] (2) It may have been a common rural proverb, Hebraic in format[69] or possibly Grecian (suggested by its iambic trimeter forms),[70] and the saying was placed on the disciples' lips by Jesus in order to date this moment: four months before harvest could be understood to be about January or early February.[71] (3) Bultmann[72] thought that this proverb minimized the interval of time between sowing and reaping (the Gospel); indeed, sowing and reaping took place simultaneously because Bultmann's realized

---

[66]Barrett, *The Gospel According to St. John*, p. 240; Carson, *The Gospel According to John*, p. 228.

[67]Bernard, *A Critical and Exegetical Commentary*, 1:154.

[68]So Beasley-Murray, *John*, p. 63.

[69]Barrett, *The Gospel According to St. John*, p. 241.

[70]Dodd, *Historical Tradition*, pp. 325-326; A. Argyle, "A Note on John 4:35," *ExpTim* 82 (1971): 247-248.

[71]Westcott, *The Gospel According to St. John*, 1:166; Brown, *John*, 1:174.

[72]Bultmann, *The Gospel of John*, p. 196.

eschatology demanded it so. That may be true, but not because of eschatology. (4) Aileen Guilding thought that the proverb pointed to the lectionary readings in the synagogue for that period of the year, but this is purely speculative.[73] Number (1) above seems to make most sense of the verse.

Verse 35 has always been of great importance to the missionary imperative addressed to Christians. One cannot say that there will yet be time in the future to do mission work; the mission call may or may not still be futuristic but it is definitely real in the present time. This opportune time may be lost forever by waiting. "Now" is the time for evangelization — as well as for education, worship, etc.

4:36. Harvest time is stressed by the notation that already the harvester was receiving his wage (μισθόν, *misthon*, means "wage" here, not "reward") and was gathering fruit for eternal life. The harvester was not waiting for the time of harvest; the harvest was already present. What was the harvest and who were the harvesters? The harvest or crop was the human beings (here the Samaritans) who became followers (disciples) of Jesus. The harvesters were Jesus (and later the disciples of Jesus [v. 38]). The goal or purpose for which the fields were harvested was eternal life (grain that was harvested has always been "preserved" or "saved" in bins; that is, its life-giving powers were preserved that those who ate it might live). Jesus was the original sower/harvester (not John the Baptist or the Old Testament prophets); he sowed the seed in conversation with the Samaritan woman and later in the Samaritans in his teaching in their village.

The sower planted in anticipation of the joy that would come in the future; the harvester reaped in the joy of the harvest that was being gathered all around.

4:37. This verse, however, has been supposed by many modern commentators to contradict verse 36. Verse 37 says, **"Thus the saying, 'One sows and another reaps' is true."** First of all, "Thus" is a poor translation, because it seems to imply that verse 37

---

explains verse 36; but, the Greek ἐν τούτῳ (*en toutō*, "in this") may refer forward (cf. 9:30; 13:35; 15:8) or backward (16:30 only, in John). Further, what does the saying in verse 37 mean? Bultmann[74] and others hold that the saying expressed the unfortunate inequality in life: one sowed but did not share in the harvest, while another shared the harvest who had nothing to do with the sowing (the verse does not really say this). More likely the saying asserted that one sowed and another reaped but the work of both was essential to a joyful harvest — and so both were equally important.[75] This latter explanation avoids verse 37's contradicting verse 36.

4:38. Jesus has sent (aorist tense) the apostles to reap that on which they had not labored (perfect tense). Others had labored and they had entered into the results of their labors. Their testimony to the Samaritans was practically nil. Jesus had done most of this testifying, but they benefited from it. Some see this passage as a sort of forecast (or "seed sowing") by Jesus and his disciples of the later "harvest" made by Philip the evangelist in Acts 8:4-8.

Firsthand and Secondhand Testimony (4:39-42)

[39]**Many of the Samaritans from that town believed in him because of the woman's testimony, "He told me everything I ever did." [40]So when the Samaritans came to him, they urged him to stay with them, and he stayed two days. [41]And because of his words many more became believers.**

[42]**They said to the woman, "We no longer believe just because of what you said; now we have heard for ourselves, and we know that this man really is the Savior of the world."**

4:39. Many of the Samaritans believed in Jesus through the testimony of the woman. Woman though she was, she brought much of a town to faith in Christ, which is more than Jesus' disciples had done thus far! The woman was an eyewitness in this verse; they, at best, were believers in Jesus because they accepted her testimony.

---

[74]Bultmann, *The Gospel of John*, p. 198.
[75]Carson, *The Gospel According to John*, p. 230.

(Faith is the acceptance of testimony!) They were exactly where we stand: dependent on the testimony of eyewitnesses in the New Testament. She had seen and/or heard a bit of the supernatural in Jesus when he told her some of the secrets of her life, and she believed. Now some of the Samaritans accept her testimony.

4:40-41. The Samaritans urged Jesus to stay with them, and he taught them for two days. Now they accepted his words about God, which on the one hand, still made them secondhand receivers of testimony; on the other hand, they saw and heard him face to face, which made them in these matters also firsthand witnesses, on a par to a small extent with the other eyewitnesses in the New Testament.

4:42. What did the Samaritans conclude about Jesus and the Samaritan woman? They did not degrade her testimony when they said **"We no longer believe just because of what you said; now we have heard for ourselves, and we know . . . ."** They confirmed her testimony. Even more Samaritans came to believe in Jesus when they saw and heard him, but this Gospel will say later that such is not the highest kind of faith (20:29). The conclusion of the Samaritans about Jesus was **"We know that this man really is the Savior of the world."** The way in which one comes to believe or comes to faith in the New Testament desperately needs fresh study by the divided world church. Too much or too little of the miraculous, and too much or too little of the human are not the roads to belief and conversion in Scripture. Even when the Samaritans saw and heard *Jesus* they did little more than believe, the same as when they heard *about* him from the woman.[76]

The title "Savior of the world"[77] is rare in the New Testament (here and 1 John 4:14; cf. 1 Tim. 1:1; 2 Tim. 1:10; Titus 1:3). The title summarized and is based on God's work of saving the world through Jesus in John 3:16-17. In the Old Testament, "savior" is applied to God occasionally (Ps 24:5; Isa 12:2; 43:3,11; 63:8.

In paganism of the first century, "savior" was a technical term that described divine or semidivine deliverers, especially the Roman emperors. Inscriptions that read "savior of the world" frequently

---

[76]Barrett, *The Gospel According to St. John*, p. 243.

[77]A significant study on "savior" is by W. Foerster and G. Foehrer, "σωτήρ," *TDNT*, 7:1003-1021. The article's use of "savior" in John is at 7:1016, and its use of the title for the Roman emperors is at 7:1010-1011.

applied to Hadrian (A.D. 117-138). Zeus and the healing god, Asclepius were regularly given the title, as were also the gods of the Mystery religions; for example, Isis and Serapis. Borchert[78] called attention to the use by early Christians of the symbol of the fish as an identifying mark: the Greek word for fish was ἰχθύς (*ichthys*), whose letters stood for Ιησους Χριστος Θεου Υιος Σωτηρ (Jesus Christ, God's Son, Savior). The term "savior" took a prominent position in the confessions of faith in the New Testament and the early church.

Note the growth in recognition of Jesus by the woman of Samaria as this chapter 4 in John unfolds; she addressed him as Jew (v. 9), lord (sir) (v. 11), prophet (v. 19), Messiah (v. 29), and (with her fellow townsfolk) savior of the world (v. 42). Note further that in this chapter three very practical issues were addressed and resolved (or at least progress was made with them): (1) racial prejudice, (2) gender prejudice, and (3) the guilt of sin.

F. JESUS' HEALING OF THE NOBLEMAN'S SON, THE SECOND SIGN AT CANA (4:43-54)

1. Introduction (4:43-45)

[43]After the two days he left for Galilee. [44](Now Jesus himself had pointed out that a prophet has no honor in his own country.) [45]When he arrived in Galilee, the Galileans welcomed him. They had seen all that he had done in Jerusalem at the Passover Feast, for they also had been there.

The purpose of this story has been debated, but it seems clear that the passage was intended to portray a kind or stage of faith not evidenced in the Gospel up to this point: faith in Jesus without the believer's having first encountered a miraculous sign. "Faith without sight" was first fleetingly noted in the previous incident of Jesus and the Samaritans when the men of the city came out to see and hear Jesus at the well after they heard the testimony of the woman

---

[78]Borchert, *John 1-11*, p. 215, n. 207.

concerning him (v. 39). Even when they believed Jesus after two days of his teaching, they believed because of his word (v. 41) which they had *heard*, not because of miraculous signs which they had *seen*. This *hearing Jesus* that produced faith in him, however, was a case of faith based upon the physical senses' reaction to physical data. Disciples of Jesus in the future would not be able to hear him teach *in person*.

4:43-45. This short paragraph constitutes a hinge on which the text turns to a new subject or emphasis. Verse 43 says simply that after two days (of teaching in Samaria) Jesus started for Galilee. In verse 44 Jesus spoke a maxim, **"A prophet has no honor in his own country,"** which was often true, and which also sounded much like the saying(s) that he quoted in Matthew 13:57; Mark 6:4; and Luke 4:24. Two problems arise immediately with verse 44. First the wording of verse 44 for "in his own country" in Greek is ἐν τῇ ἰδίᾳ πατρίδι (*en tē idia patridi*); *patris* means "home land" or "home town." (The Synoptics also used *patris* to mean "home *town*," Nazareth, but John seemed to use it to refer to Jesus' "home *land*"). Second, the next verse (v. 45) goes on to state that Jesus was welcomed in Galilee by those who had seen all that he had done in Jerusalem at the recent Passover feast which they had also attended. The maxim seems out of place or even untrue, because the Galileans gave him honor, not dishonor, when he arrived there this time. Why did the author place end to end acceptance of Jesus in Galilee, and the usual rejection of a prophet in his own home country? Numerous solutions to the problems have been offered.[79] (1) The *patris* referred to Judea at Bethlehem.[80] Against this view: (a) the Fourth Gospel set forth Nazareth as the place from which Jesus derived (1:45-46; 7:41,52; 19:19). (b) Judea rejected him and Galilee accepted him; so, this would be where the opposition was mild and approval was strong. (2) Jesus' real *patris* was heaven.[81]

---

[79]See Carson, "Current source criticism of the Fourth Gospel: some methodological questions," *JBL* 97 (1978): 424, n. 50.

[80]Westcott, *The Gospel According to St. John*, 1:77-78; Hoskyns, *The Fourth Gospel*, pp. 259-260; Barnabas Lindars, *The Gospel of John*, New Century Commentary of the English Bible (Grand Rapids: Eerdmans, 1972), pp. 200-201.

[81]Robert H. Lightfoot, *St. John's Gospel*, p. 35.

This was accurate, but it spiritualized or allegorized the whole passage. (3) Perhaps the best solution saw *patris* as identical with Galilee, but Galilee as it represented Jewish identity, even Judean interests, as over against Samaritans; thus, Galilee and Judea, together, were pitted over against Samaria, not Judea against Galilee.[82] Samaria had just received Jesus, but Galilee's reception was based on miracles that they had recently witnessed him perform in Jerusalem — and that was not the kind of faith that Jesus prized (2:23-25).

2. The Healing of the Nobleman's Son (4:46-54)

[46]Once more he visited Cana in Galilee, where he had turned the water into wine. And there was a certain royal official whose son lay sick at Capernaum. [47]When this man heard that Jesus had arrived in Galilee from Judea, he went to him and begged him to come and heal his son, who was close to death.

[48]"Unless you people see miraculous signs and wonders," Jesus told him, "you will never believe."

[49]The royal official said, "Sir, come down before my child dies."

[50]Jesus replied, "You may go. Your son will live."

The man took Jesus at his word and departed. [51]While he was still on the way, his servants met him with the news that his boy was living. [52]When he inquired as to the time when his son got better, they said to him, "The fever left him yesterday at the seventh hour."

[53]Then the father realized that this was the exact time at which Jesus had said to him, "Your son will live." So he and all his household believed.

[54]This was the second miraculous sign that Jesus performed, having come from Judea to Galilee.

4:46-47. The site of this healing marked Jesus' return to Cana where his first miracle (water to wine) had been performed. Some

---

[82]Carson, *The Gospel According to John*, pp. 235-236.

see a Cana-to-Cana cycle of Jesus' activities here,[83] but if so, the text
makes little of it. A man met him, who was greatly agitated, because
his son was severely sick of a fever and near to death. The man is
called a βασίλικος (*basilikos*, v. 46) from Capernaum. The term may
be an *adjective* (royal) or a *noun*.[84] Many exegetes, therefore, have
viewed the man as an officer in the army or government service
(such as a revenue collector) of Herod Antipas (4 B.C.–A.D. 39), who
was not really a king, though he did belong to the royal house of
Herod the Great, and sometimes was called king by the people (cf.
Mark 6:14). If so, he very likely was a Gentile, though the text never
calls him that. Some have attempted to identify him and this whole
story with the centurion in Matthew 8:5-13 and Luke 7:1-10, but the
accounts differ in important ways. That he was Chuza (Luke 8:3) or
the Manean (Acts 13:1), as older exegetes often suggested, is surely
not accurate. The royal official had heard that Jesus was returned
from Judea and was at Cana, so the official left his ill son, traveled to
Jesus at Cana, and begged him to come and heal his son.

4:48. Jesus exclaimed, **"Unless you people see miraculous signs
and wonders you will never believe."** Note the plural "you people,"
which meant that Jesus addressed more persons than just the official. The sentence also meant that faith based solely on seeing miracles was never enough; it is not so much faith, as sight. One who
witnessed a miracle did not so much believe as know. The testimony was, in such cases, directly and objectively encountered by
one's own senses, and not through and dependent on the tongue
and/or pen of another person. Such faith the Samaritans possessed
but not the Galileans — and others. Note that the miraculous
"signs" were also viewed as wonders (τέρατα, *terata*).

4:49. The officer begged Jesus with renewed urgency to come
down (Cana is situated well above Capernaum which is on the
shore of the Sea of Galilee; the sea is some six hundred and eighty
feet below sea level.)[85] to his house and heal his child before he

---

[83]Borchert, *John 1–11*, p. 219.

[84]*BAGD*, p. 136. Josephus used the term to describe the relatives and
officials of the Herods (*Antiquities* 10:7:5; 15:8:4), as well as of their troops
(*Life* 400f.).

[85]See Michael Avi-Yonah (ed.), *The World of the Bible* (New York:
Educational Heritage, 1964), 5:35.

died. The officer operated on at least two assumptions: (1) that Jesus had to be present to effect a healing on his son; so Jesus must accompany the official to his home in Capernaum where the sick boy lay; (2) that Jesus was powerless to effect any kind of cure or relief beyond death (chapter 11 will set this misunderstanding aright). One should not fault this man's faith too much, because others, such as Mary and Martha, had the same two flaws (11:21,22, 32,39).

4:50. Jesus replied with a command, "Go!" (an imperative, rather than the mild "You may go" in NIV). "Your son lives" (or "is living"), Jesus added. The royal official **took Jesus at his word** (literally, "believed the word which Jesus said to him") and departed. This was the kind of faith that Jesus was always seeking: acceptance of his word or testimony without hesitation and without first *seeing* a miracle. This is the highest type of faith encountered by Jesus thus far in this Gospel, even a bit more advanced than the Samaritans, because this official had not had the benefit of even two days of teaching from Jesus as the Samaritans had had.

4:51-52. While the official was on the way down from Cana, he met his servants coming up to tell him about the child's healing. He inquired of the servants what time his son was suddenly healed. (Most healings are a bit slow, but this one was quick.) They informed him that it was about 1:00 P.M. (if they were reckoning by usual time: day beginning at sunrise, or about 7:00 P.M. if they reckoned by a supposed Roman time beginning at noon).[86]

4:53. At any rate, the *basilikos* knew that it was Jesus who did the healing of his son across some 18-22 miles.[87] The report of the servants showed the officer/father that the work of Jesus was instantly and totally effective. When the father realized this truth, **he and all his household believed.** This statement introduced into the New Testament for the first time the language of "household belief," a new paradigm in Christian missions and conversion, cf. Acts 10:2; 11:14; 16:15, 31; 18:8. Notice that a household "believed"; that is, the statement "and all his household" is regulated by the verb ἐπίστευσεν

---

[86]See W.M. Ramsay, "About the Sixth Hour," *Expositor* 7 (1893): 216-223; J. Miller, "The Time of the Crucifixion," *JETS* 26 (1983): 155-166.

[87]See Borchert, *John 1-11*, p. 221 on the mileage.

(*episteusen*). There was no way to become a disciple of Jesus or a part of that community without one's having believed[88] — and that still is true.

In verse 50 the *basilikos believed the word* and in verse 53 "*he and all his household believed.*" Are these lines a demonstration or at least evidence of growth in faith on the part of the *basilikos*? Possibly so. That should not surprise a student of the New Testament because growth in a Christian was expected in the apostolic age. The Christian mind and life were not formed instantaneously by a miraculous gift of faith that could never be enlarged (or shrunk) in one's future. This kind of determinism simply is not in the New Testament. Rather the expectation of growth and progress, in the life of a disciple of Jesus, is!

4:54. Since John 2:23 and 4:45 mentioned more than two miracles done by Jesus, this healing of the official's son could not be accurately called Jesus' **second miraculous sign**; so say several commentators. This is to overlook the contents of these several statements about miracles by Jesus. John meant here "the second miraculous sign that Jesus performed *in Cana.*"

---

[88]So Borchert, *John 1-11*, p. 221.

JOHN 5

G. JESUS AND THE MAJOR JEWISH FESTIVALS (5:1-12:50)

1. A Feast, the Sabbath, and Jesus' Healing at the Pool in Jerusalem (5:1-47)

The Healing on the Sabbath (5:1-9a)

[1]Some time later, Jesus went up to Jerusalem for a feast of the Jews. [2]Now there is in Jerusalem near the Sheep Gate a pool, which in Aramaic is called Bethesda[a] and which is surrounded by five covered colonnades. [3]Here a great number of disabled people used to lie — the blind, the lame, the paralyzed.[b] [5]One who was there had been an invalid for thirty-eight years. [6]When Jesus saw him lying there and learned that he had been in this condition for a long time, he asked him, "Do you want to get well?"

[7]"Sir," the invalid replied, "I have no one to help me into the pool when the water is stirred. While I am trying to get in, someone else goes down ahead of me."

[8]Then Jesus said to him, "Get up! Pick up your mat and walk." [9]At once the man was cured; he picked up his mat and walked.

[a]2 Some manuscripts *Bethzatha*; other manuscripts *Bethsaida*   [b]3 Some less important manuscripts *paralyzed—and they waited for the moving of the waters. [4]From time to time an angel of the Lord would come down and stir up the waters. The first one into the pool after each such disturbance would be cured of whatever disease he had.*

A number of commentators have sought to transpose chapters 5 and 6, but this opinion has not been widely adopted, and the sense has not been improved by the suggestion. Both chapters seem to be the opening part of a larger unit of the Gospel, 5:1–12:50. Following the lead of Aileen Guilding,[1] Borchert[2] called this section of the book the Festival Cycle because the Jewish feasts in this segment of the Gospel formed the settings for the evangelist's message.

5:1. An unnamed "feast of the Jews" introduces chapter 5, and in 5:9b the Sabbath is noted and serves as the cylinder around which to wind the dialogue in chapter 5. John hangs chapter 6 on the Passover festival (6:4), chapters 7–9 on the Feast of Tabernacles (7:2), and chapter 10 on the Feast of Hanukkah or Feast of Dedication (10:22). Chapter 11 closes with the Passover near at hand (11:55-56), and chapter 12 opens 6 days before Passover (12:1).

Jesus left Galilee for Jerusalem and attended an unnamed feast. Beside a pool lay many disabled people who waited for its waters to be stirred so that the first one to enter the waters might be healed (It is never indicated how often the stirring of the waters occurred). Jesus there encountered a man who had been an invalid for thirty-eight years and so could never enter the pool fast enough to be healed. Jesus healed the man and commanded him to take up his pallet and walk. Jesus then slipped away into the crowd.

The word for feast (ἑορτή, *heortē*) was without the definite article in nearly all the earliest Greek manuscripts and versions. If the definite article had been read, then there would have been strong grounds for understanding this festival as a Passover, or possibly as Tabernacles, which was often referred to as "the Feast" (הֶחָג, *hahag*).[3]

5:2. In Jerusalem there was "at the Sheep, a pool." To these words, a word such as πυλή (*pylē*, "gate") may be added and read "There is in Jerusalem, at the Sheep (Gate), a pool, which in Aramaic is called ...."

Also in 5:2 the name of this pool is written variously: Bethesda, Bethsaida, Belzetha, and Bethzatha. The last two do not have strong support in the manuscripts. The second has the best manuscript support but was the name of a town in Galilee and so may

[1]Aileen Guilding, *The Fourth Gospel*; on the contrary, Robert T. Fortna, *The Fourth Gospel and Its Predecessor* (Philadelphia: Fortress, 1988), p. 300, n. 141, saw no real significance in the festivals in John.

[2]See Borchert, *John 1–11*, 1:224.

[3]Barrett, *The Gospel According to St. John*, p. 251.

have been the product of transcriptional variation. The first (Bethesda) may be the best reading (so NIV), though Metzger and his group of textual experts chose Bethzatha (with a low rating, D, for this reading);[4] however, Metzger noted that the Copper Scroll at Qumran contained a reference to a pool at *Betheshdathayim*, a word with a dual ending, probably because there were actually two pools at the site in Jerusalem.[5] This word from Qumran certainly corroborated the reading Bethesda.[6]

5:3. The pool, which has been excavated, had five colonnaded porches (v. 2), so that many lame persons could have been sheltered within its precincts (v. 3) as they awaited the stirring of its waters and the possibility of being healed by these waters. These five colonnaded porches have been allegorized as symbols of the five books of Moses, which are now ineffective for healing and saving.[7]

5:4. An unknown copyist supplied this verse as an explanation for stirring of the waters (mentioned in 5:7), and was translated thus in the King James Version: "For an angel went down at a certain season into the pool, and troubled the water; whosoever then first after the troubling of the water stepped in was made whole of whatsoever disease he had." However, none of the early manuscripts contain this verse at all, so it is not a legitimate part of the New Testament. The NIV puts a translation of 5:4 in a footnote.[8] The verse probably began as a marginal note explaining the local superstition and why the lame man thought he needed someone to help him get into the pool first (v. 7).

---

[4]Metzger, *A Textual Commentary*, p. 208.

[5]See J.T. Milik in M. Baillot, J.T. Milik, and Roland de Vaux, (*Discoveries in the Judean Desert of Jordan*, III), *Les Petites grottes de Qumran Textes* (Oxford: Clarendon, 1962), p. 271.

[6]Cf. David Wieand, "John V.2 and the Pool of Bethesda," *New Testament Studies* 12 (1966), pp. 392-404; Joachim Jeremias, *The Discovery of Bethesda.* (Louisville, KY: Southern Baptist Seminary, 1966); also E.J. Vardaman, "The Pool of Bethesda," *The Dead Sea Scrolls in English*, 4th ed., (London: Penguin, 1995), p. 377.

[7]Carson, *The Gospel According to John*, p. 242.

[8]See Metzger, *A Textual Commentary*, p. 209, and Zane C. Hodges, "Problem Passages in the Gospel of John. Part 5: The Angel at Bethesda — John 5:4," *BSac* 136 (1979): 25-39.

5:5. Notice that wherever he went, Jesus did not fraternize with
only the upper classes who were wealthy, educated, and powerful,
even in Jerusalem. Instead he fellowshipped with the disabled: "the
blind, the lame, the paralyzed," (v. 3) and often helped them. In the
present case the man had been lame **for thirty-eight years.** This
"thirty-eight" is not to be allegorized in terms of the Israelites'
thirty-eight year journey from Kadesh Barnea to the brook Zered
(Deut 2:14).[9] Actually, if John had wanted to show that the years of
the lame man's infirmity were the same years as Israel's wandering
in the wilderness, it would have been more accurate for him to
have written *forty* than thirty-eight.[10]

5:6. When Jesus asked the lame man if he wanted to get well,
there was a momentary misunderstanding by the lame man, who
did not immediately answer "yes" or "no," but began to explain
why he had not been able to be healed, since he could not enter
the troubled water fast enough. The text says nothing of the healed
man's response: shock, joy, disbelief, gratitude, or a combination of
several of these; nor is anything recorded as to how and why he had
been paralyzed (5:14 may be such a clue to this latter question).

5:7-8. Over so long a time of sickness and helplessness, the man
had developed a limited view of God's love and power: that God
could (or would) heal only a few who were really able to help themselves; the rest God could (or would) not assist. The lame man also
sensed his having been alone, as if human beings as well as divine
had forsaken him (v. 7). The man, therefore, had become pes-
simistic and sought to charge fellow human beings and God
himself with his plight. In reply, Jesus did not argue, pity, lecture,
or fault him with ignorance and moroseness; instead, he commanded him to get up, pick up his mat[11] and walk — and the man
was cured. Notice that Jesus did not even call for faith in him by
the lame man. On the lame man's part, faith was exhibited by the

---

[9]Michael Baumgarten, *Geschichte Jesu* (Braunschweig: G. A. Schwetschke,
1859), pp. 139-140; Bultmann, *The Gospel of John*, p. 241, n. 7.

[10]Bernard, ICC, 1:229.

[11]*krabbaton* — the word was probably Egyptian in origin and appeared in
Mark and John but not in Matthew and Luke. The term, therefore, has a
special bearing on the problem of the relation of the four Gospels to one
another.

man's immediately doing what Jesus commanded: getting up, picking up, and walking – and the man kept on walking right on through the city. This healing, therefore, was quite like the previous one of the nobleman's son in Cana (4:43-54): in both cases the principal person involved simply took Jesus at his word and acted on his command – without question or hesitation.

The jarring twist to this otherwise delightful story lay in the opening line of the next paragraph.

Violations of the Sabbath and the Healed Man's Defense (5:9b-15)

The day on which this took place was a Sabbath, [10]and so the Jews said to the man who had been healed, "It is the Sabbath; the law forbids you to carry your mat."

[11]But he replied, "The man who made me well said to me, 'Pick up your mat and walk.'"

[12]So they asked him, "Who is this fellow who told you to pick it up and walk?" [13]The man who was healed had no idea who it was, for Jesus had slipped away into the crowd that was there.

[14]Later Jesus found him at the temple and said to him, "See, you are well again. Stop sinning or something worse may happen to you." [15]The man went away and told the Jews that it was Jesus who had made him well.

5:9. The healing of the paralytic was a wonderful performance – until John added that *it took place on the Sabbath day*. All of the Jewish festivals, viewed in the light of Exodus 23,[12] were, like a Sabbath celebration, a holy convocation before God. Part of this celebration of every festival was freedom from work so as properly to observe the occasion. This was especially true of the Sabbath day. In the Babylonian and Jerusalem Talmuds, a very large volume contains the Sabbath regulations concerning work or works that rabbinical debate had forbidden to be done on that day. The Jews have calculated the number of obligatory commands in the whole Old Testament at 613, but the regulations to be kept with reference

---

[12]So Borchert suggested (*John 1–11*, 1:230, Excursus 5).

to Sabbath day observance numbered over 2,000! To observe the Sabbath day conscientiously, therefore, became an intolerable burden. It may be true that not all the rules in the Talmudic tractate called *Shabbath* existed in the early first century, but too many of them did, and these Jesus met head on in the controversy evoked by Jesus' healing on the Sabbath in John 5.

In the second part of this verse the lame man obeyed Jesus: he got up, picked up his mat, and walked. The man's carrying his mat (probably made of straw and light enough to be rolled up and carried on one's shoulder or under one's arm) and his walking evidenced the completeness of his cure, just as the thirty-eight years had attested to the seriousness of his illness.[13]

5:10. Immediately, "the Jews" saw him carrying a mat, and so said to him, **"It is the Sabbath; the law forbids you to carry your mat."**[14] They paid no attention to the wonderful and helpful deed that Jesus had just performed on the man who had been a cripple for thirty-eight years. Surely a little celebration, such as pallet-carrying, was in order, even on a Sabbath.

5:11-13. The healed man did what he had previously done: blame his problem on someone else. The healed man's defense was in these words: **"The man who made me well said to me, 'Pick up your mat and walk.'"** Naturally they asked who gave him such a command (v. 12), but the healed man did not know the healer or the healer's name, because Jesus had **slipped away** (ἐξένευσεν, *exeneusen*) **into the crowd that was there** (v. 13). Borchert[15] noted that the man's ignorance about Jesus who had healed him called to mind the familiar "secret" or "hidden" theme of Jesus' Messiahship in Mark, which William Wrede set forth in 1901 in his *The Messianic Secret.*[16] The healed man's defense against the charge of Sabbath-breaking was very weak, since he could not identify his healer/commander. Notice that the healed man was charged with Sabbath-breaking, not Jesus (v. 10).

---

[13]Barrett, *The Gospel According to St. John,* p. 254.

[14]On the law against burden-bearing on the Sabbath day see Strack and Billerbeck, *Kommentar,* 2:454-461.

[15]Borchert, *John 1-11,* 1:234.

[16]William Wrede, *The Messianic Secret,* (Greenwood, SC: Attic Press, 1971); cf. James L. Blevins, *The Messianic secret in Markan research, 1901-1976* (Lanham, MD: University Press of America, 1981).

5:14-15. Jesus later found the man in the temple and told him to stop sinning lest something worse should happen to him. The man went away and told the Jews that it was Jesus who had made him well, thereby casting the blame for breaking Sabbitical laws on his healer. It is not always true that the helper is thanked or appreciated (Luke 17:17-18).[17] Notice, however, what a tremendous testimony to Jesus the man's report to the Jews finally turned out to be: it was Jesus who had made him whole.[18]

Why should Jesus have spoken the words in verse 14, **"Stop sinning or something worse may happen to you"**? What is the meaning of "his sinning" and "a worse thing happening to him"? (1) One answer sees Jesus here as connecting sickness and suffering to sin;[19] or at least that this man's illness resulted from his very own sin.[20] (2) As in 9:3 and 11:4, the illness was to the glory of God.[21] (3) For the sin of becoming an informer to the Jews, the healed man might be severely punished,[22] though the same man had already done this without apparently too much punishment. (4) Further sin and its correlating punishment may refer to the final judgment day and the punishment handed out there[23] — this would surely be the "something worse" that "might happen to him."[24]

Violations of the Sabbath and Jesus' Defense (5:16-18)

[16]**So, because Jesus was doing these things on the Sabbath, the Jews persecuted him. [17]Jesus said to them, "My Father is always at his work to this very day, and I, too, am working." [18]For this reason the Jews tried all the harder to kill him; not only was he**

---

[17]Cf. Carson, *The Gospel According to John*, p. 243.

[18]See Foster, *Studies*, 1:453-454.

[19]Bultmann, *The Gospel of John*, p. 243.

[20]McGarvey and Pendleton, *The Fourfold Gospel*, p. 198.

[21]Carson, *The Gospel According to John*, p. 246; Barrett, *The Gospel According to St. John*, p. 255.

[22]J.L. Martyn, *History and Theology in the Fourth Gospel* (New York: Harper & Row, 1968), p. 55.

[23]Borchert, *John 1-11*, 1:235.

[24]Schnackenburg, *The Gospel according to St John*, 2:98.

**breaking the Sabbath, but he was even calling God his own
Father, making himself equal with God.**

5:16. In verse 10 the healed man was accused of violating the
Sabbath day by carrying his bed; his defense was that he did so in
compliance with the command of the one who had healed him
(v. 11). In verse 15 the healed man dropped from the story; presumably no charge against him was afterwards pursued.

Jesus, however, was open to charges of healing on the Sabbath
and of causing others to bear a burden on the Sabbath, though
these accusations were apparently not officially made (in court) at
this time. In verse 16 the Jews (Jewish leaders) were persecuting
Jesus because he was doing these things. "Persecuting" and "doing"
are in the imperfect tense — Jesus "kept on doing" such things and
the Jews "kept on persecuting."[25] John did not say what these "persecutions" of Jesus were; hassling from the audience, threats to Jesus
(and his disciples), spying on him in public and in private, etc. were
possibilities. John did not at this time further stress the Sabbath
question because he intended to pursue another and greater question, namely, the christological nature and work of Jesus.

Verses 16-18 have been said to introduce the controversy scenes
in the Festival portion of the book.[26] Jesus' person and relation to
the Sabbath were in the spotlight, and the turning of attention
from the healed man to Jesus marked the shift of the Jewish
leaders' hostility to Jesus. The charges against him relative to the
Sabbath, however, were speedily escalated to a much more serious
accusation, an accusation that led eventually to his crucifixion. The
argument that follows is, therefore, central to Jesus and to this
book about him.

5:17-18. Jesus responded in a way that precipitated the real conflict with the Jews: his heavenly Father always was at work to that
moment, so he too, was working. This statement seemed extreme
to a Jew. It justified Jesus' work on the Sabbath and it placed Jesus
on a par with God. The Synoptics show a different approach in
treating the alleged violations of the Sabbath by Jesus. In the

---

[25]BDF says the usage here was iterative, p. 325.
[26]Borchert, *John 1-11*, 1:235.

Synoptics Jesus is greater than the Sabbath because he is Lord over it. Here he seemed to some Jews to violate several commands, and also asserted that God worked on the Sabbath, and so he did as God did. What was here being asserted publicly for the first time by Jesus was the relation of Jesus to God, or in other words, the deity of Jesus.

Jesus defended his right to work on the Sabbath, saying, **"My Father is always at his work to this very day, and I, too, am working."** The Sabbath was introduced in Genesis by God himself, who was said to have rested on the seventh day from his creation labors (Gen 2:2) though let it be noted that no command for *mankind's* observance of the Sabbath was given before it was revealed to *Israel* as a part of that *nation's* laws (Exod 20:8; Deut 5:12); i.e., the command to observe the Sabbath was not in force from the beginning. A number of ancient authors observed the seeming contradiction of verse 17 (God's continual working) and Genesis 2:2 (God's resting on the Sabbath day). Jewish attempts to reconcile the tension between the two positions included the following: (1) God's physical activity, such as that at the creation, did come to an end, but not his moral activity, such as judging good and evil persons.[27] (2) As the Sabbath commandments concerning burden bearing did not prohibit one from carrying things about in one's own house, so God may create within his own homestead (the universe) even on the Sabbath without violating the Sabbath regulations.[28] Pagan thought also asserted that God worked continually,[29] though, the philosophers' "unmoved (axis of the) mover" suggests the idea of rest in God.

Jesus' Discourse on the Sabbath and His Work (5:19-29)

[19]**Jesus gave them this answer: "I tell you the truth, the Son can do nothing by himself; he can do only what he sees his Father doing, because whatever the Father does the Son also does. [20]For the Father loves the Son and shows him all he does. Yes, to your**

---

[27]*Genesis Rabbah* 8c.

[28]*Exodus Rabbah* 30(89a); see Philo, *Concerning Cherubim* 90.

[29]Cicero, *De officiis/On Oaths* — literally, *On Things Fitting* 3:28:102.

amazement he will show him even greater things than these. ²¹For just as the Father raises the dead and gives them life, even so the Son gives life to whom he is pleased to give it. ²²Moreover, the Father judges no one, but has entrusted all judgment to the Son, ²³that all may honor the Son just as they honor the Father. He who does not honor the Son does not honor the Father, who sent him.

²⁴"I tell you the truth, whoever hears my word and believes him who sent me has eternal life and will not be condemned; he has crossed over from death to life. ²⁵I tell you the truth, a time is coming and has now come when the dead will hear the voice of the Son of God and those who hear will live. ²⁶For as the Father has life in himself, so he has granted the Son to have life in himself. ²⁷And he has given him authority to judge because he is the Son of Man.

²⁸"Do not be amazed at this, for a time is coming when all who are in their graves will hear his voice ²⁹and come out — those who have done good will rise to live, and those who have done evil will rise to be condemned.

In verse 12 the question of the personal identity of Jesus stands out, "Who is the fellow who told you to pick it up and walk?" Afterwards, when Jesus' identity was learned as the one who performed the Sabbath miracles, he was not praised for his divine kindness, but criticized sharply for his good work. In verses 19-20 it made Jesus the object of doing what God did, while Jesus was acknowledged with power to do all that the Son saw the Father do.

5:19. In verses 19-29 Jesus makes the revelation concerning the Father known to the common people, the essence of which is that what Jesus learned from the Father he revealed to the people. What the Father has, he shows to the Son, and what the Father does, the Son does. This is to authenticate the nature and work of Jesus. It is no wonder that everyone who hears the Son and the Father are held to be condemned if they refuse to obey them because the Father and Son hold the same standards, truths, lifetime measures, etc. Jesus continues in verses 24-29 by telling the world that whoever hears him has been blessed with eternal life, and he has been given authority to judge because he is the Son of Man.

In verse 18 the Jews are not slow to see the implications of how the Son and Father love one another.

5:20. It means that the Son is loved extraordinarily by the Father and Jesus himself is willing to die at the hands of common people to make this truth obvious. This was not Jesus' way of making people jealous but of challenging his disciples to love God as God loved them.

5:21-23. The Son can do nothing but what he sees the Father do. Just as the Father raised the dead, so he has given power to the Son to raise the dead. Further, the Father judges no one but has entrusted all judgment to the Son, that all may equally honor the Father and the Son. No higher claims to deity could be made than what Jesus here asserts: the power of life over death, and the authority to execute eternal judgment.

5:24. Jesus goes on to assert a new truth, that whoever hears the word and believes him who sent the Son will not be condemned but has crossed over from death to life.

5:25-27. The Father and the Son both have life in themselves. That is why the Father and the Son can both promise eternal life to those who believe God's word. The Father raised the dead and gave life to all those who accepted God's word. The Son accepts the same persons that the Father accepts and to the Jews' amazement the Son can do even greater things (v. 20) than heal a lame man and rule over the Sabbath. Whoever hears the word of God and believes him whom God sent can receive eternal healing of the soul.

5:28-29. In fact the time is coming when the dead will hear the voice of God and those who hear will live. Surely this implies a resurrection. Jesus expresses it stronger in verses 28f when he says that all in the graves will hear his voice, and they that hear will be raised to life. Two views of the resurrection jostle one another here: (1) as in the case of Lazarus (11:43) Jesus can summon the dead and give them physical life (2) the word of Jesus can give spiritual life to these who are dead in sin. Too much should not be made in the distinction of the two views because both are true and both are needed.

Jesus' Defense and the Four Witnesses (5:30-47)

[30]"By myself I can do nothing; I judge only as I hear, and my judgment is just, for I seek not to please myself but him who sent me.

[31]"If I testify about myself, my testimony is not valid. [32]There is another who testifies in my favor, and I know that his testimony about me is valid.

[33]"You have sent to John and he has testified to the truth. [34]Not that I accept human testimony; but I mention it that you may be saved. [35]John was a lamp that burned and gave light, and you chose for a time to enjoy his light.

[36]"I have testimony weightier than that of John. For the very work that the Father has given me to finish, and which I am doing, testifies that the Father has sent me. [37]And the Father who sent me has himself testified concerning me. You have never heard his voice nor seen his form, [38]nor does his word dwell in you, for you do not believe the one he sent. [39]You diligently study[a] the Scriptures because you think that by them you possess eternal life. These are the Scriptures that testify about me, [40]yet you refuse to come to me to have life.

[41]"I do not accept praise from men, [42]but I know you. I know that you do not have the love of God in your hearts. [43]I have come in my Father's name, and you do not accept me; but if someone else comes in his own name, you will accept him. [44]How can you believe if you accept praise from one another, yet make no effort to obtain the praise that comes from the only God[b]?

[45]"But do not think I will accuse you before the Father. Your accuser is Moses, on whom your hopes are set. [46]If you believed Moses, you would believe me, for he wrote about me. [47]But since you do not believe what he wrote, how are you going to believe what I say?"

[a]*39* Or *Study diligently* (the imperative)   [b]*44* Some early manuscripts *the Only One*

5:30-36. Jesus has made astonishing claims of deity. What proof or evidence could he offer in support of his claims? Jesus therefore singles out four major witnesses which give credence to his ministry. (1) The first is Jesus himself. Jesus well knew how that one's self-witness didn't really count in the courts, so he did not rely totally on his own testimony. (2) We move to the second form of testimony, namely John the Baptist. John's testimony pointed ultimately to Christ who is the Lamb of God. The form of John's testimony is rational; that is, it does not take the form of any miracle nor that of any miraculous manifestation. Testimonies to Jesus are of a verbal kind, not just of feelings or dreams. (3) The third source of testimony to Jesus was his works done before God and man. These showed Jesus to be as much divine as human because they were on a miraculous order. And yet they were not merely of a subjective order in which an event could mean anything.

5:37-38. (4) The fourth form of testimony is really the highest and rarest, because it is the testimony of the Father to the works of the Son. The Father bears testimony to the works of the Son in a way that He does not to any others. Jesus said that the Jews of his time had never heard God's voice nor seen his form, nor did God's word dwell in them, because they did not believe the form of the one whom God sent. Jesus was somewhat severe in his critique of his contemporaries, but they deserved it.

5:39-40. Jesus said, **"You diligently study the Scriptures because you think that by them you possess eternal life. These are the Scriptures that testify about me, yet you refuse to come to me to have life."** Notice that life is granted through the knowledge of and obedience to written words. Notice also that this does not conform to the mode of seeking life today, which often employs visions, dreams, reliance on the physical, psychics etc., not in Christ, the living, unchanging Word of God. The Old Testament Scriptures constitute the highest manner of the ancient testimony of God to his Son. Notice that the Old Testament Scriptures are classical written documents; that is, the Father's testimony to the Son is solid, readable, even rationalistic and reliable as compared with, for example, supernatural "revelation" in the form of the flights of birds, yellow spots on the liver of animals and other weird attempts at deducing God's testimony. Scriptures always lead to life, yet Jesus' contemporaries refuse to seek life by him.

Jesus pointed out that part of the testimony of antiquity to himself was the Old Testament, and a vital part of that Old

Testament was the Pentateuch, traditionally said to be authored by Moses. But the Jews disallowed the testimony of Moses to him and so rejected Jesus as a source of life.

5:41-47. Jesus did not accept the praise of men, though the Jews did constantly. They were unable to accept Moses' testimony because of its link to Jesus. Jesus said that the real accuser is not one's neighbor or himself but the word of God. This word will commend or condemn by its own standards of perfection; hence, to seek salvation apart from God's word is an impossibility. The Jews relied upon themselves rather than God. Even Christians who seek a salvation of their own will fail to realize it, and notice that salvation is a response to the gospel in the form of word (cf. Rom 1:16 or 1 Cor 1:21).

JOHN 6

2. The Passover and Jesus' Explanation of the Exodus (6:1-71)

The Background (6:1-4)

[1]Some time after this, Jesus crossed to the far shore of the Sea of Galilee (that is, the Sea of Tiberias), [2]and a great crowd of people followed him because they saw the miraculous signs he had performed on the sick. [3]Then Jesus went up on a mountainside and sat down with his disciples. [4]The Jewish Passover Feast was near.

6:1. The Sea of Galilee was referred to by several names in the first century. One of these was the "Sea of Tiberias," a name derived from the most prominent city on its shores. This city of Tiberias was built by Herod Antipas about AD 20 in honor of the Roman Emperor, Tiberius Caesar, and was located on the west shore. Tiberias was a Hellenistic city, and we have no record of Jesus ever visiting it. Tiberias escaped eradication in the Roman War against the Jews (AD 66-70) and became the capital of the province after the destruction of Jerusalem. John's use of the designation **Sea of Tiberias** (6:1; 6:21; and 21:1) is unique in the New Testament, and serves as an indication of a later date for the writing of this Gospel, well after AD 70. The "Sea" is actually a large freshwater lake.[1]

Since this is the second Passover[2] after Jesus began his ministry, **after this** refers to the time after his second year of ministry, the

---

[1]This lake is also called "Chinnereth" (KJV) or "Kinnereth" (NIV) in Num 34:11; Deut 3:17; Josh 13:27 and 19:35. Luke 5:1 refers to it as the Lake of Gennesaret, a Greek variation of Chinnereth.

[2]First Passover approximately April in John 2:13 (see previous comments); the second in John 6:4. While many take the "Feast" of 5:1 to be the Passover, we conclude it is not.

choosing of the Twelve and the Sermon on the Mount.[3] The **far shore** ("other side" as in NASB, et al.) is likely Bethsaida (as in the Synoptics and in John 1:44; 12:21).

6:2. The multitude or **the great crowd** gives evidence that Jesus' popularity was nearing its zenith. John explains why the people followed — **because they saw the miraculous signs he had performed on the sick**. No doubt some of the crowd had pure motives in following Jesus; perhaps others followed out of curiosity. The Jews in general were expecting a Messiah who would perform great deeds, and in Jesus they were seeing amazing things that made their hearts race as they journeyed to Jerusalem.

6:3. Which **mountainside** is this? Some have speculated that it was what is now known as the Golan Heights.[4] Had Jesus intended to escape the crowd, which had not even allowed for time to eat,[5] by climbing the hill with his disciples? They had probably set out to secure some time for themselves when the crowds interrupted them.

6:4. John dates this scene and helps our chronology by telling us that the **Passover Feast was near**. All three times in John, this is referred to as the "Jewish Passover" (John 2:13; 6:4; and 11:55). Because John consistently labels the Passover as "Jewish," it is likely that Christians had given up the practice of celebrating the Passover at the time of John's writing.

Jesus' Feeding of the Five Thousand (6:5-13)[6]

5When Jesus looked up and saw a great crowd coming toward him, he said to Philip, "Where shall we buy bread for these

---

[3]See use of "after this" elsewhere in John's writings, e.g., John 2:12; 3:22; 5:1; 6:1; 7:1; Rev 4:1; 7:1,9; 15:5; 18:1; and 19:1

[4]E.g., F.F. Bruce, *John*, p. 142.

[5]McGarvey and Pendleton, *Fourfold Gospel*, p. 374; William Barclay, *The Gospel of John*, The Daily Bible Study Series (Philadelphia: Westminster, 1956), 1:203; Butler, *Gospel of John* (Joplin: College Press, 1961, 1965), p. 227; William Hendriksen, *Expositions of the Gospel According to John*, New Testament Commentary (Grand Rapids: Baker, 1954), p. 216; et al.

[6]Leon Morris, *Commentary on the Gospel of John*, The New International Commentary on the New Testament (Grand Rapids: Eerdmans, 1971), p.

people to eat?" ⁶He asked this only to test him, for he already had in mind what he was going to do.

⁷Philip answered him, "Eight months' wages* would not buy enough bread for each one to have a bite!"

⁸Another of his disciples, Andrew, Simon Peter's brother, spoke up, ⁹"Here is a boy with five small barley loaves and two small fish, but how far will they go among so many?"

¹⁰Jesus said, "Have the people sit down." There was plenty of grass in that place, and the men sat down, about five thousand of them. ¹¹Jesus then took the loaves, gave thanks, and distributed to those who were seated as much as they wanted. He did the same with the fish.

¹²When they had all had enough to eat, he said to his disciples, "Gather the pieces that are left over. Let nothing be wasted." ¹³So they gathered them and filled twelve baskets with the pieces of the five barley loaves left over by those who had eaten.

*7 Greek *two hundred denarii*

6:5-6. The feeding of the 5,000 is one of the few accounts included in all four of the Gospels (see Matt 14:15-21; Mark 6:35-44; Luke 9:12-17). Philip's role in this and other narratives is unique in John's Gospel. First Philip was introduced as following Jesus and bringing his friend Nathaniel (John 1:43-48). Here Philip comments on the price of food (vv. 5,7). Later, in John 12:21,22, we will learn of Philip's role in an incident where some Greeks wanted to meet Jesus and of Philip's introduction of them to Andrew. Finally, in John 14:8,9, Philip makes a request to be shown the Father.

Jesus probably addresses Philip because he was the disciple nearest to him at the time. The same Greek word used for **test** (πειράζων, *peirazōn*) is translated elsewhere as "tempt." Here it shows Jesus' method of training his disciples by challenging them with responsibility.

6:7. Philip calculated quickly **that eight months' wages would not buy enough bread for each one to have a bite!** The figure in

338, "This is the one miracle, apart from the resurrection, that is recorded in all four Gospels."

the Greek text is actually 200 denarii. The silver denarius was commonly used for a day's wage in the ancient world. Thus 200 denarii, would have been 200 days' wages for a common laborer, or about eight month's pay (KJV, "200 pennies"). This would have the equivalent of several thousands of dollars in modern buying power.

6:8-9. Andrew reappeared bringing a boy with a small lunch. Andrew was introduced in John 1:40,44 as an early follower of Jesus and recruiter of his brother, Peter. We will see him again in John 12:22 helping Philip with Greek guests. While the word ὀψάρια (*opsaria*) came to mean fish in general, here it most likely means cooked fish tidbits or cooked fish filets.[7] Tenney suggests that they were "probably pickled fish used as relish, much as sardines are used now for hors d'oeuvres."[8]

6:10-11. There was plenty of grass means that it was springtime. And, according to custom, **the men sat down**. John's word here is gender specific, 5,000 **men** (ἄνδρες, *andres* — plural of ἀνήρ,[9] a "man" in contrast to women or children) sat down to hear Jesus. It is common to multiply the 5,000 to as many as 15,000 since Matthew 14:21 says, "besides women and children."[10] However, it is unlikely that all these men took their entire families into such a remote place to listen to a rabbi. A more reasonable total number might be 6,000-8,000.

After giving thanks, Jesus **distributed** [the bread first] **to those who were seated as much as they wanted**. The important point, aside from the obvious miracle, is the latter — they received **as much as they wanted!**[11] John's theological point is that there is no lack when Jesus is providing. This sets up the coming comparisons to the manna in the wilderness. As with the manna, there is no lack, for all could eat until they were full (see Exod 16:12,18).

6:12-13. Not only did they eat their fill, there were leftovers (understated in the NIV Study Bible note, "abundant supply"). It's

---

[7]LSJ, "cooked or prepared food," p. 1283.

[8]Merrill C. Tenney, *John: The Gospel of Belief* (Grand Rapids: Eerdmans, 1953), p. 112.

[9]BAGD, pp. 66-67. As with Matthew, John is aware that the audience was not men only, because Jesus' command is that the **people** (ἀνθρώπους, *anthropous*, cf. NRSV) sit down, a gender-inclusive term in Greek.

[10]See n. on p. 105 in Thomas and Gundry, *NIV Harmony*.

[11]See Hendriksen's description of the scene in *Exposition*, pp. 222-223.

one thing to feed 5,000 men, but it's another to have pieces of food that would fill twelve wicker baskets (κοφίνους, *kophinous*). Hendriksen notes, "Wastefulness is sinfulness."[12] This is echoed by Butler, "What a lesson for the poor stewardship for present day followers of Jesus!"[13]

Jesus, Not That Kind of King (6:14-15)

[14]After the people saw the miraculous sign that Jesus did, they began to say, "Surely this is the Prophet who is to come into the world." [15]Jesus, knowing that they intended to come and make him king by force, withdrew again to a mountain by himself.

6:14-15. Human nature prompted the title declaration by the crowd. They saw in Jesus the fulfillment of their messianic expectations. Part of this was their expectation of the coming **Prophet**, who had been promised by Moses (Deut. 18:15-19). This Prophet was to be greater than any previous prophet, the ultimate manifestation of God's spokesman. Ironically, the people were correct in this identification. John develops the theme of Jesus as the eschatological Prophet elsewhere. In John 1:21 the readers were introduced to the concept of the expected Prophet by learning that John the Baptist denied being this person. The Samaritan woman was able to discern Jesus' prophetic vocation (4:19).[14] John has indicated that Jesus acknowledged his prophetic role in the editorial comment of 4:44. The controversy of whether or not Jesus is the Prophet/Messiah comes to a head again in 7:40-52.

They were going to **make him king** over a physical order and no room would be left for the Messiah that Jesus really was, i.e., a being of totally spiritual order. The first century Jews of Palestine looked for a military Messiah, a savior like Judas Maccabeus. As Judas had run the Syrian Greeks out of the Promised Land 200 years earlier, they wanted a military general/king to rid Israel of

---

[12]Ibid., p. 223.

[13]Butler, *John*, p. 229.

[14]A similar identification is made by the blind man healed by Jesus in John 9:17.

the hated Romans. Surely a man who could miraculously feed thousands could also lead them to victory!

The meaning here is "to seize" (ἁρπάζειν, *harpazein* — a present infinitive) him in order to make things happen their way. This word has a violent background ("a ferocious animal *has dragged* Joseph *away*" in Gen. 37:33 in the LXX) and is used of forcefully taking another man's property (Matt 12:29). It is used in Jude 23 "to snatch" something out of the fire. Jesus, therefore, immediately retreated from the people into the hills to be by himself and prevent this forced coronation.

From this point on in John, the character of Jesus' ministry is drastically altered. He is the "Son of Man," but the "Son of Man" is henceforth the great servant of God. Up to now (vv. 1ff.), Jesus has revealed himself as a "Son of Man," but few in his audience had thought through what kind of "Son of Man" he meant[15] (see above discussion on 1:51). The people had in mind a physical kingdom and a physical king (associating "Son of Man" with the eschatological figure of Daniel 7:13,14), but Jesus had in mind a purely spiritual king and kingdom. In the "Bread of Life Discourse" that follows, Jesus begins to say this clearly, with the result that many of his would-be followers leave him (v. 66).

Jesus' Walking on the Sea of Galilee (6:16-21)

[16]**When evening came, his disciples went down to the lake,** [17]**where they got into a boat and set off across the lake for Capernaum. By now it was dark, and Jesus had not yet joined them.** [18]**A strong wind was blowing and the waters grew rough.** [19]**When they had rowed three or three and a half miles,[a] they saw Jesus approaching the boat, walking on the water; and they were terrified.** [20]**But he said to them, "It is I; don't be afraid."** [21]**Then they were willing to take him into the boat, and immediately the boat reached the shore where they were heading.**

[a]*19* Greek *rowed twenty-five or thirty stadia* (about 5 or 6 kilometers)

---

[15]See Carson's discussion of John's use of "Son of Man," *The Gospel According to John*, p. 164.

6:16-21. Mark 6:45 says Jesus "compelled" (ἀναγκάζω, *anankazō*, "force, urge or insist") his disciples to "get into the boat." John says they **set off . . . for Capernaum**; Mark says they left for Bethsaida. Which is correct? Apparently Jesus had directed them to wait at Bethsaida Julius (northeastern side of the Sea) but they finally gave up and went on toward Capernaum without him.[16] **By now it was dark** ("dark" and "darkness" are common themes in Johannine writings: 1:5; 3:19; 6:17; 8:12; 12:35,46; 20:1; 1 John 1:5,6; 2:8,9,11; Rev 8:12; 9:17; 16:10). The formula for a storm is cool mountain air rushing down onto the warm, moist air of the lake (696 feet below sea level). This resulted in turbulence! Rowing one mile is a challenge, but to row over **three or three and a half miles,**[17] in a storm had to be exasperating.

Then, Jesus walked on the Sea of Galilee. As skeptics have taunted, "Did he just walk along the beach as they hugged the shoreline? Did he just know where the rocks were (and they didn't)?" Matthew and Mark clearly answer by specifying that Jesus was "walking on the lake." This seems to be an event without precedent. His disciples had walked to their boat *on the shore* of the sea while Jesus dismissed the crowd and set out *on the sea!* When Jesus came to them, he was **walking on the water; and they were terrified** (ἐφοβήθησαν, *ephobēthēsan*, from φοβέομαι, *phobeomai* — intransitive "be afraid"). They would have been terrified because it was dark, a strong wind was blowing, and they had never seen anything like this. They knew this was impossible! Only when Jesus commanded, **don't be afraid** (μὴ φοβεῖσθε, *mē phobeisthe* — present imperative) did they take him on board. Apparently two miracles[18] took place here: (1) Jesus walked on water and (2) the boat was immediately at the safety of the shore.

---

[16]See D.A. Carson, *Matthew*, Expositor's Bible Commentary (Grand Rapids: Zondervan, 1984), 8:342-343. Matthew 14:34 and Mark 6:53 record that they arrived at Gennesaret. Although the exact site Matthew and Mark have in mind is uncertain, the broad plain on the west side of the lake was known by this term, and would have included Capernaum.

[17]Literally, 25 or 30 stadia. A στάδιον, *stadion* was a little over 600 feet.

[18]Hendriksen (*Exposition*, p. 227) says four miracles: Jesus walks on the sea; he causes Peter to walk on the sea; he reveals himself as the master of the storm; he conquers space in landing on shore instantly. This is based on a conflation of the Gospel accounts.

This little narrative, found in two of the other Gospels (Matt 14:22-36; Mark 6:45-56), is used by John to give two christological teachings. First, there is an intended connection between the two miracles of this chapter and the Exodus experience of Israel. The miraculous provision of manna by God in the wilderness has now been replicated by Jesus. This feeding is a sign of God's providential care. But further, the mastery of the sea that God demonstrated by parting the Red Sea has also been shown by Jesus' walking on the water. Mastery of the sea was a sign of God's sovereignty and omnipotence (see Exod 15:6-8). This Exodus connection is a major background for the following "Bread of Life" discourse.

Second, the words of Jesus are significant here. The disciples are told not to be afraid because, "ἐγώ εἰμι" (*egō eimi*), "I am" (NIV, "It is I"). Jesus' "I am" statements in the Gospel of John form a claim to deity based on the Divine Name of God (cf. Exod 3:14, and see comments below on John 8:58).

The Crowds' Search for Jesus (6:22-25)

²²The next day the crowd that had stayed on the opposite shore of the lake realized that only one boat had been there, and that Jesus had not entered it with his disciples, but that they had gone away alone. ²³Then some boats from Tiberias landed near the place where the people had eaten the bread after the Lord had given thanks. ²⁴Once the crowd realized that neither Jesus nor his disciples were there, they got into the boats and went to Capernaum in search of Jesus.

²⁵When they found him on the other side of the lake, they asked him, "Rabbi, when did you get here?"

6:22-24. Fact: only one boat was available to the disciples. Fact: Jesus did not leave in it. Fact: He's gone! Implied Fact: If he had walked around the shore, the crowd would have seen him. The crowd again sensed that a miracle has occurred.

Then some boats from Tiberias landed . . . very likely blown off course by the wind that had been in the face of the disciples . . . **where the people had eaten the bread after the Lord had given**

thanks. The term for giving thanks (εὐχαριστέω, *eucharisteō*) almost becomes a formula. This influences our understanding concerning the connections between the "bread of life" and the Lord's Supper, known as the "eucharist" in some Christian traditions.

Where did all the boats in verse 24 come from? Possibly they were blown in from Tiberias. Why did they go to Capernaum? Likely it was well known as Jesus' most recent base of operations. These would have arrived very early, perhaps between 3 and 6 A.M.[19] **Here** is the synagogue in Capernaum (see v. 59). The expected answer from Jesus would have been something like, "Oh, I just walked along the shore . . . ." However, that is not true, and therefore not an option for Jesus. But instead of answering the question directly, he uses their bewilderment as a jumping off point for the famous "Bread of Life" speech.

The Discourse on the Bread of Life, Part 1 (6:26-34)

[26]Jesus answered, "I tell you the truth, you are looking for me, not because you saw miraculous signs but because you ate the loaves and had your fill. [27]Do not work for food that spoils, but for food that endures to eternal life, which the Son of Man will give you. On him God the Father has placed his seal of approval."

[28]Then they asked him, "What must we do to do the works God requires?" [29]Jesus answered, "The work of God is this: to believe in the one he has sent."

[30]So they asked him, "What miraculous sign then will you give that we may see it and believe you? What will you do? [31]Our forefathers ate the manna in the desert; as it is written: 'He gave them bread from heaven to eat.'[a]"

[32]Jesus said to them, "I tell you the truth, it is not Moses who has given you the bread from heaven, but it is my Father who gives you the true bread from heaven. [33]For the bread of God is he who comes down from heaven and gives life to the world."

[34]"Sir," they said, "from now on give us this bread."

[a]31 Exodus 16:4; Neh. 9:15; Psalm 78:24,25

---

[19]Hendriksen, *Exposition*, p. 230.

6:26-29. John presents the crowd as having a certain degree of mixed motives here. There is a motive that sees Jesus as a meal ticket, the new Moses who could conjure up bread in the wilderness. Jesus confronts this attitude of freeloading directly, and surely this hit home with some. But there is a deeper motive at work, and Jesus recognizes it, too. There is a spiritual need in these people, and now he speaks to that hunger. The people specifically request a miraculous sign (albeit a self-serving one) that will be sufficient for them to believe in him.

At issue here (as elsewhere in John) is the very nature of faith. For the current audience of Jesus, there must be a parade of miraculous signs to compel belief (v. 30). Not unrelated is their conviction that Jesus should assign them some specific tasks so that they might be pleasing to God (v. 28). Jesus demolishes both of these misconceptions with a single stroke. The audience is called to believe in Jesus himself, **to believe in the one he** [God] **has sent** (v. 29). This response has the effect of saying, "Work by *believing!*"[20]

Jesus claims that God has placed his seal of approval (ἐσ–φράγισεν, *esphragisen* – aorist of σφραγίζω, *sphragizō*) on him. The Jews should have recognized Jesus' seal through the miracles he performed.[21] As Nicodemus has already noted in John, no one could do the signs Jesus had done without God's approval (3:2). The "sealing" is both God's stamp of approval and his mark of identification to serve as credentials for Jesus.[22] He is the certified, authorized, "franchise" distributor of the bread of life.

6:30-34. What follows shows a bit of the method Jesus often used to interpret the Old Testament. Jesus understood himself to be a fulfillment of the manna from the Exodus. But this was not in the usual prophecy/fulfillment sense, for nowhere does the Old

---

[20]This is similar to the reasoning in Acts 2:37; 8:36; and 9:6 – baptism is never called a work; believing is. What irony! The response in John 6:30, 31 was not about the theology of works, but about the identity and credentials of the one sent.

[21]Butler, *John*, p. 238.

[22]See BAGD, p. 796. BAGD claims that in this verse σφραγίζω takes on a sense of "endue with power from heaven," but surely this is an interpretive gloss that goes far beyond the meaning of the word. Similarly the NLT renders this phrase as "God the Father has sent me for that very purpose." This unnecessarily weakens the force of this verb.

Testament promise that God would send an eternal, messianic manna at a later date. Jesus' method here is a typological interpretation of the manna. In this typology the manna stands for God's miraculous and gracious provision for his people (see Ps 78:23-24). The manna is a *type*, an identifiable pattern. The *type* of manna is fulfilled in the *antitype*, Jesus. Jesus was not physical food. He was a spiritual provision by a gracious God. The rabbis taught that in the new age the gift of manna would be restored — and therefore the people would know that all has been restored.[23] But with Jesus there is much more than food aplenty. There is eternal food that sustains "eternal life" (v. 27). There is living water that sustains "eternal life" (4:14). This will be taken out of the realm of typology and explained below as a matter of faith. One must "believe" in the Son to gain eternal life (v. 40) and to be a participant in the coming resurrection (v. 54).[24]

Ironically the people ask to be given this Jesus-manna, not quite knowing what he is talking about (v. 34). Perhaps for them the **true bread** (v. 32) or the **bread of God** (v. 33) would be miraculous, self-replenishing bread that they could keep in their pantries at home. The true bread is neither manna nor barley loaves. They have made a category error, for the bread is a Somebody.

Their mistake is similar to that of the woman who asked for the "living water" that Jesus claimed to control (4:15), not realizing that this "water" was the Holy Spirit (7:39). The implicit claim is that Jesus is far superior to Moses,[25] who was merely able to facilitate temporary and physical water and bread relief. The provision of God through Jesus is for supernatural water and bread, a spiritual nourishment that cannot be depleted.[26] Jesus clearly identifies the

---

[23]F.F. Bruce, *John*, pp. 151-152.

[24]Note that Peter understands this typology perfectly (v. 68). He knows that Jesus is not talking about manna, but about himself.

[25]McGarvey and Pendleton suggest that the Jews are musing that Moses fed millions in the wilderness for 40 years, while Jesus only fed thousands in a day. If he were less than Moses, he definitely would be less than the Messiah! (*Fourfold Gospel*, p. 375).

[26]See John 1:12, where the initial comparison between Jesus and Moses occurs. Cf. 1 Cor. 10:3-4 where Paul advances a similar typological argument to connect the supernatural water and bread of the Exodus to the elements of the Lord's Supper.

bread of life and its source. It was **not Moses who** gave the bread of life **from heaven.** It was God. It was God then; it is God now.

The contrasts in Jesus' teaching with the historical precedent and the expectations of his audience may be charted[27] accordingly:

	The Experience of Israel in Exodus	The Expectations of Jesus' Audience	Jesus' Offer in the Bread of Life Discourse
Frequency	Manna given daily	Eat loaves, want daily	Eat Bread once
Giver	Moses	Prophet like Moses	Prophet like Moses, but ultimately God
Recipients	Jews	Jews	All men and women
Spiritual Lesson	Ate & learned nothing	Ate & learned nothing	Learn Christ
Eternal Result	Died	Will die in sins	Live forever

The Discourse on the Bread of Life, Part 2 (6:35-40)

[35]**Then Jesus declared, "I am the bread of life. He who comes to me will never go hungry, and he who believes in me will never be thirsty.** [36]**But as I told you, you have seen me and still you do not believe.** [37]**All that the Father gives me will come to me, and whoever comes to me I will never drive away.** [38]**For I have come down from heaven not to do my will but to do the will of him who sent me.** [39]**And this is the will of him who sent me, that I shall lose none of all that he has given me, but raise them up at the last day.** [40]**For my Father's will is that everyone who looks to the Son and believes in him shall have eternal life, and I will raise him up at the last day."**

6:35-37. I am the bread of life — so, the giver of the bread is *himself* the bread! He is claiming to eternally supply for one of humankind's greatest needs: bread/food. He has also promised to supply eternal thirst-quenching (cf. 4:14, 7:38). This is the first of seven specific "I am" (ἐγὼ εἰμι, *egō eimi*) statements with predicate complements in John. All of them make a particular christological claim as to the nature of Jesus. These statements in John are as follows:

---

[27]See similar chart in Hendriksen, *Exposition*, p. 233.

1. I am the bread of life (6:35,41,48,51).
2. I am the light of the world (8:12; 9:5).
3. I am the gate for the sheep (10:7,9).
4. I am the good shepherd (10:11,14).
5. I am the resurrection and the life (11:25).
6. I am the way, the truth, and the life (14:6).
7. I am the true vine (15:1,5).[28]

Contrary to popular understanding, Jesus says that seeing is not necessarily believing (v. 36). Many had seen Jesus[29] yet refused to believe in him. Others had believed in him, but not with a true faith (2:23-25). If Jesus hadn't raised their ire by now, this declaration would have triggered some animosity in the crowd.

Jesus declares that "everyone who receives me" would, in turn, have eternal life. **Will never** in the NIV here and in verse 35 translates οὐ μη (*ou mē*) with the subjunctive mood (called an "emphatic negation" construction in Greek grammars[30]). Such language hammers home the eternal commitment of Jesus to guard those who believe in him.

Verse 37 brings up an interesting question, "How does God give anyone to Jesus?" Several possibilities might be suggested:

A. God determines who will be saved and delivers those individuals to his Son, Jesus. Salvation is ultimately a decision of a sovereign God, and not dependent upon human free will.[31]
B. God draws them to himself and his Son by His love which has been shed abroad in our hearts (cf. Rom. 5:5; John 3:16).
C. God gives them to the Son through a combination of his divine drawing, and our human turning. People come to Jesus of their own free choice. This explanation is to be preferred. That the freedom of choice is the human's prerogative is evident from

---

[28]Other occurrences of the ἐγὼ εἰμι without a predicate complement are 4:26, 6:20, 8:58, and 18:6. This will be discussed below with comments on 8:58.

[29]"Me" in referring to their seeing Jesus is implied and may not have been in the original text. See Metzger, *Textual Commentary*, p. 213.

[30]E.g., H.E. Dana and Julius R. Mantey, *A Manual Grammar of the Greek New Testament* (New York: Macmillan, 1955), pp. 266-267. It can be translated "will certainly not."

[31]See Carson, *The Gospel According to John*, p. 290. Carson says, "Jesus' confidence in the success of his mission is frankly predestinarian."

many other Scriptures and *this context*. Human beings exercise this prerogative until the end of their life on earth. Even after having become a member of the body of Christ (the church), we continually choose to remain in the fold, or are consequently lost. In exercising this choice, one must continually "show his faith by his works" (cf. Jas 2:18).[32] Jesus **will never drive away** anyone who comes to him, yet "man's rejection *by* God is caused by man's rejection *of* God."[33] (See comments below on v. 43. Cf. John 15:2; 1 Cor 9:27; 10:12; Rev 3:16.)

6:38-40. A strong christological statement dominates verses 38-40. Here Jesus declares that it is God's will that all **who come to** him truly do receive **eternal life** and will be **raised up at the last day** (vv. 39, 40, 44, and 54; his power to raise the dead was established in John 5). The clause, **I have come down from heaven,** is repeated six times in this chapter (vv. 33, 36, 41, 50, 51, 58). It reminds us again of the manna typology, the bread that came down from heaven. This is an explicitly supernatural claim, that although Jesus was human, he was the heavenly Word of God incarnate (cf. 1:14).

Why did Jesus come down from heaven? While we make the answer to this very complex at times, Jesus states it very simply: **to do the will of him who sent me.** There is no conflict between the wills of Father and Son; they are one. In verse 39 Jesus' will = save those individuals given to him by God. In verse 40 Father's will = save those who believe. God "gives" individuals to Jesus. Jesus in turn guards the ones who come to him and believe. The Greek text of verse 40 means literally, "the one looking[34] and believing." Both of these actions are present participles, implying ongoing action. This looking and believing is done so that they **shall have eternal life** (see comments above on verse 27). God is "not wanting anyone to perish, but everyone to come to repentance" (2 Pet. 3:9).

---

[32]Butler, *John*, p. 242; see also Seth Wilson, *Learning from Jesus* (Joplin, MO: College Press, 1979), pp. 315-316. Cf. Carson, *The Gospel According to John*, p. 290.

[33]Butler, *John*, p. 242.

[34]See Carson's comments on the word for "looking," θεωρέω, *The Gospel According to John*, p. 292. Carson ties this "looking" closely to the companion participle, "believing."

Conflict Concerning Bread from Heaven and Flesh and Blood (6:41-59)

[41]At this the Jews began to grumble about him because he said, "I am the bread that came down from heaven." [42]They said, "Is this not Jesus, the son of Joseph, whose father and mother we know? How can he now say, 'I came down from heaven'?"

[43]"Stop grumbling among yourselves," Jesus answered. [44]"No one can come to me unless the Father who sent me draws him, and I will raise him up at the last day. [45]It is written in the Prophets: 'They will all be taught by God.'[a] Everyone who listens to the Father and learns from him comes to me. [46]No one has seen the Father except the one who is from God; only he has seen the Father. [47]I tell you the truth, he who believes has everlasting life. [48]I am the bread of life. [49]Your forefathers ate the manna in the desert, yet they died. [50]But here is the bread that comes down from heaven, which a man may eat and not die. [51]I am the living bread that came down from heaven. If anyone eats of this bread, he will live forever. This bread is my flesh, which I will give for the life of the world."

[52]Then the Jews began to argue sharply among themselves, "How can this man give us his flesh to eat?"

[53]Jesus said to them, "I tell you the truth, unless you eat the flesh of the Son of Man and drink his blood, you have no life in you. [54]Whoever eats my flesh and drinks my blood has eternal life, and I will raise him up at the last day. [55]For my flesh is real food and my blood is real drink. [56]Whoever eats my flesh and drinks my blood remains in me, and I in him. [57]Just as the living Father sent me and I live because of the Father, so the one who feeds on me will live because of me. [58]This is the bread that came down from heaven. Your forefathers ate manna and died, but he who feeds on this bread will live forever." [59]He said this while teaching in the synagogue in Capernaum.

[a]*45* Isaiah 54:13

6:41-43. The similarities between this account and the story of Israel in the wilderness become even more pronounced at this point. John tells us that the people "grumble" (Greek verb γογγύζω, *gongyzō*), the very verb used by the LXX for the complaining Israelites (see Exod 17:3, Num 14:27, Ps 106:25, et al.). Jesus' hearers don't want spiritual food; they want belly-filling food. They don't want to listen to someone who claims to be from heaven; they want a king who will rule on earth.

Jesus enters this conflict or debate concerning bread from heaven versus physical flesh and blood. The controversy turned on the identity of Jesus, his origin. **The Jews** (probably leaders of the synagogue in Capernaum[35]) asked, "How could Jesus, the son of Joseph and Mary, be from heaven?" They thought they knew Jesus' origin and nature. He ate and drank daily, and he was otherwise a normal human being. Even Christians have had trouble with this theological matter for many centuries, trying to reconcile the simultaneous humanity and divinity of Jesus.

Jesus is addressing the hometown crowd. (Nazareth was not far from his current home base of Capernaum.) **Joseph** may or may not have been alive at this time.[36] **Stop grumbling among yourselves** — now we have the complete Exodus scene!

6:44. The word **draws** implies resistance. Note the use of ἕλκω (*helkō*) in John and elsewhere in the New Testament:

> John 6:44 — Father *draws* him
> John 12:32 — I will *draw* all men to myself
> John 18:10 — Simon Peter *drew* his sword
> John 21:6 — unable to *haul* the net of fish aboard
> John 21:11 — Simon Peter *dragged* the net ashore
> Acts 16:19 — *dragged* Paul and Silas into the marketplace
> Acts 21:30 — they *dragged* him [Paul] from the temple
> James 2:6 — *dragging* you into court[37]

As mentioned above in the discussion of verse 37, John presents conversion as the result of divine drawing and human turning.

---

[35]Hendriksen, *Exposition*, p. 237, alludes to commentators who suggest members of the Sanhedrin in Jerusalem. But this is unlikely with the Passover nearing and the unnecessary roundtrip to Galilee; see also F.F. Bruce, *John*, p. 155.

[36]Although his absence at the Cana marriage (ch. 2) would seem to indicate Joseph was already dead when Jesus began his ministry.

[37]See other examples from the LXX: he *drew* me out of mighty waters (2 Sam 22:17); I *draw* breath [= pant] (Ps 119:131); he *drags* him in a net (Hab 1:15); they *were dragged* with violence (3 Mac. 4:7).

There is no question but that the divine drawing of verse 44 is a compulsion that our wills initially resist. We are not expected to find a God who hides himself. We respond to the self-revealing God who draws all men and women to himself. John makes plain the central role of Jesus in this process. When Jesus is "lifted up" (when he dies on the cross), he *draws* all men and women to himself (12:32). For John the preaching of the cross is the central element of God's bringing people to him. Salvation is from God's initiative, not ours. While we deny the "irresistible grace" required by the "total depravity" of the Calvinists,[38] we must readily admit that (1) the process of salvation is initiated by God's action, and (2) it meets with initial resistance in every one of us. God does not, however, overrule our will.

6:45. It is written in the Prophets: 'They will all be taught by God.' The Old Testament verse Jesus seems to have in mind is Isaiah 54:13, "All your sons will be taught by the LORD," but the concept is encountered elsewhere in the Old Testament (e.g., Ps 25:4-5; 94:12; Isa 2:3; Jer 16:21; Micah 4:2; Zeph 3:9; Mal 1:11; cf. 1 Cor 2:13). We see a wonderful interweaving of heavenly and human responsibility in the second part of the verse, **everyone who listens to the Father and learns from him comes to me.**

6:46-48. Only Jesus knows the Father and has seen him (see 1:14,18; cf. hope for the redeemed to see Jesus in his glory in 17:24, 1 John 3:2). In the course of this argument, Jesus knows what he is talking about based on intimate experience. The NIV translates ἀμὴν ἀμὴν λέγω ὑμῖν (*amēn, amēn, legō hymin*, amen, amen, I say to you) **I tell you the truth.** This is the third time in this section that John has used this clause (6:26,32,47, cf. 53).

The one believing **has everlasting life** — now![39] Verse 48 states the basis for this truth very succinctly, **I am the bread of life.** Jesus is Creator and the source of life![40]

---

[38]Contra Hendriksen, *Exposition*, pp. 238-239; Leon Morris, *The Gospel of John*, p. 372; et al.; compare Carson, *The Gospel According to John*, p. 293; see also R.C. Foster's excellent treatment of the passage in *Studies in the Life of Christ.*

[39]Hendriksen, *Exposition*, p. 240; Bruce, *John*, p. 157.

[40]McGarvey and Pendleton assess this as a restatement of his main proposition in the sermon (*Fourfold Gospel*, p. 388).

6:49-51. Jesus is trying to get them to analyze the reason that **their forefathers ate the manna in the desert, yet they died**. Just enjoying God's blessings did not save them. Neither was physical bread the answer. The miracle of manna was a powerful, supernatural demonstration of God's provision, but all the people who ate that bread died.

Jesus' claim is that **I am the living bread . . . If anyone eats of this bread, he will live forever. This bread is my flesh . . .** The language of Jesus at this point moves to terms that are more and more explicitly tied to our understanding of the Lord's Supper. In John's account of the *Last Supper* (chs. 13-17) he has no mention of the institution of the *Lord's Supper*. These sections of chapter 6 are both a foreshadowing of that event, and provide some of the theological basis for our understanding of the Eucharist.

Must we understand verse 51 and the verses that follow (53-58) in a sacramental way? In other words, is there something about the physical eating of the loaf and drinking of the cup on a weekly basis that guarantees our salvation? Or, on the other hand, if the church prohibits participation in the Lord's Supper to a person, is that person being denied salvation? Such understandings may be found in Roman Catholicism and other Christian traditions, but do not really seem to be the intent of the text here. Participation in the Lord's Supper is not an exercise in magic. The emblems of Communion are not "salvation pills" that must be taken weekly to ward off condemnation to hell. "Feeding on Jesus" (v. 57) equals believing in Jesus. As already demonstrated above, John's central message is that eternal life is the result of faith. There is no change in emphasis here. We are to believe so fully in Jesus that we have assimilated him into our life. We feast on him in the sense of "man does not live on bread alone but on every word that comes from the mouth of the LORD" (Deut 8:3; Matt 4:4; Luke 4:4). Jesus' **flesh** (σάρξ [*sarx*], not σῶμα [*sōma*] as in Mark 14:22) that was sacrificed on the cross (Matt 20:28; Gal 2:20; Eph 5:2) is this bread.

6:52. Then the Jews began to argue sharply among themselves . . . another understatement in the NIV translation. The word used for argue (μάχομαι, *machomai*) sometimes meant to have a literal fight on the level of combat (Acts 7:26), but in the verbal sense means to have a heated contentious quarrel (cf. 2 Tim 2:24). The lines are being drawn between believers and unbelievers.

6:53. Jesus has no interest in backpedaling or softening his claims and demands. His hearers are offended even more when Jesus asserts, **"unless you eat the flesh of the Son of Man and drink his blood."** This is a serious claim that even the earliest Christians debated one another over — and still do. The Reformation battles over transubstantiation versus consubstantiation versus simple memorial have never been totally resolved in the larger Christian community. Yet it is easy to see that some churches have memorialized the Lord's Supper to the point that it has become an optional exercise, done monthly, quarterly, annually, or not at all. Surely this is an overreaction to the sacramental theology of Roman Catholicism. Participation in the Lord's Supper is a tangible means of fellowship with Jesus, whom we have believed upon for salvation.

In verse 63, Jesus says, "the words I have spoken to you are spirit and life." Compare this carefully with verse 53, which says, **unless you eat the flesh of the Son of Man and drink his blood, you have no life in you.** Yet verse 63 says, "the flesh profits nothing. The words that I have spoken to you are spirit and life." Notice that the flesh and blood did not produce life, but the words of Jesus did, and this is the real solution to the Eucharist controversy. What gives life are the words of Jesus. The heart of all his words, which he came to say and enact, was his death, burial, and resurrection. Even more to the core of the matter, what gives life is the person of Jesus himself, the Risen Lord. John says that the death and resurrection of Jesus is the source of life for all Christians. It is not a magical formula, nor an emotional phenomenon, nor a mystery that is incomprehensible, but it is the heart of the gospel that saves everyone who accepts it, namely the death, burial, and resurrection of Jesus.

Rejection and Acceptance of Jesus (6:60-71)

[60]**On hearing it, many of his disciples said, "This is a hard teaching. Who can accept it?"**

[61]**Aware that his disciples were grumbling about this, Jesus said to them, "Does this offend you? [62]What if you see the Son of Man ascend to where he was before! [63]The Spirit gives life; the flesh counts for nothing. The words I have spoken to you are spirit[a] and they are life. [64]Yet there are some of you who do not believe." For**

Jesus had known from the beginning which of them did not believe and who would betray him. [65]He went on to say, "This is why I told you that no one can come to me unless the Father has enabled him."

[66]From this time many of his disciples turned back and no longer followed him.

[67]"You do not want to leave too, do you?" Jesus asked the Twelve.

[68]Simon Peter answered him, "Lord, to whom shall we go? You have the words of eternal life. [69]We believe and know that you are the Holy One of God."

[70]Then Jesus replied, "Have I not chosen you, the Twelve? Yet one of you is a devil!" [71](He meant Judas, the son of Simon Iscariot, who, though one of the Twelve, was later to betray him.)

[a]63 Or *Spirit*

In John 6 Jesus is at the height of his popularity. He has done a great feeding miracle (vv. 1-15). He has to escape from the large crowds, leading to the miracle of walking on water (vv. 16-21). The crowds seek him out to make him king (v. 15) and to have another free meal (vv. 25-26). This sets the scene for the famous "Bread of Life" discourse in which Jesus makes the greatest public claims he has made so far in the book.

6:60-71. The result is a defining moment for "would-be disciples." Who will stay, and who will leave? In what follows we may discern three types of disciples of Jesus, two who are false, and one who is a true disciple.

The first type of false disciple is the one who counts the cost and turns away (vv. 60,66). This disciple understands that being a follower of Jesus involves steadfast allegiance to him, even to his claims of deity and to being the one who gives eternal life. But this disciple refuses to accept these demands, and voluntarily withdraws from the ranks of disciples. He will accept free meals but will not submit to the Lordship of Jesus. He retains his integrity, but loses his soul.

Judas personifies the second type of false disciple (vv. 70-71). This disciple knows the cost and falsely stays. Such persons stay in the fellowship of disciples (the church), but refuse to submit fully to the Lordship of Jesus. They are like the false guest at the wedding feast (Matt 22:11-14) or the hypocrites that are so soundly condemned by Jesus.

Peter serves as the example of a true disciple in this text. He knows the cost of believing in Jesus, yet also knows that no one else has **the words of eternal life** (v. 68). Jesus alone has the "message that brings eternal life," the message that frees us from sin and alienation from God, the message of gracious truth that saves our souls from eternal destruction. There is no other way!

This chapter ends on a note of foreshadowing that one of the inner twelve disciples of Jesus would betray him (vv. 64,65,70,71). John tells us that person is **Judas, the son of Simon Iscariot**, introduced for the first time here in the Gospel of John. We learn a number of things about this enigmatic figure from John that are not found in the other Gospels. For example, we gain some clue to the meaning of **Iscariot**. This is apparently a family name, for Judas's father is **Simon Iscariot**.[41] While the exact derivation of the name "Iscariot" is uncertain, a likely explanation is that it is a Hellenized form of the Hebrew phrase "man of Kerioth." If Judas were from Kerioth (a town in southern Judea) he would have been the only Judean among the twelve, for the rest were all Galileans. In verse 70 Jesus calls Judas a **devil** (διάβολος, *diabolos*), perhaps better translated here as "adversary." Judas is the one who acts in the spirit of the Great Adversary, Satan, who opposes the work of Jesus by diabolical means. More often John refers to Judas as the "betrayer" (6:64; 12:4; 13:2; 18:2,5). In John 13:2 the connection between Judas and the betrayer and the Devil/Satan is stated explicitly.

With the end of chapter 6 the tone for John's Gospel is changed. Jesus is no longer the popular icon of the people, but rather the one whose life is in danger (7:1). To be a follower of Jesus means to accept his claim to deity, and to trust in him for salvation and eternal life. These are hard demands, and many would-be disciples have left. John has drawn the lines between believers and unbelievers more clearly than ever.

---

[41]Judas is also identified as the son of Simon Iscariot in John 13:2 and 13:26. Interestingly, John 14:22 identifies another disciple named Judas as Judas not Iscariot, probably a reference to the disciple known as Thaddaeus in Mark and Matthew, and Judas the son of James in Luke and Acts.

JOHN 7

3. Jesus at Tabernacles (7:1-52)

Introduction: Question If Jesus Would Go to This Feast (7:1-13)

¹After this, Jesus went around in Galilee, purposely staying away from Judea because the Jews there were waiting to take his life. ²But when the Jewish Feast of Tabernacles was near, ³Jesus' brothers said to him, "You ought to leave here and go to Judea, so that your disciples may see the miracles you do. ⁴No one who wants to become a public figure acts in secret. Since you are doing these things, show yourself to the world." ⁵For even his own brothers did not believe in him.

⁶Therefore Jesus told them, "The right time for me has not yet come; for you any time is right. ⁷The world cannot hate you, but it hates me because I testify that what it does is evil. ⁸You go to the Feast. I am not yet^a going up to this Feast, because for me the right time has not yet come." ⁹Having said this, he stayed in Galilee.

¹⁰However, after his brothers had left for the Feast, he went also, not publicly, but in secret. ¹¹Now at the Feast the Jews were watching for him and asking, "Where is that man?"

¹²Among the crowds there was widespread whispering about him. Some said, "He is a good man."

Others replied, "No, he deceives the people." ¹³But no one would say anything publicly about him for fear of the Jews.

^a*8 Some early manuscripts do not have* yet.

7:1-2. John 7 contains several distinct views of Jesus, ways of looking at him and evaluations of him. Chapter 7 also deals with the relationship of Jesus to another Jewish festival.[1] In particular, these opening verses contain the debate as to whether or not Jesus would go to **the Jewish Feast of Tabernacles**, also called the "Festival of Booths."[2] In this weeklong festival the Jews remembered God's provision for the nation during the 40 years in the wilderness, and gave thanks to God for the late summer harvest (see Lev 23:34-43; Deut 16:13-15). Tabernacles was one of the three great pilgrimage festivals[3] for which all Israelite men were expected to go to Jerusalem (see Deut 16:16). During this feast the Jews were to live in temporary huts to reenact their ancestors' interim residence in the wilderness before entry into the Promised Land. From Passover (6:4) to Tabernacles (7:2) is six months. This would bring us to the fifteenth day of the Jewish month of Tishri. This would likely be equivalent by modern reckoning to October 12, A.D. 29.

7:3-4. Jesus' brothers are unnamed here, but Mark 6:3 lists James, Joseph, Judas, and Simon (as well as sisters).[4] **You ought to leave here and go to Judea, so that your disciples may see the miracles you do** — the wisdom was sound, at least from a worldly viewpoint. **Since** (εἰ, *ei*) in verse 4 more properly means "if." *Ei* occurs 49 times in the Gospel of John and is translated "since" only one other time in the NIV translation of the book.[5] It is a conditional marker that deals with "present reality," at least as it is perceived in the eyes of some.[6] The NRSV text here is more accurate, "If you do these things, show yourself to the world."

---

[1]See the helpful chart and comments in Craig L. Blomberg, *Jesus and the Gospels* (Nashville: Broadman & Holman, 1997), p. 302.

[2]Apparently also known as the "Feast of the LORD," Lev. 23:39.

[3]The other two were Passover and Pentecost (also known as the Feast of Weeks).

[4]Epiphanius (A.D. 298-403, bishop on Cyprus) maintained that the "brothers" were Joseph's children by a previous marriage. Jerome (A.D. 340?-420, assistant to the Pope) believed that they were "cousins." Helvidius (A.D. 385, layman in Rome who denied the perpetual virginity of Mary) claimed that the "brothers" were normal children of Joseph and Mary.

[5]The "since" of the NIV is a poor choice here. Perhaps the translators intended the statement to come across as ironic, but the affirmation of the "since" clause certainly clashes with John's flat statement as to the unbelief of Jesus' brothers in verse 5.

[6]Notice the following examples from elsewhere in John: "If (as some say) you are the Christ, tell us plainly" (10:24); "If (as some have claimed) I

Show yourself to the world because many significant Jewish leaders would normally be in Jerusalem for this important feast, thus making it a prime opportunity for a demonstration of power and a claim to be Messiah. The **world** (κόσμος, *kosmos*) has a deeper significance for John's readers than public display. The *kosmos* in John is humankind as morally alienated from God (see 1:10, cf. 1 John 5:19).[7] Jesus cannot be a part of this world (8:23). Jesus did not come to impress the world, but to redeem and save the world (1:29; 3:16 and many others). This relationship to the *kosmos* creates a clear distinction between Jesus and his brothers, for they are aligned to the world by their unbelief (7:7).

7:5. If we did not know the rest of the story, the words — **for even his own brothers did not believe in him** — would be extremely discouraging. These brothers did not believe until after the resurrection,[8] but later became leaders in the Jerusalem church (see Gal 2:9). John continues to develop his important theme of belief versus unbelief. In this case unbelief is not a characteristic of nameless disciples, but of the family of Jesus itself.

7:6. He told his brothers **the right time for me has not yet come**, meaning that he would not go *at that time*. The word used for "time" (καιρός, *kairos*) is found only here and in verse 8 in John, but it is a relatively common New Testament word. It has the meaning here of "appropriate time" or "opportunity" (cf. 2 Cor 6:2). Jesus did wait and go later (v. 10), obviously waiting in order to save his physical life from meaningless early destruction (remember verse 1 which clearly states the danger to his life in Jerusalem). **For you any time is right**; in other words, any time is safe for the brothers to go. They encouraged him to go, but Jesus delayed his journey so that he would not die at the wrong time, in the wrong place, for the wrong reason. He was fully aware that such a premature death would not fulfill God's purpose.

---

said something wrong, testify as to what is wrong" (18:23); "If (as I perceive to be the case) you have carried him away, tell me where you put him" (20:15). See *BDF*, p. 189.

[7]See the article by John Painter, "World," in *Dictionary of Jesus and the Gospels* (Downers Grove, IL: InterVarsity, 1992), especially p. 890.

[8]All of them have become believers and part of the community of disciples in Acts 1:14. First Corinthians 15:7 records a special postresurrection appearance of Jesus to James.

7:7. By saying, **the world cannot hate you, but it hates me because I testify that what it does is evil,** the author again plays upon the distance between the world/*kosmos* and Jesus. Jesus' brothers are in no danger from unbelieving humanity, because they are a part of this unbelieving world. John has already shown us that Jesus' condemnation of the world's evil was rejected by many (3:19-20). Ironically, in order for Jesus to save the world from sin, the world first had to accept its sinful, unbelieving, condemned state. It was this denial of a need for salvation that kept many from being saved, and still does so today. The drowning man cannot be saved as long as he thinks he can swim to shore himself.

7:8-9. I am not yet going to this Feast . . . has a textual note in the NIV. It is probable that the original text read "I am not going to the feast" (cf. NRSV). "Not yet" seems to have been added by a later copyist to avoid the apparent contradiction of having Jesus make this statement in verse 8 and then proceed to go to the feast in verse 10. The actual language here makes such changes unnecessary. Jesus told his brothers he was not going **because for me the right time has not yet come.** He does not confide with his brothers what would constitute the proper opportunity. Therefore, Jesus decided to stay **in Galilee,** as Bruce says, "not to run before the Father's guidance nor yet lag behind it."[9]

7:10. Jesus finally went to the feast, although **not publicly, but in secret.** In John he does not return to Galilee again until after his resurrection (21:1). Here there is a sense of Jesus as the "Hidden Messiah," a theme which is much more developed in the Synoptic Gospels (cf. v. 4). Jesus does not act secretly out of cowardice or because he is naturally sneaky. God is directing him, and he goes when God reveals to him that it is the proper time. There will be an appropriate time and place for him to reveal himself in Jerusalem as the Messiah, but not yet.

7:11-13. Meanwhile, he was expected in Jerusalem. The religious leaders of **the Jews were watching for him** apparently for an opportunity to arrest him. The crowds of festival pilgrims were also expecting him. Among the common people **there was widespread whispering about him,** because it was unsafe to speak openly about

---

[9]Bruce, *John*, p. 173.

Jesus (v. 13, cf. 9:22). The crowd's reaction to Jesus had turned from rejection (6:66) to speculation about his true character. There was a clear difference of opinion. Some were able to affirm him as a **good man**. Others dismissed him as a "deceiver." The word translated **deceiving** is πλανάω (*planaō*), and is often translated "lead astray" (cf. Matt 24:24). Ironically there *was* mass deception at work here, but Jesus was not the guilty party. The true deceiver will be identified later, the "father of lies" (8:44; cf. Rev 12:9).

Jesus' Discourses Spoken during the Feast (7:14-36).

[14]Not until halfway through the Feast did Jesus go up to the temple courts and begin to teach. [15]The Jews were amazed and asked, "How did this man get such learning without having studied?"

[16]Jesus answered, "My teaching is not my own. It comes from him who sent me. [17]If anyone chooses to do God's will, he will find out whether my teaching comes from God or whether I speak on my own. [18]He who speaks on his own does so to gain honor for himself, but he who works for the honor of the one who sent him is a man of truth; there is nothing false about him. [19]Has not Moses given you the law? Yet not one of you keeps the law. Why are you trying to kill me?"

[20]"You are demon-possessed," the crowd answered. "Who is trying to kill you?"

[21]Jesus said to them, "I did one miracle, and you are all astonished. [22]Yet, because Moses gave you circumcision (though actually it did not come from Moses, but from the patriarchs), you circumcise a child on the Sabbath. [23]Now if a child can be circumcised on the Sabbath so that the law of Moses may not be broken, why are you angry with me for healing the whole man on the Sabbath? [24]Stop judging by mere appearances, and make a right judgment."

[25]At that point some of the people of Jerusalem began to ask, "Isn't this the man they are trying to kill? [26]Here he is, speaking publicly, and they are not saying a word to him. Have the authorities really concluded that he is the Christ[a]? [27]But we know where

this man is from; when the Christ comes, no one will know where he is from."

[28]Then Jesus, still teaching in the temple courts, cried out, "Yes, you know me, and you know where I am from. I am not here on my own, but he who sent me is true. You do not know him, [29]but I know him because I am from him and he sent me."

[30]At this they tried to seize him, but no one laid a hand on him, because his time had not yet come. [31]Still, many in the crowd put their faith in him. They said, "When the Christ comes, will he do more miraculous signs than this man?"

[32]The Pharisees heard the crowd whispering such things about him. Then the chief priests and the Pharisees sent temple guards to arrest him.

[33]Jesus said, "I am with you for only a short time, and then I go to the one who sent me. [34]You will look for me, but you will not find me; and where I am, you cannot come."

[35]The Jews said to one another, "Where does this man intend to go that we cannot find him? Will he go where our people live scattered among the Greeks, and teach the Greeks? [36]What did he mean when he said, 'You will look for me, but you will not find me,' and 'Where I am, you cannot come'?"

[a]26 Or *Messiah*; also in verses 27, 31, 41 and 42

7:14. It has been eighteen months since Jesus has set foot in Jerusalem. He waits until the midpoint of the feast to make a public appearance in the temple. It was common for rabbi/teachers to teach in one of the spacious courtyard areas of the temple, and he assumes this role.

7:15. The first exchange recorded by John is with **the Jews**, meaning the Jewish religious leaders. They sarcastically challenge Jesus' right to teach, since they know he is not highly educated. By this they mean that he has not studied with any of the prominent rabbis in Jerusalem (as Paul had, see Acts 22:3). The KJV has "How knoweth this man letters?" How can he be a man of letters without going to college? Perhaps they noticed his rural dress and his Galilean accent. From a human perspective, they are correct, for Jesus would have had no more education than that given in the synagogue school of his hometown, Nazareth (see Acts 4:13 for a similar reaction to John and Peter).

7:16-19. My teaching is not my own. It comes from him who sent me — i.e., God. Jesus immediately raises the stakes of this dispute. This is not a war of words between two rabbinical schools. It is much more than a learned discussion. It is a matter of the acceptance or rejection of divine revelation, a Word from God himself.

Jesus begins his defense by stating a timeless principle. The one with the obedient heart, with a desire to do God's will, is the one who will make a correct judgment about the validity of Jesus' message. His overall point is that the problem of the Jewish people has never been a lack of God's Word. It has been the failure to obey that Word due to disobedient and unbelieving hearts. They have the law of **Moses**, but even so **not one of you keeps the law**. This disobedient spirit to the law is clearly perceived by Jesus, who accuses them of seeking to murder him (an intention to violate the sixth commandment). Reference to the law and attempts to kill Jesus already appeared in John 5:18.

7:20. Now the dialog shifts from Jesus and the Jewish religious leaders to Jesus and the crowd. The crowd begins not by answering Jesus' charge of law breaking, but by a personal attack against Jesus: **You are demon-possessed**. This is more than an accusation of insanity, but a slanderous charge of spiritual complicity with the devil. Tied to this is a diagnosis of paranoia, **Who is trying to kill you?** John shows that at this point the plot to kill Jesus is a tightly held secret, hatched and protected by the religious leaders.

7:21-24. Jesus responds by referring to the last miracle he had performed in Jerusalem, **I did one miracle** (John 5:1-14). The healing of the lame man at the Pool of Bethesda had occurred on the Sabbath (5:9,16) and accounts for what follows.

Jesus answers the unspoken charge of Sabbath-breaking by using an example at the core of Jewish practice: **circumcision** (an issue frequent in Paul, but occurring only here in John). Jesus corrects a commonly used argument that Moses gave the sign of circumcision, when it was more specifically given by God through **the patriarchs** (Abraham, Gen 17:9-14). The Jewish practice of circumcision on the eighth day (see Lev 12:3) necessarily came into conflict with the commandment to keep the Sabbath if the day of circumcision was a Sabbath. In this case, circumcision had been put above Sabbath, and this put the Jews in technical violation of the fourth commandment. Jesus' argument with them is that if they can see the necessity of breaking the Sabbath in order to get circumcision done on the right day, why should they object if God heals a person on the Sabbath? **Why are you angry with me for healing the whole man on the Sabbath?** The obvious logic is whether to fix the whole person versus fixing a single sex organ. **Stop judging by mere appearances and make a right judgment.** Contrary to the whining unrepentant, we are *commanded* to judge. The key is to judge with God's perspective (Matt 7:1). Jesus should not be judged by his lack of education or by the rumors about him, but by what he says and does.

7:25-27. At this point John again switches the discussion to another group, **the people of Jerusalem,** i.e., hometown festival participants. Someone in this group verbalizes a rumored plot, that the Jewish religious leaders were **trying to kill** Jesus. How could Jesus' **speaking publicly** go unchallenged? (Again the simultaneously private/public nature of Jesus' ministry is highlighted, cf. vv. 4,10.) A reason for this lack of challenge is tentatively offered as a rhetorical question in verse 26: perhaps the authorities have concluded Jesus really is the Messiah.[10] In so asking, the topic of discussion now shifts from the issue of Sabbath-breaking to the question of the true identity of Jesus.

For these Jerusalem residents the possibility that Jesus might be the Messiah has a large problem. According to their expectation, **when the Christ comes, no one will know where he is from.** The origin of Jesus is a crucial factor in his validation as Messiah. The Jews well knew that their Messiah would not be self-appointed, a "self-made man." God would control his origin. For us, the readers, John has already clearly told where Jesus came from (1:1,14). In the narrative, however, conflicting expectations of the source of the Messiah are very important. One group expects the Messiah to

---

[10]See Carson, *The Gospel According to John*, p. 317. As Carson notes, this is the first time in John that the possibility of Jesus' being the Messiah is discussed in Jerusalem.

come out of nowhere.[11] Later in this chapter another group asserts that the Messiah would come out of Bethlehem (v. 42).

7:28-29. Jesus **cried out** (κράζω, *krazō*) as if out of frustration at the peoples' unnecessary ignorance.[12] He challenges them by saying **Yes, you know me, and you know where I am from.** Likely, this is intended to be an ironic statement,[13] i.e., that Jesus meant "You have no idea where I am really from." While they might have known that he was from Galilee, the general populace still had not accepted his ultimately divine origin. This question will return again at the end of this section when the Jewish leaders have council (7:45-52).

7:30-32. The response to Jesus now is one of confusion. Some **tried to seize him**, probably to detain him for official arrest. This is unsuccessful because of what for John is a simple reason, **his time had not yet come**; i.e., God prevents it. The **whispering such things** (i.e., messianic speculation) made some of **the chief priests** (Sadducees) **and the Pharisees** jealous, and therefore they sought to overlook their long-standing rivalry[14] and cooperate in arresting him. A false Messiah would certainly be a discouraging nuisance to the Pharisees, and any type of Messiah was a threat to the Sadducees and their temple monopoly. So, they **sent temple guards to arrest him**, but we do not learn of the failure of this expedition until verse 45.

In the midst of these detention attempts, John records that some in the crowd **put their faith in him**, meaning, in context, that they believed Jesus to be the Messiah. This belief was prompted by Jesus' miraculous signs, however, and John has already shown that faith based on the excitement of miracles may be an inadequate faith (2:23-25).

---

[11]Justin Martyr vs. Trypho the Jew discusses their view that the Messiah will not even know he is the one until Elijah suddenly comes to anoint him and make him manifest to all.

[12]Borchert says the time of discussion is over and it's time for an announcement (*John 1–11*, p. 286).

[13]Hendriksen, *Exposition*, 2:17-18, concludes that Jesus intended irony in the statement and gives a number of reasons to support this conclusion, i.e., that Jesus meant "You have no idea where I am really from."

[14]See Butler, *John*, 2:29.

7:33-36. Jesus states, **"I am with you for only a short time, and then I go to the one who sent me. You will look for me, but you will not find me; and where I am, you cannot come."** These cryptic comments were surely confusing to the audience as the following discussion among the Jews illustrates. John's point is that the perception of the Jewish religious leaders seemingly never rises above the material world. They can only speculate that Jesus intends to travel to other countries, **our people scattered among the Greeks.**[15] It is this limited, materialistic perspective that prevents them from understanding what the true mission of Jesus is. The readers know that Jesus is referring to his coming death and ascension.

Jesus' Discourses Spoken on the Last Day of the Feast and the Audience's Response to It (7:37-52).

[37]**On the last and greatest day of the Feast, Jesus stood and said in a loud voice, "If anyone is thirsty, let him come to me and drink.** [38]**Whoever believes in me, as**[a] **the Scripture has said, streams of living water will flow from within him."** [39]**By this he meant the Spirit, whom those who believed in him were later to receive. Up to that time the Spirit had not been given, since Jesus had not yet been glorified.**

[40]**On hearing his words, some of the people said, "Surely this man is the Prophet."**

[41]**Others said, "He is the Christ."**

Still others asked, "How can the Christ come from Galilee? [42]**Does not the Scripture say that the Christ will come from David's family**[a] **and from Bethlehem, the town where David lived?"** [43]**Thus the people were divided because of Jesus.** [44]**Some wanted to seize him, but no one laid a hand on him.**

[45]**Finally the temple guards went back to the chief priests and Pharisees, who asked them, "Why didn't you bring him in?"**

---

[15]εἰς τὴν διασποράν – the Diaspora or dispersion of the Jews following the exile. See James 1:1; 1 Peter 1:1. Barclay sees this as an unintentional prophecy on the part of the Jews that Jesus intended to reach the Gentiles with the gospel (*The Gospel of John*, p. 258).

[46]"No one ever spoke the way this man does," the guards declared.

[47]"You mean he has deceived you also?" the Pharisees retorted. [48]"Has any of the rulers or of the Pharisees believed in him? [49]No! But this mob that knows nothing of the law — there is a curse on them."

[50]Nicodemus, who had gone to Jesus earlier and who was one of their own number, asked, [51]"Does our law condemn anyone without first hearing him to find out what he is doing?"

[52]They replied, "Are you from Galilee, too? Look into it, and you will find that a prophet[b] does not come out of Galilee."

[a]42 Greek *seed*   [b]52 Two early manuscripts *the Prophet*

7:37-39. John now changes the scene to the **last and greatest day of the Feast**. Whether this is the seventh day (the last day of the Feast proper) or the eighth day (a winding-down, "special Sabbath" that had become attached to Tabernacles by this time) has been much debated by scholars.[16] However, what is important to John is not this debate, but that it is the **last day** of the feast. It is the finale for the Feast of Tabernacles in the Gospel of John, for it will not be celebrated again in this book. Yet it is also Tabernacles' closing act symbolically in that Jesus is fulfilling the intent of the Feast of Tabernacles and making it obsolete. From the author's perspective, writing 20-25 years after the destruction of the Jerusalem temple, the grand celebrations and pageantry of Tabernacles were but a distant memory. While there would certainly be some poignancy and sentimental nostalgia associated with the lost temple observance of Tabernacles, for John there are no regrets, *because Jesus would accomplish what Tabernacles anticipated.* To appreciate this fulfillment, one must understand both the elements of the temple celebration of Tabernacles and the scriptural references that are included in this passage.

In Jesus' day the Jerusalem celebration of Tabernacles involved a daily fetching of water from the Pool of Siloam in a golden pitcher, and a ritual pouring out of the water at the temple altar. The

---

[16]For a thorough discussion of both positions see Hendriksen, *Exposition,* 2:21-22.

purpose of this ceremony was to remind the nation of Israel of God's miraculous provision of water out of rocks while they were in the desert wilderness (Exod 17:1-7; Num 20:1-11; cf. Deut 8:15; Wisdom 11:4). But for the Jews God's supplying of water was more than a past, historical event tied to the wilderness experience. The Scriptures repeatedly portrayed God as the one who provides spiritual water to the spiritually thirsty and looked ahead to a time when there would be an ultimate fulfillment of this thirst-quenching. Notice these texts (as well as Ps 107:9; Isa 35:7; cf. Rev 7:14,17; 21:6):

> *For I will pour water on the thirsty land,*
> *and streams on the dry ground;*
> *I will pour out my Spirit on your offspring,*
> *and my blessing on your descendants.*
> Isaiah 44:3

> *Come all you who are thirsty,*
> *Come to the waters;*
> *and you who have no money,*
> *come, buy and eat!*
> Isaiah 55:1

Jesus echoes Isaiah when he announces, "**If a man is thirsty, let him come to me and drink**." John weaves his editorial guidance into the words of Jesus to teach us that neither Tabernacles nor the offer of Jesus were really about water, but about **the** [Holy] **Spirit, whom those who believed in him were later to receive**.

Jesus ties this together by describing his offer of water/Spirit as having a scriptural antecedent, **streams of living water will flow from within him**. Attempts to find an Old Testament quotation to match this text have been unsuccessful.[17] A possible reference may be found in Nehemiah 8 and 9. Here the context is of a reinstituted celebration of the Feast of Tabernacles (Neh 8:13-18). In this case certain elements of the Feast are extended over the entire month (Neh 8:18). Toward the end of the month, although after the Feast proper, there was a well-planned day of national repentance (Neh 9).

---

[17]The best suggestions include Zechariah 14:8a, "On that day living water will flow out from Jerusalem" and Isaiah 58:11b, "You will be like a well-watered garden, like a spring whose waters never fail."

This day included a thoughtful rehearsal of the history of Israel from Abraham to Israel's current unsatisfactory situation (Neh 9:5-38). This retelling of Israel's story included mention of the miraculous water from rock (Neh 9:15,20) and a remarkable mention of God giving his "good Spirit to instruct them" while in the wilderness.[18] It is surely this sort of reference that Jesus has in mind when he combines water, Spirit, and Scripture in verse 38.

Sometimes overlooked in attempting to unravel these problems of interpretation is the magnitude of the blessing promised to future believers in verses 37-39. Since the resurrection and glorification of Jesus, believers are assured of the gift of the Holy Spirit, the everflowing river of living spiritual water in their hearts. As Jesus says elsewhere, "Blessed are those who hunger and thirst for righteousness, for they will be filled" (Matt 5:6). The gift of the Holy Spirit to all believers is one of the major differences between the Old Testament and the New Testament. For the people of God under the Old Covenant, the Holy Spirit was a future promise, but for the people of God under the New Covenant, the Holy Spirit is a present reality. *How gracious God is to allow us to have our spiritual thirst quenched by his Holy Spirit!*

The final section of this chapter serves to sum up some of the various estimations of Jesus that have been presented. In verse 12 there were those who said **He is a good man,** but also those who disagreed and said **he deceives the people** (cf. v. 47). In verse 20 he was given the insulting title of **demon-possessed.** His public speaking while under threat of arrest and death in verse 26 identifies him as a *brave man,* but more importantly his preaching has convinced some that he was **the Prophet**[19] (v. 40), i.e., Moses' pledged prophet of Deuteronomy 18:15-19. The befuddled temple police decide that he was a *unique man,* for **No one ever spoke the way this man does** (v. 46). Most importantly, some have decided that Jesus is **the Christ** (v. 41). This is the decision the author wants his readers to make also, the stated purpose of his book (20:31).

---

[18]For this interpretation based on Nehemiah, I am in debt to D.A. Carson, both on the level of personal conversations and on the presentation he has made in his commentary, *The Gospel According to John,* pp. 326-328 (MSK).

[19]See comments on 1:21; 6:14.

7:40-44. These verdicts are not without controversy, however. There are those who contend Jesus could not be **the Christ** because he does not meet all the qualifications. This is the third time in this chapter that Jesus has met some of the people's messianic expectations, only to have those same credentials disputed by others. Some disqualified Jesus as Messiah because he did not make a sudden dramatic appearance (v. 27). Some believed that Jesus was the Christ because of his miracles (v. 31), yet others explained this as demon possession (v. 20). Now some have been convinced by his preaching that he is the Christ (v. 41), but others argue against this because of Jesus' seeming lack of Davidic blood and Bethlehem birthplace (v. 42). Although we know from the other Gospels (see Matt 1:1,20; Mark 10:47-48; and Luke 1:27,32, 2:4), from Paul (see Rom 1:3 and 2 Tim 2:8), and perhaps from Hebrews (see Heb 7:14) that Jesus was from the house of David, the author is silent concerning this challenge. We also know from Matthew and Luke that Jesus was born in Bethlehem as the Messiah should have been, yet again John is silent. Why?

Some have suggested that this is another case of John's use of irony, that by recording these objections the unbelievers are ironically confirming what the reader should know: that David was an ancestor of Jesus, and that Jesus had been born in Bethlehem, so Jesus meets these messianic qualifications.[20] While this may be possible, the irony here is so subtle as to be missed by most readers. A nonironic interpretation is to be preferred. This leaves us with three options, which will be discussed in turn.

1. *Jesus really was not born in Bethlehem, and was not a descendant of David.* This position is popular among those who see most of the material of the Gospels as historically unreliable. For them, John's lack of correction of this misapprehension creates a serious contradiction between John and the Synoptic Gospels. Therefore, this position contends that the early church created the Bethlehem story and/or the Davidic genealogy. This was done as a part of its defense of Jesus as the Messiah to the Jewish community. This makes John's seeming denial of these

---

[20]E.g., Carson, *The Gospel According to John*, pp. 329-330.

things much more historically reliable.[21] Yet this seems unlikely. As already discussed, Jesus' Davidic ancestry is mentioned in all three Synoptic Gospels, as well as in Paul's letters, so its attestation is both early and widespread. As for the Bethlehem connection, there seems to have been only a marginal expectation among the Jews that the Messiah would be born there, and only Micah 5:2 may be cited as Old Testament prophecy for this. As C.H. Dodd has suggested, if anything, it seems that the Bethlehem requirement was revived by the early church because they knew that Jesus had indeed been born there.[22]

2. *John did not know whether or not Jesus had been born in Bethlehem or was a descendant of David.* While this cannot be ruled out conclusively, it must be seen as almost ludicrously unlikely. John was a close associate of Jesus throughout his ministry, and tradition even connects him with Jesus' mother, Mary, after the resurrection. He had apparently been a disciple of John the Baptist, who was Jesus' cousin. He wrote after the other Gospel authors, and even if he did not have access to Matthew and Luke, he certainly must have been aware of most of their material (if not all).

3. *John chose not to base his argument for Jesus as Messiah upon Davidic lineage or Bethlehem birthplace.* As Dodd says, for John's presentation "Jesus is not the Messiah of Jewish expectation . . . ."[23] John presents a Messiah of spiritual, not national salvation. He is an object of faith, not a tool of military vengeance. John has already shown Jesus resisting this national savior role (6:14-15). He is the Lamb of God who takes away the sins of the world, not the new David, the warrior king. While this explanation is admittedly an argument from silence, it does fit the overall context of John the best.

7:45-52. John concludes this chapter with an insider's version of the resulting meeting of the Jewish religious leaders (**chief priests**

---

[21]For a thorough discussion of this possibility see John P. Meier, *A Marginal Jew: Rethinking the Historical Jesus*, Vol. I, *The Roots of the Problem and the Person* (New York: Doubleday, 1991), pp. 214-219. Meier himself concludes that it was unlikely that Jesus was born in Bethlehem, but that his Davidic ancestry was likely.

[22]C.H. Dodd, *The Fourth Gospel*, p. 91.

[23]Ibid.

and Pharisees). We are probably to understand that this is at least an informal meeting of the Jewish High Council known as the Sanhedrin, although the actual term συνέδριον (*synedrion*) is not used by John until 11:47.

The leaders are first thwarted by the **temple guards**' failure to arrest Jesus. The reason given by these policemen is that **no one ever spoke the way this man does**. While this makes perfect sense to the reader, it is a lame excuse for the religious leaders. John emphasizes their elitist attitude and arrogance in belittling the temple guards: they have been deceived and are no better than the ignorant and accursed **mob**, the gullible and unwashed masses.

A member of the council speaks up who is already known to us, Nicodemus (cf. 3:1-9; 19:39). He challenges the mounting frustration of the council by asking, **Does our law condemn anyone without first hearing him to find out what he is doing?** Nicodemus is demanding both the rule of law (not elitist power politics) and due process (not mob lynching or secret judgments).

While the courage of Nicodemus is admirable and shows that he must have had considerable clout in the council, they do not listen to this voice of reason and justice. The reply to Nicodemus is another angry *ad hominem* response, an attack against both Jesus and Nicodemus himself. For this group of urban elites, it is impossible that a Galilean bumpkin could be the Messiah, or even someone worth listening to. They extend this insult by suggesting that Nicodemus is as stupid as a loutish Galilean if he has fallen for Jesus.

Nicodemus is told to **look into it**, presumably to check and see if there is any scriptural basis for a prophet to come from Galilee. If he had, the answer would be that there had been prophets from Galilee,[24] but perhaps no clear text that promised a great prophet or the Messiah coming from this region. At this point, however, they have no interest in scriptural arguments. They simply want to remove this outsider who has threatened their status quo.

---

[24]An example usually suggested is Jonah (2 Kgs 14:25).

JOHN 8

Textual Parenthesis: The Woman Taken in Adultery (7:53–8:11)

[53]Then each went to his own home.

[1]But Jesus went to the Mount of Olives. [2]At dawn he appeared again in the temple courts, where all the people gathered around him, and he sat down to teach them. [3]The teachers of the law and the Pharisees brought in a woman caught in adultery. They made her stand before the group [4]and said to Jesus, "Teacher, this woman was caught in the act of adultery. [5]In the Law Moses commanded us to stone such women. Now what do you say?" [6]They were using this question as a trap, in order to have a basis for accusing him.

But Jesus bent down and started to write on the ground with his finger. [7]When they kept on questioning him, he straightened up and said to them, "If any one of you is without sin, let him be the first to throw a stone at her." [8]Again he stooped down and wrote on the ground.

[9]At this, those who heard began to go away one at a time, the older ones first, until only Jesus was left, with the woman still standing there. [10]Jesus straightened up and asked her, "Woman, where are they? Has no one condemned you?"

[11]"No one, sir," she said.

"Then neither do I condemn you," Jesus declared. "Go now and leave your life of sin."

Because it is unlikely that this section was part of the original text of the fourth Gospel, many commentaries have chosen to leave John 7:53–8:11 out of their discussion[1] or to treat it in an

---

[1]For examples see Butler, *John* (although see his excellent discussion, 2:42-43), and Robert Kysar, *John's Story of Jesus* (Philadelphia: Fortress, 1984).

appendix.[2] Several reasons may be given which lead to the conclusion that this was a later addition to the text:

1. Many of the oldest and best manuscripts of John do not have this text and proceed seamlessly from 7:52 to 8:12.[3]

2. Among those manuscripts that do have 7:53–8:11, some have it at different locations, including after 7:36, after 7:44, after 21:25, or even after Luke 21:38.

3. Thematically it seems out of place in John. There is no other place in John where the topic of adultery or sexual sin comes up. In general "sin" in John is not so much behavioral but much more the general attitude of unbelief (cf. John 16:8-9).

4. The vocabulary of this passage is very unlike the rest of the book. About 9% of the words do not occur elsewhere in John. This is quite a high percentage for John, where the vocabulary tends to be repetitious and limited.[4] Of the 15 non-Johannine words, four are not found elsewhere in the New Testament.[5]

---

[2]For examples of the appendix approach see Bruce, *John*, pp. 413-418 and C. K. Barrett, *The Gospel According to St. John*, 2nd ed. (Philadelphia: Westminster, 1978), pp. 589-592.

[3]This passage is missing in such important manuscripts as the papyrus text, $\mathfrak{P}^{66}$, in both Codex Sinaiticus and Codex Vaticanus, in important later manuscripts such as minuscule 33, and in early versions such as the Syriac and some old Latin translations.

[4]Compare this with other passages in John of similar length. John 1:1-12 contains only one word not used elsewhere in the book, less than 1%. At the other extreme, John 21:1-12 has 16 words not used elsewhere in the book, about 6% of the words for this passage. This relatively high percentage is partly because of the fishing narrative and the somewhat technical vocabulary associated with it.

[5]The 15 words occurring only here are ἐλαιῶν (*elaiōn* = olives, 8:1; the location "Mount of Olives" is found nowhere else in John), ὄρθρου (*orthrou* = early morning, 8:2), γραμματεῖς (*grammateis* = Scribes, 8:3; although "Pharisees" occurs 20 times in John, nowhere else is the expression "Scribes and Pharisees" used), μοιχεία (*moicheia* = adultery, 8:3), αὐτοφώρῳ (*autophōrō* = in the very act, 8:4; only here in the NT), μοιχευομένη (*moicheuomenē* = commiting adultery, 8:4), κύψας (*kypsas* = bending, 8:6), κατέγραφεν (*kategraphen* = writing down, 8:6; only here in the NT), ἐπέμενον (*epemenon* = kept on, continued, 8:7), ἀνέκυψεν (*anekypsen* = straightened up, 8:8,10), ἀναμάρτητος (*anamartētos* = without sin, 8:7 only here in the NT), κατακύψας (*katakypsas* = bending, 8:8; only here in the NT), πρεσβυτέρων (*presbyterōn* = older ones, 8:9), καταλείφθη (*kataleiphthē* = was left, 8:9), κατέκρινεν (*katekrinen* = condemn, 8:10,11).

5. Stylistically, leaving out this section does no damage to the flow of the text. If we read from the end of 7:52 and go immediately to 8:12, it merely seems that Jesus is continuing his public discussions during the Feast of Tabernacles. A more subjective side to this is that the style seems somewhat unlike John, and more like that of the Synoptic Gospel authors.[6]

For these and other reasons, most scholars agree that the story of the woman caught in adultery was not part of the Fourth Gospel as it came from the hand of the author.

But having said that, what do we do with this section? While probably not from John, it appears to be a somewhat free-floating piece of Jesus material that was preserved by the early church. Although there is no way to prove this, we might say this text seems to be *authentic Jesus material.*[7] All of the arguments for this conclusion will be subjective, but they boil down to this point: *it seems exactly like the sort of thing Jesus would do.* Therefore, although the source of this section is uncertain and this uncertainty should be acknowledged, it contains a unique picture of the ministry of Jesus that deserves commenting upon.

7:53–8:2. The scene changes to a new day. Apparently Jesus has spent the night on the Mount of Olives, a large hill directly east of Jerusalem proper. It has been noted that this sequence is suggestive of Passion Week in the Synoptic Gospels, where Jesus was in Jerusalem during the day, but retired each night to Bethany (on the other side of the Mount of Olives).[8] Perhaps this period at the end of Jesus' ministry is a more likely original setting for the incident.

8:3-6. Jesus is immediately confronted with a situation that thrusts upon him the position of a judge. **The teachers of the law**

---

[6]Both of the expressions "Scribes and Pharisees" and "Mount of Olives" are more at home in the Synoptic Gospels. Likewise the vocative διδάσκαλε (*didaskale*) is more at home in the Synoptics (28 times), for John uses the Hebrew/Aramaic "Rabbi" (1:38,49; 3:2,26; 4:31; 6:25; 9:2) or "Rabbouni" (20:16). John uses the vocative διδάσκαλε only in parenthetical, explanatory translations (1:38; 20:16).

[7]Bruce Metzger says that John 7:53–8:11 "has all the earmarks of historical veracity" (*Textual Commentary*, p. 220). Kurt and Barbara Aland say that it "represents a very early tradition" (*The Text of the New Testament*, trans. Erroll F. Rhodes [Grand Rapids: Eerdmans, 1987], p. 302).

[8]Carson, *The Gospel According to John*, p. 334.

(Scribes) are not mentioned elsewhere in John, but are often the allies of the Pharisees in the Synoptic Gospels. The Scribes were a class of Jews with professional knowledge in the Law, and were frequently called upon to make legal judgments in the community.[9] They smugly challenge Jesus to perform in an area where they are the acknowledged experts.

The accusers claim the woman was **caught in the act**. The expression **in the act** (ἐπ' αὐτοφώρῳ, *ep' autophōrō*) is found only here in the New Testament, but is relatively frequent in classical Greek. It literally means "in self-detection," but here means "during the undeniable act." This **act** was **adultery**. The author uses both the noun for adultery in verse 3 and the verb in verse 4. Someone had observed and apprehended this woman during the physical act of sexual infidelity. This rather embarrassing admission leaves us with several questions. Who caught her? Her husband? And where is the man involved, the other guilty party? We have no definite answers to these questions, but the editorial comment, **They were using this question as a trap, in order to have a basis for accusing him**, leaves us with the impression that the entire thing was a set-up, a matter of voyeuristic spies bursting out of closets at the indelicate illegal instant.

The accusers are not seeking to debate the woman's guilt or innocence (no one questions her guilt). They are attempting to thrust Jesus into the role of the sentencing judge. They remind him of the ancient and powerful legal code, that **Moses commanded us to stone such women**. Presumably the reference is to Leviticus 20:10, which decreed death for both the man and the woman judged to be guilty of adultery. This text, however, did not prescribe the method of execution. Their demand for stoning betrays their blood lust, for stoning was little more than mob lynching during this period of Roman occupation. The Roman overlords did not permit the Jews the legal authority for execution (John 18:31). Stoning was community justice at its worst, with too many executioners for the Romans to take effective action against the perpetrators.

The reader is left with a great deal of anticipation. What will Jesus do? Will he engage these legal scholars in an argument based

---

[9]See the excellent article by G.H. Twelftree, "Scribes," in *Dictionary of Jesus and the Gospels*, pp. 732-735.

on technicalities that might save the woman (such as a demand that her sex partner also be produced)? Will he break new legal ground that lessens this terrible penalty for adultery? Jesus does neither. Without a word he squats down and begins to write on the ground.

8:7-8. We are really given no hint as to what Jesus writes. Suggestions have included the Ten Commandments, or perhaps words that are clues to secret sins of the accusers. Telling us is not important to the writer, however. What are important are the spoken words of Jesus, "**If any one of you is without sin, let him be the first to throw a stone at her.**" The word for **without sin** (ἀνα–μάρτητος, *anamartētos*) is found only here in the New Testament, but simply means "non-sinful." Christians know that all men and women are sinners (see Romans 3:23). Ironically, the only legitimate candidate for hurling a rock at this woman is the speaker, Jesus himself, the sinless Lamb of God (John 1:29, cf. Heb 4:15).

8:9-11. Why do they leave? The text says that the words of Jesus cause the accusers to depart, in traditional order beginning with the oldest. The KJV includes the phrase, "being convicted by *their own* conscience,"[10] implying that these were men who could still feel some shame for their actions. Whether or not this is the case, none of them rises to the moral challenge issued by Jesus. None of them makes a claim to sinlessness by launching the first death rock. They withdraw in silent procession, admitting no guilt and discarding their human pawn, the terrified woman, like roadside litter.

The new cast of characters includes only two: Jesus and the woman. The Scribes and Pharisees are gone. Apparently the crowd has gone. There seem to be no disciples around Jesus. Jesus asks, "**Woman, where are they? Has no one condemned you?**"[11] The prosecution has abandoned its case, in effect moving for dismissal

---

[10]Although this reading, καὶ ὑπὸ τῆς συνειδήσεως ἐλεγχόμενοι, is included in the King James Version (and its modern derivative, the New King James Version) it is unlikely that it was originally part of the story of the adulterous woman. It is found in only a few Greek manuscripts, all very late, but did make its way into the *Textus Receptus*, the Greek text upon which the KJV is based.

[11]Again there is a considerable expansion of 8:10 in the KJV (based on the *Textus Receptus* Greek readings). This version tells us that Jesus "saw none but the woman," and that he asked "Woman, where are those thine accusers."

by their walkout. But one possible threat remains for her: the Rabbi Jesus. Indeed, Jesus now assumes the role of judge that has been thrust upon him. But he "rules from the bench," **neither do I condemn you.**" This judicial sense is developed even more as he commands her to **Go,** as if to say "you are free to go."

Does this mean that Jesus the Judge is winking at a serious sin, marital infidelity? Not at all. To "not be condemned" does not mean there is no guilt. In this case, it means the woman is indeed guilty, but has been forgiven. Jesus reminds the woman of this fact by his final words: **leave your life of sin,** perhaps more accurately translated, "sin no longer," or even, "quit sinning." Jesus has not rescued her so that she could be more careful and not get caught the next time she engaged in illicit sex. He is asking for her to demonstrate a heart of repentance, for repentance and forgiveness always go hand in hand in the Bible (see Mark 1:4; Luke 17:3-4; Acts 2:38; 8:22).

4. The Light of Tabernacles and Jesus' Great Confrontation with the Jews (8:12-59)

Jesus' Discourse at the Temple Treasury: Jesus the Light of the World and the Authority of His Testimony to Himself (8:12-20)

[12]When Jesus spoke again to the people, he said, "I am the light of the world. Whoever follows me will never walk in darkness, but will have the light of life."

[13]The Pharisees challenged him, "Here you are, appearing as your own witness; your testimony is not valid."

[14]Jesus answered, "Even if I testify on my own behalf, my testimony is valid, for I know where I came from and where I am going. But you have no idea where I come from or where I am going. [15]You judge by human standards; I pass judgment on no one. [16]But if I do judge, my decisions are right, because I am not alone. I stand with the Father, who sent me. [17]In your own Law it is written that the testimony of two men is valid. [18]I am one who testifies for myself; my other witness is the Father, who sent me."

[19]Then they asked him, "Where is your father?"

"You do not know me or my Father," Jesus replied. "If you knew me, you would know my Father also." [20]He spoke these words while teaching in the temple area near the place where the offerings were put. Yet no one seized him, because his time had not yet come.

8:12. If we leave out the adulterous woman passage (7:53–8:11) and proceed from 7:52 immediately to 8:12, we are left with a scene change, but apparently we are still in the context of the Feast of Tabernacles. This is important, because the temple celebration of Tabernacles in Jesus' day also included a ceremony in which four huge candlestick-torches were lit in the Court of the Women. The light of these candles was said to be so brilliant as to be seen all over the city of Jerusalem.[12] This indicates that this scene probably takes place after dark on the final day of the Feast. Therefore, Jesus has tied his claims to two of the great symbols of Tabernacles, the Water Ceremony (7:37-38), and this Light Ceremony (v. 12).

Jesus' statement here is the second of the great "I am" passages in John, **"I am the light of the world."**[13] This claim should not be unexpected for the reader of John, for Jesus as the Word of God has already been identified as a true and living light (1:4,5,7,8,9). John has already used light as a metaphor for the opposite of sin and evil (3:19-21). Light signifies the revelation of God, in particular the revealing of human sinfulness (which is appropriately seen as the sort of activities that are more comfortably done in darkness than light). Jesus promises that those who follow him **will never walk in darkness**, meaning that his believers will be freed from lives of sin. And this is a light not dependent upon having enough oil to burn, or fresh batteries, or a paid up electric bill. It is **the light of life.** Just as Jesus is the "Living Water" and the "Living Bread," he is the "Living Light," the eternal, unquenchable source of God's revelation.

---

[12]For a full account of the lighting of these candles see Barrett, *Gospel According to St. John*, p. 335.

[13]The first of the "I am" claims are those in chapter 6 associated with bread: "I am the bread of life" (6:35,48), "I am the living bread that came down from heaven" (6:51).

8:13. The public opponents are now **the Pharisees**. They failed in their attempt to have Jesus arrested (7:32) and have apparently come to Jesus for a public confrontation. They change their approach and attack the very credibility of his message and claim because he appears to have no supporting witnesses (see Deuteronomy 19:15).

8:14-18. Jesus responds by taking the discourse to a higher plane, to the spiritual level. His **testimony is valid** (ἀληθής, *alēthēs* = "true") because it has an "other-worldly" collaborating witness. This heavenly source for Jesus' mission is not developed at this point, but is used to point to the other, hidden witness to Jesus' claims, **the Father**. This variously understood "fathers" of Jesus and of his opponents will be a central element in the discussion that follows.

Jesus' statement, **"I pass judgment on no one"** may be the reason the story of the adulterous woman was inserted at this point in the text.[14] The statement itself, however, is seemingly at odds with Jesus' role as judge elsewhere in John (e.g., 3:19, 5:22, 9:39). The verb for **pass judgment** is κρίνω (*krinō*). Sometimes this apparent contradiction is explained as being caused by a dual meaning for *krinō*, either a legal, judicial sense or a casual sense of personal preference.[15] But such explanations are not necessary, for this text itself explains what Jesus means. He accuses the Pharisees of judging **by human standards** (literally, "according to the flesh"). Jesus' statement is intended to be elliptical, assuming this same phrase.[16] He is saying **I pass judgment on no one** [by human standards]. This is in keeping with his next statement, **if I do judge my decisions are right** [not humanly fallible and imperfect[17]] **because I am not alone. I stand with the Father who sent me** [his judgments are divine and therefore perfect].

---

[14]Brown, *John*, 1:340.

[15]See Bruce, *John*, p. 189.

[16]See Bultmann, *The Gospel of John*, p. 281.

[17]It is not necessary to read into this an Augustinian conclusion that human or "fleshly" judgments are inescapably sinful and bad because of the fallen, sinful nature of the flesh. An example of this is Carson's comment, "they are resorting to the criteria of flesh, of fallen mankind in a fallen world, without the compelling control of the Spirit (*The Gospel According to John*, p. 339).

Human judgments are always imperfect because of our finite knowledge and inability to reliably tell the difference between the truth and the lie. We are often fooled by the appearance of a situation. Such is the mistake of the Pharisees here. They judge Jesus upon his appearance and upon the basis of their prejudices. To them he is an unschooled Galilean peasant making extravagant claims. Their limited and biased human decision is to reject his claims. God, however, is never limited to this perspective. God always knows all the facts. God can instantly determine what is true and what is a lie (Rev 16:7). When Jesus claims to stand with the Father in the matter of judgment, he is claiming perfect judgment.

8:19-20. The identity of Jesus' Father will be a central point in the discussion that follows. John has already told us that Jesus' claim that God was his Father is considered blasphemy by his opponents (5:18). Jesus' answer here contains a central truth of the Gospel, that *truly knowing Jesus is equivalent to knowing God.*

The author identifies the location of this dialog as the **place where the offerings were put** (NRSV: "treasury"). Although this location cannot be pinpointed with certainty, it is likely a meeting area within the temple's Court of the Women.[18] This spot would have given the temple police an excellent opportunity to arrest Jesus (7:32). John gives a theological reason for their failure to do so, **because his time** [and therefore God's time] **had not yet come.**

Jesus' Attack on the Jews Who Disbelieved and the Origin of His Testimony and the Problem of Who He Is (8:21-30)

[21]**Once more Jesus said to them, "I am going away, and you will look for me, and you will die in your sin. Where I go, you cannot come."**

[22]**This made the Jews ask, "Will he kill himself? Is that why he says, 'Where I go, you cannot come'?"**

[23]**But he continued, "You are from below; I am from above. You are of this world; I am not of this world.** [24]**I told you that you**

---

[18]Note Mark 12:41, speaking of the same temple location in the story of the widow's offering. The fact that the widow was there would mean that this could not be one of the inner locations of the temple precincts where women were no allowed to go.

would die in your sins; if you do not believe that I am the one I claim to be,ᵃ you will indeed die in your sins."

²⁵"Who are you?" they asked.

"Just what I have been claiming all along," Jesus replied. ²⁶"I have much to say in judgment of you. But he who sent me is reliable, and what I have heard from him I tell the world."

²⁷They did not understand that he was telling them about his Father. ²⁸So Jesus said, "When you have lifted up the Son of Man, then you will know that I am the one I claim to be and that I do nothing on my own but speak just what the Father has taught me. ²⁹The one who sent me is with me; he has not left me alone, for I always do what pleases him." ³⁰Even as he spoke, many put their faith in him.

ᵃ24 Or *I am he*; also in verse 28

8:21-24. The dialog resumes although the time and place are indefinite. Presumably we are still in the temple precincts during the Feast of Tabernacles. Jesus begins by speaking of **going away**. This future "going away" (ὑπάγω, *hypagō*) has already been mentioned (7:33) and will continue to be an important theme in John (cf. 13:33). Jesus teaches that his time with the Jews is brief, and that he will go back to where he came from, to God (13:3). They are prevented from following him because of their **sin**. "Sin" is singular here (v. 21), because Jesus is speaking of the primary sin that disqualifies them, the sin of unbelief (v. 24).

The contrast between Jesus and his antagonists is laid out very clearly in verse 23. Jesus is **from above** (God/heaven). Those challenging him are **from below** = the **world** (*kosmos*). To follow Jesus is to believe in him and to overcome the deadly sin of unbelief. To remain in the world is to **die in** one's **sins**.

The "I am" focus of the text now begins to emerge even more clearly. What the NIV renders as **believe that I am the one I claim to be** in Greek is simply "believe that I am" (ἐγώ εἰμι, *egō eimi*). Here Jesus is not saying "I am _____." There is no predicate nominative, no noun complement for the verb. It is simply "I am." The full implications of this demand for faith will be unpacked in conjunction with verse 58.

8:25-29. In response to the "I am" claim of verse 24, they specifically ask Jesus, **"Who are you?"** While this might seem like an honest query, it is more likely an attempt to trick Jesus into saying something incriminating. Yet the question has a deeper significance for the reader of John. The "Who are you?" question was asked first of John the Baptist (1:19). Significantly, the Baptist responded, "I am not the Christ." John's answer, "I am not . . ." (ἐγώ οὐκ εἰμί, *egō ouk eimi*) is the opposite of Jesus' claim in this section, "I am" (*egō eimi*). At the end of the book (21:12), after the resurrection, the question "Who are you?" occurs a last time, but this time it need not be asked because the disciples *know* who Jesus is; he is the Lord.

Jesus' answer here is that he has been hiding nothing. He is the one speaking a word of judgment concerning them. Yet this judgment comes from his "sender" (God), and Jesus' job is to **tell the world**. John editorially alerts the reader that there is a level of misunderstanding at this point. The hearers do not understand that the one who sent Jesus is **his** [heavenly] **Father**. Jesus is aware of this misunderstanding, and responds to it with a prophetic word: **When you have lifted up the Son of Man** [i.e., after his crucifixion], **then you will know who I am** [literally, "that I am"]. The question of his identity will be answered unequivocally by the resurrection. The resurrection will be an unmistakable confirmation of the "I am-ness" of Jesus.

8:30. John tells us that **many put their faith in him** (NRSV: "many believed in him"). This is not the faith of serious, contemplative reflection, but rather an instantaneous, fickle faith of the hour. John often uses this expression to measure crowd reaction (see 4:39; 7:31; 10:42; 11:45; 12:42). Yet the rejection of Jesus that follows in 8:31-59 by this same group indicates that this is in no way "saving faith." It is not a deeply held, God-blessed commitment to follow Jesus no matter what the cost (cf. v. 12). Perhaps we would be more accurate if we translated **many put their faith in him** as *he was very popular with many*. This popularity is a lose-lose situation for Jesus. He loses because popularity is the wrong kind of "faith," not the true faith of discipleship. He also loses because this popularity is dangerous for him. It is directly tied to the jealousy and fear of the religious leaders and their attempts to arrest him. Jesus confronts this shallow acceptance head on in the next section.

Truth, Sin, Freedom, and the Children of Abraham (8:31-59)

³¹To the Jews who had believed him, Jesus said, "If you hold to my teaching, you are really my disciples. ³²Then you will know the truth, and the truth will set you free."

³³They answered him, "We are Abraham's descendants[a] and have never been slaves of anyone. How can you say that we shall be set free?"

³⁴Jesus replied, "I tell you the truth, everyone who sins is a slave to sin. ³⁵Now a slave has no permanent place in the family, but a son belongs to it forever. ³⁶So if the Son sets you free, you will be free indeed. ³⁷I know you are Abraham's descendants. Yet you are ready to kill me, because you have no room for my word. ³⁸I am telling you what I have seen in the Father's presence, and you do what you have heard from your father.[b]"

³⁹"Abraham is our father," they answered.

"If you were Abraham's children," said Jesus, "then you would[c] do the things Abraham did. ⁴⁰As it is, you are determined to kill me, a man who has told you the truth that I heard from God. Abraham did not do such things. ⁴¹You are doing the things your own father does."

"We are not illegitimate children," they protested. "The only Father we have is God himself."

⁴²Jesus said to them, "If God were your Father, you would love me, for I came from God and now am here. I have not come on my own; but he sent me. ⁴³Why is my language not clear to you? Because you are unable to hear what I say. ⁴⁴You belong to your father, the devil, and you want to carry out your father's desire. He was a murderer from the beginning, not holding to the truth, for there is no truth in him. When he lies, he speaks his native language, for he is a liar and the father of lies. ⁴⁵Yet because I tell the truth, you do not believe me! ⁴⁶Can any of you prove me guilty of sin? If I am telling the truth, why don't you believe me? ⁴⁷He who belongs to God hears what God says. The reason you do not hear is that you do not belong to God."

⁴⁸The Jews answered him, "Aren't we right in saying that you are a Samaritan and demon-possessed?"

⁴⁹"I am not possessed by a demon," said Jesus, "but I honor my Father and you dishonor me. ⁵⁰I am not seeking glory for myself; but there is one who seeks it, and he is the judge. ⁵¹I tell you the truth, if anyone keeps my word, he will never see death."

⁵²At this the Jews exclaimed, "Now we know that you are demon-possessed! Abraham died and so did the prophets, yet you say that if anyone keeps your word, he will never taste death. ⁵³Are you greater than our father Abraham? He died, and so did the prophets. Who do you think you are?"

⁵⁴Jesus replied, "If I glorify myself, my glory means nothing. My Father, whom you claim as your God, is the one who glorifies me. ⁵⁵Though you do not know him, I know him. If I said I did not, I would be a liar like you, but I do know him and keep his word. ⁵⁶Your father Abraham rejoiced at the thought of seeing my day; he saw it and was glad."

⁵⁷"You are not yet fifty years old," the Jews said to him, "and you have seen Abraham!"

⁵⁸"I tell you the truth," Jesus answered, "before Abraham was born, I am!" ⁵⁹At this, they picked up stones to stone him, but Jesus hid himself, slipping away from the temple grounds.

ᵃ33 Greek *seed*; also in verse 37   ᵇ38 Or *presence. Therefore do what you have heard from the Father.*   ᶜ39 Some early manuscripts *"If you are Abraham's children," said Jesus, "then*

8:31-32. Jesus now turns to the "believers" among the Jews, the ones with whom he is currently popular (according to our analysis above, v. 30). To these, Jesus now issues a new challenge, a call to discipleship. If they desire to truly be his **disciples**, they must **hold to** [his] **teaching**. The translation of the NIV (**hold to my teaching**) is particularly obscuring here, for the actual reading is more like the NRSV's "continue in my word." To be a disciple of Jesus, you must continue/remain/live in his word. This is more than studying Jesus' teachings or memorization of Scripture. Remember, John has presented Jesus as the Living Word of God (1:1,14). To "live in his word" means that we have a living relationship with Jesus.

In verse 32 we have some of the most famous words in the Gospel of John, **you will know the truth, and the truth will set you free**. These words have often been used in political settings to speak of national or personal freedom. Jesus, however, is not speaking of political truth or of political freedom. His call is to God's truth and to God's freedom.

What does it mean to **know the truth**? There is a close parallel here between "you will know that I am" (γνώσεσθε ὅτι ἐγώ εἰμι, *gnōsesthe hoti egō eimi*) in verse 28 and the **you will know the truth** (γνώσεσθε τὴν ἀλήθειαν, *gnōsesthe tēn alētheian*) in verse 32.[19] This truth is neither abstract nor propositional. It is personal. Jesus *is* the Truth (1:14; 14:3). Knowing him (v. 28) = believing in him (v. 24) = knowing the truth (v. 32). It is more than knowing some important facts about Jesus. It is knowing Jesus in an intimate, personal way. Such "knowing the Truth" is a primary characteristic of the Christian.[20]

Jesus promises that such a relationship **will set you free**. The verb here for **will set free** is ἐλευθερόω (*eleutheroō*). The word implies freedom from slavery, not political freedom. In this case, Jesus is speaking of spiritual slavery, the slavery of sin.

8:33. The listening Jews understand exactly that Jesus means freedom from slavery, although they again miss the spiritual dimension of his message. They retort that they **have never been slaves of anyone**. What selective memories! The history of Israel as a nation began with its rescue by God from the slavery of Egypt (see Exod 20:2; Deut 5:6; 6:12; 8:14; 13:5; Josh 24:17; Jer 34:3; Micah 6:4)! Doubtlessly the answer of the Jews is a proud assertion of national freedom, an illusion held despite the collar and chain of the Roman overlords. Yes, we are forced to pay taxes to Rome, and Roman legions occupy our country, but we are not their slaves!

8:34-38. Jesus does not engage in a political argument. He brings them back to the spiritual reality. Much more than freedom from Rome, they need freedom from **sin** (cf. Rom 6:16-18). Jesus as **the Son** offers this freedom. But he offers them more than the status of being freed slaves. They may be sons with a permanent place in the household of God. Jesus says that their sin is characterized by their refusal to **have room for my word**. This is the reverse of Jesus' description of his disciples as those who "remain in my

---

[19]Barrett, *The Gospel According to John*, p. 344.

[20]Bultmann, *The Gospel of John*, 435n. As Bultmann suggests, this characteristic is also mentioned in 1 John 2:21 and 2 John 1.

word" (v. 31). It is this stubborn refusal that keeps them enslaved by sin, and this enslavement may be seen in their readiness **to kill** Jesus. While such a charge is surprising to the reader, who has been told that this is a group of believers (v. 31), this perception of Jesus will be borne out in this passage (v. 59). Jesus goes further by revealing an underlying cause of this, that his **Father** is not their **father**.

8:39-41. The Jewish believers initially respond to this topic of parentage by reasserting **Abraham is our father**. Several things are implied in this claim. First, there was the immense pride of the Jews in the antiquity of their known ancestry. They were able to trace their genealogy back 2,000 years to a man who had a unique relationship with God. Second, Jesus' charge that they suffer enslavement is answered by this claim. Abraham is their true father, therefore they are his true sons. **We are not illegitimate children**, they say. We are from the legitimate line of Abraham, Isaac, and Jacob, not the bastard line of Ishmael. Third, there is a personal challenge to Jesus in the assertion that **Abraham is our father**. Presumably, as a Jew, Abraham is the "father" of Jesus. If Jesus is now talking about having a different "father" (v. 38), his very Jewishness is being called into question.

Jesus again brings the discussion back to the spiritual level. It is not good enough to be a physical descendant of Abraham if they are not spiritual descendants of Abraham. Abraham was obedient to the word and call of God, but when they hear Jesus speak God's word, they **are determined to kill** him. This is because on the spiritual level they are obeying a different father than the Father Abraham obeyed (and whom Jesus obeys).

Now they begin to understand that Jesus is speaking of spiritual matters. **"We are not illegitimate children,"** literally, "We are not born of fornication" (KJV). As with Abraham, **The only** [spiritual] **Father we have is God himself**.

8:42-45. Now Jesus' cryptic comments about the two fathers are clearly explained in very strong terms. Jesus can claim God as Father both because of origin (**I came from God**) and because of message (he is **telling the truth**). Their response to him indicates that they have a different father. They contemplate murder and reject the truth, showing that their spiritual father is **the devil**, not God.

The devil is given a lengthy description here. He is (1) **a murderer**, (2) one without regard for truth, (3) one devoid of truth, (4) a practicing **liar**, (5) and **the father of lies**. Jesus says that lying is the devil's **native language**, what moderns might call a "pathological liar." The last phrase, **because he is a liar and the father of lies** means literally "because he is a liar and the father of it" (cf. KJV). The "it" may refer to the word "liar," thus "the father of the liar," or, in context, "the father of liars." This fits better with the context of Jesus calling the devil the "father" of his hearers at the beginning of verse 44. When the Jews reject Jesus' message of truth they are accepting the devil as their moral and spiritual father, not God.

The word translated **devil** is διάβολος (*diabolos*), from which we get our word "diabolic." It means literally "slanderer," or "one who tells lies about other people."[21] Elsewhere in John it is used to refer to Judas, the false disciple (6:70; 13:2). It is a particularly fitting word for this section about lying and liars. The devil is also called a **murderer from the beginning**. The text does not explain exactly to what this is referring. Most commentators assume "the beginning" is a reference to the Garden of Eden,[22] and that Satan is a "murderer" by causing Adam and Eve to lose access to the Garden's tree of life (Gen 3:24), thus "killing" them (see Rom 5:12).

8:46. Can any of you prove me guilty of sin? The verb translated "prove guilty" (ἐλέγχω, *elenchō*) has a legal sense here, "Can any of you make a charge of sin against me stick?"[23] This is an important question both in the narrative and to the readers of the Gospel of John. Jesus must be the sinless, perfect Lamb of God to serve as a suitable sacrifice for the sins of the world (cf. Heb 4:15, 1 John 2:2). Jesus is only guilty of **telling the truth**, a truth they have rejected because of unbelief.

8:47. This verse gives a theological reason for the entire controversy. The opponents of Jesus have not believed him because they **do not belong to God** (literally they "are not from God."). This is

---

[21]*Diabolos* is equivalent to the Hebrew term שׂטן (*stn* or *satan*). This Hebrew word "Satan" is used in John 13:27. Both terms refer to Satan's role as the "Accuser," but have the connotation of the "slanderous accuser."

[22]E.g., Barrett, *The Gospel According to St. John*, p. 349; Carson, *The Gospel According to John*, p. 353.

[23]See a similar, legal use of ἐλέγχω in James 2:19.

180° from Jesus who came "from God" (v. 42). It is an additional way of saying that they have another father, not God.

8:48. Rather than try to convict Jesus of sin, the Jews answer with insults. The argument is now *ad hominem*, directly against Jesus on the personal level. How remarkably things have changed! Remember, these Jews were identified earlier as "believers" (v. 32), meaning (at least) those who had a favorable, popular opinion of Jesus. Now they have been deeply insulted by Jesus' charge that they are children of the devil. They respond by calling him **a Samaritan**, a bigoted, racially based slur in this context. The animosity between the Jews and their cousins, the Samaritans, would make this insult somewhat like calling a conservative American a "communist" during the height of the Cold War. They also accuse Jesus of being **demon-possessed** (literally, "you have a demon"). This is not a new charge (see 7:20). In effect they are saying, "Yes, there are two fathers here, but it is you who have the devil as your father." The implication is that Jesus is talking nonsense, craziness that can only be explained by the presence of the demonic.

8:49-51. Jesus immediately denies the charge of demon-possession. Again, Jesus claims that he is being persecuted merely for doing the will of God. But then he raises the stakes of the argument dramatically. He has already promised that the one who **keeps** his **word** will be free from sin (vv. 31-32). Now he adds the further implication that the one who **keeps** his **word** will escape **death**, the terrible future that the devil brought upon humankind (see comments on v. 44). The language at this point is actually much stronger than the NIV rendering, literally "he will certainly not see death, forever!" This is the equivalent of "eternal life" frequently mentioned in John (cf. 5:24).

8:52-53. The *ad hominem* attack is renewed, but now the Jewish opponents give some argumentation for their charge that Jesus is suffering from demonic madness. Their point is that even a child would know that the greatest and most faithful of the Jewish ancestors were people who died normal deaths.[24] Jesus' declaration that his message offers victory over death is seen as a claim to superiority

---

[24]The two possible exceptions being Enoch and Elijah, but they are not mentioned here.

over these faithful ancestors. Therefore they scold him with an angry and patronizing question, "Just **who do you think you are?**"

8:54-56. Jesus answers by returning to the theme of "knowing God." To know Jesus is to know God (cf. v. 19), because Jesus truly knows God. Jesus cannot deny this knowing relationship with God, for to do so would make him **a liar** and transfer his spiritual parentage to the devil.

The calmness of Jesus in the midst of this heated exchange is very striking. He only states facts and consequences. There is no self-serving, passionate oratory. Any "glory" he receives comes from God himself. In this, Jesus presents himself as the Ultimate Disciple of God, "**I know him and keep his word.**" Likewise, we, the readers, are being taught that we may know God by knowing Jesus (v. 19), and therefore we may keep God's word by keeping Jesus' word (v. 31). To be disciples of God we must simply be disciples of Christ.

Jesus finishes his answer by returning to Abraham. Yes, Abraham died, but with his eyes of faith Abraham anticipated the ministry of Jesus the Messiah. We have no exact biblical basis for Jesus statement, "**Abraham rejoiced at the thought of seeing my day.**" It may be an allusion to Abraham's typologically prophetic words to his son Isaac, "God himself will provide the lamb . . ." (Gen 22:8), for certainly Abraham must have rejoiced when the God-provided ram was discovered and the death of his son was averted. But there is more here than Jesus' mastery of Scripture. His words imply a relationship with Abraham as if he personally witnessed the patriarch's gladness when God gave Abraham foresight of the future Messiah.

In a larger sense, however, Jesus is giving us an important truth. The Old Testament (Abraham and the prophets) should be understood as anticipatory to Jesus himself. The Old Testament looks forward to the coming of God's Messiah with gladness and joy (cf. 1 Pet 1:10-12).

8:57. The Jewish opponents immediately pick up on the implication that Jesus has personal, intimate knowledge of Abraham. How could he be a friend of Abraham's? Abraham died nearly 2,000 years earlier and Jesus is not even **fifty years old**. The arithmetic just does not compute! Seemingly, they have caught Jesus in an obvious contradiction that would prove he is deluded and crazy.

8:58. At this point Jesus makes one of the most sensational statements in all of the recorded Gospels, and one of the most staggering statements in John, **"before Abraham was born, I am."** Unfortunately the NIV's unnecessary overtranslation here mars the beauty of the actual text, "before Abraham was, I am" (KJV, many others). This is the climax of the "I am" statements in John. Here the "I am" has two very important implications.

First, the "I am" (ἐγὼ εἰμί, *egō eimi*) is an intentional play upon the divine name of God found in the Old Testament. At the burning bush, when Moses asked God what his name was, the answer was "I am who I am" (Exod 3:14). In Hebrew, this name is יהוה (*YHWH*), which is sometimes transliterated as "Jehovah." It is based upon the Hebrew verb for "being," and so God's personal name revealed to Moses is literally "the I am." Here, as in verses 24 and 28, there is no complement for the verb. The statement is not "I am (something)." It is just **"I am."** Jesus has already said that one must "believe that I am" (v. 24) and "know that I am" (v. 28). To make these demands is to claim the name of God for personal use. In some ways Jesus is saying, "I am the '*I am.*' I am God."

Second, this claim has other enormous theological implications. By saying "before Abraham was, I am," Jesus is asserting his transcendence over time and history. He does not say "I was there with Abraham." In effect, he says "I *am* there with Abraham, and even before." Time does not limit God, and it does not limit Jesus. As John has said, "In the beginning was the Word" (1:1; cf. Rev 22:13).

We must be careful here. For us these theological truths can be dangerously overstated as in the simplistic bumper-sticker theology that says, "Jesus is Jehovah." Although we may not completely understand all the distinctions, Jesus does not remove everything that separates the Father from the Son. In fact if there is no difference between the Father and the Son, much of what Jesus has said in this chapter is nonsense: God is not his Father; he is his own "father." The Father did not send him; he sent himself. He does not know the Father; he knows himself. This results in a loss of the humanity of Jesus, a loss that orthodox Christianity has never tolerated. At the end of the day we must affirm both the full humanity and the full divinity of Christ, and that is precisely one of the major agendas of the Gospel of John.

8:59. Time for talking is now over as far as the Jews are concerned. They understand exactly what is at stake in Jesus' claim to be "I am." He has gone far beyond being an irritation to them. He is now a dangerous blasphemer, a threat that cannot be ignored. Mob violence mentality takes control, and preparations for a stoning/lynching begin. But this is not the time, place, or method for Jesus' death, so the text says he **hid himself** and he gets away safely (implying a miraculous escape).

JOHN 9

5. Healing of the Man Born Blind (9:1-41)

As is usual for John, a series of discourses is followed by a miracle account or "sign" (σημεῖον, *sēmeion*). The pattern of material for John has been called a sermon then a sign. Jesus' capacity to perform such miraculous signs was a testimony to his true identity (see 7:31; 9:16; cf. 6:14), although the exclusively sign-based faith seems to always be an inadequate faith for Jesus (2:23-24, cf. 6:2, 30). Also standard is a thematic connection between the discourses and the accompanying signs. Here Jesus' claim to be the "light of the world" (8:12) is followed by the healing of a blind man, the sixth sign.[1] John recounts the miracles of Jesus in much more detail than the Synoptic Gospels. This chapter is a good example, for it not only tells of the healing itself, but also of the ensuing controversies the healing caused.

The Setting (9:1-5)

[1]As he went along, he saw a man blind from birth. [2]His disciples asked him, "Rabbi, who sinned, this man or his parents, that he was born blind?"

[3]"Neither this man nor his parents sinned," said Jesus, "but this happened so that the work of God might be displayed in his life. [4]As long as it is day, we must do the work of him who sent

---

[1]The earlier "signs" are: 1. Water to Wine at Cana (2:1-11), 2. Healing the Royal Official's Son at Capernaum (4:43-54), 3. Healing the Lame Man in Jerusalem (5:1-14), 4. Feeding the 5,000 Men near the Sea of Galilee (6:1-15), 5. Walking on the Water (6:16-21).

me. Night is coming, when no one can work. ⁵While I am in the world, I am the light of the world."

9:1-2. John begins this story with no definite time or location. Presumably we are to understand the time as being near or during the Feast of Tabernacles (continuing from chapters 7 and 8), and the location being somewhere in the temple precincts. While moving along with his disciples, Jesus sees the blind man. This man apparently had a regular station for begging (v. 8), so it is likely that Jesus and his disciples had seen him before. It is not, therefore, the chance encounter with a blind man, but rather the question of the disciples that sets off this series of events.

The disciples ask, **"Rabbi, who sinned, this man or his parents . . . ?"** They assume that the blindness is much more than a physical disability. For them it is a curse of God caused by sin. The only question is whether this was a personal sin or an ancestral sin. A possible implication here is that the disciples believe he was conceived as a result of premarital sex, therefore his blindness would be the result of the sin of his parents.[2]

While it is correct that Scripture draws a connection between sin and physical suffering (see Exod 20:5; Deut 28:15; Ezek 18:4), it is incorrect to conclude that each and every instance of physical ailment or disability is the direct result of sin.[3] We know from our own experience that sinful lifestyle choices may lead to disease (e.g., AIDS contracted through sexually immoral behavior), but that certainly not all disease may be traced to sinful behavior (e.g., AIDS contracted through blood transfusion). We all suffer because of our own sins, and because of the general sinfulness of our culture, but this does not mean that degree of disability or illness is a measure of a person's moral failure. To hold such a view is a way to justify a lack of mercy and compassion to those who are suffering, since it assumes they suffer justly because of God's punishment for sin. Elsewhere, Jesus refuses to accept such a theology of sin and suffering (Luke 13:2-5).

---

[2] Cf. 2 Samuel 12:13-14 where the sin of David and Bathsheba is forgiven, but results in the death of their adulterously conceived child.

[3] See the thorough discussion of this topic in Hendriksen, *Exposition*, pp. 72-73.

9:3-5. Rejecting this "sin causes blindness" theology, Jesus offers an entirely different explanation for the man's disability. His blindness is an opportunity that **the work of God might be displayed in his life.** But does this mean that God somehow caused years of suffering in this man to set up a miracle for Jesus? Although verse 3 is often overtranslated in such a way as to give this impression (e.g., NRSV: "*he was born blind* so that God's works might be revealed in him"), this is not a necessary translation. A literal translation of verse 3 would be:

> *Jesus answered, "Neither this man sinned nor his parents,*
> *but in order that the works of God might be revealed in him."*

Jesus does not really comment on the cause of the man's blindness, but does say that the blindness will be used to reveal **the works of God.**

The additional comment of Jesus here tied this story to the "light of the world" discourse of chapter 8. Jesus and his disciples[4] must work during "daylight" (his lifetime) because there will come a time when his work will be finished (**night** = his death). In this case **the work of him who sent me** is to heal a blind man, hard evidence that Jesus is **the light of the world.**

The Healing (9:6-7)

[6]**Having said this, he spit on the ground, made some mud with the saliva, and put it on the man's eyes.** [7]**"Go," he told him, "wash in the Pool of Siloam" (this word means Sent). So the man went and washed, and came home seeing.**

---

[4]The KJV renders 9:4 as "I must work the works . . ." whereas most modern translations have something like the NIV's "We must do the work . . . ." The difference comes from the reading of the Greek *Textus Receptus,* which has the first person singular pronoun ("I") versus the choice of the modern Greek texts of the first person plural pronoun ("we"). The actual evidence in the early manuscripts is mixed, with such important witnesses as the Codex Alexandrinus and Minuscule 33 supporting "I," and Papyrus[66] and the Codex Vaticanus supporting "we." In this case the textual critic's rule of "the harder reading is to be preferred" comes to play, for it is easy to see why a scribe might have changed the text from "we" to "I," but difficult to see why a scribe would change it from "I" to "we."

9:6-7. Jesus' healing has some unusual elements. First, the blind man does not request the healing. It is initiated by Jesus. Second, while spit is used in two healings found in Mark (7:33; 8:23), there is no other healing where saliva is mixed with dirt to make a muddy ointment.[5] Third, the blind man is an active participant in the process by obeying the command to go and **wash in the pool of Siloam**.[6] This is an important detail for the story, because it means that he never actually sees Jesus until much later.

Siloam is the name of a public pool of water located about 600 yards south of the temple precincts. Its water source is the Gihon spring and it was fed through a tunnel carved during the reign of Hezekiah (cf. Isa 8:6). **Siloam** is significant to the narrative of John in several ways. First, John includes for the reader an interpretation of the Hebrew background of the word Siloam. It comes from the Hebrew verb *shalach* meaning **Sent**. John includes this detail but does not give a precise explanation as to why it is important. Probably he has in mind Jesus as the "sent one" of God (cf. v. 4). Second, water from the pool of Siloam was used in the water ceremony for the Feast of Tabernacles (see comments on 7:37-39). Therefore, there may be an intended connection to Jesus' claim at the feast to be the superior "Living Water"; i.e., he uses even the famous pool of Siloam for his purposes. Third, the waters of this pool were thought to have therapeutic power in ancient Jerusalem.[7] Clearly, however, it is not the waters of Siloam that heal the blind man. It is Jesus.

Interrogations of the Man (9:8-34)

Questions Posed by the Neighbors and Friends (9:8-12)

[8]**His neighbors and those who had formerly seen him begging asked, "Isn't this the same man who used to sit and beg?"** [9]**Some claimed that he was.**

---

[5]The ancient world, with its different hygienic standards, understood saliva to have certain medicinal powers. See various accounts in Barrett, *The Gospel According to St. John*, p. 358.

[6]This is more like the Old Testament healing of Naaman the leper (2 Kgs 5) than any of the other miracles of Jesus.

[7]See the section on Siloam in the article "Archeology and Geography" by Rainer Riesner in *Dictionary of Jesus and the Gospels*, pp. 41-42.

Others said, "No, he only looks like him."

But he himself insisted, "I am the man."

[10]"How then were your eyes opened?" they demanded.

[11]He replied, "The man they call Jesus made some mud and put it on my eyes. He told me to go to Siloam and wash. So I went and washed, and then I could see."

[12]"Where is this man?" they asked him.

"I don't know," he said.

9:8-9. The location of this scene is uncertain, but presumably the man has returned to his usual begging station in the temple area.[8] Jesus is no longer there, but there are others who quickly observe that the man is no longer blind. Some refuse to recognize a miracle in their midst and reason that it is not their blind man but a case of mistaken identity, one who **looks like him**. But the healed man will not allow this nonsense and insistently claims **I am the man**.

9:10. The "opening of the eyes" doubtlessly has deeper significance for the Gospel of John. Obviously it refers to physical restoration, but there is an intended symbolic meaning, too. To have one's eyes opened spiritually is to come to faith (cf. 12:40), to become a believer. The elimination of blindness was a true sign of the presence of God, for it was a miracle that could not be copied by false spiritual powers (see 10:21).

Here the crowd demands to know how the man received his ability to see. For him to say, "I just got better," or, "I don't know," would not be good enough. Either there is trickery afoot or something marvelous, and they must know.

9:11-12. In his simple yet persistent way the healed man relates the facts as he knows them: Jesus applies mud, commands washing in Siloam. He washes then sees. That's all he knows. He does not even know where Jesus has gone.

Preliminary Quizzing by Some Pharisees (9:13-17)

[13]**They brought to the Pharisees the man who had been blind.** [14]**Now the day on which Jesus had made the mud and opened the**

---

[8]The word "home" in the NIV's translation of 9:7 is a curious translation, not based on the Greek text.

man's eyes was a Sabbath. [15]Therefore the Pharisees also asked
him how he had received his sight. "He put mud on my eyes," the
man replied, "and I washed, and now I see."

[16]Some of the Pharisees said, "This man is not from God, for
he does not keep the Sabbath."

But others asked, "How can a sinner do such miraculous
signs?" So they were divided.

[17]Finally they turned again to the blind man, "What have you
to say about him? It was your eyes he opened."

The man replied, "He is a prophet."

9:13-15. The plot thickens. We now learn a crucial detail: all this
happened on a Sabbath day. The unusual process of this healing
will now be used as evidence of breaking the Sabbath. Jesus did
some mud-mixing (= work) and mud-daubing (= more work). At
Jesus' command the man walked to the pool of Siloam[9] (= still more
work) and washed off the mud (= even more work). All of this
strenuous "work" does not go unnoticed by the next group to question the healed man, some **Pharisees.**

Why do these folks defer to the Pharisees? Undoubtedly they
see this as a religious issue, and so they consult accessible religious
authorities. But there is no indication that the crowd has anticipated what would happen when the Pharisees were brought into
the situation.[10] That is, there is a shift from an investigation regarding the validity of a miracle to a case of Sabbath-breaking.

For a second time the man recounts his version of the healing,
this time even more briefly, "**He put mud on my eyes, I washed,
and now I see.**"

---

[9]A "Sabbath day's journey" was considered to be 2,000 cubits, or 2,000
paces (see BAGD under ὁδός, p. 553, cf. Acts 1:12), or roughly 1,000
yards. A walk from the temple precincts to the pool of Siloam and back
would have exceeded this distance, although this fact is not mentioned in
John 9.

[10]That the crowd had not begun to see this as a potential case of
Sabbath-breaking is not a conclusion shared by all authors. See Bruce,
John, 211-212, for one who agrees. For the view that the case is taken to
the Pharisees precisely because it was Sabbath-breaking, see Robert Kysar,
John's Story of Jesus (Philadelphia: Fortress, 1984), pp. 49-50.

9:16-17. The dialog quickly presents the two polarized views of Jesus: (1) he is a Sabbath-breaker and therefore a sinner outside of God's will, or (2) he is a miracle-worker and therefore an agent of the power of God. The presupposition that causes the conundrum is the belief that God would not use a sinful person as his miracle-working instrument.

Because they are divided on this issue, they turn back to the blind man to hear his opinion of Jesus. This is a sneaky attack upon him, an attempt to catch *him* in some sort of inconsistency. His answer, while inadequate, is very simple, **"He is a prophet."** This indicates the healed man is of the second opinion, that Jesus is some type of instrument of God. Historically prophets such as Elijah and Elisha were known to be miracle-workers, but the healed man's statement may mean nothing more than *he is God's man.*

The Man's Parents Questioned by the Jews (9:18-23)

[18]**The Jews still did not believe that he had been blind and had received his sight until they sent for the man's parents.** [19]**"Is this your son?" they asked. "Is this the one you say was born blind? How is it that now he can see?"**

[20]**"We know he is our son," the parents answered, "and we know he was born blind.** [21]**But how he can see now, or who opened his eyes, we don't know. Ask him. He is of age; he will speak for himself."** [22]**His parents said this because they were afraid of the Jews, for already the Jews had decided that anyone who acknowledged that Jesus was the Christ[a] would be put out of the synagogue.** [23]**That was why his parents said, "He is of age; ask him."**

[a]*22 Or Messiah*

9:18-19. The name of the interrogators now shifts from the Pharisees to **the Jews.** Whether or not this is a new, different group is open for some debate, but John is likely using "the Jews" as an alternate title for "the Pharisees."[11] These authorities now attempt

---

[11]On the side that the "Pharisees" of 9:13 and the "Jews" of 9:18 are the same group see Carson, *The Gospel According to John*, p. 368; Barrett, *The*

to solve their problem by questioning the validity of the miracle. They have deduced that since Jesus is an obvious Sabbath-breaker/ sinner, he could not have performed a God-powered miracle. Some sort of deception must be involved. Perhaps the whole thing is a setup and the man was never blind in the first place. John ties this action to his overall presentation by the simple words **did not believe**. Unbelief is still the heart of the matter.

The authorities summon **the man's parents**. They demand two things from them: positive identification of the man as their blind son and an explanation as to his current ability to see. The unspoken agenda is to catch them in a discrepancy that shows that there was no healing.

9:20-23. The parents give their testimony in the simplest terms. Yes, this is our son. Yes, he was born blind. But, no, we do not know how he received his sight nor will we offer any opinion about the source of the healing. You must ask him.

Why have they abandoned their son? John tells us that they are well aware of the danger here. **The Jews** (= the Pharisees) have already threatened anyone who confesses Jesus as Christ. Such persons were to **be put out of the synagogue** (ἀποσυνάγωγοι, *aposynagōgoi*, a word used only by John in the New Testament). The parents of the healed man dearly want to avoid this, even at the cost of deserting their son.

It is difficult for us to appreciate how devastating it was for a first century Jew to be "cast out of the synagogue." This was much more than dismissal or excommunication or disfellowshiping by a church today. A modern Christian who is "put out of a church," has the option of joining another church across the street and getting a fresh start. But even though first century Jerusalem had dozens of synagogues, to be **put out** of one was to be put out of all. As Butler says, "The excommunicated Jew was literally cut off from all social, religious, economic, or fraternal associations. His family counted him as dead."[12] For the Jewish community this ostracized

---

Gospel According to St. John, p. 360; Bruce, *John*, p. 214; even Bultmann, *The Gospel of John*, p. 335. (Although I have no way of knowing for certain, apparently Dr. Bryant saw two different groups by the way he constructed his outline of the book — MSK.)

[12]Butler, *John*, 2:89. For other references in John to being cast out of the synagogue see 12:42 and 16:2. Cf. Luke 6:22.

individual was like a Gentile, no longer a legitimate son of the covenant. This was an enormous threat for the parents of the healed man.

As many commentators have noted, this synagogue excommunication had a deeper significance for the early readers of John. By the time John's Gospel was published, the lines between synagogue and church had been drawn.[13] To confess Jesus as the Christ was grounds for expulsion from the Jewish synagogue. It is likely that many of these first readers had experienced this drastic action. After the destruction of the Jerusalem temple in AD 70, the synagogue took on even greater significance as a center for Jewish life. To be kicked out of the locus of one's heritage and existence was more like losing one's citizenship and identity than losing one's church membership.

The Man Questioned a Second Time by the Jews, and Excommunicated (9:24-34)

[24]A second time they summoned the man who had been blind. "Give glory to God,[a]" they said. "We know this man is a sinner."

[25]He replied, "Whether he is a sinner or not, I don't know. One thing I do know. I was blind but now I see!"

[26]Then they asked him, "What did he do to you? How did he open your eyes?"

[27]He answered, "I have told you already and you did not listen. Why do you want to hear it again? Do you want to become his disciples, too?"

[28]Then they hurled insults at him and said, "You are this fellow's disciple! We are disciples of Moses! [29]We know that God spoke to Moses, but as for this fellow, we don't even know where he comes from."

[30]The man answered, "Now that is remarkable! You don't know where he comes from, yet he opened my eyes. [31]We know

---

[13]For discussion as to whether or not synagogue expulsion for Christians was a practice introduced much later (thus making verses 22-23 an anachronistic reference to the author's time) see Carson, *The Gospel According to John*, pp. 369-372.

that God does not listen to sinners. He listens to the godly man
who does his will. ³²Nobody has ever heard of opening the eyes of
a man born blind. ³³If this man were not from God, he could do
nothing."

³⁴To this they replied, "You were steeped in sin at birth; how
dare you lecture us!" And they threw him out.

ᵃ24 A solemn charge to tell the truth (see Joshua 7:19)

9:24. Having gotten nothing from the parents, the authorities
turn back to the healed man. **"Give glory to God,"** they demand of
him. This does not mean that they have been convinced of the
validity of the miracle. It is their way of urging him to quit lying
(see the NIV footnote). As Dodd has written, "The formula seems
to be an exhortation to full and frank confession of truth."[14] For
them the truth is still to be revealed because they **know this man**
[Jesus] **is a sinner.**

9:25. With his stubborn, bulldog determination the healed man
sticks to his story. He does not know enough to make a judgment
on the sinfulness of Jesus, but he knows what happened to him. For
the last time he tells his story, this time in two basic steps, **"I was
blind but now I see."**

9:26-27. Still unsatisfied, the authorities demand further details.
They are hoping either to uncover evidence of a hoax or perhaps
to bully the man into denouncing Jesus. The answer of the healed
man now shifts in tone. He no longer responds with a respectful,
factual answer. He replies with defiance (*No, I won't tell you again!*)
and ironic sarcasm (*Are you desiring to become his disciples?*). This
baiting question works as intended by pushing the anger button of
the authorities and causing them to drop all false appearances of
impartiality.

9:28-29. The interrogation is at an end, for now **they hurled
insults at him**. This *ad hominem* attack must have reminded some of
John's early readers of their own experiences with the synagogue.

---

[14]Dodd, *Fourth Gospel*, p. 81. Dodd gives an example from the Jewish
Mishna of a condemned Jew urged to confess and give glory to the Lord
on the way to the place of execution. As Dodd says, "God is glorified by a
full confession."

The verb translated **hurled insults** is λοιδορέω (*loidoreō*, literally "to give abuse"). Elsewhere in the New Testament the verb is used to characterize Jesus as the abused one who did not return abuse (1 Pet 2:23) and by Paul to remind the Corinthians that he and his companions answered abuse with blessings (1 Cor 4:12).

As expected the authorities respond with hostility to the question about becoming Jesus' disciples. They accuse the healed man of being a disciple of Jesus (a false charge, at least at this point), indicating their obstinate belief that they are victims of a hoax concocted by Jesus and his disciples. Unable to debunk the "hoax," however, they resort to asserting their own credentials. They shout, **"We are disciples of Moses."** This was particularly true of the Pharisees (v. 13) who held to both the written law of Moses and the oral traditions associated with him. The yelling is almost like a one-sided version of a shouting match between two groups of fans at a sporting event: We're number one! We're winners and you're a loser! God spoke directly to our guy, but your guy? We don't even know where he came from! He has no credentials! He's a nobody!

9:30-33. The healed man is not battered into silence or compliance. He responds to the insults rationally but defiantly. He picks up on their claim that Jesus' origin is unknown by exclaiming, **"Now that is remarkable!"** He goes on to explain that which he thinks should be obvious to religious authorities. If Jesus does a Godlike miracle, he must be from God. Jesus is **the godly man who does** [God's] **will**, not a sinner. The word translated **godly man** is θεοσεβής (*theosebēs*, used only here in the New Testament) meaning "a God-worshiper" or "devout." This is a word used of Job in the LXX (Job 1:1), the one who "fears God."

The man's argument for Jesus turns upon medical evidence. **Nobody has ever heard of opening the eyes of a man born blind**. The implication is that his blindness was a congenital defect, a missing of some of the necessary equipment, although he certainly does not have this type of modern sophistication. Even today with our marvelous medical technology, there is no way to bring true sight to someone who is born with unformed eyeballs. Such creative restoration can only be done by the power of God. He will not let them escape the facts. He will not allow them to win through *ad hominem* attack. He demands that they acknowledge the miracle.

9:34. Inadvertently the authorities give their answer to the original question of the disciples, "Who sinned, this man or his parents?" (v. 2). **"You were steeped in sin at birth,"** literally "you were born entirely in sin." In other words both the man and the parents were and are hopeless sinners. They have found no holes in the man's story, no evidence of a hoax or mistake. Because they cannot win any other way, **they threw him out,** meaning they expelled him from the synagogue. This is likely full-blown excommunication, the act dreaded by the man's parents (vv. 22-23).[15]

Who Sees and Who Is Blind? Jesus' Answer (9:35-41)

[35]**Jesus heard that they had thrown him out, and when he found him, he said, "Do you believe in the Son of Man?"**

[36]**"Who is he, sir?" the man asked. "Tell me so that I may believe in him."**

[37]**Jesus said, "You have now seen him; in fact, he is the one speaking with you."**

[38]**Then the man said, "Lord, I believe," and he worshiped him.**

[39]**Jesus said, "For judgment I have come into this world, so that the blind will see and those who see will become blind."**

[40]**Some Pharisees who were with him heard him say this and asked, "What? Are we blind too?"**

[41]**Jesus said, "If you were blind, you would not be guilty of sin; but now that you claim you can see, your guilt remains.**

Clearly this story is about more than giving sight to a blind man. It is also about his odyssey of faith. The healed man begins by seeing Jesus as just a man (v. 11). He progresses until he sees Jesus as a prophet (v. 17). Finally he sees Jesus as the Son of Man, the one who must be believed and worshiped (v. 38). Physical sight without spiritual sight (faith) is still inadequate.

---

[15]For a summary of different durations of synagogue excommunication see Brown, *John*, 1:374. Although Brown is able to distinguish three types (one week, one month, permanent), it should be admitted that the evidence for this is later than the first century, and it is doubtful that there was any type of temporary excommunication at the time of Jesus' ministry.

9:35-38. The word of the healed man's excommunication has gotten back to Jesus, so Jesus seeks him out. We should remember that this man has never physically seen Jesus before, so he would only recognize him by voice. Again, Jesus initiates the contact and the conversation. Cutting through all the controversy, he simply asks the man, **"Do you believe in the Son of Man?"** There is no question but that "Son of Man" is assumed here to be a messianic title, the one sent from God (v. 4).[16] Obviously, the man knows that Jesus is the one who healed him. Therefore, when Jesus presents himself to him as the necessary object of faith, the man quickly responds with faith and worship (meaning he fell down before Jesus).

It may seem to us that this response is easy and natural, yet we should not be so quick with this conclusion. The man has received much from Jesus (his sight), yet he has lost much because of Jesus (his synagogue membership, which he would have finally been able to exercise as a whole man). His response is simple and beautiful, **"Lord, I believe."** This is the uncoerced confession of faith that Jesus seeks, and the type of confession that John seeks from his readers (cf. 20:31).

9:39. Jesus openly affirms that his ministry causes a **judgment** or a division among the people. Some believe and some don't. Now he reveals the true significance of his claim to be the "Light of the World." He is the spiritual Light. Some gain sight (faith) because of him. Others end up with no spiritual sight (unbelief) because of him. Such words are reminiscent of Isaiah, who frequently looks forward to the messianic period as a time when the blind receive sight (see also Isa 29:18; 35:5; 42:7):

> *I will lead the blind by ways they have not known,*
> *along unfamiliar paths I will guide them;*
> *I will turn the darkness into light before them*
> *and make the rough places smooth.*
> (Isaiah 42:16)

9:40-41. Jesus' conversation with the healed man seems to have been a private chat, but now we learn that there were plenty of eavesdroppers. **Some Pharisees** were there, and they pick up

---

[16]For a recent study of the "Son of Man" references in John see Ham, "The Title 'Son of Man,'" *SCJ*, 1: 67-84.

on the last pronouncement of Jesus. In one of the most ironic moments in the fourth Gospel, they ask, **"Are we blind, too?"** Spiritually blind Pharisees? This seems inconceivable to them, like an airline pilot who does not know how to fly, a truck driver who does not know how to drive, or a basketball star who does not know how to make a layup. The Pharisaic vocation was to be a spiritual guide for the nation of Israel.

Jesus recognizes a certain enlightenment among his adversaries, but shows that this makes their lack of faith all the more culpable. To be confronted by a mighty act of God (the healed blind man) and still reject Jesus cannot go unnoticed, so their **guilt remains** (literally, their "sin remains"). Again, the line is drawn between believers and unbelivers.

JOHN 10

6. The Feast of Dedication and the Shepherd Analogy (10:1-42)

There is no clear break between Jesus' words in 9:41 and 10:1, but this seems to be a new section with a new setting. In chapters 7-9 we were in Jerusalem during the Feast of Tabernacles. At 10:22 we are clearly at the Feast of Dedication, about three months after Tabernacles. But there are at least two reasons that we may see a section break beginning at 10:1. First, the subject matter has changed radically, with the topic of Jesus as the Shepherd being found on both sides of 10:22. This is in contrast to the topic of Jesus as the Light of the world in chapter 9, although admittedly the blind man of chapter 9 is referred to in 10:21. Second, the beginning words of Jesus at 10:1 are ἀμὴν ἀμὴν (*amēn amēn*, "I tell you the truth" in NIV). These are often the opening words of a response by Jesus to a question or comment from his audience. Yet there is no corresponding audience remark here, suggesting that we are breaking in on such a scenario.[1] While some may disagree, we will treat chapter 10 as a bridge unit of material set sometime between the Feast of Tabernacles and the Feast of Dedication.[2]

Jesus, the Sheepgate, and the Shepherd (10:1-21)

The age-old business of tending sheep would have been very familiar to most everyone in the ancient world. The key players in

---

[1]For detailed discussion of the sequence of events in chapters 9 and 10 see Brown, *John*, 1:388-390.

[2]For reasons to attach 10:1-21 to chapter 9 see Carson, *The Gospel According to John*, pp. 379-380.

this extended metaphor are the **shepherd** (v. 2), who is the daily caretaker and perhaps the owner of the sheep; the **sheep** (v. 2), who are understood both individually and as a **flock** (v. 12); the **watchman** (v. 3), who opens the door for the legitimate shepherd; the **thief** (v. 1), who illegitimately steals sheep; the **hired hand** (v. 12), who abandons the sheep at the first sign of danger; and the **wolf** (v. 12), who terrorizes and scatters the sheep. The primary setting is the **sheep pen** (v. 1), an enclosure for the nighttime safety of the animals with a single entrance or **gate** (v. 1).

Figures from Shepherd Life (10:1-6)

[1]"I tell you the truth, the man who does not enter the sheep pen by the gate, but climbs in by some other way, is a thief and a robber. [2]The man who enters by the gate is the shepherd of his sheep. [3]The watchman opens the gate for him, and the sheep listen to his voice. He calls his own sheep by name and leads them out. [4]When he has brought out all his own, he goes on ahead of them, and his sheep follow him because they know his voice. [5]But they will never follow a stranger; in fact, they will run away from him because they do not recognize a stranger's voice." [6]Jesus used this figure of speech, but they did not understand what he was telling them.**

10:1. The sheep-herding analogy is introduced with the "anti-shepherd," the one who is a **thief and robber**.[3] This one violates the safety of the **sheep pen** by stealth, climbing over the walls. It is not

---

[3]The distinction between these two words is difficult to maintain in English translation. "Thief" (κλέπτης, *kleptēs*, from which we get the word "kleptomaniac") is one who steals another's property. Judas is referred to as a thief in John 12:6. "Robber" (λῃστής, *lēstēs*) also has the connotation of thievery, but more along the lines of a highwayman, outlaw, bandit, or pirate. See John 18:40 where Barabbas is identified as a *lēstēs*. Some scholars have maintained that such persons were bandit/revolutionaries, but cf. Luke 10:30 where the word is simply used of rural bandits who prey upon their own people.

clear that Jesus has any individual or group in mind as the **thief.**[4]
The point seems to be more that there is only one legitimate way to
enter, and that is through **the gate** (θύρα, *thyra*, the word from
which we get our English word "door"). Presumably there is but a
single entry to the sheep pen. One who attempts to enter by any
other way has only the goal of "sheep-stealing" in the sense of
taking sheep away through false, deceptive leadership.

10:2-3. In contrast to the thieves, the **shepherd of the sheep**
enters by the gate/door. He is recognized by the **watchman** (θυρωρός,
thyrōros, literally a "doorkeeper"). Such recognition comes about
because he is the true shepherd and not some type of imposter. His
legitimacy is further validated by the fact that the **sheep listen to
his voice.** The relationship between the shepherd and his sheep is
so deep and longstanding that he can **call** them **by name.** The
depiction here is of a shepherd beginning the workday by gaining
entrance through the night watchman and calling each of his
beloved sheep by names he has given to them (Fuzzy? Wooly?
Sparky?) . They respond to his summons, and he leads them out to
their daily grazing area. The story pictures a community sheep pen
where several flocks are housed together. During the night the
sheep from various flocks may have intermingled. This shepherd
does not separate his sheep by walking through the pen, but by
standing at the gate and calling their names.

10:4-5. The pastoral scene is developed even further. Now the
sheep are gathered outside the sheep pen and the shepherd leads
them to pasture. An important detail here is the ancient practice of
the shepherd leading his sheep rather than driving them.

10:6. John labels this speech as a παροιμία (*paroimia*), translated
as **figure of speech.** In the book of John a *paroimia* is not just any
type of figure of speech, it is a "concealed saying" with a hidden
meaning[5] requiring interpretation. John uses *paroimia* as the opposite

---

[4]See Carson, *The Gospel According to John*, pp. 381-382, for a detailed but
ultimately unconvincing argument that "thieves and robbers" is a reference
to the religious leaders of Israel who were "fleecing the sheep." Carson
bases this on his reading of Ezekiel 24 and other Old Testament passages.

[5]See the Apocryphal Sirach 39:3 where the author speaks of the wise
man who seeks out the "hidden meanings" (ἀπόκρυφα, *apokrypha*) of
paroimia.

of παρρησία (*parrēsia*) which means to speak "plainly," or without figures of speech (cf. John 16:25, 29). To understand this as a "parable" is probably somewhat misleading. John never uses the Greek word for "parable" (παραβολή, *parabolē*); it is found only in the Synoptic Gospels. To be sure this is an allegorical saying and some of Jesus' parables are allegories (e.g., the Sower Parable), but the presentation is quite different here. Allegory "speaks of one thing in the guise of another."[6] Jesus does not intend to rehearse farming techniques here, but to take standard shepherding practices and use them to illustrate his ministry.

The basic allegorical framework has been set up (shepherd = leader and protector, sheep = followers and dependents). Jesus goes on to expand and even modify the allegory because **they did not understand what he was telling them.**

Explaining the Figure (10:7-18)

Jesus is the Sheepgate (10:7-10)

[7]Therefore Jesus said again, "I tell you the truth, I am the gate for the sheep. [8]All who ever came before me were thieves and robbers, but the sheep did not listen to them. [9]I am the gate; whoever enters through me will be saved.[a] He will come in and go out, and find pasture. [10]The thief comes only to steal and kill and destroy; I have come that they may have life, and have it to the full.

[a]*9 Or kept safe*

10:7-9. Jesus begins unpacking the allegory by stating that he is the **gate**. This is the third great "I am + identifier" claim of Jesus in the book of John. He has claimed to be the "bread of life" (6:48). He has claimed to be the "light of the world" (8:12). Now he asserts **"I am the gate for the sheep**" (v. 7) and simply **"I am the gate**" (v. 8). As John Ashton has maintained, all of these "I am (something)" statements are "miniature Gospels."[7] That is, these

[6]Janet Martin Soskice, *Metaphor and Religious Language* (Oxford: Clarendon, 1985), p. 55.

[7]Ashton, *Fourth Gospel*, p. 186.

metaphorical descriptions of Jesus are all insights into his mission as the one who comes to give life to believing humankind (see v. 10, cf. 3:16, 20:31).

In this case the **gate** is not so much an armor-plated security door as it is a limited, unique entryway. Jesus says **"whoever enters through me** (the gate) **will be saved."** The important verb translated "save" is used relatively infrequently in John.[8] Here it is a future passive form (σωθήσεται, *sōthēsetai* from the verb σῴζω, *sōzō*). The future tense indicates a promise for Jesus' hearers and for John's readers. For a sheep "salvation" is characterized by the idyllic state of safe passage and ready pasture. For the believer "salvation" is to be under the perfect shepherding care of God, to trust him for every need. As elsewhere in John, Jesus is presented as the only true way to gain access to this matchless relationship with God.

The image of Jesus as the gate or door contributes to a controversial aspect of John's Gospel: the exclusive claims of the gospel. It is fashionable today to speak of many ways of accessing God. In our age of tolerance as a virtue, many want to say that all religious roads end up at the same place. Buddhism, Islam, Native American Spirituality, African Traditional Religions, Mormonism; all of these are spiritual journeys that sincere seekers may travel to find God. To think that one religion is superior to others smacks of the social error of intolerance. And to even suggest that one religion is true and others are false is narrow-minded bigotry that has no place in our postmodern ethic. Yet that is precisely what is going on here. Jesus is not just a new way or a better way to God. He is **the gate**, the *only way* to God (see comments with 14:6; cf. Acts 4:12). It is this truth that makes his statement the "Gospel in miniature."

10:10. As Jesus has already made clear, there are those who do not have the best interests of the flock at heart. These thieves come to **steal and kill and destroy.** Jesus, on the other hand, brings **life** and it is life **to the full.** The word translated **to the full** is περισσός (*perissos*), and is a rather straightforward comparative word. It is

---

[8]The Greek verb σῴζω is used in John 3:17; 5:34; 10:9; 11:12; 12:27 and 12:47 for a total of 6 occurrences. Compare this with 13 times for Matthew, 13 times for Mark, and 15 times for Luke.

much better translated "abundant" or simply "more."[9] What is this "more-life," though?

It is common to interpret abundant life as meaning that the Christian believer enjoys a superior life than that of the nonbeliever. Presumably this means the believer is happier, more content, and even more materially blessed than his nonbelieving neighbor is. This verse may be pushed to say that Christianity is not a life of self-denial, but of self-affirmation. The "abundant life" becomes a justification for a life of "Christian hedonism."

Yet such an interpretation would be in contradiction to both the experience of believers who have suffered horribly for their faith and for the general call to self-denial that is found elsewhere in the teaching of Jesus.[10] A more correct meaning of *perissos* would see the "abundant life" as equivalent to the frequent expression in John, "eternal life." This life is abundant in the sense that it is inexhaustible. It never runs out. And it is never-ending because it comes from the eternal, inexhaustible God. Therefore it may be superior to the unbeliever's life in that it is full of hope and of the blessings of God. We have victory over sin because of the "super-abundance" of God's grace (Rom 5:20).[11] There is a sense that living the God-directed life is akin to following the instruction manual rather than rebelliously making our own way. Eugene Peterson has aptly rendered this final phrase of verse 10 as "more and better life than they ever dreamed of."[12]

Jesus is the Good (or Model) Shepherd (10:11-18)

[11]"I am the good shepherd. The good shepherd lays down his life for the sheep. [12]The hired hand is not the shepherd who owns

---

[9]To translate *perissos* as "more" or "greater" is the most common usage in the New Testament. For example see Matthew 5:37,47; Luke 7:26; 12:48; 1 Corinthians 12:23; Hebrews 6:17.

[10]For example see the injunction to deny self and bear one's cross found in all three of the Synoptic Gospels: Matthew 16:24; Mark 8:34; Luke 9:23. Luke tells us that this self-denial is to be a daily occurrence.

[11]In Romans 5:20 Paul uses a word related to *perissos* to describe grace, the verb ὑπερπερισσεύω (*hyperperisseuō*), meaning "to super-abound," even beyond "more-ness."

[12]Eugene Peterson, *The Message* (Colorado Springs: NavPress, 1993).

the sheep. So when he sees the wolf coming, he abandons the sheep and runs away. Then the wolf attacks the flock and scatters it. [13]The man runs away because he is a hired hand and cares nothing for the sheep.

[14]"I am the good shepherd; I know my sheep and my sheep know me — [15]just as the Father knows me and I know the Father — and I lay down my life for the sheep. [16]I have other sheep that are not of this sheep pen. I must bring them also. They too will listen to my voice, and there shall be one flock and one shepherd. [17]The reason my Father loves me is that I lay down my life — only to take it up again. [18]No one takes it from me, but I lay it down of my own accord. I have authority to lay it down and authority to take it up again. This command I received from my Father."

10:11. Now we get the fourth great "I am (something)" claim of John's Gospel, **"I am the good shepherd,"** repeated in verse 14. To be "good" in this sense is more than the opposite of "bad." The word translated **good** is καλός (*kalos*), and has the connotation of "beautiful" or "lovely." In what sense, though, is Jesus the "beautiful shepherd"? Raymond Brown and others have pointed out that for Greek speakers *kalos* referred to an ideal, perfect beauty. Thus Brown's translation is "I am the model shepherd."[13] Jesus is describing himself as the ideal, model shepherd to whom other human shepherds should be compared. This text, then, certainly speaks to those called to "shepherd" the flock today.

The word translated **shepherd** is ποιμήν (*poimēn*). To understand Jesus as the Great Shepherd (Heb 13:20) is a cherished image in the church, found in some of the earliest known Christian art in the Roman catacombs. The early church remembered Jesus as its shepherd (see Matt 9:36; 26:31; 1 Pet 2:25), and applied Old Testament passages to him that pictured God as shepherd (particularly Psalm 23). To be a shepherd or pastor is also a function of church leadership (*poimēn* is the word translated "pastor" in Ephesians 4:11), and John surely intends his readers to use the Jesus the Model Shepherd as a standard by which to evaluate their own leaders.

---

[13]Brown, *John*, 384, 386.

Jesus cuts to the chase with his description of what it takes to be the **Good Shepherd.** He **lays down his life for the sheep,** meaning he would be willing to die voluntarily for his sheep. On the lips of Jesus these words are prophetic of his coming crucifixion. For John's readers these words and the explanations that follow are also standards by which church leaders should evaluate themselves.

10:12-13. Jesus contrasts the model shepherd with the **hired hand.** The Greek word translated **hired hand** is μισθωτός (*misthōtos*), meaning "one who works for money." Such a person was neither a slave nor an owner, but only a casual laborer with no personal interest in the sheep. At the first sign of danger such a person **runs away.**[14]

In some church traditions this condemnation of the "hireling" has been used as an argument against paying pastors or ministers. Yet surely this pushes the analogy far beyond Jesus' intention. No one would argue with the position that ministry motivated solely by money is unacceptable. Pastors should not be mercenaries for money, hired guns working for the highest bidder. And it is true that the church has always had some workers of independent means who did not need to be paid for their ministry, but this has been the exceptional situation, not the norm. To deny the validity of paid ministry does not square with other teachings in the New Testament (see Luke 10:7; 1 Tim 5:18). The church has a duty to adequately compensate those whom it employs in full-time ministry. Ministers may be called to suffer for the Gospel, but should this be economic suffering at the hands of the church that has called them to serve it?

Another character in this analogy is the **wolf.** The wolf has an important characteristic for this analogy. It kills and eats sheep, and they are defenseless against it. Because of this the wolf inspires fear among the sheep (and the hired hand), so when sheep see or smell a wolf coming they run in all directions. A reality of the church is that there will always be "wolves" (= nonbelievers) around who are not sheep. These wolves will prey upon the trust and innocence of Christians, and will seek to destroy the fellowship of the church by

---

[14]The bravery of the shepherd and cowardice of the hired hand would have surely reminded the Jewish readers of the fearless exploits of David the shepherd as related in 1 Samuel 17:34-36.

driving believers apart. The terrifying image of wolves in the sheep flock is used elsewhere as a metaphor for evil persons who come into the church with predatory motives rather than as fellow believers (Matt 7:15; Acts 20:29).

10:14-15. Jesus explains the shepherd/sheep illustration a little more with some additional insights. Just as a crucial dynamic in shepherding is that the sheep **know** and trust the shepherd, so it is with Jesus and his true disciples. The word translated **know** here is the common Greek verb γινώσκω (*ginōskō*). To "know" a person in this *ginōskō* sense means to have an intimate relationship built on experience. In the Gospel of John, those who refuse to **know** Jesus in this way are "of the world," and beyond salvation (see 1:10). But this is a two-way relationship, for Jesus' "knowledge" of his disciples (= commitment to them) is so great that he will die for them. This is a divine relationship patterned after the way Jesus' **Father** knows him (cf. 8:55).

10:16. In slightly cryptic fashion Jesus expands the sheep/shepherd analogy to portray the Good Shepherd as being something of a sheep baron. His business is bigger than it may seem, for he has more than one pen full of sheep. These **other sheep** are surely a reference to believers outside of the nation of Israel, the coming Gentile church. But ultimately there will be only **one flock**/church, for there is only **one shepherd** (cf. Eph 2:14-16). In the early church a primary cause for disunity was the Jew/Gentile division (see Acts 15). In the modern church we manage to find all kinds of things to divide the church, but the principle of Jesus still remains. In the end we are **one flock** because we have **one shepherd** (cf. Eph 4:3-6).

10:17-18. This is a deeply theological comment on the relationship between the **Father** and Jesus his Son. This relationship is characterized as love built on complete obedience (cf. Heb 5:8). Jesus willingly offers his life of his **own accord**. But the **Father** has cooperated in this mission by granting Jesus the necessary **authority** both to **lay down** his life (sacrificial death) and **to take it up again** (resurrection).

Are we left, then, with understanding that the relationship between Jesus and the Father is one of love earned by obedience, a type of merit theology? Surely not, for just as we cannot earn our salvation through works, it seems ridiculous to imagine that Jesus earns the Father's affection by his obedient deeds. There is something much deeper afoot here. Part of what Jesus is saying is that he does something God could not do without him. The immortal God cannot die, but the human Jesus can die for the sins of the world. Through Jesus God is able to do what he dearly wants to do: redeem his beloved children from sin. Jesus does this with his eyes fully open as to the dreadful personal cost, but also being aware of the commanded necessity of his sacrificial act.

Response to Jesus' Explanation: Rejection of Jesus by the Jews (10:19-21)

[19]**At these words the Jews were again divided. [20]Many of them said, "He is demon-possessed and raving mad. Why listen to him?"**

[21]**But others said, "These are not the sayings of a man possessed by a demon. Can a demon open the eyes of the blind?"**

10:19. Ironically, while Jesus has just spoken of future unity between Jews and Gentiles, now there is a schism within his Jewish hearers. The polarization that Jesus' words seem to bring to his listeners has only become more intense.

10:20. The unbelievers issue another *ad hominem* attack. Don't listen to anything this man says because he **is demon-possessed and raving mad**. These two items were tied closely together for John's original readers. The accusation would have been particularly offensive to any self-respecting Jew in the ancient world. It is a description of a pagan prophet, one who has abandoned Judaism and converted to heathen practices. This is the man who has given over to a pagan god (the δαιμόνιον, *daimonion*, cf. Acts 17:18). The result is that he speaks madly (from the verb μαίνομαι, *mainomai*). In Wisdom 14:28 this word is used to describe the raving ecstasy of pagan worship. So the opponents are saying, in effect, "We don't have to even listen to this man because he is, after all, crazy!"

Why listen to him? This is both the question of Jesus' opponents in this story, and John's question to the reader. Why listen? Because, as Peter said, Jesus has "the words of eternal life" and is the "holy one of God" (6:68, 69).

10:21. Those aligned with Jesus are not buying this *ad hominem* attack. They still remember that Jesus healed the blind man, and that no one could show the healing to be a fraud. For them this goes far beyond demonic power, and would certainly not be the accomplishment of a crazy person. **Can a demon open the eyes of the blind?** As in verse 20 the question has a rhetorical function for the reader. In the text this ends the section, but we are not left to wonder what the answer might be. The form of this sentence in Greek expects a negative answer, therefore the answer is "No, of course not!"

Jesus at the Feast of Dedication (10:22-39)

Jesus the Messiah (10:22-31)

²²**Then came the Feast of Dedication**ᵃ **at Jerusalem. It was winter,** ²³**and Jesus was in the temple area walking in Solomon's Colonnade.** ²⁴**The Jews gathered around him, saying, "How long will you keep us in suspense? If you are the Christ,**ᵇ **tell us plainly."**

²⁵**Jesus answered, "I did tell you, but you do not believe. The miracles I do in my Father's name speak for me,** ²⁶**but you do not believe because you are not my sheep.** ²⁷**My sheep listen to my voice; I know them, and they follow me.** ²⁸**I give them eternal life, and they shall never perish; no one can snatch them out of my hand.** ²⁹**My Father, who has given them to me, is greater than all**ᶜ**; no one can snatch them out of my Father's hand.** ³⁰**I and the Father are one."**

³¹**Again the Jews picked up stones to stone him,**

ᵃ**22** That is, Hanukkah   ᵇ**24** Or *Messiah*   ᶜ**29** Many early manuscripts *What my Father has given me is greater than all*

10:22-23. The scene has now clearly shifted to **the Feast of Dedication** and Jesus is back in the Jerusalem Temple. The **Feast of Dedication** is mentioned only here in the New Testament (ἐγκαίνια, *enkainia*, meaning literally "rededication"). As the NIV footnotes indicate, this is the festival known today as "Hanukkah." This is an eight-day festival beginning on the twenty-fifth of the Jewish month of Kislev (usually falling in our month of December).

Hanukkah is the celebration of a major event in Jewish history (see 1 Macc 4:36-61). In 164 BC Judas Maccabeus drove the Syrian Greeks out of Judea and reestablished Jewish control over Jerusalem and the temple. Judas and his men cleaned out the temple, which had been used for pagan worship by the Syrians. They rebuilt the holy altar (which had been used to sacrifice pigs) and declared an eight-day feast. According to Jewish legend, they could only find one container of undefiled oil for the temple candlestick (menorah), enough for one day. But through a miracle of God the lights burned for the entire eight days, thus giving rise to a popular name for Hanukkah, the "Festival of Lights." The **Feast of Dedication** was a nationalistic celebration, yet a hollow one at this time of Imperial Roman domination.

John mentions that it was **winter**, the rainy season in Palestine. This explains why Jesus is operating in **Solomon's Colonnade**, one of the large covered porches in the temple precincts (see Acts 3:11; 5:12).

10:24. Jesus is encircled by **the Jews**, apparently his Jewish opponents (cf. v. 31). In the midst of the nationalistic atmosphere of Dedication, they confront Jesus and demand that he make a declaration about his messiahship. This must be done **plainly** (παρ–ρησία, *parrēsia*), which is somewhat the opposite of παροιμία (*paroimia*, "hidden saying") in verse 6. The motives of these Jews are uncertain to the reader. Perhaps they are secretly hoping that Jesus might claim the heritage of the Festival of Lights and become the new Judas Maccabeus in response to Roman oppression. But it is clear in the narrative that follows that Jesus does not see them as legitimate believers (vv. 25-26).

10:25. "**I did tell you . . . .**" In the Gospel of John there is no record of Jesus openly claiming to be the Messiah to the Jerusalem crowds previous to this verse (although see 1:41; 4:25-26). But rather than verbally claiming to be the Messiah, Jesus points out that **the miracles I do in my Father's name speak for me**. "Miracles" is an NIV overtranslation of the Greek word ἔργα (*erga* = works, deeds). Certainly "miracles" are among his deeds, but his claim is that everything he has done is a proclamation and confirmation that he is the

Messiah. Those now challenging him are without excuse for their unbelief, because the miraculous deeds of Jesus are obvious signs of God's approval of him (see 3:2; 7:31).

10:26. Jesus returns to the analogy of the first half of chapter 10: he is the shepherd, his followers/believers are his sheep. Jesus says, **"You do not believe because you are not my sheep."** The language here is troubling to Christians who do not believe in unconditional predestination. Those of us in this position would be more comfortable if Jesus had said, "You are not my sheep because you do not believe."[15] Yet there is no grammatical ambiguity in this verse, no possibility of Greek sleight of hand to moderate the force of this language. As difficult as it may seem to us, there is a sense in John that faith is ultimately under the control of God (i.e., omnipotence) and not all are willing to believe (see comments at 12:39). Yet we should also recognize that the sheep analogy is rather fluid, and to read a full-blown doctrine of predestination into this text is not justified.

10:27-29. In verse 10 Jesus said that he came to give his sheep "abundant life." Now this is explained more completely. He gives **eternal life** (ζωὴν αἰώνιον, *zōēn aiōnion*). This promised life is a gift; it is not earned by the sheep/followers of Jesus. Here we get two of the characteristics of **eternal life**. First, those who have it will **never perish** (οὐ μὴ ἀπόλωνται, *ou mē apolontai*). This is an emphatic construction in Greek, meaning, "They will certainly never be destroyed." This is the language of immortality. A second characteristic of **eternal life** is that **no one can snatch them out of my hand**. For Jesus this is because these sheep are his with the consent and cooperation of the Father, and **no one can snatch them out of my Father's hand**. Salvation can never be stolen or taken away. This is true "eternal security," that we rest safely in the arms of God without any fear that the Destroyer, Apollyon,[16] can either destroy us or steal us from God.[17] Who can separate us from the love of God? None! (Rom 8:38-39).

---

[15]For an exposition of this verse from a predestinarian point of view see Carson, *The Gospel According to John*, p. 393; Leon Morris, *The Gospel According to John*, The New International Commemtary of the New Testament (Grand Rapids: Eerdmans, 1971), p. 520.

[16]Revelation 9:11. This name, Apollyon ('Απολλύων) is from the same verbal root as the word translated "perish" in John 10:28.

[17]There is no need to read a doctrine of eternal security here that

10:30. The enormity of the statement, **"I and the Father are one,"** within the context of the Gospel of John is difficult to over-state. There are several reasons for this. First, this is a type of "I am" statement for Jesus, this time "we are." There is a continued reference to the divine name of Jehovah God, I AM (see comments on 8:58). Second, there is a further divine claim in obvious allusion to the famous *Shema* of Deuteronomy 6:4, "Hear O Israel: The LORD our God, the LORD is one." This was the monotheistic bed-rock of the Jewish religion, that there was only one God. Yet Jesus has now included himself in this monotheistic confession. He does not mean that he has achieved some type of mystical unity with God that might be more at home with Hinduism. He is speaking of the very essence of his relationship with the Father, that there is a sameness about them. The theological math here is that $1 + 1 = 1$ (cf. 1:1). And yet a third element in this should be noted. Jesus does not say, "I am the Father." Although he makes a mighty claim here, he continues to maintain a certain level of distinction between the Father and himself.

10:31. For a second time the mighty claims of Jesus cause the unbelieving Jews to prepare for a mob action, a stoning/lynching (cf. 8:59).

Jesus the Son of God (10:32-39)

³²but Jesus said to them, "I have shown you many great miracles from the Father. For which of these do you stone me?"

³³"We are not stoning you for any of these," replied the Jews, "but for blasphemy, because you, a mere man, claim to be God."

---

amounts to "once saved, always saved." Such a doctrine cannot be logically separated from the doctrine of God's unconditional election. As John Calvin himself wrote, "But we are not to forget that the stability of our sal-vation is not in us but in the secret election of God." It is true that many Christians understand faith to be a day-by-day thing, and live in fear of dying on a "bad day." This is a misconception. God views the whole of a person's life and does not base his judgment of our saved relationship on any one day. God's grace is sufficient to cover anything up to a personal rejection of his provision in Christ. We should rejoice in the promise here of the permanent, divine nature of our salvation, a salvation that cannot be destroyed or taken away by Satan or anyone else.

³⁴Jesus answered them, "Is it not written in your Law, 'I have said you are gods'^a? ³⁵If he called them 'gods,' to whom the word of God came — and the Scripture cannot be broken — ³⁶what about the one whom the Father set apart as his very own and sent into the world? Why then do you accuse me of blasphemy because I said, 'I am God's Son'? ³⁷Do not believe me unless I do what my Father does. ³⁸But if I do it, even though you do not believe me, believe the miracles, that you may know and understand that the Father is in me, and I in the Father." ³⁹Again they tried to seize him, but he escaped their grasp.

^a*34* Psalm 82:6

10:32. Rather than make an immediate escape, Jesus asks these Jewish unbelievers to justify their desire to kill him. **Many great miracles** is literally "many good works." Jesus knows that he has *said* many things to infuriate them, but what has he *done* that would deserve death? His actions have been **from the Father**.

10:33. The Jews do not deny that Jesus has done great deeds, but this is not their complaint against him in this case. They think he must die for the religious crime of blasphemy.[18] Blasphemy is deliberate disrespect for God and was a capital offense according to Jewish Law (Lev 24:16). The blasphemous offense was that Jesus made a **claim to be God**. One might quibble over the exact nature of Jesus' statement in verse 30, "I and the Father are one," but they are correct in seeing this as a potentially blasphemous declaration. If Jesus is just a **mere man** his claims are offensive, delusional, and punishable by death.

10:34-36. What follows is one of the most difficult passages for interpretation in all the New Testament. In response to the objection from the Jews that he has claimed to be God, Jesus quotes Psalm 82:6, "**I have said you are gods**." We may identify at least three separate issues in attempting to understand this passage.

First, does Jesus intend us to understand that he is no more than a human being with a special relationship to God? Or, conversely,

---

[18]This is the only place where the term "blasphemy" (βλασφημία) is used in the book of John, but this charge against Jesus is also found in the Synoptic Gospels. See Matthew 9:3; 26:65; Mark 2:7; 14:64; Luke 5:21.

does he mean that there are many other humans who have similar status with God as he does? The key to answering these questions is to look more closely at Psalm 82. In a somewhat poetic way, this short psalm is a pointed message to the corrupt judges of the nation of Israel.[19] They "defend the unjust and show partiality to the wicked" (Psalm 82:2). The word of God to them in 82:6 is a reminder that while they are "gods" (i.e., entrusted with godlike authority to judge) and "sons of the Most High" (a parallel expression to "gods," but a bit more human), they are still very mortal (82:7) and therefore subject to the ultimate judgment of God himself (82:8). The logic of Jesus, therefore, is that if Jewish Scripture itself refers to human judges as "gods," he has every right to refer to himself as **God's Son**. For Jesus, this is even more justified because **the Father set** [him] **apart as his very own and sent** [him] **into the world**. Jesus' point is that he can hardly be accused of blasphemy if he has Scriptural precedent for his terminology.

A second issue is the question as to why Jesus says this Old Testament passage is in the **Law** when it is actually in the Psalms. Did Jesus (or John) make a mistake here? But to see Jesus as making a common human error is unnecessary here. While the **Law** is most specifically the first five books of the Old Testament, the concept had a range of meaning for first century Jews. It could refer to the specific legal code of books like Leviticus, or the books attributed to Moses (Genesis through Deuteronomy), or even Jewish Scripture in a broader sense. This last meaning is intended by Jesus here, and would have included the Psalms. This may be seen in Jesus' qualification of the **Law** as the writings of those **to whom the word of God came**.

Third, we should consider the implications of the parenthetical statement, **and the Scripture cannot be broken**. This verse has been a key text for those who hold to a doctrine of biblical inerrancy. The battle cry of inerrantists has been "Scripture cannot be broken!"[20]

---

[19]For an alternate interpretation that the "gods" of Psalm 82 are not the judges of Israel but the angels of God's heavenly court, see Ashton, *Fourth Gospel*, pp. 147-150. Although Ashton cites some interesting material from Qumran, he is ultimately unconvincing in explaining why the "gods" of Psalm 82 would be charged with corruption if they were angels, or why the psalmist would be giving his readers a picture of God scolding angels at all.

But is this a justified use of the text or illegitimate proof-texting? As one who is a friend of the doctrine of inerrancy, my views here are certainly biased. Over a century ago, Charles Hodge defined the doctrine of inerrancy as the position that Scripture is "free from all error whether of doctrine, fact, or precept." While some of the terminology used by defenders of inerrancy may be of relatively recent origin, the idea that Scripture is without error has been the historic position of the church until the last two centuries. This comes from the view that God is an active participant in the writing of Scripture. Since God can neither make mistakes nor be deliberately deceptive, we must conclude that Scripture is without error. According to inerrantists, this position may be traced back to Jesus himself as demonstrated in this verse.

Having said these things, it should be admitted that there are some difficulties in using this verse as the cornerstone for a doctrine of inerrancy. First, it is a parenthetical, side comment of Jesus with little exposition. If John had chosen to lift this comment up a bit higher or do more with it, we would feel more secure about using it as a primary support for such a crucial doctrine. Second, Jesus does not really say that "Scripture is without error." He says that **Scripture cannot be broken** (from the verb λύω, *lyō*, meaning "break, destroy, or loose"). The obvious meaning of this verb is to say something like "Scripture cannot be thwarted" or "Scripture

---

[20]The literature on inerrancy is vast and of vastly varying quality. The classic treatment is still to be found in B.B. Warfield, *The Inspiration and Authority of Scripture* (Phillipsburg, NJ: Presbyterian and Reformed, 1948). This is a compilation of articles written by Warfield during the time he was a professor at Princeton Theological Seminary from 1887-1921. John 10:35 was Warfield's key text. A survey of the current state of the inerrancy question is found in D. A. Carson, "Recent Developments in the Doctrine of Scripture," in *Hermeneutics, Authority, and Canon*, eds. D. A. Carson and John D. Woodbridge (Grand Rapids: Zondervan, 1986): 1-48. Other useful books for those wishing to research the topic of inerrancy include Norman L. Geisler, ed., *Inerrancy* (Grand Rapids: Zondervan, 1980). See particularly the article by Paul D. Feinberg, "The Meaning of Inerrancy." See also Ronald Youngblood, ed., *Evangelicals and Inerrancy: Selections from the Journal of the Evangelical Theological Society* (Nashville: Nelson, 1984) and Roger R. Nicole and J. Ramsey Michaels, eds., *Inerrancy and Common Sense* (Grand Rapids: Baker, 1980).

cannot be annulled" (NRSV). Yet there is more here than such a simplistic reading of *lyo*. Jesus has quoted Scripture as an answer to his critics, and his exact intent is to dare them to say, "Well, Scripture is wrong in this case." It would seem that something like our doctrine of inerrancy is shared by *both Jesus and his Jewish opponents*. To disavow any sort of doctrine of inerrancy is to hold a different view of Scripture than that of Jesus as found in this text.

10:37-38. Jesus makes one last appeal for faith from his opponents. He says that even if they are not willing to accept Jesus for what he says and who he is, they cannot neglect **the miracles**. If they would begin with this type of faith, they **may learn and understand** the central truths that **the Father is in** [Jesus] **and** [Jesus] **is in the Father.** Start with accepting that God was doing the miraculous through Jesus, and move to deeper faith.

10:39. Jesus has talked his way out of being stoned to death (v. 31), but now there is an attempt **to seize him**, probably a "citizen's arrest" to turn him over to the proper authorities. He does not allow this but escapes, although we are not told specifically that this is a miraculous escape.

Jesus in Retrogression and Progression Simultaneously (10:40-42)

⁴⁰Then Jesus went back across the Jordan to the place where John had been baptizing in the early days. Here he stayed ⁴¹and many people came to him. They said, "Though John never performed a miraculous sign, all that John said about this man was true." ⁴²And in that place many believed in Jesus.

10:40. Jesus retreats to a safe place, the former site of John the Baptist's activities (probably "Bethany across the Jordan," see 1:28). This is in the region called Perea, meaning, literally, "across [the Jordan]." This region was nominally controlled by Herod Antipas, the ruler of Galilee, rather than the Roman governor.

10:41-42. The influence of John the Baptist is still present in this place when Jesus arrives. They remember that John had spoken about Jesus (see 1:15,26-27,32-34,36; 3:27-30). The result is that this becomes a community of believers in Jesus.

JOHN 11

7. Lazarus and the Passover Plot (11:1-57)

Chapter 11 of John is the celebrated story of bringing a dead man named Lazarus back to life. For the careful reader, however, it is more than a dramatic miracle account. It is one of the most important explorations of the subjects of life, death, and resurrection found anywhere in Scripture.

Lazarus (11:1-44)

Setting (11:1-6)

¹Now a man named Lazarus was sick. He was from Bethany, the village of Mary and her sister Martha. ²This Mary, whose brother Lazarus now lay sick, was the same one who poured perfume on the Lord and wiped his feet with her hair. ³So the sisters sent word to Jesus, "Lord, the one you love is sick."

⁴When he heard this, Jesus said, "This sickness will not end in death. No, it is for God's glory so that God's Son may be glorified through it." ⁵Jesus loved Martha and her sister and Lazarus. ⁶Yet when he heard that Lazarus was sick, he stayed where he was two more days.

11:1-3. John quickly sets the scene for the following story. A dear friend of Jesus has become seriously ill and his sisters have relayed this information to Jesus. Jesus is probably still in Perea where we left him in chapter 10. Bethany is a village on the backside of the Mount of Olives, about 1 ½ miles east of Jerusalem. It is not the same as the Bethany in the Jordan River Valley (1:28), but a small village on the road to Jericho.[1]

Positioning the Mary/Martha/Lazarus household within the context of other New Testament accounts is an interesting challenge. We know from Luke 10:38-42 that Jesus had previously enjoyed the hospitality of this family. In John 12:1-10 there is another story involving this trio that tells of Mary's expensive anointing of Jesus (hinted at in v. 2). In Matthew 26:6-13 and Mark 14:3-9 a similar story is told, although the setting is the house of Simon the leper, and the woman is not identified as Mary. In Luke 7:36-50 there is another similar story about a woman washing Jesus' feet with her tears in the house of a man named Simon. This has led some to conclude that Lazarus and Simon the leper are the same person, or that Martha was married to Simon the leper. We have no way of proving or disproving either of these claims, and so they must remain interesting speculations.[2] At any rate, Mary, Martha, and Lazarus are presented as close personal friends of Jesus, and their house in Bethany may have served as Jesus' local headquarters when he was visiting Jerusalem.

Lazarus was a relatively common name in the ancient Jewish world, occurring also in Josephus and in Luke 16:20. It is a first century version of the Old Testament name "Eleazar," meaning "God is a help." This was the prestigious name of one of the sons of Aaron (see Exod 6:23).

11:4-6. The reader is confronted with an unexpected reaction from Jesus. We, the readers, expect him to rush over to Bethany and heal Lazarus before it is too late. Yet he delays **two more days**. John indicates that the human heart of Jesus aches to go to Bethany immediately for he **loved**[3] **Martha and her sister and Lazarus** (cf.

---

[1]Modern Bethany is named "El 'Azariyeh," an Arabic version of the name "Lazarus." It is the site of an ancient church and a tomb that is traditionally shown to tourists and pilgrims as the tomb of Lazarus. Nearby burial inscriptions have been found that include the names Mary, Martha, Lazarus, and Simon (cf. Matthew 26:6), but this proves nothing more than that these were common names in ancient Palestine.

[2]See discussion of this issue in David A. Fiensy, *The Message and Ministry of Jesus* (Lanham, MD: University Press of America, 1996), p. 275. For an attempt to reconcile the various anointing stories see Brown, *John*, 1:449-454.

[3]The word for "loved" here is the Greek verb ἀγαπάω (*agapaō*). It has no

v. 36). Jesus seems to know that Lazarus will die, but that this series of events **will not end in death**. There is a larger purpose here, to demonstrate **God's glory** and the resulting glorification of **God's Son**.

The Greek word for **glory** is δόξα (*doxa*), and is used by John in several ways. First, in general, it refers to the self-existent, unique splendor and power of God. This is the sense in verse 4, **God's glory**. Second, the proper recognition of this *doxa*/glory by human beings may have the sense of "praise." This is partially the sense in 7:18, where the healed blind man is commanded to "Give glory to God." It is also the thrust of 11:40, where Jesus informs Martha that her act of faith would allow her to "see the glory of God." Third, there is a type of *doxa*/glory that is granted by God. In particular this is the *doxa*/glory that God gives to his Son, Jesus. It is this glory that is being referred to in verse 4, **that God's Son may be glorified through it**. It is also seen in 8:54, "My Father, whom you claim as your God, is the one who glorifies me." God is the source of such glory, but God's Son reveals this divine glory to humankind (see 1:14). This divine glory is particularly seen in the miracles of Jesus (2:11). A fourth type of *doxa*/glory is the praise given by people to other people for human accomplishments. This cannot compare with the glory of God. Jesus rejects this type of praise/glory when it is only on the human level and fails to take God into account (see 5:41,44 where the NIV translates *doxa* as "praise"). Now, Jesus anticipates a painful episode, the death of his friend, but also knows that God will use the agonizing occasion to reveal his glory to those who believe (v. 40).

Jesus' Discussion with the Disciples (11:7-16)

[7]Then he said to his disciples, "Let us go back to Judea."

[8]"But Rabbi," they said, "a short while ago the Jews tried to stone you, and yet you are going back there?"

[9]Jesus answered, "Are there not twelve hours of daylight? A man who walks by day will not stumble, for he sees by this world's

---

implied sexual overtones, but refers to spiritual, unselfish love. This goes against Mormon claims that Mary and Martha were among the wives of Jesus.

light. ¹⁰It is when he walks by night that he stumbles, for he has no light."

¹¹After he had said this, he went on to tell them, "Our friend Lazarus has fallen asleep; but I am going there to wake him up."

¹²His disciples replied, "Lord, if he sleeps, he will get better." ¹³Jesus had been speaking of his death, but his disciples thought he meant natural sleep.

¹⁴So then he told them plainly, "Lazarus is dead, ¹⁵and for your sake I am glad I was not there, so that you may believe. But let us go to him."

¹⁶Then Thomas (called Didymus) said to the rest of the disciples, "Let us also go, that we may die with him."

11:7-8. After waiting two days, Jesus announces that the time has come to return to Judea (the region of both Jerusalem and nearby Bethany). Jesus does not immediately tell his disciples that this return is related to Lazarus, and they seem to assume he wants to return to Jerusalem itself, perhaps to resume his teaching ministry in the temple. The disciples recognize this as a dangerous proposition and remind Jesus that "a short while ago the Jews tried to stone you" (8:59; 10:31).

11:9-10. The answer of Jesus to the disciples' warning and reluctance seems puzzling, but may be readily understood. In short, Jesus is saying that as far as his ministry is concerned, it is still daylight (= safe) and therefore they may return to Judea in safety.[4] This is a reminder, however, that this period of safety will not last long. A typical daylight period is divided into **twelve hours**, and then darkness comes. As Bultmann explains, "he must use to the full the short time that still remains to him on earth"[5] (cf. 9:4).

11:11-13. John relates a miscommunication between Jesus and his disciples. Jesus tells them that Lazarus is **asleep**, and they eagerly take this statement at face value. If the problem with Lazarus were merely illness-induced slumber, he would naturally wake up after his body had healed sufficiently. But the narrator

---

[4]See Butler, *John*, 2:141.
[5]Bultmann, *The Gospel of John*, p. 399.

informs us that Jesus was using **sleep** as a euphemism for **death**, a frequent figure of speech in the Bible.[6]

11:14-15. Because of the confusion Jesus breaks out of the sleep/death metaphor to tell them **plainly** that, "**Lazarus is dead.**" The reader is not told how Jesus has learned that Lazarus had died, so we are left to assume that this is a demonstration of supernatural knowledge by Jesus. But again we are reminded that Jesus knows more than the simple *fact* of his friend's death. He also knows the *purpose* of his death. What happens next has the purpose of causing belief, bringing a deeper, saving faith to the disciples (and to the readers, cf. 20:30-31). If Jesus had healed a sick Lazarus, there would have doubtlessly been approval of Jesus and *doxa*/praise for him. But to witness the miracle of reviving a corpse would leave no room for any doubt that God himself was behind these mighty acts of Jesus. This was to the glory of God (v. 4).

11:16. The disciples are beginning to put this all together. The known facts are simple: Judea is dangerous, Lazarus is dead, and Jesus is determined to go to Bethany. Although Jesus has indicated in figurative language that he intended to bring Lazarus back to life ("I am going there to wake him up," v. 11), it is not at all clear that the disciples have understood or believed this. Perhaps they interpret Jesus' travel plans as a dangerous but understandable desire to be with an esteemed family during a time of tragedy.

Thomas, however, does not waste time in analyzing Jesus' motives. At what may have been a point of wavering and indecision among the disciples, he boldly confronts them, "**Let us also go, that we may die with him.**" His words stand as both a foreshadowing of the coming death of Jesus and as a challenge to the readers: true faith in Jesus is a faith that would be willing to die for him. Elsewhere Jesus exhorts his followers to shoulder their crosses and

---

[6]Cf. Luke 8:52. There is a sense that death is a type of "sleep," for the believer knows that resurrection follows (see 1 Cor 15:51). However, this euphemistic way of referring to death as sleep is not always theologically or eschatologically driven. We still refer to a veterinarian "putting a dog to sleep" when we mean that the dog is "put to death" or "killed." For other New Testament references to death as sleep in the New Testament see Matt 27:52; Acts 7:60; 13:36; 1 Cor 7:39; 11:30; 15:6,18,20; 1 Thess 4:13-15; 2 Pet 3:4.

"follow me" (Matt 16:24), which is much more than a call to put up with the annoying people in one's life. The cross was a well-known instrument of death and Jesus was calling would-be followers to die with him. Likewise, Paul reminds us "I die every day" (1 Cor 15:31), and that "I have been crucified with Christ" (Gal 2:20). As Francis of Assisi wrote in the 13th century:

> . . . it is in giving that we receive
> It is in pardoning that we are pardoned
> It is in dying that we are born
> To Eternal Life.

This is the first appearance of **Thomas** in John. The name **Thomas** is related to the Aramaic word for "twin." John supplies his Greek name, **Didymus**, which also means "twin." Apparently this man was one of a pair of twins, although we do not have any record of his twin brother or sister.[7] "Twin" was a nickname like "Shorty" or "Red." There is extensive early tradition that Thomas's given name was Judas, but this information does not appear in the New Testament. Thomas is often remembered by Christians as the Great Doubter (because of his actions in 20:24-29) but this is an incomplete picture of him. He should be remembered here for his bravery and loyalty. He will not allow his Lord to face death alone.

Jesus and Martha: Jesus the Resurrection and the Life(11:17-27)

[17]On his arrival, Jesus found that Lazarus had already been in the tomb for four days. [18]Bethany was less than two miles[a] from Jerusalem, [19]and many Jews had come to Martha and Mary to comfort them in the loss of their brother. [20]When Martha heard

---

[7]In the Coptic *Gospel of Thomas* the introduction reads, "These are the secret words which the living Jesus spoke, and (which) Didymus Judas Thomas wrote" (B. Metzger translation). Some scholars have contended that this indicates the author of this book believed that *Jesus and Thomas were twin brothers!* This is also a claim of the much later apocryphal *Acts of Thomas*, which reads, "But the Lord said to him: I am not Judas which is also called Thomas but I am his brother." The Greek version of the *Acts of Thomas* refers to Thomas as the "twin brother of Christ." Such references are doubtlessly fanciful elaborations on Thomas's name (the "twin").

that Jesus was coming, she went out to meet him, but Mary stayed at home.

²¹"Lord," Martha said to Jesus, "if you had been here, my brother would not have died. ²²But I know that even now God will give you whatever you ask."

²³Jesus said to her, "Your brother will rise again."

²⁴Martha answered, "I know he will rise again in the resurrection at the last day."

²⁵Jesus said to her, "I am the resurrection and the life. He who believes in me will live, even though he dies; ²⁶and whoever lives and believes in me will never die. Do you believe this?"

²⁷"Yes, Lord," she told him, "I believe that you are the Christ,ᵇ the Son of God, who was to come into the world."

ª*18* Greek *fifteen stadia* (about 3 kilometers)   ᵇ27 Or *Messiah*

11:17-20. The Bethany situation is quickly established for the reader. Jesus arrives on the scene four days after the body of Lazarus has been put in a tomb. This was not a burial as we are accustomed to, where a corpse is placed in a casket and buried under six feet of dirt in a cemetery. Ancient tombs in this region were often small rooms or expanded caves (see v. 38) carved out of the relatively soft rock and used by families for many generations. Because there was no way for the ancient Palestineans to delay the decomposition of a corpse along with its unpleasant odor, burial was usually done quickly, sometimes on the day of death.

Although the body is buried, the period of mourning is still in full swing. John records that **many Jews** from Jerusalem have come **to comfort** the bereaved sisters of Lazarus. The grief is such that only Martha comes to greet her famous friend, Jesus. Her sister, Mary, stays behind.

We are not told who these **Jews** are, except they seem to be from the city. They are not pictured as antagonistic here, but on a mission of mercy. Later, some of them become believers (v. 45). That John would record their attendance here means that they are not just any Jews, but "important Jews." Their presence testifies to the status of the family of Lazarus among the Jewish society in and around Jerusalem.

11:21-22. "If you had been here my brother would not have died." Martha's words to Jesus are both a grief-generated scolding and a statement of faith: "Why weren't you here when I needed you?" and "You have access to God's power over even the worst illness." Her further statement, "**I know that even now God will give you whatever you ask**," is more difficult to understand. Some interpreters have understood this as an expectant prodding for Jesus to bring Lazarus back from the dead.[8] Yet this seems unlikely in light of Martha's later reluctance to open the tomb (v. 39). More likely this is a statement meaning, "even though you didn't get here in time to heal my brother, I still believe you are able to heal severe sickness through the power of God."

11:23-24. Martha interprets Jesus' words as something other than a prediction of Lazarus' imminent resuscitation. She thinks Jesus is just sharing comforting words at the time of death, playing upon the popular Jewish belief in a final resurrection. For her it is as if Jesus is saying, "You'll see Lazarus again some day, when God brings us all back to life!" This statement puts Martha in the sphere of the ancient Pharisees rather than the Sadducees when it comes to a belief in resurrection (see Acts 23:6-8; cf. John 5:28-30). Such a belief was commonly held among the general Jewish population. This may indicate that the **Jews** of verse 19 were primarily Pharisees, and that Martha had been given similar words of hope for the future many times already. Perhaps there is a certain disappointment for Martha here, a fear that the best Jesus can do is to mouth "funeral words" that she has already heard many times.

11:25-26. But Jesus has much more to offer than a fuzzy hope in a future resurrection. He stuns Martha and the reader with a double-barreled "I am" statement: "**I am the resurrection and the life.**" This is the fifth great "I am + identifier" statement in John.[9] He is not a prophet awaiting the final resurrection. His claim is that he *is* the living resurrection.

The Greek word for resurrection is ἀνάστασις (*anastasis*[10])

---

[8]E.g., Butler, *John*, 2:145.

[9]The earlier "I am + identifier" claims are "I am the bread of life" (6:48 and elsewhere in chapter 6), "I am the light of the world" (8:12), "I am the gate/door" (10:7,8), and "I am the good shepherd" (10:11,14).

[10]From which we get the name "Anastasia" = the resurrection one, i.e., the one hoping in resurrection.

meaning, literally, to "stand up." It can have the sense of "getting up" after one falls down (cf. Luke 2:34). Most often in the New Testament it is applied to the future event of The Resurrection, a time when all human beings will come alive again for purposes of eternal judgment (see John 5:29; Acts 24:15). Jesus goes far beyond this common Jewish belief in future resurrection, however, to assert that the power of resurrection exists in his very person (see Phil 3:10). It is through Jesus' own victory over death that we have access to a future resurrection of our own (1 Cor 15:21-22).

The Scriptures teach the biblical doctrine of bodily resurrection. That is, although we will all die, after death God will bring us back to life. We will receive new, resurrection bodies (1 Cor 15:44). This gives purpose and hope to life and to eternity. This is because of our Lord Jesus who is **"the resurrection and the life."** As C.E. Warner put it many years ago in a little poem:

> And Death's not the end — 'neath the cold black sod —
> 'Tis the Inn by the Road on our way to God.

11:27. The response of Martha is not an off-base rambling, unrelated to the issues of life and death. It is precisely what Jesus is looking for. He has promised victory over death for those who believe in him (v. 26). Believe in him how (or what)? Martha's answer has three parts, and each part is an essential element to full belief in Jesus. First, one must believe that Jesus is the **Christ/ Messiah**. This means he is the promised and chosen one of God. His ministry is not an accident or the result of an enterprising young man seizing an opportunity. It is part of the plan of God as promised by God's prophets in the Old Testament. Second, one must believe that Jesus is the **Son of God**. He is more than an obedient human tool of God. He is God in human flesh (1:14). Third, Jesus has **come into the world**. This means that the "invasion" of the Christ into the human sphere is not a future event but clearly present to Martha in her current experience.

This confession of Martha is remarkably similar to some other passages. It reminds us of the "Good Confession" of Peter, "You are the Christ, the Son of the Living God" (Matt 16:16; cf. Mark 8:29; Luke 9:20). The readers of John will notice later that the statement of Martha is given as the purpose of the book in 20:31: "But these things are written that you may believe that Jesus is the

Christ, the Son of God, and that by believing you may have life in his name."

Jesus and Mary and the Grieved (11:28-37)

²⁸And after she had said this, she went back and called her sister Mary aside. "The Teacher is here," she said, "and is asking for you." ²⁹When Mary heard this, she got up quickly and went to him. ³⁰Now Jesus had not yet entered the village, but was still at the place where Martha had met him. ³¹When the Jews who had been with Mary in the house, comforting her, noticed how quickly she got up and went out, they followed her, supposing she was going to the tomb to mourn there.

³²When Mary reached the place where Jesus was and saw him, she fell at his feet and said, "Lord, if you had been here, my brother would not have died."

³³When Jesus saw her weeping, and the Jews who had come along with her also weeping, he was deeply moved in spirit and troubled. ³⁴"Where have you laid him?" he asked.

"Come and see, Lord," they replied.

³⁵Jesus wept.

³⁶Then the Jews said, "See how he loved him!"

³⁷But some of them said, "Could not he who opened the eyes of the blind man have kept this man from dying?"

11:28-31. Mary's failure to accompany her sister to greet Jesus is unexplained. However, when Martha informs Mary that Jesus had been "asking for you," she goes to him immediately. John's description emphasizes the suddenness of her exit. It is done ταχέως (*tacheōs*[11] = quickly or rapidly). It is as if Mary has been waiting for some sign of concern from Jesus. This hasty departure does not go unnoticed, and the Jews who follow her ensure that the following events are done with an audience present.

11:32. Mary's words to Jesus are identical to the first statement

---

[11]From which we get the word "tachometer," literally a device to "measure speed."

of Martha, "**Lord, if you had been here, my brother would not have died**" (cf. v. 21). The author gives the impression that the sisters had dealt with their grief by discussing this together. Many times they had said to themselves, "If only Jesus had been here!" For them Lazarus had been the victim of unfortunate circumstances as much as deadly illness. Mary's action of falling **at his feet** shows that she bears no grudge, but still holds Jesus in high esteem and respect.

11:33-36. John does not present a Jesus who is inhumanly impervious to emotional display. It is a time of **weeping** for Mary and the crowd.[12] The Greek word for weeping is κλαίω (*klaiō*), meaning to shed tears as a deep emotional response (rather than for physical pain). This universal crying causes Jesus to be **deeply moved in spirit**. The Greek word for **deeply moved** is ἐμβριμάομαι (*embrimaomai*), also used in verse 38. The word is rare in the New Testament. It may be used for giving a strict warning (Matt 9:30; Mark 1:43) or even scolding (Mark 14:5). Here it refers to a highly charged emotional state that Jesus experienced **in** his **spirit**, that is, internally. John says that Jesus was also **troubled** (ταράσσω, *tarassō*), meaning he was very disturbed. This word is used elsewhere to describe the angelic troubling of the waters of the healing pool (5:7) and the troubled emotional state of Jesus when he announces that one of the disciples is a traitor (13:21). Jesus is near the emotional breaking point.

From a human point of view, then, it is not at all surprising to learn that **Jesus wept**. This is not the same word for weeping as in verse 33, but δακρύω (*dakryō*) meaning that the tears begin to flow. What sort of human being would he be if he could ignore the pain of Mary and Martha, and block out his own personal heartache over the death of his friend Lazarus? And for once **the Jews** do not attack Jesus or attempt to discredit him. They see him through their own tears and empathize with this wonderful person by exclaiming, "**See how he loved him!**" The human Jesus was not immune to these emotions, nor did he try to be. We should not be either. When death strikes, it is natural and acceptable to let the

---

[12]The readers will be reminded of this scene when they encounter another Mary weeping at a tomb in 20:11.

tears flow. It is not a sign of a lack of faith. To do otherwise may be an unnatural repression of a God-sanctioned emotional release.

11:37. A second comment from some of the Jewish crowd is both ironic and a foreshadowing of what is to come. It is ironic in that some from this group may have been involved in the mistreatment of the blind man in chapter 9. Now they seem to accept it as a true miracle. It is foreshadowing in that the trouble that came to Jesus as a result of the healing of the blind man is merely a taste of what is to come on the heels of the raising of Lazarus. For John, the Lazarus miracle will be the event that causes the Jewish authorities in Jerusalem to kill Jesus (see 11:50; cf. 12:10-11).

Jesus' Raising of Lazarus (11:38-44)

³⁸**Jesus, once more deeply moved, came to the tomb. It was a cave with a stone laid across the entrance. ³⁹"Take away the stone," he said.**

"But, Lord," said Martha, the sister of the dead man, "by this time there is a bad odor, for he has been there four days."

⁴⁰**Then Jesus said, "Did I not tell you that if you believed, you would see the glory of God?"**

⁴¹**So they took away the stone. Then Jesus looked up and said, "Father, I thank you that you have heard me. ⁴²I knew that you always hear me, but I said this for the benefit of the people standing here, that they may believe that you sent me."**

⁴³**When he had said this, Jesus called in a loud voice, "Lazarus, come out!" ⁴⁴The dead man came out, his hands and feet wrapped with strips of linen, and a cloth around his face.**

Jesus said to them, "Take off the grave clothes and let him go."

11:38. The description of the tomb may indicate a relatively high degree of family wealth. It is described as a cave (σπήλαιον, *spēlaion*, from which we get the word "spelunker"). The author says the covering stone laid across the entrance. The verb to describe this is ἐπίκειμαι (*epikeimai*), meaning literally to "lay upon" (KJV) or "lay over." Although this term could be used for a cave in a hillside, it implies a cave whose mouth is in relatively flat ground.

11:39. While the weeping of Jesus may have engaged the sympathies of the crowd, the command, "**Take away the stone,**" must have alarmed them. Surely these were the ravings of a lunatic, for, as Martha reminds Jesus, the four-day old corpse was now decomposing. There is an element of dark humor here, eloquently brought out by the old KJV translation, "Lord, by this time he stinketh."

11:40-41a. The objections of Martha are immediately taken by Jesus to the arena of faith. She must believe in him, and in this case to believe is to obey. This is the point of decision for the grieving sister. She has no logical reason to do as Jesus has asked, for he has not explained himself to her. She must think that Jesus wants to see the body of his friend one last time, even in its decomposed state. Everything in her Jewish background[13] and upbringing would be telling her to keep the tomb closed. But Jesus offers her a chance to **see the glory of God** (see discussion under v. 4). She moves beyond fear and traditions and gives the word, **so they take away the stone**.

11:41b-42. Jesus prepares for the miracle by praying. His prayer is opened by giving thanks (εὐχαριστέω, *eucharisteō*), a tremendously valuable lesson for all believers. His faith is so complete that in the midst of his sorrow and grieving he gives thanks to the God who hears and answers prayers. **Heard** and **hear** (from the verb ἀκούω, *akouō*) are not so much about the reception of audible sensation, but about God's responding to a human prayer request. The reader knows that God's willingness to **always hear** Jesus in his pursuit of confirming miracles is a sign that Jesus is not a sinner (see the comment of the healed blind man, 9:31). Those who see with eyes of faith will understand that such miracles are proof that Jesus has been **sent** by God.

11:43-44. Dramatically Jesus switches from his prayer voice to his summoning voice and yells, "**Lazarus, come out.**" The yelling is not because he must summon Lazarus's soul out of Hades, but for the benefit of the crowd. When Jesus had requested the cover stone be removed from the tomb, they must have assumed he intended to enter it. Much to their astonishment Jesus not only doesn't enter, but someone comes out of this place that should only contain corpses and bones. And this can be none other than

---

[13]Contact with a corpse could make a Jewish person ceremonially unclean. See Numbers 5:2; 19:13.

Lazarus, still wrapped in the burial garb,[14] which apparently does not allow him to see or walk very well. He is probably stumbling around dangerously, but the dumbfounded crowd does not react. It is left to Jesus to give the practical order, "**Take off the grave clothes and let him go**," a command that was doubtlessly carried out immediately by Lazarus's joyful sisters.

The description of Lazarus as a **dead man** is illogical. How can a dead man walk out of a cave? However, John's wording is a little more nuanced than the NIV translation indicates. The Greek word here is τεθνηκώς (*tethnēkōs*, from θνήσκω, *thnēskō*). It is a perfect participle and should be translated "the one having died." There is no denial of the death of Lazarus. This is not some hoax cooked up by Jesus and his followers. There is also no changing of the fact that Lazarus *had died*. For the rest of his graciously continued life he could be described as "Lazarus who had died."

And so is the abrupt ending of the most dramatic miracle in the ministry of Jesus: the un-rotting and revival of a corpse. Jesus has truly validated his claim to be "the Resurrection and the Life." He has authority even over death.

The Passover Plot to Kill Jesus (11:45-53)

[45]**Therefore many of the Jews who had come to visit Mary, and had seen what Jesus did, put their faith in him. [46]But some of them went to the Pharisees and told them what Jesus had done. [47]Then the chief priests and the Pharisees called a meeting of the Sanhedrin.**

"What are we accomplishing?" they asked. "Here is this man performing many miraculous signs. [48]If we let him go on like this, everyone will believe in him, and then the Romans will come and take away both our place[a] and our nation."

---

[14]There is a bit of foreshadowing and contrast here to the empty tomb scene of Jesus in John 20:3-7. Here the burial clothes are left behind. John particularly records the detail that the face cloth (σουδάριον, *soudarion*) that blinds the resurrected Lazarus has been neatly folded by Jesus and left in the tomb.

⁴⁹**Then one of them, named Caiaphas, who was high priest that year, spoke up, "You know nothing at all! ⁵⁰You do not realize that it is better for you that one man die for the people than that the whole nation perish."**

⁵¹**He did not say this on his own, but as high priest that year he prophesied that Jesus would die for the Jewish nation, ⁵²and not only for that nation but also for the scattered children of God, to bring them together and make them one. ⁵³So from that day on they plotted to take his life.**

ᵃ*48 Or temple*

As is often the case in John, a miraculous sign of Jesus is met with belief (many of the Jews, v. 45) and with unbelief (the Sanhedrin, v. 47). But from this point on in the fourth Gospel the unbelief is linked with a plot to kill Jesus.

11:45. The **Jews who had come to visit Mary** are to be understood as residents of Jerusalem. John indicates that Jesus now has a strong contingent of believers in the city. Why would John mention Mary here and not Martha? Although the NIV translation, **come to visit Mary**, is grammatically possible, it is not the best choice in this instance. The word translated "**to**" (πρός, *pros*) is a preposition that may also be translated "with."[15] Thus the NRSV translation, "who had come with Mary," fits the context better. These were the Jewish friends of Mary who walked with her from the house to Jesus and then to the tomb (v. 31). Some of these Jews understood the purpose of the miracle and became believers.

11:46-48. Word of the Lazarus miracle gets back to some of the Pharisees who were members of the Jewish High Council (the **Sanhedrin**[16]). We are not told if these informants were believers or

---

[15]Cf. John 1:1-2, the Word was "with" God.

[16]Only here does John use this quasi-technical term, συνέδριον, *synedrion*, which the NIV renders as "Sanhedrin." For other occasions in the New Testament where *synedrion* refers to this Jewish High Council see Matt 26:59; Mark 14:55; 15:1; Luke 22:66; Acts 4:1; 5:21; 22:30 (and several other times in Acts). For further information on the Sanhedrin of Jesus' day see the article "Sanhedrin" by G.H. Twelftree in *Dictionary of Jesus and the Gospels*, pp. 728-732.

unbelievers, but the reaction to the news is unbelief. This startling news causes the leading Pharisees and their rivals the **chief priests** (= Sadducees) to convene the Sanhedrin.

The tone of the meeting is near panic. The NIV translation is particularly misleading and muddled here. They do not ask, "**What are we accomplishing?**" "**Here is a man performing many miraculous signs.**" A better rendering would be "What should we do, because this man continues to do many miraculous signs?" or, even better, "How should we respond to the continuing miracles coming from Jesus?" One wonders why they feel the need to "do" anything in response. If the miracles are true signs of God's power and glory, why not accept them with worship and praise? The answer to this is in verse 48. This is one of the most historically illuminating verses in all the New Testament.

The question has often been asked in recent years, "Why was Jesus killed?" Although his death is attributed to "the Jews," there is nothing inherently Jewish about this. We have no basis for believing that the Jews of the ancient world were a murderous and bloodthirsty lot. To the contrary, the vast majority of Jews all across the Roman Empire made a sincere effort to live according to the righteous standards of God as outlined in the Law of Moses.

John, who may have had inside information about the proceedings of the Sanhedrin,[17] tells us that the Jewish leaders react out of their fear of a two-part potential scenario: Jesus will become the leader of a revolutionary army of the general citizenry and then the Roman legions will come and ruthlessly crush this rebellion. They see this as a lose-lose situation: the people will lose their **nation** and the religious leaders will lose their **place**. By "**place**" John means the Jerusalem temple, which was both the international center and symbol of Judaism, and the economic engine that made Jerusalem prosperous. Without the temple the Sadducees in particular would see their income stream dry up overnight.

Jesus, then, was seen as a threat to the national, religious, and economic survival of temple Judaism. John intends the reader to again reflect that this is ultimately a matter of faith. There no

---

[17]See John 18:15, where the author indicates that he was a known face in the house of the High Priest.

longer seems to be a question as to whether or not the miracles of
Jesus were a sign of the powerful work of God in their midst. The
question is whether or not the God of the Jews was more powerful
than the mighty Roman Empire with its seemingly invincible
armies. Jewish traditions were full of stories of faithful leaders like
Deborah and Barak, Gideon, David, and Judas Maccabeus, who led
God-powered military victories against overwhelming odds. However, the tacit conclusion of these Jewish leaders around AD 30 was
that Rome was more powerful than Jehovah.

11:49-50. The **high priest** and leader of the Sanhedrin lays out
the basis for a plan of action with this chilling statement, "**It is
better . . . that one man die . . . than that the whole nation
perish.**" His statement confirms that the Sanhedrin believed
national survival was at stake. This way of thinking is a precursor to
the modern philosophy called "utilitarianism." The originator of
this type of philosophy is usually seen as the Englishman, Jeremy
Bentham (1748-1832). Bentham is best known for advocating that
decisions of government should be made according to the principle
of "the greatest happiness for the greatest number." This seemingly
enlightened principle is actually terribly misguided, for the people
of God must make moral decisions based on the unchanging and
absolute principles of God, not the perceived advantages of a
majority of the population. Murder is always wrong and never justified, even for national survival. How can God honor a course of
action based on a disregard for one of his commandments?

This high priest is identified as **Caiaphas**. Caiaphas is one of the
few Bible characters for whom we have physical confirmation of his
existence. In December 1990 the Caiaphas family tomb was discovered by a road construction crew working south of the Old City of
Jerusalem.[18] This tomb contained several ossuaries (boxes carved
from limestone to hold bones). Each intact ossuary held the bones
of several people. One of these had the bones of a man approximately 60 years old. It was the most deluxe of the ossuaries, with
beautiful and intricate decorative carvings. On the back of this
stone box was scratched (rather crudely) the name "Joseph bar

---

[18]See the double issue of *Jerusalem Perspective* 38 & 39 (July–October,
1991) devoted exclusively to this amazing find. See also *Biblical Archaeology
Review* 18 (September/October 1992): 28-36, 38-44, 76.

Caiaphas." This is the exact name given by Josephus for the high priest during the time of Jesus, and these are almost unquestionably his actual 2,000 year-old bones. In one of the supreme ironies of history we have uncovered the tomb and bones of the man who feared Lazarus's deliverance from a similar tomb, and who was powerless to keep Jesus in another similar tomb.

11:51-52. The author presents an interesting ironical twist of his own. For him the words of Caiaphas are unwittingly prophetic. Despite Caiaphas's evil intent, it is ultimately a good thing for Jesus to die. Jesus' death, however, was not to serve the special interests of the Sanhedrin and the high priests. It was to redeem and unite all the people of God from all nations. Elsewhere John reminds his community that, "He is the atoning sacrifice for our sins, and not only for ours but also for the sins of the whole world" (1 John 2:2). As Fred Craddock has written, "[The] scene is part of a drama so large the characters have no idea of the real parts they play."[19]

11:53. The NIV has given an unusual sense for this verse, that the Sanhedrin now made plans **to take his life**. The text simply says that they planned "to kill him." There is no longer any hope for reconciliation, nor for a delay that would allow them to forget their plot. Certainly some of these Sanhedrin members are good men. They must have been horrified at the prospect of being accessories to murder. But the political climate and the power of the high priest stifles any protests they might have made. Even good men and women lack the courage to stand up against gross injustice at times.

Retreat of Jesus (11:54-57)

⁵⁴Therefore Jesus no longer moved about publicly among the Jews. Instead he withdrew to a region near the desert, to a village called Ephraim, where he stayed with his disciples.

⁵⁵When it was almost time for the Jewish Passover, many went up from the country to Jerusalem for their ceremonial cleansing before the Passover. ⁵⁶They kept looking for Jesus, and as they stood in the temple area they asked one another, "What do you

---

[19]Craddock, *John*, p. 89.

think? Isn't he coming to the Feast at all?" [57]But the chief priests and Pharisees had given orders that if anyone found out where Jesus was, he should report it so that they might arrest him.

11:54. Jesus responds to this dangerous threat by temporarily withdrawing to a remote village named Ephraim. The exact site of this town is uncertain, but it is often associated with a village on the edge of the desert of Judea, about 12 miles NE of Jerusalem.[20] Such a place would have been very much off the beaten path, and therefore a momentary safe haven.

11:55-57. John finishes this section by setting the scene for the next act. Passover is near and Jesus is expected in Jerusalem. When will he arrive? It is not just his admirers who look for him, though. John tells us that the Sanhedrin has built an informant network **so that they might arrest him**. The drama builds. It all comes down to this final Passover. How will it play out? That is the story John now wants to tell.

---

[20]For discussion of the several possible sites for Ephraim see Brown, *John*, 1:441. The *Oxford Bible Atlas* gives the Aramaic name of this village as "Aphaireme" (p. 87).

JOHN 12

8. Preparation for Passover and Death (12:1-50)

Mary's Anointing of Jesus (12:1-11)

¹Six days before the Passover, Jesus arrived at Bethany, where Lazarus lived, whom Jesus had raised from the dead. ²Here a dinner was given in Jesus' honor. Martha served, while Lazarus was among those reclining at the table with him. ³Then Mary took about a pint[a] of pure nard, an expensive perfume; she poured it on Jesus' feet and wiped his feet with her hair. And the house was filled with the fragrance of the perfume.

⁴But one of his disciples, Judas Iscariot, who was later to betray him, objected, ⁵"Why wasn't this perfume sold and the money given to the poor? It was worth a year's wages.[b]" ⁶He did not say this because he cared about the poor but because he was a thief; as keeper of the money bag, he used to help himself to what was put into it.

⁷"Leave her alone," Jesus replied. "It was intended that she should save this perfume for the day of my burial. ⁸You will always have the poor among you, but you will not always have me."

⁹Meanwhile a large crowd of Jews found out that Jesus was there and came, not only because of him but also to see Lazarus, whom he had raised from the dead. ¹⁰So the chief priests made plans to kill Lazarus as well, ¹¹for on account of him many of the Jews were going over to Jesus and putting their faith in him.

[a]3 Greek *a litra* (probably about 0.5 liter)   [b]5 Greek *three hundred denarii*

12:1-2. As we approach the final Passover, the author is careful to give chronological guideposts. It is now six days before Passover. Although there is some difference of opinion among interpreters, the Passover likely began the next Thursday night.[1] This would place the Bethany meal on the previous Friday evening. Thus verse 2 refers to a Sabbath meal, for the Jews counted sundown as the beginning of a new day (whereas we reckon the new day's start as sunrise). This would mean that Jesus and his companions had planned their travel in order to make it to Bethany before the day of rest, rather than be perceived as Sabbath breakers.[2] The host for the dinner is unnamed by John, but we learn from the Synoptic accounts that it was the home of a man named Simon.[3] The author makes it clear that Martha/Mary/Lazarus are closely tied to the Simon household, for Martha is among those serving and Lazarus is among the dinner guests. The word used to describe Martha's serving is διακονέω (*diakoneō*), the same verb used for Martha in Luke 10:40. It is the verb form of the word from which we get the term "deacon," which means "servant" or "minister."

12:3. Without warning Mary begins to pamper the feet of Jesus with an extravagant lotion. John (a likely eyewitness to this event) describes the lotion as **a pint of pure nard, an expensive perfume**. The actual measurement is a λίτρα (*litra*, Latin = *libra*), a Roman "pound." This is equivalent to approximately 325 grams. In equivalent liquid measure a Roman *libra* would be roughly .5 liters or a **pint** according to our modern standards. **Nard** was a highly prized perfume imported from the Himalayan region of India. Its color may range from amber to deep blue. Nard's aroma is characterized as a heavy, sweet-woody and spicy animal odor. Such out-of-the-ordinary luxuries were highly prized in the ancient world by both men and women.[4]

---

[1]For one who believes this meal was on Saturday night see Brown, *John*, 1:447. For complete discussion of the problems of harmonizing John's chronology for this week with that of the Synoptic Gospels, see Carson, *The Gospel According to John*, pp. 455-458.

[2]Butler, *John*, 2:167.

[3]See Matthew 26:6 and Mark 14:3. Both of these accounts identify this man as "Simon the leper." For discussion on the possible relationships between Martha, Mary, Lazarus, and Simon see the notes above on 11:1.

[4]See the references to nard in the luxurious royal court of Solomon

The author emphasizes Mary's lavish extravagance. She is not miserly with her treasure. She applies so much costly nard to Jesus' feet that she must use her hair to mop up the excess.[5] The author also records that the experience was a pleasant one for all present, for **the house was filled with the fragrance of the perfume**. Mary is presented to us as an example of no-holding-back devotion and unashamed humility.

12:4-6. Not everyone is impressed by Mary's display of humble devotion. **Judas Iscariot** (who has already been foreshadowed as the betrayer in 6:71) raises a seemingly valid objection. According to him the nard that was just used as foot lotion could have been sold for **a year's wages**. The actual amount in the Greek text is 300 denarii. A denarius was a small silver coin, often used in the Roman world as a day's wage for an unskilled laborer. In terms of equivalent buying power from the U.S.A. of the late twentieth century, Judas's complaint is that Mary just wasted $15-20,000 worth of nard.[6]

John is quick to point out, however, that Judas is not speaking as a champion of the poor. He is a **thief** who ironically was the group's **keeper of the money bag** or treasurer. He shed no tears for the poor, but for his own lost opportunity to access a large sum of money that could have been embezzled. John is aware that Judas misappropriated the group's funds, but does not tell us how he arrived at this knowledge. It may be that there had been minor incidents in the past where Judas had been caught in obvious discrepancies, or it may be that this came out after Judas's death when

---

found in Song of Solomon 1:12; 4:13-14. This attests to the antiquity of this costly aromatic oil.

[5]Both Mark 14:3 and Matthew 26:7 record that the nard was applied to Jesus' head rather than his feet. While some have seen this as an irreconcilable contradiction of details, this view is unnecessary. It seems reasonable that she applied the nard to both his feet and his head. Both acts would have been interpreted as gestures of hospitality. The attention to feet demonstrated by Mary anticipates the foot-washing lesson of Jesus in chapter 13, thus this particular detail is more important to John than the anointing of Jesus' head.

[6]See John 6:7 where Philip notes that it would take more than 200 denarii to feed the crowd of 5,000+, even minimally. The value Judas attributes to Mary's nard is 1.5 times as much (300 denarii). Cf. Mark 14:5, where others present estimate that Mary's nard was worth more than 300 denarii.

someone else would have assumed this responsibility of group treasurer. At any rate, the author's comments help the reader appreciate the defective moral character of this person and thereby understand how he could become a traitor.

12:7-8. Jesus refuses to tolerate Judas's criticism of Mary, even
his insincere version that the cash value of the nard could have
been used for benevolent purposes. Jesus states, **"It was meant that
she should save this perfume for the day of my burial."** This translation of the NIV is probably accurate in intent, but somewhat far
afield of the original text. Jesus is telling Judas and the other critics
to hush up because Mary should be allowed to treasure her act of
devotion without the taint of criticism. It will become even more
precious to her at the time of Jesus' death and burial.[7]

Jesus' justification for approving of Mary's incredibly costly foot
treatment is that **"You will always have the poor among you, but
you will not always have me."** This is not a statement about the
inevitability of poverty or the futility of relief efforts. It is a lesson
in priorities. There comes a time when devotion to God and the
Son of God must take priority over all else. If we immerse ourselves
in social action but neglect our relationship with our Lord Jesus, we
have "missed what is better."[8] In this case the opportunities for personal interaction with Jesus are rapidly escaping, for **the day of
[Jesus'] burial** is less than a week away. Mary is the one who intu-
itively understands this, who will not be at the burial saying, "I wish
I had told him I loved him before he died." She seizes the opportunity at hand and acts out her love for her Lord in full public view.

12:9-11. The news that Jesus has returned to Bethany reaches
Jerusalem quickly, and **a large crowd of Jews** (presumably Jerusalem
residents) now hikes over to Bethany. This time they are not only
interested in seeing Jesus (cf. 11:56), but would like also to see the
miracle man, Lazarus. Such curiosity is understandable, but has the
reverse effect upon the Jewish religious leaders. They now add

---

[7]This is a suggestion of Barrett, *The Gospel According to St. John*, p. 414,
although Barrett has some reservations about this interpretation. He notes
that the Greek verb used here is τηρέω (*tēreō*) which means "to keep," but
comments that it would be unusual for *tēreō* to be used in the sense of "to
keep a memory."

[8]See Luke 10:42, where Mary teaches the same lesson of the priority of
devotion to Jesus in a different context.

Lazarus to their list of enemies and make **plans to kill** [him] **as well**. Why this insane jealousy? Because many **were going over to Jesus**. Literally, **many of the Jews** were "deserting" (NRSV). The religious leaders refuse to see this as anything but a win-lose situation. If Jesus is "winning" by gaining more believers, then they are "losing" by the attrition of compliant citizens. The religious leaders' refusal to believe has blinded them to the mighty activities of God, which the common Jews readily perceive.

Jesus' Triumphal Entry (12:12-19)

[12]**The next day the great crowd that had come for the Feast heard that Jesus was on his way to Jerusalem.** [13]**They took palm branches and went out to meet him, shouting,**

"**Hosanna!**[a]"

"**Blessed is he who comes in the name of the Lord!**"[b]

"**Blessed is the King of Israel!**"

[14]**Jesus found a young donkey and sat upon it, as it is written,**

[15]"**Do not be afraid, O Daughter of Zion;**

see, your king is coming,

seated on a donkey's colt."[c]

[16]**At first his disciples did not understand all this. Only after Jesus was glorified did they realize that these things had been written about him and that they had done these things to him.**

[17]**Now the crowd that was with him when he called Lazarus from the tomb and raised him from the dead continued to spread the word.** [18]**Many people, because they had heard that he had given this miraculous sign, went out to meet him.** [19]**So the Pharisees said to one another, "See, this is getting us nowhere. Look how the whole world has gone after him!"**

[a]*13* A Hebrew expression meaning "Save!" which became an exclamation of praise   [b]*13* Psalm 118:25, 26   [c]*15* Zech. 9:9

The "triumphal entry" is found in all four Gospel accounts with varying components.[9] Some of John's unique details include the

---

[9]The other triumphal entry accounts are in Matthew 21:1-11; Mark 11:1-11; and Luke 19:28-44.

mention of palm branches (v. 13), the editorial reflection upon the significance of the event (v. 16), and the response of the Pharisee observers (v. 19). John uses the triumphal entry to highlight the popular support for Jesus from the crowds. He explains this popularity as being a result of the raising of Lazarus. On this "Palm Sunday" the "triumphal procession" of Jesus is an impromptu, joyous celebration. It is not a formal affair sanctioned by the Sanhedrin or the Roman officials in Jerusalem. It is spontaneously staged by the common folk, the people astounded by the word that Jesus "called Lazarus from the tomb" (v. 17).

12:12. The next day would be Sunday (which began at sundown on Saturday evening according to ancient standards). The **great crowd** was a normal phenomenon at Passover time in the first century. These are pilgrims coming to Jerusalem via the Jericho road to the east. This was a common route for Jewish festival pilgrims coming from Galilee or Perea, and the post-Sabbath day throng was likely in the tens of thousands, if not the hundreds of thousands.[10] This is the third and final Passover feast recorded by John.[11]

12:13. The exact significance of the **palm branches** is not explained, but presumably they are intended to assist in giving a spontaneous royal welcome (cf. Rev 7:9). Palm branches would have been in plentiful supply near Jerusalem, even for this large crowd. John effectively conveys the joy and excitement that must have rippled through the people, as they waved their palm branches and shouted their praises to God. Since the time of the Maccabees, two centuries earlier, palm branches had been a symbol of Jewish nationalism.

---

[10]In a well-known passage, Josephus estimates that during a Passover shortly before the outbreak of the Jewish War of A.D. 66-70, at least 2,700,200 people participated in the paschal meal at Jerusalem. This estimate was made by having the temple priests keep track of the number of lambs sacrificed for Passover in the temple, and assuming that each lamb represented at least 10 people, the minimum number to celebrate the feast. This is in Josephus's work, *Wars of the Jews*, 6.9.3. Elsewhere Josephus puts this number at 3,000,000 (*Wars* 2.14.3). Since all Jewish men were expected to go to the Jerusalem temple for Passover, it is possible that 500,000 or more came from Galilee alone.

[11]The first two are mentioned at John 2:13 and 6:4. (See n. 2, p. 155.)

The words of the crowd are taken mainly from Psalm 118:25-26, a traditional psalm used by pilgrims on their way to the temple. **Hosanna** is a Hebrew term meaning "Please save us." For John to have the people say, "**Blessed is he who comes in the name of the Lord,**" is theologically important, because it means that some of the Jews understand what is going on. Jesus has not come in his own name, but with God's obvious blessing and in God's name. This is because he was to reveal God to his people (1:18). At least part of his wild popularity at this point must be attributed to his avoidance of self-glorification. He is no self-promoter with an agent and a public relations consultant. He is not trying to leverage his popularity into a lucrative contract. Yet, despite this humility, the crowd also acclaims him personally by roaring, "**Blessed is the King of Israel!**" In this they can only be talking about Jesus, for there was no king over Jerusalem in those days. This is the man who just brought a dead person back to life! Surely he would make a fine king!

12:14-16. John includes no information about the procurement of a steed for the procession, but merely says **Jesus found a young donkey and sat upon it**. For John, the donkey's importance is to be found in its connection to prophecy (Zech 9:9). He explains carefully that the significance of this act was not understood at the time, but only after Jesus' glorification (= death/resurrection). This is a valuable insight into the ways that the early church interpreted the actions of Jesus. In many cases, apparently, a rereading of the Old Testament provided insights into the things Jesus did and that were done to him (12:16; cf. 2:22; 7:39). Later we will learn that the Holy Spirit was a guiding influence for the disciples in this interpretive process (16:13).

In this case the author indicates that both the acclamation of the crowd (based on Psalm 118) and the choice of a donkey (based on Zechariah 9) are elements of a larger, divinely orchestrated plan. Although spontaneous, it is not accidental that the crowd adores Jesus. And the donkey is not just a convenient ride. It is a necessary and prophetic action that demonstrates the continuing humility of Jesus.

12:17-18. John's picture of the mechanics of the procession includes some details not present in the Synoptic accounts. Here he shows that the procession is not only made up of Jericho Road pilgrims, but also of people coming out of the city **to meet him**. John continues to emphasize their fascination with and fixation upon the miracle of Lazarus. It is a **miraculous sign** (σημεῖον, *sēmeion*), precisely what the crowds want (3:2; 7:31) and the authorities fear (11:47-48).

12:19. The **Pharisees** continue the hostile whining of the whole Sanhedrin (11:48) and the chief priests (12:10). In their view, this unfortunate and misguided popularity of Jesus has now reached epidemic proportions, and their efforts to squash the uprising have been futile. It is no longer a movement of the lower classes or of the bumpkinish Galileans. Now, they observe, **the whole world has gone after him**. For John this is a theologically significant comment. As already noted, **the world** (κόσμος, *kosmos*) in John usually represents humankind as morally alienated from God (see comments on 7:3-4). For the world to follow Jesus means that the signs are beginning to accomplish their purposes and that Jesus' mission to save the world is being fulfilled.

Gentiles Prompt Jesus' Announcement of His Hour (12:20-36)

[20]Now there were some Greeks among those who went up to worship at the Feast. [21]They came to Philip, who was from Bethsaida in Galilee, with a request. "Sir," they said, "we would like to see Jesus." [22]Philip went to tell Andrew; Andrew and Philip in turn told Jesus.

[23]Jesus replied, "The hour has come for the Son of Man to be glorified. [24]I tell you the truth, unless a kernel of wheat falls to the ground and dies, it remains only a single seed. But if it dies, it produces many seeds. [25]The man who loves his life will lose it, while the man who hates his life in this world will keep it for eternal life. [26]Whoever serves me must follow me; and where I am, my servant also will be. My Father will honor the one who serves me.

[27]"Now my heart is troubled, and what shall I say? 'Father, save me from this hour'? No, it was for this very reason I came to this hour. [28]Father, glorify your name!"

Then a voice came from heaven, "I have glorified it, and will glorify it again." [29]The crowd that was there and heard it said it had thundered; others said an angel had spoken to him.

[30]Jesus said, "This voice was for your benefit, not mine. [31]Now is the time for judgment on this world; now the prince of this world will be driven out. [32]But I, when I am lifted up from the earth, will draw all men to myself." [33]He said this to show the kind of death he was going to die.

[34]The crowd spoke up, "We have heard from the Law that the Christ[a] will remain forever, so how can you say, 'The Son of Man must be lifted up'? Who is this 'Son of Man'?"

[35]Then Jesus told them, "You are going to have the light just a little while longer. Walk while you have the light, before darkness overtakes you. The man who walks in the dark does not know where he is going. [36]Put your trust in the light while you have it, so that you may become sons of light." When he had finished speaking, Jesus left and hid himself from them.

[a]34 Or Messiah

12:20-22. John includes a unique story at this point, one not found in the other Gospels. Some Greeks make a request to see Jesus. These are not Greek-speaking Jews, but Gentiles who have come to Jerusalem for Passover. The descriptive detail that they went up to worship implies that they have also ascended the Jericho Road to Jerusalem, perhaps implying that they have come from the Gentile-rich area of Galilee.

The Galilean source of these Greeks seems to be confirmed by John's careful explanation that they attempted to contact Jesus through Philip and Andrew. Both of them are Galileans (see 1:44), and the original readers would likely notice that these two are the only disciples with Greek names. **Philip** means "horse aficionado" and was a noble military name (the famous name of the father of Alexander the Great). **Andrew** means "masculine one," "courageous one," or, in our modern idiom, "macho one." It is somewhat unlikely that these were the names these two were given at birth, but more likely they were names they had adopted themselves. This might indicate that Philip and Andrew had embraced Greek ways (become "Hellenized") including both clothing and haircut. Such visible markers must have identified them to the curious Greeks.

12:23-26. At this point Jesus faces a crucial decision. Surely he knows that his teachings have universal application and appeal (remember he claimed to be the "Light of the World," 8:12). Here is an opportunity to move beyond the resistant nation of Israel and perhaps find a more receptive audience with a door open to world-wide exposure. At an earlier point in his ministry Jesus may have welcomed this break, but now it is a temptation that must be resisted, for the time for public teaching is over. As he puts it, **"The hour has come for the Son of Man to be glorified."** By this he means that the time for his death has now come. He knows this and has determined in his heart that he will not try to avoid it.

Even as he is confronted head on with his coming death, Jesus uses the situation as a teaching occasion. His point is for his disciples to profit by observing his obedient and self-sacrificing model. He does this by introducing a series of three paradoxes:

1. Seeds become productive by "dying." When a grain of wheat produces a mature wheat plant with a head full of grain, the original seed grain no longer exists. In the economy of God *life comes by death*.

2. For men and women, holding on to life too selfishly will result in losing it. If our life is lived for God, we have **eternal life**. In the economy of God it is only by *spending life that we attain true life*.

3. This attitude toward life may be demonstrated by service to Jesus (and therefore to God). It is this servant who will be honored by God. In the economy of God *greatness comes only by service*.

In this final paradox Jesus includes a striking promise to his followers. We follow Jesus by serving him, and by serving him we maintain our relationship with him. And Jesus, who has made repeated "I am" claims throughout the fourth Gospel, now gives this pledge, **"Where I am, my servant also will be."** This is but a taste of a mighty vow that Jesus will expand upon in chapter 14: his true follower/servants will have a share in his "I am-ness."

12:27-28. Jesus reveals some of his own inner struggle at this time, a struggle that the Synoptic Gospels include in the Gethsemane accounts.[12] The human instinct for survival is horrified

---

[12]Matthew 26:36-45; Mark 14:32-43; Luke 22:39-46. For John Gethsemane (which he does not name) is only used as the place of betrayal by Judas. John does not include the "agony of prayer" in the garden (18:1-11).

at the thought of death, and Jesus rightly says, **"Now my heart is troubled."** The word translated "heart" by the NIV actually means "soul" or "life" (ψυχή, *psychē*). Jesus is saying more than that he is emotionally troubled. He is saying that the very core of his human person is naturally resistant to the coming pain and death. This is a spiritual battle, a battle between survivalistic instincts God has purposely built into humans, and the course of obedience that calls Jesus to the cross.

Therefore, Jesus voices the natural passions of a human when he asks if he should pray, **"Father, save me from this hour."** For him to say this means that it is a course he has considered (and considers again in Gethsemane according to the Synoptics). But he immediately dismisses this choice and proclaims his submission and obedience by stating, **"No, it was for this very reason I came to this hour."** This decision for a "No" to disobedient selfishness is given over to God at once in the form of a prayer, **"Father glorify your name!"** As the revival of dead Lazarus was for the glory of God and the glorification of God's Son (11:4), so the coming passion will be for God's glory as well as the Son's (v. 23).

The atmosphere must have been highly charged and full of tension at this point. As a result of the resisted temptation to turn to the Greeks, Jesus publicly gives an emotional presentation of his inner turmoil. This pressure is relieved by the audible voice of God, **"I have glorified it** [God's name] **and will glorify it again."** God has not abandoned Jesus, but rather gives heavenly approval to the obedient course of action to which he has committed himself.[13]

12:29. At the very few points in Scripture where God communicates through an audible voice, this voice is described as having supernatural resonance, often compared to thunder.[14] John's point is that the crowd is aware of an unusual, divine communication, but does not understand the message. They wait for clarification.

---

[13]In the total Gospel material this is the third time that God gives such audible approval to the ministry of Jesus. The first is at his baptism, which is only alluded to in John 1:32-34. The second is at the Transfiguration, an event that John has chosen not to record, but found in all three of the Synoptic Gospels.

[14]For examples of the voice of God as thunder see Exodus 19:19; 20:18-19; 1 Samuel 7:10; 2 Samuel 22:14; Job 37:2,4,5; 40:9; Ezekiel 1:24; Revelation 14:2; cf. Acts 22:9; Sirach 46:17.

12:30-32. Jesus explains that the voice was for the **benefit** of the crowd, literally, "this voice came for you, not me." God is confirming what Jesus has already stated, that the timing of events is on track. Jesus now defines this crucial season in three ways:

1: It is **the time for judgment on this world**. The Greek word for **judgment** is κρίσις (*krisis*). If we leave it in an untranslated state, the result is striking: *Now is the **crisis** of this world*.[15] The coming death of Jesus is a crisis/judgment for the world in that it reveals the depth of human depravity. As George Beasley-Murray comments, "In the murder of the Son of Man sin is exposed in its most dreadful form."[16] As far as the world is concerned, unbelieving humanity has rejected the Son of God.

2: It is the time when **the prince of this world will be driven out**. The act of murder represented by the coming crucifixion will not be a victory for Satan, but a defeat. In the events of the resurrection and the coming of the Holy Spirit, humans will no longer be held in the power of Satan, the grip of sin. Satan himself has been judged and condemned (see 16:11).

3: It is the time for Jesus to be **lifted up from the earth**. So there is no misunderstanding as to the meaning of this phrase, John informs us that this is a metaphor for Jesus' death by crucifixion. But rather than withdraw in horror, the terrible/wondrous death of Jesus **will draw all men** to him.[17] The statement is hyperbolic, not absolute, for we know in the Gospel of John itself that not all become believers. Jesus' demonstration of love will become a powerful draw to all who look upon his life without prejudice.

12:34. The crowd has recovered enough feistiness to engage Jesus in skeptical controversy one more time. Here is one of the greatest turning points in this entire book. Thousands have just given Jesus a triumphal procession fit for royalty. Now he is speaking of death and exaltation (being "lifted up"). They want to discuss his plans for national liberation, but he talks about his demise. They confront him by pointing out that the Old Testament promised

---

[15]This is not completely legitimate, because the Greek word κρίσις does not have a true sense equivalent to the English word "crisis."

[16]Beasley-Murray, *John*, p. 213.

[17]For the previous references to Jesus being "lifted up" see 3:14 and 8:28.

that the Messianic King would **remain forever** (see Dan 7:14). They end their outburst with a ringing question, **"Who is this 'Son of Man'?"** This is an example of the sort of questions that John leaves rattling in the minds of the readers. The rest of the book will serve to answer this.[18]

12:35-36. Rather than engage in controversy at this point, it is as if Jesus shrugs and smiles and offers one last piece of advice for the crowd: *The time is short, you must believe.* The coming darkness will overwhelm them, and there is only one hope. If they believe in Jesus (**"trust in the light"**), they will be able to resist this dark spiritual oppression, for they will be **sons of light**. With this Jesus slips away.

The Tragedy of Unbelief, Past and Present (12:37-43)

[37]**Even after Jesus had done all these miraculous signs in their presence, they still would not believe in him.** [38]**This was to fulfill the word of Isaiah the prophet:**

"Lord, who has believed our message
    and to whom has the arm of the Lord been revealed?"[a]

[39]**For this reason they could not believe, because, as Isaiah says elsewhere:**

[40]**"He has blinded their eyes**
    and deadened their hearts,
so they can neither see with their eyes,
    nor understand with their hearts,
    nor turn — and I would heal them."[b]

[41]**Isaiah said this because he saw Jesus' glory and spoke about him.**

[42]**Yet at the same time many even among the leaders believed in him. But because of the Pharisees they would not confess their faith for fear they would be put out of the synagogue;** [43]**for they loved praise from men more than praise from God.**

[a]*38* Isaiah 53:1   [b]*40* Isaiah 6:10

---

[18]For another example see Pilate's resounding but unanswered question, "What is truth?" (18:38).

John 12:37-50 is a pivotal section for the book. It serves as a theological summary where the author reflects on the first half of the story. C.H. Dodd has identified this as the transition between what he calls the "Book of Signs" (chapters 2-11) and the "Book of the Passion" (chapters 13-20). For Dodd the first half of John has been an expansion of his statement in the prologue:

> He was in the world, and though the world was made through him, the world did not recognize him. He came to that which was his own, but his own did not receive him.[19]

This is unquestionably one of the most theologically challenging passages in the book of John. It is a penetrating discussion by the author of the root cause of unbelief. For the non-Calvinist it is a passage that must be wrestled with honestly and fully. We (non-Calvinists) tend to attribute unbelief to some sort of spiritually knuckleheaded stubbornness. We are persuaded that faith is a logical, reasonable response to evidence that compels belief. We naively hold on to the conviction that anyone can be converted if they are given enough evidence. John is telling us here that faith is a more complex issue than this. John wants to answer this question, "Why did the majority of Jews fail to believe that Jesus was the Messiah?" There are three factors that come out in his discussion.

12:37-38. First, John observes that there are some for whom even multiple spectacular miracles are not sufficient to cause faith. To borrow a statement from another Gospel, "They will not be convinced even if someone rises from the dead" (Luke 16:31). John couples this observation with a quotation of Isaiah 53:1. The point of the Isaiah text is that even though **the arm of the Lord** [has] **been revealed** (i.e., miraculous signs), we may still shake our heads and ask, **"Who has believed?"**

12:39-41. Second, John takes this a step further by observing **they could not believe**. He reinforces this by a modified quotation of Isaiah 6:9-10, a text famous in the New Testament for its prophecy of the spiritual hard-heartedness of the nation of Israel.[20]

---

[19]Dodd, *Fourth Gospel*, p. 380.

[20]For other full or partial citations of Isaiah 6:9-10 in the New Testament see Matthew 13:13-15; Mark 4:12; Luke 8:10; Acts 28:26-27; and Romans 11:8. Allusions to Isaiah 6:9-10 are found in Mark 8:18 and John 9:39.

The point is that they do not believe because God has blinded them and hardened their hearts to prevent repentance and healing. According to John, this unbelief is part of God's plan. This is left unexplained here, and we must turn to other New Testament passages to understand it fully. Romans 11:11-12 teaches us that the general unbelief of the nation of Israel was a necessary means to bring the Gospel to Gentiles. I would contend that Isaiah 6:9-10 does not say that God ordains unbelief so much as that he uses it.[21] If there had not been strong unbelief among the Jewish religious leaders, the atoning death of Jesus for the sins of the world might have been avoided, and Jesus would not have become the "Savior of the World" (John 4:42; cf. 1 John 4:14).

Even the coming death and resurrection of Jesus will not be enough for all to believe and this was foreseen by God. As John points out, Isaiah himself had a basic understanding of this astounding unfaith. Isaiah experienced unbelieving rejection in his own ministry, but even more **he saw Jesus' glory** [death/resurrection] **and spoke about him.**

12:42-43. Third, John informs us that parallel to this general spirit of unbelief is a significant group of believers. These believers even include many of **the leaders** of the Jews. But we are to be disappointed if we expect them to act decisively on behalf of Jesus. John tells the reader that the spirit of unbelief is accompanied by a climate of fear. The unbelief is so strong that believers will not be tolerated, but **put out of the synagogue.** John has already shown us examples of this in the story of the healing of the blind man. The man's parents refuse to make any public statement of belief because they are afraid of synagogue expulsion (9:22-23). The man himself holds on to a stubborn faith in his miracle and is expelled (9:34).

Unquestionably John is prodding some of his readers here. Among the first century synagogues there were still those who were in this position. If they came out as believers in Jesus, they risked expulsion as well as the ostracism and economic consequences associated with this expulsion. John chides them by asking, what is more important, **praise from men** or **praise from God**? Even today

---

[21]According to his sermon notes, Dr. Bryant would agree with this statement completely.

there is a need for taking a bold stand for Jesus. Religion may be considered a private matter in our culture, but we must never let our Christianity be hidden away like the light under a basket. We must let our "light shine before men, that they may see [our] deeds and praise [our] Father in heaven" (Matt 5:16).

The Call to Faith Still Stands (12:44-50)

⁴⁴**Then Jesus cried out, "When a man believes in me, he does not believe in me only, but in the one who sent me. ⁴⁵When he looks at me, he sees the one who sent me. ⁴⁶I have come into the world as a light, so that no one who believes in me should stay in darkness.**

⁴⁷**"As for the person who hears my words but does not keep them, I do not judge him. For I did not come to judge the world, but to save it. ⁴⁸There is a judge for the one who rejects me and does not accept my words; that very word which I spoke will condemn him at the last day. ⁴⁹For I did not speak of my own accord, but the Father who sent me commanded me what to say and how to say it. ⁵⁰I know that his command leads to eternal life. So whatever I say is just what the Father has told me to say."**

John brings Jesus before the crowd one last time to summarize his message to the crowds. The points of this brief message have all been given before, and the reader is intended to be reminded of them now. Jesus follows a circular pattern here, beginning and ending with his relationship with the Father.

1. Belief in Jesus amounts to belief in the Father (vv. 44-45).
2. Jesus has a mission from the Father to enlighten the world (v. 46).
3. Jesus came to save the world, not to condemn it (v. 47).
4. There will be consequences for those who reject Jesus and his message (v. 48).
5. This consequence is because Jesus' message and mission come from the Father (vv. 49-50).
6. Therefore, rejection of Jesus is a rejection of the Father himself (implied).

This is a good example of the type of argumentation found in John. First a premise is stated (point #1). Then various logical steps are taken based on this premise (points #2-5). Finally, Jesus arrives back where he started (implied point #6). The ultimate message is that *belief in Jesus is belief in the Father and, likewise, rejection of Jesus is rejection of the Father.* This is not because Jesus has a special version or vision of God. It is much more than that. It is because Jesus is the Father's direct action of revealing himself to men and women. You cannot accept some of the teachings of Jesus and reject his claims to be God's Son. What Jesus says and who Jesus is are part of the same whole and cannot be divided.

This ends any sort of public ministry for Jesus in the book of John. His remaining time will be spent with his disciples and in the actual passion events of his trials, crucifixion, and subsequent resurrection appearances to his believers.

JOHN 13

II. JESUS' MANIFESTATION OF HIMSELF IN HIS DEATH AND RESURRECTION (13:1-21:25)

Chapter 13 begins the second half of the book of John, what C.H. Dodd dubbed the "Book of the Passion." No longer do we see Jesus in the public courts of the temple engaged in dialog with the crowd. No longer do we see Jesus performing mighty signs.[1] Now he spends private time with his disciples leading up to his arrest, trials, crucifixion, burial, and resurrection appearances.

A. JESUS' MANIFESTATION OF HIMSELF TO HIS DISCIPLES IN HIS FAREWELL DISCOURSES (13:1-17:26)

A unique feature of the book of John is the inclusion of the so-called "Farewell Discourses," also called the "Upper Room Discourses." These chapters contain a wealth of material not found in the other Gospels. From the second half of chapter 13 through chapter 16 the material consists primarily of Jesus giving personal instructions to his disciples concerning future events. It is a particularly rich source of material concerning the work and nature of the Holy Spirit. Chapter 17 is an instructive prayer, where Jesus intercedes for his disciples and the future church. As Carson has noted, John's pattern in chapters 2-12 is to present a sign/miracle and then explain it through Jesus' following discourses. In this case the pattern is reversed. Now the explanation is given first (chapters

---

[1]John's word for "miraculous sign" (σημεῖον, sēmeion) is not used again until the explanatory editorial comment of 20:30. This is in contrast to nine appearances of sēmeion in chapters 2-12, Dodd's "Book of Signs."

13–17) followed by the greatest sign of all (the death/resurrection of Jesus).[2]

1. At the Last Supper (13:1-38)

John's version of the Last Supper is obviously different yet strikingly similar to the versions found in the Synoptic Gospels. The most glaring difference is that John makes no mention of the institution of the Lord's Supper. We must remember, however, that the "Bread of Life Discourse" of John 6 contains distinct connections to the Lord's Supper. Therefore, apparently, John has deemed that material as a sufficient way of informing his readers of this significant event.

Jesus' Washing of His Disciple' Feet (13:1-17)

[1]It was just before the Passover Feast. Jesus knew that the time had come for him to leave this world and go to the Father. Having loved his own who were in the world, he now showed them the full extent of his love.[a]

[2]The evening meal was being served, and the devil had already prompted Judas Iscariot, son of Simon, to betray Jesus. [3]Jesus knew that the Father had put all things under his power, and that he had come from God and was returning to God; [4]so he got up from the meal, took off his outer clothing, and wrapped a towel around his waist. [5]After that, he poured water into a basin and began to wash his disciples' feet, drying them with the towel that was wrapped around him.

[6]He came to Simon Peter, who said to him, "Lord, are you going to wash my feet?"

[7]Jesus replied, "You do not realize now what I am doing, but later you will understand."

[8]"No," said Peter, "you shall never wash my feet."

Jesus answered, "Unless I wash you, you have no part with me."

---

[2]Carson, *The Gospel According to John*, p. 455.

[9]"Then, Lord," Simon Peter replied, "not just my feet but my hands and my head as well!"

[10]Jesus answered, "A person who has had a bath needs only to wash his feet; his whole body is clean. And you are clean, though not every one of you." [11]For he knew who was going to betray him, and that was why he said not every one was clean.

[12]When he had finished washing their feet, he put on his clothes and returned to his place. "Do you understand what I have done for you?" he asked them. [13]"You call me 'Teacher' and 'Lord,' and rightly so, for that is what I am. [14]Now that I, your Lord and Teacher, have washed your feet, you also should wash one another's feet. [15]I have set you an example that you should do as I have done for you. [16]I tell you the truth, no servant is greater than his master, nor is a messenger greater than the one who sent him. [17]Now that you know these things, you will be blessed if you do them.

[a]1 Or *he loved them to the last*

13:1. John notes the time of the next event as **just before the Passover Feast.** According to ancient Jewish reckoning, the Passover Feast day would have run from sundown Thursday until sundown on Friday. This has caused some scholars to take the position that John understands the "Last Supper" to have taken place on Wednesday evening, just before Passover. This cannot be reconciled with the Synoptic accounts, which clearly identify the Last Supper as a Passover meal (e.g., Luke 22:15).[3] But this is an easily explained contradiction. John does not say "the day before Passover" but "just before." The episode he relates next, Jesus washing the disciples' feet, is done immediately before the meal really begins.[4] This symbolic act of humility was a preliminary way for Jesus to demonstrate **the full extent of his love.** The complete demonstration will come on the cross.

---

[3]For extended discussion of this position see Barrett, *The Gospel According to St. John,* pp. 48-51, 437.

[4]Carson, *The Gospel According to John,* p. 460. For an exhaustive discussion of the problem of the timing of the Last Supper and the Crucifixion in relation to the Passover see Hendriksen, *Exposition,* 2:222-227.

John alerts the reader to a coming painful reality: Jesus will **leave this world** but his believers remain **in the world**. As stated already the world for John is sinful humanity alienated from God. The term "world" (κόσμος, *kosmos*) is a very significant one in the Farewell Discourses, occurring 35 times in chapters 14-17, nearly half of the occurrences for all of John.[5] In these chapters Jesus discusses thoroughly what it will mean for his disciples to be left behind in a world where sin still has a powerful grip on humanity.

Therefore, two of the great themes for the following chapters are introduced here: "leaving" and "love." Jesus' disciples, both his supper companions and the future church, must understand that his "leaving" was necessary and resulted in the presence of the Holy Spirit among believers. They must also understand that "love" is the controlling ethic for Jesus' disciples. Everything that happens in the community of believers is governed by love.

13:2. The NIV introduces unnecessary confusion into the text by saying **the evening meal** *was being served* (emphasis added). A literal translation would be "dinner was taking place." The event has begun, but the eating has not necessarily started. The unexpected washing of feet comes first.[6]

John tells us that **Judas Iscariot** has already made the decision to betray Jesus (see comments on Judas under 6:71). John does not include an account of Judas's meeting with the high priests to agree to the terms of Jesus' betrayal (see Luke 22:1-6). This meeting has already taken place. John is more interested in the spiritual forces at work. Judas did not concoct the idea for betrayal by himself. It was "put into [his] heart" by the devil (NRSV). Yet John does not imply that Satan somehow was able to override Judas's own will in this matter. He has already portrayed Judas as a money-hungry thief (12:6). His love of money is the overriding factor, negating any loyalty he may have felt for Jesus.

13:3. John takes care to remind the reader that Jesus has no insecurity when it comes to his status or his future. He has **all things under his power**, a remarkable statement of the omnipotence given

---

[5]These three chapter contain almost 20% (35 out of 186) of the occurrences of *kosmos* for the entire New Testament.

[6]The KJV translation, "supper being ended," is based upon an inferior Greek text, generally rejected by modern scholars.

to Jesus (cf. Matt 28:18; Phil 3:21). We are to remember that Jesus is not a victim in the events that follow, but a willing participant.

13:4-5. Jesus' secure relationship with the Father allows him to assume a very submissive role: that of the foot-washing servant. Because washing feet is not considered a normal feature of hospitality today, it is difficult for moderns to understand exactly how humiliating this act would have been. It was a necessary job, but one normally done by a household slave or servant. Jesus not only does the task, he assumes the full "costume" of a servant, stripped to his undergarment with a towel tied around his waist. One can imagine the drop-jawed disciples silently submitting to Jesus' scrubbing. It goes without comment that one of those having his feet bathed was Judas the betrayer. For the reader this lurking threat continues to hang over the scene.

13:6-9. There is one disciple, however, who finds his voice. Initially Peter sees nothing symbolic about the foot washing. His view is only of Jesus strangely and inappropriately acting the part of a slave, so he blurts out, **"you shall never wash my feet."** Jesus' response seems cryptic to us on first hearing, **"Unless I wash you, you have no part with me."** But this pushes Peter (and us) to a deeper understanding of the entire episode. We must admit that while Peter is impulsive and stubborn at times, he is no blockhead. He immediately recognizes what Jesus is offering, and he cannot get enough of it.

13:10-11. Jesus' answer to Peter is that only his feet need washing. Guests normally bathed before they came to dinner so only their feet would need washing once they arrived at the home of the host. Jesus is playing upon this social reality to provide a lesson for his disciples. The "cleansing" he is really concerned about is spiritual cleansing (cf. 15:3). Jesus can make them completely, utterly clean and pure (KJV, "clean every whit"). In this Jesus is referring to his atoning work on the cross, "the blood . . . [which] purifies us from every sin" (1 John 1:7). Believers will wear "white robes" (i.e., perfectly clean) which have been "washed in the blood of the Lamb" (Rev 7:14, cf. 22:14).

Yet, in the midst of this excellent lesson and promise, the plot continues. And the terrible fact is that Jesus must admit that not every one of the disciples is clean. While Peter actively resists the washing of Jesus at first, Judas passively rejects it without a word. Judas may have feet without a speck of filth upon them, but his heart is still dirty.

13:12-17. As we will see in chapters 13-17, the time for semi-cryptic comments from Jesus is past. Now he takes special care to ensure that his disciples understand his actions and words. His teaching point in the foot washing is **an example** of the relationships he expects in the future community of his believers. If he, the greatest of them, willingly serves them, then there is no excuse for any of them to disdain service. It is the same lesson as the Synoptic Gospels teach: "whoever wants to become great among you must be your servant, and whoever wants to be first must be slave of all" (Mark 10:43-44). This attitude of service must be based in love, and that will be the next teaching topic (v. 34, cf. v. 1).

But some will object that this message is out of date. How can we expect people to act as humble servants when our world honors the rich and the powerful?[7] Service takes time and effort, and it requires an attitude of humility. In the Roman Empire power and wealth were idolized, pity and humility were signs of weakness. Jesus' demand for a servant's heart is never outdated nor inappropriate. Our reward does not come from the world's adulation or from our control and mastery of other people. Our reward comes from having an obedient heart and in the confidence that we will be blessed by God.

Note: some Christian traditions have seen verse 14 as a continuing command for the church and, therefore, practice foot washing as a part of their worship activities. No one should object to such a foot washing service, and those who have never participated in one have missed a great lesson in humility and service. Yet it is difficult to make a case for this as an expected continuing practice of the church on the same level as baptism or the celebration of the Lord's Supper. The biggest reason for this conclusion is the lack of evidence that the early church practiced foot washing in this way. There is no evidence in the book of Acts (or any other New Testament book for that matter) that the primitive, apostolic church per-

---

[7]Rarely a world-class servant like Mother Teresa of Calcutta is honored, but this is the exception to the rule.

formed foot washing on a regular basis. For this reason it is seen as an instructive and beneficial exercise, but not a required one.

Jesus' Prediction of Judas' Betrayal (13:18-30)

[18]"I am not referring to all of you; I know those I have chosen. But this is to fulfill the scripture: 'He who shares my bread has lifted up his heel against me.'[a]

[19]"I am telling you now before it happens, so that when it does happen you will believe that I am He. [20]I tell you the truth, whoever accepts anyone I send accepts me; and whoever accepts me accepts the one who sent me."

[21]After he had said this, Jesus was troubled in spirit and testified, "I tell you the truth, one of you is going to betray me."

[22]His disciples stared at one another, at a loss to know which of them he meant. [23]One of them, the disciple whom Jesus loved, was reclining next to him. [24]Simon Peter motioned to this disciple and said, "Ask him which one he means."

[25]Leaning back against Jesus, he asked him, "Lord, who is it?"

[26]Jesus answered, "It is the one to whom I will give this piece of bread when I have dipped it in the dish." Then, dipping the piece of bread, he gave it to Judas Iscariot, son of Simon. [27]As soon as Judas took the bread, Satan entered into him.

"What you are about to do, do quickly," Jesus told him, [28]but no one at the meal understood why Jesus said this to him. [29]Since Judas had charge of the money, some thought Jesus was telling him to buy what was needed for the Feast, or to give something to the poor. [30]As soon as Judas had taken the bread, he went out. And it was night.

[a]18 Psalm 41:9

The drama of betrayal is now played out in detail. Jesus is perfectly aware of the intended action of Judas and its result. Jesus now begins to force Judas's hand. The rest of the disciples are only partially aware of what is going on, and their bewilderment is apparent.

13:18. Jesus begins this sequence by reminding the disciples that there is an unfortunate exception among them (v. 10). Just as not all of them are "clean," so also not all of them will be blessed as obedient servants (v. 17). Jesus teaches them that this is not an unforeseen development, but a fulfillment of Scripture, and therefore part of God's plan. The Scripture he quotes is Psalm 41:9, a moving revelation of David's heartbreak over the treachery he experienced from close friends who were really enemies.

13:19-20. Jesus is concerned that the disciples understand that his coming betrayal and death are in no way a thwarting of his plans. He anticipates their disappointment and confusion, but gives them a reassurance that will be understood at a later time. It is crucial that they continue to believe in him (literally, "believe that I am," *egō eimi*). If they maintain this faith, they become the end product of Jesus' mission from God. To those who want to discredit the church of today as being something Jesus never expected, we must answer that *to create a community of believers was an intended purpose of Jesus' ministry.*

13:21. As mentioned above, this is the time and place for Jesus to quit talking in figures of speech or giving little clues about the future. He has given hints already about the presence of a traitor among the band of disciples (see 6:70-71). Now John, the eyewitness, relates that Jesus is nearly overcome by the emotional distress this knowledge is causing him (**troubled in spirit**) and solemnly testifies, **"one of you is going to betray me."** The human Jesus does not seek to keep this horror to himself, but shares his troubles with his beloved disciples.

13:22-26. The NIV captures the essence of this scene well by saying the disciples stared at one another. The truth has dawned upon them: the real danger is from within their own crew! In order to appreciate fully what happens next, it is necessary to visualize the likely physical arrangement of this meal.[8]

---

[8]For examples of this style of dining where the participants recline on couches around a central serving table see William H. Stephens, *The New Testament World in Pictures* (Nashville: Broadman, 1987), pp. 390-393. See also the description in Craig S. Keener, *The IVP Bible Background Commentary: New Testament* (Downers Grove, IL: InterVarsity, 1993), p. 298.

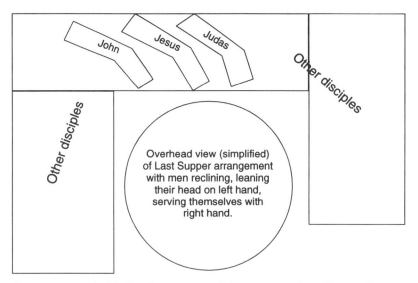

Overhead view (simplified)
of Last Supper arrangement
with men reclining, leaning
their head on left hand,
serving themselves with
right hand.

Jesus was probably in the center of this group of reclining diners. We are told that **the disciple whom Jesus loved** (= John) was **reclining next to him.** Literally, the text says he was "reclining on Jesus' chest."[9] This would mean that he was in front of Jesus, on his "chest" side. We also surmise that Judas was on the other side of Jesus, just behind him. This is because Jesus is able to easily speak to Judas and serve him with a piece of bread without any extraordinary effort (13:26-27).

If we understand this arrangement, we are better able to understand the sequence of events at this point. First, Jesus announces that one of the disciples is a traitor. Second, the dumbfounded disciples stare at each other. Third, Peter prompts his friend John to get a private reading on the identity of the traitor. John is able to do this because his head is just inches from Jesus' head. Fourth, Jesus tells John that he will identify the traitor by giving him a piece of bread. Fifth, he gives the bread to Judas, on his other side. If we accept this reconstruction of events we may project some of the other elements of this scene.

Why, then, did the disciples do nothing to stop Judas? The answer seems to be that they do not know what is happening. Only John knows, and he says nothing. One wonders if the author is

[9]Cf. KJV, "leaning on Jesus' bosom."

revealing here a secret burden he has carried for many years. He was the one who received an answer from Jesus to the question, "Who is it?" Yet he did nothing. Was he paralyzed by fear? Was he unwilling to believe Jesus' word that there was a traitor? Did he suffer from previous intimidation by Judas? Or was he simply too apathetic to act? We do not know, but all of us who have failed many times to do the right thing at the right time can easily put ourselves in John's place.

Another element that becomes clearer is the relationship between Jesus and Judas. These two were considered close friends. They are reclining right next to each other at the Passover meal, and Jesus even serves Judas (a sign of intimacy). For the majority of disciples this act is not seen as unusual, so we may assume that Jesus had handed Judas food many times before. What heart-stopping disappointment Jesus must have felt in Judas! Judas allows the influence of Satan and his own love of money to cause him to betray a very close friend.

13:27-30. There is another person besides John and Jesus who knows exactly what is going on, and this is Judas. Surely he could overhear Jesus' comment that the one to whom Jesus gave the dipped bread was the traitor. By accepting the bread, he removes all pretenses, all deception between Jesus and himself. He has the capacity to refuse the bread and, therefore, renounce his money-loving treachery. But he doesn't. By taking the bread he confirms his role as betrayer, and Satan has won a complete victory in his life. The influence of Satan is so triumphant at this point that John describes it as a demonic possession: **Satan entered into him.** Ironically for Judas the bread of the Last Supper was not "Christ's body broken for him," but his commitment to self-serving allegiance and evil actions.

Judas's departure has no effect upon the disciples, confirming our scenario that only Jesus, John, and Judas hear this private conversation and understand the actions. They hear Jesus say, **"What you are about to do, do quickly,"** but do not associate these words with the earlier pronouncement of a traitor in their band. They assume that Jesus is sending Judas on an errand of some type. John finishes this section with the chilling statement, **And it was night.** It is much more than the period after sundown. It is the darkest spiritual period in all of human history. Satan has flexed his mighty muscles of spiritual evil and stolen a disciple from the Son of God. It is clear to John that Satan is deceptively orchestrating the events leading to the crucifixion of Jesus. Why else would such a monstrous, unthinkable deed have been done? Humans are capable of terribly evil things, but satanically inspired evil is beyond any rhyme or reason. As Paul notes many years later, "None of the rulers of this age understood it, for if they had, they would not have crucified the Lord of glory" (1 Cor 2:8). Truly, it was night.

Jesus' Prediction of Peter's Denial; The New Commandment (13:31-38)

[31]When he was gone, Jesus said, "Now is the Son of Man glorified and God is glorified in him. [32]If God is glorified in him,ᵃ God will glorify the Son in himself, and will glorify him at once.

[33]"My children, I will be with you only a little longer. You will look for me, and just as I told the Jews, so I tell you now: Where I am going, you cannot come.

[34]"A new command I give you: Love one another. As I have loved you, so you must love one another. [35]By this all men will know that you are my disciples, if you love one another."

[36]Simon Peter asked him, "Lord, where are you going?"

Jesus replied, "Where I am going, you cannot follow now, but you will follow later."

[37]Peter asked, "Lord, why can't I follow you now? I will lay down my life for you."

[38]Then Jesus answered, "Will you really lay down your life for me? I tell you the truth, before the rooster crows, you will disown me three times!

ᵃ32 Many early manuscripts do not have *If God is glorified in him.*

13:31-33. The reader cannot miss the density of the concept of "glory" in this passage. We have already discussed the noun form for glory, *doxa* (see comments under 11:4). In verses 31-32, the verb form, "glorify," is used five times in quick succession. The Greek verb for glorify is δοξάζω (*doxazō*). It means to glorify, to give praise, to exalt, to attribute greatness or magnificence. As we have seen in John, Jesus often uses the terminology of "glory" to refer to his coming death and resurrection. In the act of sacrificial death Jesus brings glory to God. In the act of resurrection and exaltation God gives glory to Jesus. In the first four times that "glorify" is used here we find a *chiasmus* to express this reciprocal relationship.[10]

A: The Son of Man is glorified   B: God is glorified
   (by God)   (by the Son)

B': If God is glorified in him   A': God will glorify the Son
   (the Son)   in himself

Jesus follows this *chiasmus* with a fifth and final explanation of the glorification intention of God: God **will glorify him at once.** By this he means that his death will be followed by immediate resurrection and exaltation with no waiting for a future, eschatological Day of Resurrection/Judgment. This immediate future is not an option for the disciples. Therefore Jesus says, **"Where I am going** [to the right hand of the throne of God], **you cannot come."**

13:34-35. As the previous paragraph is dense with the concept of *glory* and *glorification*, these two verses are thick with the concept of love. They are some of the most enduring verses in all of Scripture, giving the cardinal command for the believing community: **you must love one another.** These are forms of the Greek verb ἀγαπάω (*agapaō*). This verb is usually translated as "love," but this English term is a poor substitute for the Greek verb. In this context *agapē* (the noun from this verb) is "unselfish love." It is "self-giving love." It is "love without expectations of returned affection." It is pure love, the love that acts simply out of the conviction that the right thing must be done for another human being. This altruistic and benevolent type of action is lacking in human society. For this reason Jesus emphasizes the necessity for his disciples to act this way toward one another, so that such a demonstration would cause the unbelieving world to notice. We are not his disciples *because* we demonstrate *agapē* love to one another, but if we *are* his disciples, this is not an option.

---

[10]Chiasmus is a term from advanced biblical interpretation that refers to an A–B, B–A literary structure. The term comes from the name of the Greek letter *chi* (χ) which looks like our English letter x. The structure looks like this when diagrammed: A   B
                                                   B   A

This great, controlling ethic of Jesus became a hallmark of the Christian community. It was later taught by both Paul (Rom 13:8; 1 Thess 4:9; cf. Gal 6:10) and Peter (1 Pet 1:22). It continued to be a favorite theme elsewhere in the writings of John (John 15:12,17; 1 John 3:11,23; 4:7,11,12; 2 John 5). The unswerving love of fellow believers is what Francis Schaeffer so aptly called the "Mark of the Christian." As Schaeffer says, it is "the mark that Jesus gives to label a Christian not just in one era or in one locality but at all times and all places until Jesus returns."[11] And this "mark" has continually renewed the church when it has been rediscovered. The Jesus People and youth of the 1960s loved to sing, "and they'll know we are Christians by our love," and they infused life and love into the church. In the nineteenth century the fathers of the Restoration Movement proclaimed:

In Essentials, Unity

In Non-Essentials, Liberty

In All Things, Love

Unfortunately, the Christian community of the late twentieth century has not been characterized by loving acceptance, but by sectarianism, distrust, and sometimes by open hostility. *Agapē* love is not the same as blanket toleration or approval of heretics and false teachers. But, as Schaeffer reminds us, "we must both distinguish true Christians from all pretenders and be sure that we leave no true Christians outside of our consideration. . . . We must include everyone who stands in the historic-biblical faith whether or not he is a member of our own party or our own group."[12]

13:36-38. In characteristically blunt fashion, Peter ignores the teaching on love to get back to something Jesus said earlier (v. 33). **"Where are you going?"** he demands to know. He does not like talk of Jesus abandoning them, and expresses his willingness to die for Jesus (cf. 11:16). But Jesus sees into his heart to see a mixture of loyalty and cowardice. He gives Peter a personal prophecy that must have broken his heart: he would soon deny his relationship with Jesus! He, in effect, would betray Jesus. We wonder how Peter interpreted these words. Did he see this as Jesus' answer to his

---

[11]Francis Schaeffer, *The Mark of the Christian* (Downers Grove, IL: Inter-Varsity, 1970), p. 8.

[12]Ibid., p. 11.

earlier question about the traitor, "Who is it?" (vv. 24-25). Is he the traitor? Peter's lack of rebuttal tells us that Jesus' words struck a chord in Peter's heart. He is fully aware of his own tendency toward unbelief and has no defense to offer.

JOHN 14

2. Promises of Jesus (14:1-31)

Chapters 14–16 continue the Farewell Discourses, but without the dramatic tension of chapter 13. Judas has now exited. Peter's outburst has been silenced. Jesus has revealed the central ethic of the Christian life, love for one another (13:34). Now the time is right for him to give the remaining disciples a "final briefing" before his own departure. These chapters contain some of the most wonderful truths of the Christian faith.

Promises of an Abode Where Jesus Is Going (14:1-4)

[1]"Do not let your hearts be troubled. Trust in God[a]; trust also in me. [2]In my Father's house are many rooms; if it were not so, I would have told you. I am going there to prepare a place for you. [3]And if I go and prepare a place for you, I will come back and take you to be with me that you also may be where I am. [4]You know the way to the place where I am going."

[a]1 Or You trust in God

14:1. The talk of traitorous betrayal in chapter 13 must have been alarming to the disciples. Jesus now reassures them, **"Do not let your hearts be troubled."** The **heart** (καρδία, kardia) is not the physical organ of blood pumping here.[1] But it is not strictly the emotional center of a person either, as we often understand it. In

---

[1]Καρδία (kardia) is never used of the physical organ in the New Testament. It generally has the figurative sense of the intellectual and volitional seat of the personality.

Jesus' day the *kardia*/heart was seen as the center of human volition or will.[2] When he says, **"Do not let your hearts be troubled,"** it would be something like a modern person saying, "Don't be wavering in your determination." This is why he follows this up with another command, "Believe in God and believe in me." This is a literal translation of John 14:1b, avoiding the somewhat weaker rendering of the NIV, "Trust in God; trust also in me." This is more than advice to trust God at a time of crisis. It is a perpetual command of Jesus for his disciples: *Believe, Believe, Believe, and never stop Believing.*

14:2-4. Jesus follows the command to believe with a promise for his disciples. His departure is for a reason: to make preparations for our eternity. The reader gains a unique glimpse of heaven. Jesus pictures heaven as the Father's **house**; a house with **many rooms.** The Greek word translated **"rooms"** is a plural form of μονή (*monē*), meaning "dwelling place" or "personal room."[3] This promise sets up the paradoxical use of *monē* in 14:23, where Jesus promises that he and the Father will have a "room" within the obedient disciple. In the future we will have our own rooms in God's "Big House." For now God willingly takes the small room of our hearts.

The final aspect of this promise is stated in extraordinary language. Jesus says the ultimate result is that where **I am** (*egō eimi*, see comments on 8:58), **you also may be.** In Greek it is clear that this is an intentional play upon the "I am" statement. Jesus hints that at his Second Coming believers will share in the "I am-ness" he presently enjoys. They will have unobstructed access to the glorious majesty of God the Father.[4] In these words Jesus is beginning to paint the big picture for the disciples of God's grand plan for the redemption of humanity.

---

[2]See Romans 10:10 where Paul notes that we "believe with our heart."

[3]The old KJV translation of *monē* as "mansion" gives a more grandiose sense to this word than is justified. This is based upon the Latin Vulgate's translation of the plural of *mone* as *mansiones.*

[4]There should be no doubt that Jesus is speaking of a Second Coming or Parousia here. Although the Gospel of John does not contain the descriptions of the Parousia found in other New Testament books, it has a strong sense of Jesus' return in glory. See John 14:18,28; 21:22-23.

Jesus the Way to the Father (14:5-12)

⁵Thomas said to him, "Lord, we don't know where you are going, so how can we know the way?"

⁶Jesus answered, "I am the way and the truth and the life. No one comes to the Father except through me. ⁷If you really knew me, you would knowᵃ my Father as well. From now on, you do know him and have seen him."

⁸Philip said, "Lord, show us the Father and that will be enough for us."

⁹Jesus answered: "Don't you know me, Philip, even after I have been among you such a long time? Anyone who has seen me has seen the Father. How can you say, 'Show us the Father'? ¹⁰Don't you believe that I am in the Father, and that the Father is in me? The words I say to you are not just my own. Rather, it is the Father, living in me, who is doing his work. ¹¹Believe me when I say that I am in the Father and the Father is in me; or at least believe on the evidence of the miracles themselves. ¹²I tell you the truth, anyone who has faith in me will do what I have been doing. He will do even greater things than these, because I am going to the Father.

ᵃ7 Some early manuscripts *If you really have known me you will know*

14:5. Thomas has not understood the spiritual nature of Jesus' promises. He may have thought that the "Father's house" Jesus referred to was the temple in Jerusalem. Did Jesus have a secret short cut to the temple? Or, does Jesus have a covert escape route? Yet his question opens the way for another grand teaching of Jesus. Thomas asks, "Is it possible *to know the way*?"

14:6. Thomas wants to know about a footpath. Jesus takes him far beyond the Jerusalem neighborhoods and side streets to give an eternal truth: "**I am the way.**" But this is only the first third of a triple "I am" statement: "**I am the way and the truth and the life.**" This is the sixth great "I am + identifier" statement in John.⁵ There

---

⁵The earlier "I am + identifier" claims are "I am the bread of life" (6:48 and elsewhere in chapter 6), "I am the light of the world" (8:12), "I am the gate/door" (10:7,8), "I am the good shepherd" (10:11,14), and "I am the resurrection and the life" (11:25).

is a sense in which these three are speaking of the same idea ("I am the true and living way"), but if we reduce the claim too quickly, we lose some of the richness and impact of the statement. Each of these declarations deserves separate discussion.

I am the way. The Greek word for "way" is ὁδός (*hodos*). On the literal level *hodos* refers to a thoroughfare for travel, whether a road, path, or highway (e.g., Mark 4:4; Luke 10:31), and by extension could refer to the journey itself (e.g., Matt 10:10). On the metaphorical level, however, *hodos* was often used to refer to the "way of life;" the life choices one makes and lifestyle one adopts (e.g., Matt 7:13; 1 Cor 12:31; Jude 11). Jesus' use of *hodos* is metaphorical, but not in the sense of "way of life." He is making a claim very similar to his statement, "I am the door/gate" (see comments on 10:7-9). Jesus is declaring that there is a single road that leads to God, and that *he is that road*. He has not come to show a "better way to God." It is not a "better way" because there is no other way. There is no wiggle-room in the statement, **No one comes to the Father except through me**. When it comes to fellowship with the Father, Jesus is the only port of entry, the only pass through the mountains, the only bridge over the river. Despite the many religious claims of our day, there is no other way.

I am . . . the truth. The Greek term for truth is ἀλήθεια (*alētheia*). The ancient concept of truth as expressed by this word was much the same as our modern concept. Truth is the opposite of falsehood. Truth is when a stated proposition matches up with factual reality. In the Greek philosophical tradition (a background for many of John's original readers), truth was to get to the nature of real being, the essence of an object. The opposite of this was that which merely "seemed" to be a certain way, only an appearance. Appearances might change, but truth does not.

The Jewish view of truth as found in the Old Testament is closely tied to the concept of "faithfulness." To say that a person is true is to say that he is faithful, reliable. In Genesis 42:16 we find the concept of reliable testimony equated with the concept of "telling the truth."

John contains a treasury of teachings on truth. Often truth is yoked with other important theological terms. In 1:14-18 John ties truth to grace resulting in the concept of "gracious truth." In this section truth is tied closely to the incarnation of Jesus. God's truth is displayed in human form in the person of Jesus. In 3:21 truth is presented as something we *do*, "living by the truth."[6] "Doing truth" is the opposite of evil works and deeds. In 4:23-24 truth is hitched to another key Johannine word, *spirit*. Acceptable worship must be done in "spirit and truth." There is no room for falsehood in spiritual worship. One cannot lie to God and expect the lie to go undetected. The idea of lying to God is really preposterous and absurd, and amounts to self-delusion. In 8:32 truth is linked with *freedom*. Jesus' disciples may become free if they "know the truth." The implications of "knowing the truth" are expressed more fully here, in verse 6. To know the truth is to know a person, Jesus Christ. He is Truth personified. When we know the truth, we really understand who Jesus is; we believe it with all our hearts; we stake our lives upon it.

I am . . . the life. This claim has already been made in combination with "I am the resurrection" (see comments on 11:25-26). The Greek word for **life** used here is ζωή (*zōē*). It can refer to simple biological viability, that which is alive as opposed to that which is dead. John began his Gospel by claiming that Jesus, as the "Word," was the creator/originator of the *zōē* life of the universe (see comments on 1:3). But John has already shown that a primary objective of Jesus' mission is to bring life to humankind (5:39-40; 10:10). How can you bring "life" to something that is already alive?

This illustrates that there are two different kinds of "life" in mind in the book. There is biological life, a gift of God to the creatures of the universe. But there is a supernatural, eternal life that transcends the limitations of biological creatures. It is this life that Jesus has in mind in verse 6; he is **the life**.

The richness of this "I am" statement is astounding. Jesus is the Way. Jesus is the Truth. Jesus is the Life. But of these, the major teaching here is that Jesus is the only Way to the Father. Jesus is the *true and living way to the Father*. The exclusive claims of the Gospel and the problems they cause for some moderns have already been

---

[6]This was a key concept for Thomas and Alexander Campbell who concluded, "Nothing can be Christian doctrine that cannot be translated into life" (i.e., doctrine = what you can live).

discussed (see comments under 10:7-9). The fact that Jesus represented the only way to the Father was central to the preaching and beliefs of the early church. The community of Jesus' disciples became known as "The Way" (see Acts 9:2; 19:9; 24:22). Paul taught that there is "one mediator" standing between God and humankind, "the man Christ Jesus" (1 Tim 2:5). John 14:6 is truly one of the primary Scriptures of the Christian faith. There is no more "long search" for God. The way to God has been revealed through the person of Jesus Christ.

14:7. This verse expands upon the Way/Truth/Life assertion of Jesus. What does it mean to have a "way" to the Father? It is not a long process of spiritual discipline. Rather, it is "knowing" the Father, an immediate relationship. But how can we "know" God? Isn't there a sense that God is *unknowable* since humankind's expulsion from the Garden, since direct two-way conversation was ruled out of bounds? The answer to this question is yes. We can never force access to the presence of God. We are in no position to make any relationship demands upon God. The only reason we can "know" God is because, as Carl F.H. Henry has taught repeatedly, God is a self-revealing God. We can know God because he has chosen to make himself known to us. And this self-revelation is perfectly and completely made in Jesus Christ (1:14; cf. Heb 1:1-2). That is why "knowing Jesus" *is* "knowing God."

14:8-12. The dialog continues as John uses the questions of the disciples to clarify the points that Jesus is making. If Jesus is the "Way" to the Father, Philip reasons that it should be simple enough for Jesus to **show** them **the Father**. The direct simplicity yet the audacity of this request is astonishing.

The word translated "**show**" is the Greek verb δείκνυμι (*deiknymi*), and here means "to demonstrate or show visually." In the book of John *deiknymi* is generally used in the sense of "showing or demonstrating something marvelous."[7] Philip is asking Jesus to "give us a chance to see the Father," a seemingly innocent request

---

[7]For other examples of δείκνυμι (*deiknymi*) in John see 2:18, where it is part of a request of the Jewish leaders for a miraculous sign; 5:20, where it is used twice to refer to the revelation of God's works; 10:32, where it refers to the demonstration of the miraculous signs of Jesus; and 20:20, where it is used for Jesus' exhibition of the marks of his crucifixion.

with enormous implications. To "see God" was considered impossible and even dangerous by the Jews. Even Moses was only permitted to see God's backside under highly controlled circumstances, and not the full glory of God. To look upon the face of God would be deadly for any mortal being (Exod 33:20). John has reminded his readers very early on that "No one has ever seen God" (1:18).

Jesus' answer is, "the way to see the Father is to watch me." As Butler has noted, the *seeing* that the disciples may do is "spiritual comprehension and not sensory perception."[8] There is no subdued radiance about Jesus at this time, no glowing in the dark on the way to the Garden of Gethsemane. He looks like any other human being. Jesus challenges Philip to consider the situation. After all the marvelous signs Jesus has done and Philip has witnessed (including the raising of Lazarus from the dead), **Don't you believe**? (v. 10). Don't you believe that everything about Jesus is a revelation of the Father?

Jesus gives Philip and the disciples the ultimate justification for his claim, a reality that may be discerned only through spiritual eyes: **"I am in the Father and . . . the Father is in me"** (cf. 10:38). Such language of the "oneness of the Son in the Father" may sound like Eastern mysticism to us at first glance, but it is an important expression of theological truth in complete harmony with what Jesus has said throughout the Gospel of John. As Bruce explains, this "mutual indwelling" means, "to see the Son is to see the otherwise invisible God."[9] The unity of the Father and Son is perfect, yet they are not identical. As the author of Hebrews has written, "The Son is the radiance of God's glory and the exact representation of his being" (1:3).

Doing Greater Works Than Jesus, Asking in Jesus' Name (14:13-14)

[13]And I will do whatever you ask in my name, so that the Son may bring glory to the Father. [14]You may ask me for anything in my name, and I will do it.

---

[8]Butler, *John*, 2:248.
[9]Bruce, *John*, p. 300; cf. Col 1:15.

14:13-14. Jesus then gives his disciples a further benefit derived from his oneness with Father God. They will be able to make requests to God in Jesus' name, and the requests will be answered.[10] The reader must be careful not to find here a vision of prayer akin to a genie in a lamp who must grant three wishes. This is not a blanket authorization for any of Jesus' disciples to use prayer for personal benefit and enrichment. There are some important qualifications to this promise.

First, sincere prayer requests must come "in Jesus' name." This does not mean that saying "in Jesus' name, Amen" at the end of a prayer is a magic formula. As Leon Morris has written, "It means that prayer is to be in accordance with all that the name stands for. It is prayer proceeding from faith in Christ, prayer that gives expression to a unity with all that Christ stands for, prayer which seeks to set forward Christ Himself."[11] Second, the answer to such requests must serve to **"bring glory to the Father."** Jesus promises involvement in the prayer requests of his disciples in order to continue his purposeful ministry of bringing glory to God. Third, we should be careful not to remove this promise from the context in which it is given. Jesus is speaking to his disciples/apostles. For every believer to appropriate this promise without qualification misses part of its purpose. Jesus promises that his disciples will be the vehicles for **even greater things** than he has done. This is certainly hyperbolic, but it does teach that signs and wonders would accompany the ministry of Jesus' disciples, a promise fulfilled in the book of Acts.

Having given these qualifications, however, a warning should be given for the extreme view that sees prayer as a powerless, almost futile exercise. Sometimes we become prayer-paralyzed to the point we are afraid to pray for anything unless we are sure that our request will be realized anyway. We overqualify our prayers and fail to pray the bold prayer of the believer. Yes, Jesus is speaking to his disciples in verse 13, but believers today may also find a powerful prayer life if they pray "in the name of Jesus."

---

[10]For a detailed analysis of the parallel passages in John in which Jesus promises to grant whatever the disciples request in his name, see Brown, *John,* 2:633-634.

[11]Morris, *John,* p. 646.

Jesus' Departure and the Spirit's Coming (14:15-31)

[15]"If you love me, you will obey what I command.[16]And I will ask the Father, and he will give you another Counselor to be with you forever — [17]the Spirit of truth. The world cannot accept him, because it neither sees him nor knows him. But you know him, for he lives with you and will be[a] in you. [18]I will not leave you as orphans; I will come to you. [19]Before long, the world will not see me anymore, but you will see me. Because I live, you also will live. [20]On that day you will realize that I am in my Father, and you are in me, and I am in you. [21]Whoever has my commands and obeys them, he is the one who loves me. He who loves me will be loved by my Father, and I too will love him and show myself to him."

[22]Then Judas (not Judas Iscariot) said, "But, Lord, why do you intend to show yourself to us and not to the world?"

[23]Jesus replied, "If anyone loves me, he will obey my teaching. My Father will love him, and we will come to him and make our home with him. [24]He who does not love me will not obey my teaching. These words you hear are not my own; they belong to the Father who sent me.

[25]"All this I have spoken while still with you. [26]But the Counselor, the Holy Spirit, whom the Father will send in my name, will teach you all things and will remind you of everything I have said to you. [27]Peace I leave with you; my peace I give you. I do not give to you as the world gives. Do not let your hearts be troubled and do not be afraid.

[28]"You heard me say, 'I am going away and I am coming back to you.' If you loved me, you would be glad that I am going to the Father, for the Father is greater than I. [29]I have told you now before it happens, so that when it does happen you will believe. [30] I will not speak with you much longer, for the prince of this world is coming. He has no hold on me, [31]but the world must learn that I love the Father and that I do exactly what my Father has commanded me.

"Come now; let us leave.

[a]*17* Some early manuscripts *and is*

14:15-17. Jesus reminds his disciples that their relationship is built upon love and obedience. In this context **what I command** = the "new commandment," to "love one another" (13:34). We are truly his disciples if we "love one another" (13:35). In 14:16-17 Jesus gives a wondrous promise for his "true disciples": the Holy Spirit. The presence of the Holy Spirit in the believer's life has already been hinted at in John. In 1:33 we are told that Jesus would be the one to "baptize" (immerse) with the Holy Spirit. In 3:5 Jesus informs Nicodemus that the New Birth involves the Holy Spirit. In 7:37-39 the Holy Spirit is presented as the one who satisfies our previously unquenchable spiritual thirst. The Farewell Discourses of chapters 13–17 contain five distinct Holy Spirit texts: 14:16-17, 26; 15:26-27; 16:7-11,13-15. One of the closing passages of John's Gospel is his account of the reception of the Holy Spirit by the disciples (20:22-23). This is tied to the forgiveness of sins, a sign of the presence and authority of Jesus continuing in the church.[12]

In this section (vv. 16-17) Jesus teaches three primary things about the Holy Spirit. First, the Holy Spirit is our *Eternal Advocate* (v. 16). The Greek word translated **Counselor** in the NIV is παρ-άκλητος (*paraklētos*, from which we get the term "Paraclete"). The common meaning of *paraklētos* in the ancient world was "one who gives legal assistance." This is what the original reader of John would have thought of. Therefore, "Advocate" (NRSV) is an acceptable translation if understood in a legal sense. "Counselor" (NIV) is also a good translation if understood in a legal sense, as one attorney might address another. He is "counselor" in the sense of "the judge appointed legal counsel for the accused." "Helper" (NASB) is also a useful translation, but not in the sense of a subordinate/assistant. A *paraklētos* is a superior or equal helper. Elsewhere John uses this term of Jesus, our advocate who "speaks to the Father in our defense" (1 John 2:1). We pay lawyers to do what we cannot do ourselves, to guide us through the legal maze of the court system. The Holy Spirit does what we could not possibly do: intercedes for us before the throne of God. Our *paraklētos* is our advocate, our heavenly lawyer interceding for us before a righteous God, who is a righteous Judge (see Rom 8:26-27).

---

[12]For complete discussion of all the Holy Spirit texts in John see my article, Mark S. Krause, "The Holy Spirit in John's Gospel," *Christian Standard* (April 20, 1986): pp. 350-352.

Second, Jesus teaches us that the Holy Spirit is the *Spirit of Truth* (v. 17). It is in the issue of truth that the Holy Spirit may seem most unlike our stereotypes of modern lawyers. Truth is very important in John's Gospel, and it is usually identified with Jesus. In John there are three related concepts: Truth, Spirit, and Freedom. As Paul says in 2 Corinthians 3:17-18, where God's Spirit is, there is freedom. The ministry of the Holy Spirit is transforming freedom. Our minds are unveiled. We see the truth. Truth is freeing, it is always freeing. Ultimate spiritual truth frees us from the unknown in our relationship to God. Ultimate spiritual freedom is knowing that you are in a right relationship with God, and this is a part of the ministry of the Holy Spirit.

Third, Jesus promises his disciples that the Holy Sprit is **in you** (v. 17). It is important to understand that the Holy Spirit is never "gotten," the Holy Spirit is only "given." He can never be "taken," but only "received."[13] Jesus tells his disciples that the world/*kosmos* cannot accept the Spirit. The Spirit is Holy, and incompatible with the world. When believers receive the Holy Spirit, they begin a new and holy existence, and sometimes this cannot even be communicated with those on the outside. The presence of the Holy Spirit may be faked, or it may be quenched and hidden. But we should remember that at the end of the day, there is no such thing as a Christian without the presence of the Holy Spirit.

14:18-21. Jesus explains this new relationship in other terms. He has already taught of the Father being in him, and he being in the Father. Now he adds a new element. Jesus' followers may be said to be "in him" and he "in them." By extension, this also means his disciples are "in the Father," because that is the position of Jesus. This relationship is defined as being **loved by** the **Father** and by the Son. The love of the Son will be actualized in the revelation of the Son to the believer; he will **show** himself to the obedient believer.

14:22. This promise of the Son being "shown" has pricked the interest of one of the disciples. He is **Judas not Iscariot**. This is probably the "Thaddeus" of the Gospels of Matthew and Mark (Matt 10:3; Mark 3:18), who seems to be called "Judas the son of

---

[13]The Holy Spirit cannot be purchased either. See the unfortunate story of Simon the Magician in Acts 8:9-25.

James" in Luke's lists (Luke 6:16; Acts 1:13). He poses an objection in the form of a question, "Why not reveal yourself to the whole world?" This is the same question/challenge that the brothers of Jesus gave to him before the Feast of Tabernacles (7:3-4).

14:23-31. Jesus' answer to Judas is rather complicated, but the most direct statements are the following. In verse 27 Jesus says, "**I do not give to you as the world gives.**" In other words, you cannot judge what I am doing by the usual standards of the world. What may seem a failure by worldly criteria is a victory in God's plans. Therefore, Judas should not expect Jesus to impress the world by gaudy fame and spectacle. In verse 31 Jesus tells his disciples that "**The world must learn that I love the Father and that I do exactly what my Father has commanded me.**" Jesus' demonstration to the world will be a display of obedience motivated by love. Thus, he will be revealed to the world, but on the Father's required terms. As Paul has written,

> And being found in appearance as a man,
> he humbled himself
> and became obedient to death —
> even death on a cross!
> *Philippians 2:8*

Jesus introduces another new element in the life of the believer in this section. He gives **peace** to the believing community. The Greek word for **peace** is εἰρήνη (*eirēnē*). Although this word had a rich background in Greek culture, John probably intends us to understand the Jewish/Hebrew sense of this word. The Hebrew equivalent for *eirēnē* is *shalom*. It means more than just a lack of active warfare, a truce between two armies. For the Jew "peace" was personal well-being characterized by having a right and blessed relationship with God. Paul can later say of Jesus, "he himself is our peace" (Eph 2:14). Jesus did not end all human wars, but he does make it possible to end the war between God and man. His death is our peace, our means of reconciliation with our Father. This knowledge of reconciliation allows the believer to **not let** his **heart be troubled** (see comments under v. 1) **and** to **not be afraid.**

Jesus ends this section by stressing the urgency of the hour. He tells them these things now because they must believe later (v. 29). It is as if he won't have any time to explain once the final events begin. **The prince of this world is coming** (v. 30). This is Satan, particularly as he controls Judas Iscariot. Jesus implies, "he's almost here" and when he gets here there will be no more opportunities to teach. He ends by telling them, **"Come now, let us leave."** This may mean that chapters 15–17 are intended to be understood as words spoken on the way to the Garden of Gethsemane, but 18:1 gives the impression that they remain in the upper room through chapter 17. More likely verse 31 is preparing them for their final walk to Gethsemane, but Jesus still has a few more things to say.

Throughout this section Jesus states that his departure is not final; he will return (vv. 3,18,28). Although it is possible to understand these as simply references to the postresurrection appearances of Jesus, this seems to be too limited a view. Jesus is teaching that there will be a second appearance of the Son to humankind; he will come a second time.

JOHN 15

3. More Commands and Promises of Jesus (15:1-27)

Chapter 15 continues Jesus' remarks to his disciples in the Upper Room. The first part of this chapter is one of the most familiar passages of Scripture in the entire Bible, Jesus' analogy of the vine and branches. Verses 1-17 are descriptive of continuing relationships within the believing community as characterized by love. This section ends with a resounding *"then"* (v. 16). If the relationship is working correctly, *then* requests made in Jesus' name will be granted. Verses 18-25 depict the other side of the coin: the future relationship with "the world." Jesus promises that his disciples will be met with an irrational hatred from the world, hatred prophesied in the Old Testament (v. 25). Finally, verses 26-27 outline the future course of the believing community. It is to be a Holy Spirit empowered witness to the world about Jesus.

*Jesus, the Vine; the Disciples, the Branches;
the New Commandment Given (15:1-17)*

¹"I am the true vine, and my Father is the gardener. ²He cuts off every branch in me that bears no fruit, while every branch that does bear fruit he prunes[a] so that it will be even more fruitful. ³You are already clean because of the word I have spoken to you. ⁴Remain in me, and I will remain in you. No branch can bear fruit by itself; it must remain in the vine. Neither can you bear fruit unless you remain in me.

⁵"I am the vine; you are the branches. If a man remains in me and I in him, he will bear much fruit; apart from me you can do nothing. ⁶If anyone does not remain in me, he is like a branch

that is thrown away and withers; such branches are picked up, thrown into the fire and burned. [7]If you remain in me and my words remain in you, ask whatever you wish, and it will be given you. [8]This is to my Father's glory, that you bear much fruit, showing yourselves to be my disciples.

[9]"As the Father has loved me, so have I loved you. Now remain in my love. [10]If you obey my commands, you will remain in my love, just as I have obeyed my Father's commands and remain in his love. [11]I have told you this so that my joy may be in you and that your joy may be complete. [12]My command is this: Love each other as I have loved you. [13]Greater love has no one than this, that he lay down his life for his friends. [14]You are my friends if you do what I command. [15]I no longer call you servants, because a servant does not know his master's business. Instead, I have called you friends, for everything that I learned from my Father I have made known to you. [16]You did not choose me, but I chose you and appointed you to go and bear fruit — fruit that will last. Then the Father will give you whatever you ask in my name. [17]This is my command: Love each other.

ᵃ2 The Greek for *prunes* also means *cleans*.

The importance of vineyards in the ancient world is difficult for modern readers to appreciate. Winemaking dates from the earliest days of human history. Genesis records Noah as the first vineyard cultivator and winemaker, with unfortunate results (Gen 9:20 ff.). The production and consumption of wine was an economic mainstay for the farmers of Palestine in Jesus' day.

Many Christians today do not drink wine, and most have little understanding of a working vineyard. Wine comes from the juice of the grapes produced by a grapevine. If left untrimmed, a grapevine will use its available energy to grow long woody branches and extend its territory, while producing a few meager bunches of grapes. Winemakers learned early on that grapevines could be tamed by vigilant pruning of branches so that comparatively few buds would be allowed to grow. When this trimming was done, the vine was forced to direct its life-giving sap into the production of grapes rather than territorial expansion. Under good conditions of both sufficient rain and plenty of sunshine, this resulted in heavy grape clusters and abundant grape juice for wine production. Major pruning was done in midwinter, when the vine would lose the least amount of its precious sap. This process of cleaning/pruning the vineyard left a bare field with small stumps at the beginning of the spring growing season. A tidy farmer not only snipped off these old branches, but also hauled them away and burned them so that his vines could grow unhindered from the mature stump each year. Effective vine dressing required that the farmer continue to prune through the growing season to keep the vine's energy focussed on a limited number of grape clusters. Even today the best grapes are produced by developed vines, 12-40 years old, with deep, healthy root systems.

With this background we are better able to understand the features of Jesus' allegorical illustration using vineyard farming. Notice the identified elements and what they represent:

Vineyard Element	Function in Vineyard	Intended to Represent	Function in the Believing Community
Vine	Brings sap from the root to give life to the branches	Jesus	Brings and sustains life to the disciples
Branches	Bear fruit	Jesus' Disciples	Continue to carry on the ministry of Jesus by demonstrating his love
Gardener	Prunes unwanted branches, hauls away and burns the rubbish	God the Father	Judges and cleanses the community

With these basics in mind, let's look at some specifics in these verses.

15:1-8. This section begins with the seventh and final "I am + identifier" statement in John,[1] **"I am the true vine"** (repeated in v. 5 as **"I am the vine"**). The specifics of this agricultural analogy would have been immediately understood by Jesus' disciples (and by John's readers) and require little explanation in the text. That

---

[1]The earlier "I am + identifier" claims are "I am the bread of life" (6:48 and elsewhere in chapter 6), "I am the light of the world" (8:12), "I am the gate/door" (10:7,8), "I am the good shepherd" (10:11, 14), "I am the resurrection and the life" (11:25), and "I am the way and the truth and the life" (14:6).

Jesus is intending an allegorical, secondary level of meaning with the analogy is quickly understood. He is not giving a lesson in farming. He is saying, "Think for a minute about the vineyard. Let me use it to portray our community. I'll start with the vine, because my function in the community is like the function of the vine in the vineyard."

But why does Jesus claim to be the "*true* vine"? The word translated "true" is ἀληθινή (*alēthinē*). This is an adjective that means something like "genuine" or "pure." If Jesus is the "genuine vine" does this suggest there is a "false vine" or "counterfeit vine?" To answer this we should consult some of the Old Testament backgrounds for the vine analogy.

Vineyard analogies are relatively frequent in the Old Testament with a variety of applications (e.g., Gen 40:9-11; Ps 128:3). It is not necessary to find a single intended background for Jesus' vine illustration. Just as the workings of a vineyard were common knowledge in the Old Testament times, so they were in Jesus' day, and thus the vineyard served as a ready source for analogy. [2] However, we should recognize that "vine" was frequently used as an analogy for the nation of Israel (e.g., Ps 80:8-19; Isa 5:1-7; Jer 2:21; Hosea 10:1), often an unfavorable analogy. Jesus is pushing his disciples to see that their future does not lie with the national "vine" of Israel, but with the "genuine vine" (himself).

An important part of this analogy is the language of "cleansing." The "cleansing" activities of the vineyard are related as a two-stage process. First, Jesus describes the gardener's task of cutting off unproductive branches (v. 2), presumably false disciples. Such branches are allowed to dry up and are then burned (v. 6). Second, in verse 2 Jesus describes the pruning of the fruit-bearing branches, meaning the thinning of buds so the remaining ones will produce larger clusters of grapes. In this case he uses essentially the same word to describe both this "cleansing" of the fruit-bearing branches (the verb καθαίρω, *kathairō*, translated prunes by the NIV [1978

---

[2] Particularly misleading is the attempt to see Jesus' vine as a transformed image of the biblical "tree of life." This requires hermeneutical sleight of hand of the first order. For this approach see Bultmann, *The Gospel of John*, p. 530.

edition has "trims clean"][3]) and the state of the disciples, who are **already clean** (the adjective καθαρός, *katharos*, v. 3).

But in what way are the disciples "clean?" It is tempting to see Jesus' reference to their "clean" state in verse 3 as a comment on the exit of Judas, the "unclean" one (13:11) who has already departed, thus "pruning" the band of disciples. This may work for the first stage of pruning, the removal of unproductive branches.[4] But it does not encompass the second stage of pruning/cleansing which is done to the good branches on an individual basis. Jesus has already pronounced the disciples "clean" after his symbolic act of footwashing (13:10-11). This is the purification of the personal life, a cleansing done by **the word** of Jesus. Commitment to following the words of Jesus will result in purity of lifestyle. Christians today are well aware that chronic sin issues in the life of the believer are terribly debilitating and self-defeating. The preoccupied and disreputable disciple will never be as "fruitful" for the Lord as the one who "throw[s] off everything that hinders and the sin that so easily entangles" (Heb 12:1).

Jesus describes the relationship between his disciples and himself as one of **remaining**. The Greek verb translated "remain" is μένω (*menō*), occurring 7 times in verses 1-8. In reference to the vineyard analogy it is clear that the branch must "remain" on the vine[5] or else it will die. Likewise, the believer must remain attached to Jesus or face spiritual death. But Jesus describes his relationship to his disciples as being more complex than that of the branch and vine, and in this the text brings out additional meanings of *menō*. *Menō* may have the sense of "dwelling" or "living" or "making a home."[6] For Jesus to "remain in us," then, is the same concept as

---

[3]Καθαίρω (*kathairō*) is an older verb, used only here in the New Testament. In the first century it was apparently being replaced by the similar word, καθαρίζω (*katharizō*) which also means "to clean."

[4]It may be objected that the Father does not "prune" Judas. If anything, Judas prunes himself. This sort of objection, however, pushes the figurative language of the allegory far beyond what it will bear. Any allegory or analogy will break down if squeezed too hard, even those of Jesus.

[5]Here the NIV and most modern versions have failed to see the idiomatic nature of the expression "in the vine." We do not speak of attached branches as being "in" a tree, but rather "on" a tree.

[6]Hence the frequent English translation "abide." For a few examples of μένω referring to staying at a certain location see John 1:38-39; 7:9; 10:40.

found in 14:23, where Jesus promises that the Father and he will "make our home" with the obedient disciple. This is a two-way relationship. Jesus promises, **"Remain in me, and I will remain in you."** He promises never to abandon his disciples. As Paul so eloquently asked, "Who shall separate us from the love of Christ?" *No one,* Paul thunders, and his answer still brings assurance and peace to the disciples of Christ today (Rom 8:35-39).

There are additional aspects to this "remaining in Christ" relationship. Jesus promises that the one who remains in him **will bear much fruit** (v. 5). It is clear that the fruit of the vine is grapes, but what is "fruit" in the life of the disciple? This is often taken by preachers to have an evangelistic sense (the production of more disciples) but this is an unlikely connotation here. The Greek word for fruit is καρπός (*karpos*), and normally refers to the edible produce of trees or plants. In the New Testament *karpos* is frequently used to refer to righteous actions, the "fruit" of one's life. John the Baptist uses fruit/*karpos* to describe actions that demonstrate a heart of true repentance (Matt 3:8, Luke 3:8). Paul uses fruit/*karpos* as an expression for desirable, righteous qualities in one's life, the "fruit of the Spirit" (Gal 5:22-23). The author of Hebrews uses fruit/*karpos* to picture the results of the disciplined lifestyle (Heb 12:11). While these examples do not necessarily determine the sense of fruit/*karpos* in John 15, this does fit the context. As Jesus also says, the one separated from him **can do nothing,** which is the opposite of bearing fruit in this verse (v. 5). It is actions that Jesus is looking for; not works to earn God's favor, but deeds of love that validate the disciple's relationship to Christ. For Jesus' followers this is tangibly **showing yourselves to be my disciples** (v. 8).

The final promise of the "remaining" relationship in this section is that it will produce a powerful prayer life. Jesus has already made specific promises about prayer requests made in his name (14:13-14). Now he outlines the qualifications necessary to claim the promise. **"If you remain in me and my words remain in you, ask whatever you wish, and it will be given you"** (v. 7). Disciples are not promised invincible prayer power apart from their relationship to Christ, but within the bounds of this relationship. We are to "remain in" him (maintain fellowship with the living Christ) and his "words" must remain in us (obedience to Christ's teachings). If our hearts are aligned with the heart of Christ, our needs will be his needs, and these needs will be supplied. This promise will be restated one more time in verse 16.

15:9-11. Now Jesus introduces another analogy to explain his intended relationship with the disciples: the Father's love for the Son. John has already taught that this love is demonstrated by the Father's willingness to give the Son all things (3:35). Jesus has taught that the correct response to the Father's love is complete obedience (10:17). This Father/Son relationship is the model for the Jesus/disciple relationship. We are to receive the love of Jesus obediently. This is how we **remain in** [his] **love**. We are unable to fully appreciate and enjoy this love and the peace it brings if we are in a rebellious state. Human experience tells us that it is difficult to receive acts of kindness from someone we have mistreated. So too it is difficult to fully receive the love of Christ if we take his forgiveness for granted. The more we obey, the more we will experience the active love of Christ in our lives. This obedient devotion works for our benefit, for in it our **joy** is **complete**. As the songwriter has written, "There is joy in serving Jesus."

15:12-13. For the second time Jesus mandates his "new" commandment: **Love each other** (see 13:34). Before Jesus explained that this community love would mark them as his disciples. Now he gives further explanation as to the nature of this love. This explanation answers some latent questions about the commandment. How should we love each other? Jesus says, **as I have loved you.** Well, how, exactly, have you loved us? Jesus says, "I am going to show you the greatest love of all. I am going to die for you."

The stirring words of verse 13 have often been quoted in eulogizing brave men and women who have given their lives to protect or save the endangered. These applications are somewhat legitimate and certainly inspiring, but not quite in harmony with the thrust of this passage. Jesus is talking about more than a spontaneous act of selfless courage. He is, first and foremost, talking about himself. He is the one who "lays down his life" (cf. 10:11,15, 17). His coming death will be the ultimate demonstration of love, a superlative act of obedience motivated by the greatest possible love. There is no reason or explanation for Christ's willing sacrifice except for his love. It is beyond rational human explanation. The paradox was aptly put by Paul when he wrote, "While we were still sinners, Christ died for us" (Rom 5:8; cf. Eph 5:2). This was not a circumstance shoved upon Jesus. It was his mission from the outset. He came to die.

The early church fathers, particularly the monastic masters, understood what this required. For Jesus' disciples to follow his pattern, we must live as if we have already chosen obedience over death. St. John of the Ladder called this the "contemplation of death." We must look death squarely in the eye and say that its threat hanging over us will never be a sufficient reason to disobey Jesus. We will love Jesus and his community of believers, no matter what the cost. As an anonymous Christian author has said so beautifully, "Only one life, 'twill soon be past. Only what's done for Christ will last." Similarly, Paul wrote, "For me to live is Christ, and to die is gain" (Phil 1:21).

15:14-17. At this point Jesus announces a new status for his disciples. They are not his **servants** but his **friends**. These two terms make for an interesting study in contrasts. The term translated "servant" by the NIV is δοῦλος (*doulos*). While the NIV has followed the KJV with this translation, this is actually the Greek word for "slave." The word implies more than the relationship implied by a waiter seeing to the needs of his customers. It is much more than a superior/inferior or employer/employee relationship. Jesus is talking about the Master/slave relationship of the ancient world, where the slave was the personal property of another person, and served without pay or reward. In one stroke Jesus has elevated these disciple-slaves to the level of "friends." This is a translation of the Greek term φίλος (*philos*). It refers to a personal companion, a "friend" in the best sense of the word. A friend is not your inferior, but your social equal. The early church understood this relationship to be a freeing one within the believing community. Within the fellowship of Jesus' disciples there was no place for ranking by wealth or social status. As Paul wrote, "There is neither Jew not Greek, slave nor free, male nor female, for you are all one in Christ Jesus" (Gal 3:28).[7]

---

[7]John 15:15 was the verse the followers of the seventeenth century reformer, George Fox, used to describe themselves. Originally they called

We are reminded again of the love of Jesus when he says, **"You did not choose me, but I chose you . . . ."** Christ befriends us while we are at odds with his purposes, while we are alienated from God. Jesus did not come to the world to hide himself and hope that someone might find him. As he says elsewhere, he came "to seek and to save what was lost" (Luke 19:10). He chooses us **to go and bear fruit.** We are not simply chosen to have blessings heaped upon us. The election of God is to service and responsibility, not to privilege. This was a lesson the "old vine" (the nation of Israel) never learned very well in the Old Testament.

Jesus ends this section by reiterating a promise and a command, each for the third time. The promise is that when we are in a fruit-bearing (= obedient) relationship, **the Father will give you whatever you ask in my name.** Finally, this relationship of obedience is summed up in a two word (in Greek) command: **Love each other.**

Hatred from the World (15:18-25)

[18]"If the world hates you, keep in mind that it hated me first. [19]If you belonged to the world, it would love you as its own. As it is, you do not belong to the world, but I have chosen you out of the world. That is why the world hates you. [20]Remember the words I spoke to you: 'No servant is greater than his master.'[a] If they persecuted me, they will persecute you also. If they obeyed my teaching, they will obey yours also. [21]They will treat you this way because of my name, for they do not know the One who sent me. [22]If I had not come and spoken to them, they would not be guilty of sin. Now, however, they have no excuse for their sin. [23]He who hates me hates my Father as well. [24]If I had not done among them what no one else did, they would not be guilty of sin.

---

themselves the "Friends of Truth;" later, simply "Friends." These are the modern Quakers, more properly called the Religious Society of Friends. The picture of Jesus' disciples in these chapters of John was crucial for the Friends. They rejected baptism, the Lord's Supper, and ordained ministry because they saw none of them being practiced by Jesus and his disciples. Their understanding of these texts also led them to practice complete equality for women in all aspects of church life.

But now they have seen these miracles, and yet they have hated both me and my Father. [25]But this is to fulfill what is written in their Law: 'They hated me without reason.'[b]

[a]*20* John 13:16   [b]*25* Psalms 35:19; 69:4

In 15:1-17 Jesus has been talking about conditions within the believing community. Now he prepares his disciples for another new reality: the future relationship between the believing community and the world.

15:18. Whereas the relationship within the community of disciples may be characterized by the word "love," the attitude of the world to this community is "hate." In 3:19-20 the readers were taught that the unbelieving world "hates" the Light that Jesus represents because it exposes its evil deeds. On the other hand, the world "loves" its evil darkness (cf. 7:7). As fruit-bearing (righteous actions producing) followers of Jesus, the world turns its ray gun of hate upon us also. Modern believers may certainly agree with this statement. Even in the supposedly tolerant society of late twentieth century America, Christianity is constantly being ridiculed and attacked. Nothing sacred to Christians is exempt from lampooning satire in the name of "art." Public stands for biblically-based morality are thrashed ruthlessly by those who disagree. But why are we surprised? Jesus promises us that lives of loving devotion to one another and obedience to him will always be a threat to the sinful world, and therefore the object of hate.

15:19-21. There is always a certain irrationality to the world's hatred of the Christian community. Why would such good people be so universally detested? Why are believers belittled for trying to teach their children the difference between right and wrong, that lying and stealing are evil and that honesty and giving are good? The irrationality cannot be explained, but the motivation behind it is spelled out by these simple words of Jesus, **"You do not belong to the world."** Paul labels these Christ-haters as "enemies of the cross" and reminds his Philippians that "our citizenship is in heaven" (Phil 3:18,20). By choosing Christ we choose to be at odds with the standards of the world. As he was "despised and rejected," so too will his disciples be. In the end this hatred is fueled by the world's refusal to be reconciled to God, or, as Jesus puts it, to **"know the One who sent me."**

15:22-25. While the hatred of the world for Christ may be irrational, it is also inexcusable. The word translated **"excuse"** is πρό–φασις (*prophasis*) and usually means "pretext" or "false appearance."[8] Jesus says that as a result of his ministry there will be no "false appearances" for the world. The world's sin will be exposed without any cover-up or justification. When it comes to sin, the world is "without excuse" (cf. Rom 1:18; 2:1).

There simply is no logical explanation for the unbelief of Jesus' opponents. They were witnesses to his miracles, but the result was that **"they hated both me and my Father."** The justification given for this is that it is a fulfillment of prophecy,[9] i.e., part of the plan of God. John has already explored the causes and effects of the unbelief of the Jews of Jesus' day (see comments under 12:37-43).

The Spirit's Mission Like That of the Disciples': to Bear Witness to Jesus (15:26-27)

[26]"When the Counselor comes, whom I will send to you from the Father, the Spirit of truth who goes out from the Father, he will testify about me. [27]And you also must testify, for you have been with me from the beginning.

15:26-27. These verses give the disciples future information about what the Holy Spirit will do and will not do. The Holy Spirit will be a witness, one who "testifies" about Jesus. The presence of the Holy Spirit will be a confirmation of the continuing presence of Jesus within the believing community after his death and resurrection. But

---

[8]The NIV translates *prophasis* as a "show" in Mark 12:40 and Luke 20:47, "pretending" in Acts 27:30, "false motives" in Philippians 1:18, and "mask to cover up" in 1 Thessalonians 2:5. Even including this rather curious rendering in 1 Thessalonians 2:5, all of these have the common thread of "false appearance."

[9]Both Psalms 35:19 and 69:4 have been suggested as the source of this quote. The LXX wording of these two passages agree with each other, but neither agrees exactly with John. That John allows this quotation to be referred to as "written in the Law" does not need to be a problem. By "law" he simply means "earlier Scripture." See Carson, *The Gospel According to John*, p. 527.

the main point of these verses is not to teach about the Holy Spirit. It is a warning to the disciples, that they should not expect the Holy Spirit to assume their designated task of being witnesses for Jesus. The Holy Spirit is powerful and beneficial for believers, but it is a complete mistake to relax and expect the Holy Spirit to do our work. No matter how we understand the work of the Holy Spirit in the process of conversion (and there are some pretty sharp disagreements in the Christian world over this issue), disciples of Jesus are entrusted with the responsibility of "testifying to him" by preaching the Gospel.

JOHN 16

4. Still More Promises and Commands (16:1-33)

Chapter 16 continues the themes of the world's hatred and disbelief, the work of the Holy Spirit, and the coming sorrow of the disciples that will lead to joy. Much of the material in chapter 16 is a restatement of what has already been said in chapter 14[1] or elsewhere in John, but there are also some unique insights in the section.

The Works of Disbelief (16:1-4)

[1]"All this I have told you so that you will not go astray. [2]They will put you out of the synagogue; in fact, a time is coming when anyone who kills you will think he is offering a service to God. [3]They will do such things because they have not known the Father or me. [4]I have told you this, so that when the time comes you will remember that I warned you. I did not tell you this at first because I was with you.

Although there is a traditional chapter division here, 16:1-4 more properly belongs with the last section of chapter 15. It continues the discussion of the dreadful reaction of the "world" to the disciples of Jesus. Jesus speaks prophetically of a future when his disciples' **time** will come (vv. 1,4; cf. v. 32). This draws a close parallel to Jesus himself, for John has already alerted us that Jesus' "time" (for suffering and death) is at hand.[2]

[1]See the chart in Brown, *John*, 2:589-3, which outlines the parallels between John 16:4b-31 and John 13:31–14:31 as well as other parallels.
[2]One of the subplots of the Gospel of John is the timing of events for

16:1-4. It is fair to ask of this passage: Why does Jesus give such a gloomy prognosis for the future? Isn't he afraid of scaring off the disciples? Jesus himself recognizes this danger and communicates some answers before the moment of crisis. First, he gives a practical answer. He says that they must know of the unpleasant future, **so that** [they] **will not go astray.** The Greek word translated "go astray" here is the verb σκανδαλίζω (*skandalizō*). It has already been used at 6:61 in the searching question of Jesus, "Does this *offend* you?" We get our term "scandalize" from this word. While it would be inappropriate to let the meaning of the much later English word "scandalize" determine the meaning of this ancient Greek word, there is some value in seeing *skandalizō* as "scandalize." In other words, Jesus is warning his disciples of the unpleasant future so that they will not be *scandalized* to the point of disbelief and apostasy. As 6:61 indicates, many would-be disciples have already been *scandalized* or "offended" and deserted Jesus. The cross and its aftermath of persecution would be a time when the resolve of the disciples is tested to the limit.[3]

Second, Jesus prepares his disciples by foretelling the absolute madness of the coming persecution. Not only will his disciples be excommunicated (put out of the synagogue[4]), but some will even be killed. The utter insanity is that these murderers will think they are **offering a service to God.** This will be fulfilled in the coming death of Jesus, a death demanded by the Jewish leaders as a

---

Jesus. In the early sections the reader is told repeatedly that Jesus' time *has not* come (2:4; 7:30; 8:20). But later, at the time of Jesus' passion, the reader is alerted that Jesus' time *has* come (12:23,27; and especially 13:1; cf. 17:1).

[3]Paul uses the noun form of this word (σκάνδαλον, *skandalon*) to describe the way in which the large majority of Jews viewed the execution of Jesus on the cross. For the first century Jews the suggestion that their Messiah would die a criminal's death was an unacceptable and offensive scandal that caused them to be unbelievers. Paul states that preaching a crucified Messiah was a "stumbling block-*skandalon*" to the Jews (1 Cor 1:23). Paul also attributes the persecution he has suffered to the "offense-*skandalon*" of the cross (Gal 5:11). For further discussion see my article, Mark Krause, "The Scandal of the Cross," *Christian Standard* (November 8, 1987): 1031-1032.

[4]For discussion on the significance of being put out of the synagogue for the ancient Jew see the comments on 9:20-23.

requirement of their Law (19:7). The book of Acts confirms that the followers of Jesus were persecuted and killed, sometimes by Jews who believed they were doing God's will (see Acts 9:1-2, cf. Gal 1:13-14). Such martyrdom of Christian believers in the name of religion has continued to the present day.

It is ironic that the later church burned, drowned, or otherwise killed many who had been judged guilty of heresy, and did so in the name of God. In 1527 Roman Catholic authorities captured the Anabaptist leader, Michael Sattler. Sattler was condemned as a heretic for rejecting infant baptism, the bodily presence of Christ in the elements of the Lord's Supper, and other standard Roman Catholic doctrines. At his trial the leading official concluded, "You desperate villain and arch-heretic, I tell you if there were no hang-man here, I would hang you myself, and think that I had done God service." Sattler was then tortured by having his tongue cut out and being burned with red-hot iron tongs. He was tied to a ladder and burned at the stake. A few days later his wife was executed by drowning. How tragic that the Christian community has been guilty of such abuses of power! The lesson is that a claim to be serving God is no justification for murder, whether it is done by Jews, pagans, or Christians.

Third, there is a spiritual reason for this coming persecution: the persecutors **"have not known the Father"** or Jesus. By this he means that they remain in a state of alienation from God. They have rejected Jesus, and thereby rejected the Father. This is precisely the opposite condition of Jesus' disciples. Jesus has announced that their relationship with him has allowed them to "know" the Father (14:7; cf. 17:25).

The Works of the Spirit (16:5-15)

[5]**"Now I am going to him who sent me, yet none of you asks me, 'Where are you going?'** [6]**Because I have said these things, you are filled with grief.** [7]**But I tell you the truth: It is for your good that I am going away. Unless I go away, the Counselor will not come to you; but if I go, I will send him to you.** [8]**When he comes, he will convict the world of guilt**[a] **in regard to sin and righteousness and**

judgment: ⁹in regard to sin, because men do not believe in me; ¹⁰in regard to righteousness, because I am going to the Father, where you can see me no longer; ¹¹and in regard to judgment, because the prince of this world now stands condemned.

¹²"I have much more to say to you, more than you can now bear. ¹³But when he, the Spirit of truth, comes, he will guide you into all truth. He will not speak on his own; he will speak only what he hears, and he will tell you what is yet to come. ¹⁴He will bring glory to me by taking from what is mine and making it known to you. ¹⁵All that belongs to the Father is mine. That is why I said the Spirit will take from what is mine and make it known to you.

ᵃ8 Or *will expose the guilt of the world*

Now back to the good news of the future: the coming of the Holy Spirit. In this section we get more specifics as to how the Holy Spirit will operate in the future community of believers. This section includes the fourth (vv. 7-11) and fifth (vv. 13-15) teachings on the Holy Spirit contained in the Farewell Discourses.

16:5. Jesus confronts his disciples by pointing out that none of them has asked, **"Where are you going?"** To the casual reader this seems to be a mistake, a forgetting of Peter's direct question (13:36) and Thomas's implied question (14:5).[5] There is no consensus solution for this difficulty among scholars.[6] However, what Jesus seems to be indicating is that the disciples are still thinking of a physical escape. For the question, "Where are you going?" the disciples expect an answer like, "Back to Galilee and then to Damascus or Antioch." They are only beginning to catch on that Jesus is "going to the Father" (see 14:28; cf. 13:3), a spiritual trek. The disciples might have mouthed the right words, but their focus was on a different realm, and therefore they have not legitimately asked the question.

---

[5]All three of these verses (13:36; 14:5; 16:5) contain the same Greek phrase, ποῦ ὑπάγεις (*pou hypageis*), which is "Where are you going?" if translated as a question.

[6]For discussion of the various proposed solutions and nonsolutions see Carson, *The Gospel According to John*, pp. 532-533.

16:6-7. Jesus knows only too well the current and future **grief** and anguish of his disciples. His continual talk about separation must have left them feeling abandoned and leaderless. But now he reveals that this is an ironical benefit in his departure. He must leave in order for the **Counselor** (that is, the Holy Spirit) to come. But, the reader might ask, why is this necessary? Why not Jesus and the Holy Spirit at the same time?

While the explanation for this necessary sequence is not given here, we may understand it in light of the larger context. The answer is not because it would have been physically or spiritually impossible for Jesus and the Holy Spirit to both be present in the realm of humankind at the same time. To believe this is to fall into the ancient heresy of "modalism," the belief that there is only one person in the Godhead who reveals himself to humanity in different ways, but may only have one identity at a time. In modalism God assumes the identity of Father at creation, Son for redemption, and Holy Spirit for sanctification. In the end, modalism teaches that heaven is empty while God is present on earth in Jesus, and again empty when God returns as the Holy Spirit. This theory would be nonsense for John, for he clearly teaches the presence of the Holy Spirit in the ministry of Jesus (1:33) as well as the presence of the Father in heaven (12:27-28).

A much better way to understand this is to see that it is a matter of timing. The time for the Holy Spirit to come is *after* the saving work of Jesus upon the cross. As Butler says, "If [Jesus] does not complete the redemptive plan in atoning death and victorious resurrection, the Holy Spirit . . . cannot come. The Holy Spirit was not to be sent to every believer until redemption had been completed."[7]

16:8-11. Jesus' teaching in these verses plays upon his identification of the Holy Spirit in legal terms, as a **Counselor**.[8] Now, however, the legal function of the Spirit is in relation to the world. As Craddock says, "The language is obviously that of a courtroom. . . . The case is clear: the world vs. Jesus of Nazareth."[9] Before Jesus has portrayed the Holy Spirit as the defense attorney for the believers

---

[7]Butler, *John*, 2:300.

[8]On the meaning of the word "Counselor" (παράκλητος, *paraklētos*) in John see the comments above under 14:15-17.

[9]Craddock, *John*, p. 119.

(14:16-17). Now the Holy Spirit is in the role of the prosecuting attorney against the world. This is pictured in three ways. First, the Holy Spirit will convict the world of sinful unbelief. Second, the Holy Spirit will convict the world of the **righteousness** of Jesus. That is, Jesus will be vindicated by his resurrection in spite of his scandalous death on the cross. Third, the Holy Spirit will convict the world of its own **judgment**. A more consistent translation here would be "condemnation." Just as the **prince of this world** (Satan) would be defeated and condemned by the death and resurrection of Jesus, so too is the unbelieving world. Unbelievers cannot escape condemning judgment (3:18) for, "Light has come into the world, but men loved darkness instead of light because their deeds were evil" (3:19).

16:12-15. In this section Jesus gives his fifth teaching on the Holy Spirit. The main subject here is the role of the Holy Spirit as a source of guidance for the disciples' future community. Jesus cannot teach the disciples everything necessary, both because his time is short and their ability to absorb the teachings is limited. Even three years of training with the disciples was insufficient. Without Jesus they would need another source of information and clarification concerning the central truths of the Gospel.

Jesus defines this role of the Holy Spirit in three ways. First, the Holy Spirit comes as the **Spirit of truth** and guides the disciples **into all truth**. In the apostolic community matters of truth and falsehood will not be subject to human opinions or majority vote. The apostles will not have to rely on their faulty human memories when it comes to the facts of his life, death, and resurrection. The Spirit will be the arbiter and authority for truth. For outsiders, the presence of the Holy Spirit in the apostolic community was unquestionably a pointer to the validity of its message (as the story of Acts 2 demonstrates). From a historical perspective, this makes considerable sense. Why would God give his only Son for the redemption of the world (3:16) without safeguarding the integrity of the message about the Son? This truth-insuring ministry of the Holy Spirit continues in the church today through the writings of the apostolic community, the New Testament. These writings embody, "**all truth**," the complete and sufficient revelation of the Son to God's people. Although the last of the apostles died over 1,900 years ago (probably John himself), the Holy Spirit actively continues to guide believers into truth through this testimony of the apostles.[10]

A second aspect of this continuing role of the Holy Spirit is the limitation of its information. The Holy Spirit is not an independent operator, but speaks **only what he hears**. But this will include new information. From the Holy Spirit the disciples will learn some aspects of **what is yet to come**. This means that after Jesus' resurrection they will be given insights into his future return in glory and judgment. This element of the ministry of the Holy Spirit is dramatically actualized in the production of the book of Revelation, a series of visions given to this same author, John, while "in the Spirit" (Rev 1:10; 4:2; 17:3; 21:10). The stated purpose of that book is to reveal "what must soon take place," i.e., future events (Rev 1:1,19; 22:6).

Third, the Holy Spirit has a continuing function of bringing **glory** to Christ. In so doing the Spirit continues to reveal the Christ by taking what is his (his true identity as the Son of God) and making it known to the disciples. In this we see a unity of purpose between the Father and the Spirit. It is a decided purpose of God to glorify the Son (13:32), and the Spirit continues with the same purpose. We also see a unity between the Spirit and the Son in that the Spirit is revealing only those things that it receives from the Son. There is no contradiction or confusion in the plan of God. The Father, Son, and Holy Spirit all work as one for the redemption of humankind through the atoning death and resurrection of Jesus and the subsequent proclamation of this good news.

Joy Greater than Trouble (16:16-33)

[16]"In a little while you will see me no more, and then after a little while you will see me."

[17]Some of his disciples said to one another, "What does he mean by saying, 'In a little while you will see me no more, and then after a little while you will see me,' and' Because I am going to the Father'?" [18]They kept asking, "What does he mean by 'a little while'? We don't understand what he is saying."

---

[10]John points to Spirit-guided reflection upon the part of the apostles at several points in his Gospel. See 12:16 for the clearest example.

[19]Jesus saw that they wanted to ask him about this, so he said to them, "Are you asking one another what I meant when I said, 'In a little while you will see me no more, and then after a little while you will see me'? [20]I tell you the truth, you will weep and mourn while the world rejoices. You will grieve, but your grief will turn to joy. [21]A woman giving birth to a child has pain because her time has come; but when her baby is born she forgets the anguish because of her joy that a child is born into the world. [22]So with you: Now is your time of grief, but I will see you again and you will rejoice, and no one will take away your joy. [23]In that day you will no longer ask me anything. I tell you the truth, my Father will give you whatever you ask in my name. [24]Until now you have not asked for anything in my name. Ask and you will receive, and your joy will be complete.

[25]"Though I have been speaking figuratively, a time is coming when I will no longer use this kind of language but will tell you plainly about my Father. [26]In that day you will ask in my name. I am not saying that I will ask the Father on your behalf. [27]No, the Father himself loves you because you have loved me and have believed that I came from God. [28]I came from the Father and entered the world; now I am leaving the world and going back to the Father."

[29]Then Jesus' disciples said, "Now you are speaking clearly and without figures of speech. [30]Now we can see that you know all things and that you do not even need to have anyone ask you questions. This makes us believe that you came from God."

[31]"You believe at last!"[a] Jesus answered. [32]"But a time is coming, and has come, when you will be scattered, each to his own home. You will leave me all alone. Yet I am not alone, for my Father is with me.

[33]"I have told you these things, so that in me you may have peace. In this world you will have trouble. But take heart! I have overcome the world."

[a]*31 Or "Do you now believe?"*

16:16. This is a bridge verse and may be seen as the end of the previous section (vv. 5-15, as with the NIV) or the beginning of the next section (vv. 17-28).

Although the NIV and most other translations use the English verb "see" twice in this verse, there are two distinct verbs being used in Greek with slightly different nuances.[11] The first verb is θεωρέω (theōreō), from which we get our English verb "theorize." It generally means to "observe" or "experience visually as a spectator." The second verb is ὁράω (horaō) which means to "see" in a broader sense, and is frequently used by John for "spiritual sight" (see 1:18,34,51; 6:46; 11:40). While these two verbs are fairly close synonyms, it is significant that both are employed here. The change of verbs indicates that there will be a change in the way Jesus is "seen" in the future. Yes, he will be physically seen after his resurrection, but spiritual sight will not allow him to be understood as before. Indeed, after the resurrection theōreō is used to describe the resurrected but unrecognized Jesus (20:14). But when the appearances of the resurrected Jesus are described, the verb horaō is always used (20:18,25,29).[12]

Moreover, Jesus' words in the verse are likely intended to have two levels of meaning for the reader. On the obvious immediate level Jesus will be taken from their sight (death and burial) and then return to their sight (resurrection appearances), all **in a little while** (i.e., in three days). But on the future, eschatological level he will be taken from human sight (ascension and exaltation in heaven) and then be returned to human sight (Second Coming). This, too, will be done "in a little while" as far as divine timekeeping goes. This is in line with the "soon-ness" of the risen Jesus in Revelation 22:12 and 22:20, who promises "Yes, I am coming soon."

16:17-18. Jesus' speech quickly causes a buzz of discussion among the disciples. The focus of conversation is neither the prophecy about coming persecution nor the promise of the Holy

---

[11]The NASB brings out this difference by translating the first verb "behold" and the second verb "see." This is helpful except for the archaic nature of the word "behold."

[12]The KJV has the additional phrase, "because I go to the Father" at the end of verse 16. This is not supported by the earliest and best Greek manuscripts, and seems to be an attempt to make Jesus' statement in verse 16 conform to the questions of the disciples in verse 17. This unnecessary harmonization by copyists apparently missed the fact that Jesus used the phrase "because I go to the Father" in verse 10.

Spirit. It is centered on Jesus' still misunderstood references to his coming departure. The disciples are confused about his future destination and about the timing of the coming sequence of events.

16:19. No disciple actually asks these questions to Jesus directly, so he verbalizes their concerns himself (as he did in verse 5). For the reader this causes the third repetition of the statement, **"In a little while you will see me no more, and then after a little while you will see me."** This is not coincidental, but points us to a declaration that John wants his readers to remember. If we recognize that the first "readers" of John would have been primarily "hearers" who heard this book read aloud in a worship service or other gathering, we better understand the importance of this repetition.[13] As mentioned above (v. 16) there is a dual level of meaning for this statement, both immediate and more distant future (eschatological). Even after hearing the Gospel of John read for the first time, the believer could leave the reading with many phrases ringing in his or her heart, including this basic point of Christian faith, "We'll see Jesus again in a little while," a promise believers may still retain securely today.

16:20. Jesus now combines two reactions he has already discussed; **grief** (= pain or sorrow, v. 6) and **joy** (15:11). These two seemingly conflicting emotions have an important connection for the future of the disciples. Their coming **grief** at his death will be painfully real, an intense experience of sorrow. As C.S. Lewis wrote in the beginning of *A Grief Examined*, "No one ever told me that grief felt so like fear." Jesus' death will bring a paralyzing fear of the future (cf. 20:19), but this will be a short-lived situation.

16:21-22. Jesus promises that this fearful grief will give way to utter joy. He illustrates this by using the analogy of a woman who endures the pain of childbirth for the joy of a new baby. I remember the birth of my first child. My wife and I had attended childbirth classes, and although the birth was agonizingly painful for

---

[13]In the first century copies of the writings of the apostles were all hand written, and therefore rare and expensive. Having even a single copy for a local congregation was a luxury. More likely, copies were passed around from congregation to congregation and read aloud in gatherings. This procedure is reflected in Revelation 1:3, where a blessing is pronounced on both the reader (singular) and the hearers (plural) of that book.

her, she knew what to expect. As a result she made it through labor with great courage, and her pain was soon forgotten when she saw her new baby daughter. That same night/morning there was a 14-year-old girl giving birth in the same hospital ward. No one had told her what to expect, and I can still hear her screams of pain and terror. Knowing in advance what to expect does help one deal with painful circumstances.

Jesus promises that the coming joy is not temporary. **No one will take away your joy.** This is the eternal joy of the believer, the complete joy that Jesus promises (cf. 15:11; 16:24; 17:13). It is not the momentary flush of happiness at a glad occasion, or the contentment that comes when one's life is at peace. It is a God-given, deeply seated joy of one's soul, a joy that thrives even in bad times (cf. Jas 1:2). As the persecuted Moravians were dubbed "God's Happy People," in the eighteenth century, so should all Christians be who find the joy of the Lord through Christ.

16:23-24. There is an apparent contradiction of thought in these verses. Why would Jesus promise a day when "asking" would be unnecessary, and then assure the disciples that anything they "ask" for will be given to them? This is a problem only in the English versions. The first **ask** of verse 23 is the Greek verb ἐρωτάω (erōtaō), which refers to the asking of a question. On the day of joy there will be no more need for Jesus to answer questions, presumably because the Holy Spirit will supply answers to the disciples (v. 13). The second **ask** in verse 23 is the Greek verb αἰτέω (aiteō), used twice in verse 24. This is asking in the sense of "making a request." As Jesus has continually promised in the Farewell Discourses, the disciples will have a mighty prayer power in his name.[14]

For a second time Jesus indicates that the future holds a "complete joy" for the disciples (see 15:11; cf. 17:13). While the nature of this joy has already been discussed above under verses 21-22, we should not leave this section without realizing that there is an intended connection between these promises and the promised Holy Spirit. The Holy Spirit is often associated with joy in the New

---

[14]On the differences between these Greek verbs translated "ask" see Merrill C. Tenney, "John," in *The Expositor's Bible Commentary*, Frank E. Gabelein, gen. ed. (Grand Rapids: Zondervan, 1981), 9:160-161.

Testament.[15] The Holy Spirit is the ultimate gift of God (see Luke 11:13). His presence in the life of the believer consummates the joyous restoration of this person to the Father.

16:25-28. Jesus admits to the disciples that he has been **speaking figuratively** (literally, "in figurative language," see comments on 10:6). Now the time has come to speak **plainly.** He now sums up his message by giving them the "plain facts" about the Father. First, he wants the disciples to know that their future prayer power is more than just God doing them a favor because of Jesus. They will have a more direct relationship. God hears and answers them because he **loves** them himself. Second, however, they must remember that this love of God is activated because of the disciples' relationship to Jesus. They have loved Jesus and believed him; two sides of the same coin. In other words, they have not come to belief grudgingly, without love. Nor have they loved him, but never really believed his claims (as one might love a small child dearly, but not believe his wild exaggerations). The disciples have both loved and believed. And what is the very core of this loving belief? Jesus also states this in simple terms: **"I came from the Father and entered the world; now I am leaving the world and going back to the Father."** Jesus was the Son of God, doing the will of God, in order to accomplish the saving purposes of God.

16:29-30. After all these explanations and repetitions the light has finally begun to dawn in the disciples' minds. Now they get it! They have moved beyond the **figures of speech** and recognize the simple clarity of God's plan in Jesus. There is no more need for questions. They fully believe that Jesus **came from God**. The author is hopeful that the reader has now progressed to this point, too. Just as the disciples believe that Jesus is God's Son, so should the readers.

16:31-32. But wait, Jesus is not convinced! The NIV has translated his words as irony, **"You believe at last!"** Most translations, however, have retained the probable question form of the Greek text, "Do you now believe?" (e.g., NRSV, NASB). Perhaps there are the beginnings of faith, but this will be severely tested in a few

---

[15]For some examples of the Holy Spirit connected with joy see: Luke 10:21; Acts 13:52; Romans 14:17; Galatians 5:22; 1 Thessalonians 1:6.

hours and the disciples will fail the test. They **will be scattered** and run home. Jesus will be abandoned by all but God. The story is not over yet.

16:33. Before his prayer (chapter 17) Jesus gives one last comforting promise, a promise that will bring the disciples inner **peace** from their coming pain and turmoil. "The world promises persecution," Jesus says, "but don't lose your courage." These again are plain words. The disciples of Christ must not back down and run away when persecution comes. This is because they have nothing to ultimately fear from the world. The sinful, unbelieving world cannot defeat God's Son. He is the light the darkened world could not overcome (1:5). Surely Jesus' voice must have risen as he boldly proclaimed, **"I have overcome the world!"** This is also a promise given to believers. As John says elsewhere, "This is the victory that has overcome the world, even our faith. Who is it that overcomes the world? Only he who believes that Jesus is the Son of God" (1 John 5:4-5; cf. Rev 3:21; 5:5).

The Greek verb translated **overcome** is νικάω (*nikaō*). It is related to the name of *Nike*, the Greek winged goddess of victory. It means to "win a victory" or to "conquer." "Overcome" conveys this idea, but on a smaller scale than the Greek verb suggests. This is the word of triumphant generals and emperors, of world conquerors. It is a word for the Julius Caesars and the Alexander the Greats of the world. And it is directed against the current king of the hill, the "prince of this world" (Satan, v. 11). By cheating death Jesus demolishes the chief stranglehold of fear that Satan maintains over humanity (see 1 Cor 15:26). "Sin reigns in death," Paul tells us (Rom 5:21), but because of the resurrection of Christ we may sing, "Where, O Death, is your victory?" and "Thanks be to God! He gives us the victory through our Lord Jesus Christ!" (1 Cor 15:55,57).

So ends the "discourse" part of the Farewell Discourses. Chapter 17 is an instructive prayer offered to the Father.

JOHN 17

5. Jesus' Prayer (17:1-26)

This chapter is often known as Jesus' "high priestly" prayer in which Jesus assumes a mediator role for his disciples according to the pattern of Jewish high priests. Many commentators have noticed parallels between this prayer and the prayer a high priest might have offered before sacrifice on the Day of Atonement.[1] This begins with Jesus' prayer for himself, and advances outward in ever widening waves:

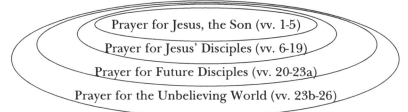

Prayer for Jesus, the Son (vv. 1-5)
Prayer for Jesus' Disciples (vv. 6-19)
Prayer for Future Disciples (vv. 20-23a)
Prayer for the Unbelieving World (vv. 23b-26)

Jesus was certainly a man of prayer. He was known to isolate himself for prayer (Mark 1:35; Luke 5:16) and sometimes to spend all night in prayer (Luke 6:12). Yet we have surprisingly few examples of the wording of Jesus' prayers. Among the most extensive of Jesus' recorded prayers are the "Lord's Prayer" (Matt 6:9-13; Luke 11:2-4) and the Gethsemane prayers (Matt 26:39,42; Mark 14:35-36;

---

[1]Butler gives a convenient summary of this in *John*, 2:322. He lists four parallels: 1. The prayer is just before Jesus gives himself as a sacrifice. 2. The prayer serves to consecrate Jesus as both a high priest and a sacrificial victim. 3. It follows the pattern of Day of Atonement prayers in beginning with the high priest (Jesus), proceeding to his colleagues (the disciples), and ending with the people (all believers). 4. There are many parallel terms between this chapter and the book of Hebrews, where the concept of Jesus as a high priest is fully developed.

Luke 22:42; cf. Heb 5:7).[2] John 17 is certainly the most extensive single prayer of Jesus found in the New Testament.

For His Glorification (17:1-5)

[1]**After Jesus said this, he looked toward heaven and prayed:**

"Father, the time has come. Glorify your Son, that your Son may glorify you.[2]For you granted him authority over all people that he might give eternal life to all those you have given him. [3]Now this is eternal life: that they may know you, the only true God, and Jesus Christ, whom you have sent. [4]I have brought you glory on earth by completing the work you gave me to do. [5]And now, Father, glorify me in your presence with the glory I had with you before the world began.

17:1a. Jesus' prayer posture is recorded here and worth noting. Whereas moderns assume that bowed heads and closed eyes are the proper praying position, Jesus prays with his head tilted up and his eyes open. While there is no way to know for sure, it is likely that Jesus and the disciples would have been standing for this time of prayer.[3]

17:1b-5. The prayer is addressed to God as **Father**, the usual way for Jesus to begin prayers in the Gospel of John.[4] This is more than intra-Trinity communication between the first and second persons of the Godhead, but rather an affirmation of Jesus' humanity. It is normal and appropriate for humans to address God as "Father," as Jesus has well taught us. He is our perfect and eternal spiritual Father, our loving yet all-powerful Master.

---

[2]For more information on the prayer life and prayer teachings of Jesus, see the article by James D.G. Dunn, "Prayer," in *Dictionary of Jesus and the Gospels*, pp. 617-625.

[3]A wide variety of prayer postures is found in the Bible, including kneeling (Acts 20:36), sitting (1 Chr 17:16), and standing with outstretched hands (1 Kgs 8:22).

[4]See John 11:41; 12:27, and 12:28 for other examples of Jesus' beginning prayers with "Father."

This section of prayer begins and ends with the theme of glorification. As already discussed, the "glorification" of Jesus is generally a reference in John to his death, resurrection, and exaltation. There is no more time for preparation or planning because Jesus acknowledges that **the time has come** (cf. 13:1). The final sequence of events is ready to begin. Jesus also prays about the other side of the plan: God's glorification. The defeat of death in the resurrection will be **completing the work you gave me to do**, and will bring glory to God.[5]

While the actual completion of this work is yet ahead for Jesus, his obedient submission to God's will is a necessary part of this victory. No human being knows for sure how he or she will respond in times of trial and temptation in advance. The proof is in the testing. The human Jesus must also meet the challenge of temptation. Will he avoid the cross and therefore thwart God's purposes for the salvation of the world? While this seems unthinkable to Christians, the true humanity of Jesus must have made the refusal of the crucifixion a possibility. Jesus' earlier statements reveal to us that this was on his mind. In 12:27 he cried out,

> Now my heart is troubled, and what shall I say? "Father, save me from this hour?" No, it was for this very reason I came to this hour.

In the Synoptic Gospels the human Jesus pours out his fears to God in the Garden of Gethsemane prayers (e.g., Mark 14:36). In the end, however, Jesus is obedient to God, and therefore wins a victory over human selfishness. As the author of Hebrews puts it,

> Although he was a son, he learned obedience from what he suffered and, once made perfect, he became the source of eternal salvation for all who obey him (Heb 5:8).

---

[5]We need not be confused by the NIV's translation of verse 4 in the past tense. In particular the word translated "have brought you glory" does not need to be understood this way. It is a Greek aorist tense verb, but the aorist tense is the "default" tense of Greek with the least time-related meaning attached to it of all the Greek tenses. While the aorist is often the equivalent of the English past tense, this does not work in verse 4. We would be perfectly correct to translate this verse as "I bring you glory on earth as I finish the work that you gave me to do."

Therefore, if Jesus' glorification functions as the beginning and ending brackets of this section, the **work** of Jesus is the inner section. The supreme result of Jesus' death/glorification is in its work of atonement. In this sense, Jesus is able to "complete his work" by giving **eternal life**. The conditions of this "eternal life" are given in verse 3, an intimate, personal knowledge of both the Father and Jesus. We are surprised to hear Jesus refer to himself in the abstract here, **know . . . Jesus Christ**, and it almost sounds as if someone else is talking. Some of this is due to the clumsiness of the NIV translation at this point, however. We would follow the sense of the original text better if we translated the second part of verse 3 this way, "that they might know you, the only true God, and the one whom you sent, Jesus Christ." This is the common and beautiful language of prayer.

A potential theological difficulty is presented by Jesus' statement in verse 2 that **eternal life** is to be given to **all those you have given him**. This sounds suspiciously like "unconditional predestination," the view that salvation is determined wholly by God apart from the human will. While there are many in the Christian world that hold to this doctrine without reservation and are therefore comfortable with seeing predestination here,[6] there are others who reject the doctrine completely, and fight to keep it out of the interpretation of verse 2.[7] Perhaps neither is justified here. If Jesus has **authority over all people**," then who is excluded from "those whom you have given him"? Jesus gives eternal life to all who believe, who truly know **the only true God** and his Son, Jesus Christ. Certainly there is a narrowing of those who will be saved from the larger category of "all people," but this reduction does not necessarily imply a predetermined selection by God. This is clarified below when Jesus identifies the "ones given to him" as those who "have obeyed your word" (v. 6).

For His Disciples (17:6-19)

⁶**"I have revealed you**ᵃ **to those whom you gave me out of the world. They were yours; you gave them to me and they have**

---

[6]See Carson, *The Gospel According to John*, p. 555.

[7]See Butler, *John*, 2:325.

obeyed your word. ⁷Now they know that everything you have given me comes from you. ⁸For I gave them the words you gave me and they accepted them. They knew with certainty that I came from you, and they believed that you sent me. ⁹I pray for them. I am not praying for the world, but for those you have given me, for they are yours. ¹⁰All I have is yours, and all you have is mine. And glory has come to me through them. ¹¹I will remain in the world no longer, but they are still in the world, and I am coming to you. Holy Father, protect them by the power of your name — the name you gave me — so that they may be one as we are one. ¹²While I was with them, I protected them and kept them safe by that name you gave me. None has been lost except the one doomed to destruction so that Scripture would be fulfilled.

¹³"I am coming to you now, but I say these things while I am still in the world, so that they may have the full measure of my joy within them. ¹⁴I have given them your word and the world has hated them, for they are not of the world any more than I am of the world. ¹⁵My prayer is not that you take them out of the world but that you protect them from the evil one. ¹⁶They are not of the world, even as I am not of it. ¹⁷Sanctify^b them by the truth; your word is truth. ¹⁸As you sent me into the world, I have sent them into the world. ¹⁹For them I sanctify myself, that they too may be truly sanctified.

ᵃ6 Greek *your name*; also in verse 26   ᵇ*17* Greek *hagiazo (set apart for sacred use or made holy)*; also in verse 19

The second section of Jesus' prayer is for his disciples. They must "remain in the world" even after Jesus departs (v. 11). In this part of the prayer Jesus repeats several of the teaching points given to the disciples in chapters 14–16, including: their belief that Jesus came from God (16:30), the promise of complete joy (16:24), and the coming hate of the world (15:18).

17:6. This verse contains a very important theological term translated **revealed** in the NIV. The Greek verb used is φανερόω (*phaneroō*), and means to "reveal" or to "show." Jesus now can say that he has "revealed" God (literally, "your name," see NIV footnote). This was done through his miracles (2:11; 9:3), and because of Jesus' intimate knowledge of God (1:18). This concept of "making God known" acts as an *inclusio*, bracketing the entire section of the prayer concerned with those other than Christ himself. Jesus begins by praying, "I have revealed you . . ." (v. 6). He ends by saying, "I have made you known . . ." (v. 26).

For discussion of the identity of the ones "given to Jesus," see the above comments on this phrase from verse 2. It should be noted that in this section "the ones given to Jesus" refers to the twelve disciples, who were doubtlessly chosen through the providential direction of God.

17:7-11. The primary thrust of this passage is to describe the believing state of the disciples. Their faith has made them ready, and contributes to it being the "right time." They are ready to be entrusted with the ministry that Jesus will leave to them. They have believed that Jesus came from the Father (v. 8), and that his message was God's message (v. 7). Even though this faith may not be perfect, it is sufficient for the hour (cf. 16:31-32).

A difficult phrase is found in verse 10, **glory has come to me through them.** Even the KJV translation, "I am glorified in them," is preferable to the NIV at this point, but an even better version is achieved if we render the "in them" with the Greek instrumental sense. This would yield, "I am glorified by them." The emphasis is not upon Jesus' receiving human recognition because of the faithful deeds of his disciples (as suggested in 13:35). Jesus is making a statement about the faith of the disciples. They have progressed in their understanding of his identity so that they have begun to "glorify" him, i.e., treat him with Godlike respect. They have recognized that he is more than a simple Galilean carpenter. He is the Son of God.

17:11-12. Jesus also prays for the protection of the disciples. Without his constant companionship and leadership, they will need to lean upon God with complete faith. Jesus also describes a protective strategy for the disciples. They must **be one.** This unity is like the unity Jesus and the Father enjoy, a deep spiritual oneness that is not negated by fighting and hostility. The unity of the apostolic community was essential to the early success of the Gospel. The motto, "United we stand, divided we fall," is nothing new, and constitutes a necessary outlook for the disciples of Christ (cf. Phil 2:2). The theme of unity will be developed further in verses 22-23.

17:13. The section of verses 13-19 takes on a more "high priestly" tone as Jesus prays pointedly about the sanctification of the disciples. Sanctification is simply to become holy. Holiness is a theme throughout this prayer (e.g., God is called "Holy Father" in v. 11). Even though the term "sanctify" is not used until verse 17, there are several aspects of holiness portrayed in these earlier verses. The first comes in this verse, Jesus' desire that they have **the full measure of my joy within them.** As mentioned in the comments under 16:23-24, there is an intended connection between Jesus' promise of "joy" and his promise of the Holy Spirit. To have complete inner joy for the believer is part of the presence and ministry of the Holy Spirit. This relationship of joy is the disciples' direct connection with God while they remain behind in the sinful world. Through the Holy Spirit the disciples are to be "sanctified by joy."

17:14-16. A second aspect to the sanctification of the disciples is in their forced separateness from the world. While they remain in the world, the **world has hated them** because, as Jesus reminds them, **they are not of the world.** A central element to the concept of holiness is to be separate. Note the words of Leviticus 20:26, "You shall be *holy* to me; for I the LORD am *holy*, and I have *separated* you from the other peoples to be mine (NRSV)."[8] The paradox of discipleship is to remain "in the world" but "not of the world" (v. 11 and vv. 14,16). How does one remain holy in a world that laughs at holiness? It is a great temptation for Christians to withdraw from the world and its painful sinfulness, to live, work, and study in a "Christian environment." While this is sometimes necessary and has advantages, we should remember that Jesus left his disciples in the world for a purpose. Jesus pointedly says, **My prayer is not that you take them out of the world . . . .** Disciples must remain separate from worldly attitudes that accept sin without a whimper, and struggle to remain spotless in a very dirty world. This is sanctification by separation.

A third way that Jesus prays for the sanctification of his disciples is by his plea for their protection. What good does it do to be clean

---

[8]For other references to holiness as separation, see Num 6:5; Isa 52:11; 2 Cor 6:17-18; Heb 7:26.

if you cannot stay clean? Likewise, what good does it do to be made holy if you cannot remain holy? Specifically, this is for protection from the **evil** (= unholy) **one**. Earlier, Jesus ties this protection to the power of God's holy name (v. 11). In the Old Testament acting in an unholy manner was sometimes seen as a profaning of God's holy name (e.g., Lev 20:3; 22:2; Ezek 20:39; Amos 2:7). Elsewhere, the name of God is seen as having protective value (e.g., Ps 5:11; 20:1). God's protection from the evil one (Satan) allows the disciples to remain holy. This is sanctification by protection.

17:17. A fourth way that Jesus prays for the holiness of the disciples is through the sanctifying power of the word of truth. This, too, is tied to the Holy Spirit, who is repeatedly referred to as the "Spirit of truth" in the Farewell Discourses (14:17; 15:26; 16:13). The Holy Spirit, working through God's word, has a purifying and sanctifying effect upon the disciples (cf. Heb 4:12). This is sanctification by truth.

In this verse the verb "sanctify" appears for the first time in the prayer. This is the Greek verb ἀγιάζω (hagiazō), occurring here and twice in verse 19.[9] While hagiazō is justifiably translated "sanctify" here, it is derived from the same root as the Greek word for "holy" (ἅγιος, hagios) and might be better understood as "make holy." Jesus has given four aspects of holiness: joy, separateness, protection, and truth.

17:18-19. Jesus now uses very priestly sounding language. He sanctifies himself, then he sees to the sanctification of his associates. His sanctification is doubly important because he will act as both the priest and the sacrifice in the coming crucifixion. As the author of Hebrews puts it, "He sacrificed for their sins [acted as a priest] once for all when he offered himself [acted as a sacrifice]" (Heb 7:27).

This section of the prayer ends with the reference to the sending of the disciples. Jesus was **sent** so that he might send others (cf. 20:21). The disciples are to be sent **into the world**, and this is why their sanctification is so important. For them, loss of holiness is a loss of purpose and mission. They must have the protective holiness of God so that, as Paul says, "when the day of evil comes, you may

---

[9]The only other use of ἀγιάζω in John is in 10:36.

be able to stand your ground" (Eph 6:13). Lack of holiness always obstructs and compromises the ministry of the disciples of Christ. Loss of holiness is a loss of joy and truth, and too often results in a complete casualty in the battle. Personal sanctification is a protective shield against the sinful landmines of the world.

For Those Who Will Believe (17:20-26)

For Unity (17:20-23)

20"My prayer is not for them alone. I pray also for those who will believe in me through their message, 21that all of them may be one, Father, just as you are in me and I am in you. May they also be in us so that the world may believe that you have sent me. 22I have given them the glory that you gave me, that they may be one as we are one: 23I in them and you in me. May they be brought to complete unity to let the world know that you sent me and have loved them even as you have loved me.

The third and final section of the prayer is for future believers and, by extension, for the world to which they will witness. This is a key text for Christians concerned with the unity of the church, and has been used extensively by ecumenical groups and by those interested in eliminating divisions within the church.

17:20. Jesus' words make it clear that there is a larger vision for the church beyond the small group of disciples in the Upper Room. The future will see people come to faith not by directly witnessing the miracles of Jesus, but by the testimony of the disciples, **their message**. The community of believers was not to end with the death and resurrection of Jesus, but to continue to a second, third, and fourth generation of disciples even down to the present day. The workings of this plan are explained by the author of Hebrews, who spells it out this way, "This salvation, which was first announced by the Lord, was confirmed to us [second-generation believers] by those who heard him [original disciples]" (Heb 2:3).

17:21. This is the key verse for the advocates of Christian unity. It gives both the basis and the purpose for unity. The basis is that

Christian believers are united through their relationship to Christ. This is a deep, personal, even mystical relationship, a spiritual bond akin to the relationship between the Father and Son. As we are all united to the same Christ, we are all part of the same family. Christ is not like the bigamist husband who has many different wives and families who do not know about each other. Christ has only one bride, only one church.

But some might ask, which church is that? Is it the Roman Catholic Church, the Orthodox Church, the Church of England, the Coptic Church, the Church of South India, the Church of Canada, or my little church down the street? This is a very difficult question to answer honestly. The answer is that Christ's church is all of these and yet none of these. Christ's church is found wherever there are true and faithful disciples, those who keep his words and model his love. Those may be found in any of the above named groups, but membership in them does not constitute a genuine disciple. Christ's disciples will be known by their love for one another (13:35), and by their loving and obedient devotion to Christ as Lord (14:15).

If relationship to Christ is the basis for unity, what is the purpose? This is also explained in this verse. The unity of the church is essential if its testimony to the world is to be believed. As the old motto states, "When the church is *one*, the world will be *won*." On a practical level we should not assume that a unified church would result in immediate conversion of every person in the world. But we know from experience and from church history that a divided church is always crippled in its presentation of the gospel. The unbeliever asks, why do I want to be a Christian if Christians are always fighting among themselves?

Although there have long been advocates of unity within the church, the sectarian spirit of others has often overshadowed unity efforts. At the close of the twentieth century, a growing number of believers are disgusted by the continuing sectarianism in the Christian world. Yes, sectarianism is alive and well. If it is the will of God that the church be one, division within the church is sinful disobedience. Bickering and division is all too easy, unity takes work. It is encouraging that the younger generation of Christians demonstrates an unwillingness to tolerate this divisive spirit, and an utter lack of understanding as to why it is so important to some. Perhaps older Christians should learn from them. The unity of Christians may happen yet, despite our best efforts to thwart it.

17:22-23. These verses are a restatement of verse 21 with a couple of new twists. First, Jesus promises to give future believers **glory**. What does he mean by this? We have already seen that "glory" is often code-language for the death, resurrection and exaltation of Jesus. This is the meaning here, too, but from a slightly different angle. The community of disciples is granted the "glory" of Jesus in that they are entrusted with the glorious message of his triumph on the cross. As Bultmann says, "he has given them his [glory] means that after his departure they are to represent him in the world; it means that the 'history' of Jesus will not become an episode in the past, but will remain continually present in the world as the eschatological event in the eschatological community."[10]

A second new element in this section is Jesus' desire that the **complete unity** of his believers would be a testimony to the world of the great love of God shown to them. They will be united in love, and this unity will be a powerful attraction to a world starved for love.

For Seeing Jesus' Glory (17:24-26)

[24]"Father, I want those you have given me to be with me where I am, and to see my glory, the glory you have given me because you loved me before the creation of the world.

[25]"Righteous Father, though the world does not know you, I know you, and they know that you have sent me. [26]I have made you known to them, and will continue to make you known in order that the love you have for me may be in them and that I myself may be in them."

17:24. Jesus now turns to the ultimate destiny of believers, their future with him. In this state they will be able to see him in his full **glory**, without any constraints imposed by his humanity. John gives a

---

[10]Bultmann, *The Gospel of John*, p. 516.

clearer picture of this elsewhere in his vision of the New Jerusalem, where "the city does not need the sun or the moon to shine on it, for the glory of God gives it light, and the Lamb is its lamp" (Rev 21:23).

This verse also contains an interesting theological insight into the eternal relationship between the Father and the Son. Jesus speaks of this as being a relationship based on love, a love that extends back **before the creation of the world**. The language here does not refer to the creation of the earth, but of the universe. This is an affirmation of the uncreated nature of Jesus, and an important text in refuting the "Arian" heresy (the belief that Christ is a divine but created being). The exaltation of Christ after the resurrection will not be just his elevation to a position of glory. It will be a return to the glory that was his since before created time began.

17:25-26. Jesus ends the prayer by addressing God one last time. First he addressed God as "Father" (v. 1, repeated in verses 21 and 24). Then he addressed God as "Holy Father" (v. 11). Finally, he addresses God as **Righteous Father** (v. 25). His designation of the Father as **righteous** (δίκαιος, *dikaios*) could be translated as "Just Father" or "Father of Justice." It places an emphasis upon God as Judge, the one who will finally reward or condemn believers and nonbelievers.

Jesus summarizes his entire mission in very simple terms here. We might highlight it this way. Problem: **world does not know** God. Solution: Jesus knows God, and can therefore reveal God to the world. Implementation: Jesus has gathered disciples who believe he came from God, and has revealed God to them. Maintenance Plan: Jesus will continue to reveal God to the world through the community of believers.

The stage is now set for the final drama, the passion of Christ.

JOHN 18

B. JESUS' TRIAL AND CRUCIFIXION (18:1–19:42)

A traditional name for the garden, trial, and crucifixion sequence is the "Passion Narrative." John's Passion Narrative reads almost like another Synoptic Gospel with varying details. His pace is fast and furious, and the dialogue is recorded in John's short, terse sentences. In this section his powers as a story-teller are evident, and, in many ways, this is the story he has wanted to tell from the beginning.[1]

Harmonizing this account and the Synoptic Gospels has been done elsewhere.[2] For us it is important to understand the sequence of events as John presents them. If we think of this as a drama, there are nine little vignettes:

1 Jesus and his disciples go to a garden (18:1).
2 While in the garden, Judas comes with a mob of temple police and others and they arrest Jesus (18:2-11).
3 After the arrest Jesus is taken to the house of Annas (18:12-14).
4 Side scene: Peter's first denial (18:15-18).
5 Return to main action: Jesus is questioned by Annas (18:19-24).
6 Side scene again: Peter's second and third denials (18:25-27).
7 Return to main action: Jesus is taken to Pilate and eventually condemned to be crucified (18:28–19:16).
8 Jesus is crucified (19:17-37).
9 Jesus is buried (19:38-42).

---

[1]One is reminded of the oft-quoted note of Martin Kähler, that the Gospels were "passion narratives with extended introductions," in *The So-Called Historical Jesus and the Historic Biblical Christ*, trans. Carl E. Braaten (Philadelphia: Fortress, 1964; German original, 1896), p. 80, n. 11.

[2]For a complete summary on the issues involved in harmonizing the trials of Jesus, see the article of Bruce Corley, "Trial of Jesus," in *Dictionary of Jesus*

1. Jesus' Arrest (18:1-11)

[1]When he had finished praying, Jesus left with his disciples and crossed the Kidron Valley. On the other side there was an olive grove, and he and his disciples went into it.

[2]Now Judas, who betrayed him, knew the place, because Jesus had often met there with his disciples. [3]So Judas came to the grove, guiding a detachment of soldiers and some officials from the chief priests and Pharisees. They were carrying torches, lanterns and weapons.

[4]Jesus, knowing all that was going to happen to him, went out and asked them, "Who is it you want?"

[5]"Jesus of Nazareth," they replied.

"I am he," Jesus said. (And Judas the traitor was standing there with them.) [6]When Jesus said, "I am he," they drew back and fell to the ground.

[7]Again he asked them, "Who is it you want?"

And they said, "Jesus of Nazareth."

[8]"I told you that I am he," Jesus answered. "If you are looking for me, then let these men go." [9]This happened so that the words he had spoken would be fulfilled: "I have not lost one of those you gave me."[a]

[10]Then Simon Peter, who had a sword, drew it and struck the high priest's servant, cutting off his right ear. (The servant's name was Malchus.)

[11]Jesus commanded Peter, "Put your sword away! Shall I not drink the cup the Father has given me?"

[a]9 John 6:39

Although this begins the section we commonly call the "Passion Narrative," John's portrayal of Jesus is quite different from that of the Synoptic Gospels. In the Synoptics Jesus is presented as an anguished victim of treachery and hate. While the treachery and

---

and the Gospels, pp. 841-854. Particularly helpful is Corley's chart comparing the accounts of all four Gospels on p. 847. See also the harmonization and discussion of Westcott, *The Gospel According to St. John,* 2:261-264.

hate are also in John (and have been there for several chapters, cf.
11:45-53), John presents Jesus as supremely confident and the
master of the situation. John does not include the prayers of agony
in the Garden. Jesus knows everything before it even happens
(18:4), so there is no surprise for him when Judas and his mob
appear. Despite being vastly outnumbered, the mob is presented
as being more afraid of Jesus than he is of them (18:6). Indeed,
Jesus is able to dictate the actions of the arresting cohort to ensure
the safety of his disciples (18:8). This confident side of Jesus, not
as well seen in the other Gospels, is continued through his trials
and crucifixion.

18:1. There is some disagreement among commentators as to
where Jesus and his disciples are "leaving" from in this verse. It is
often assumed that they left the upper room at the end of chapter
14 (see comments at 14:31), and that chapters 15–17 take place
somewhere between the upper room and the garden.[3] This interpretation is unlikely, however, for nothing in chapters 15–16 hints at a
discourse while walking, or pausing somewhere outdoors for the
prayer of chapter 17. It is more likely that 14:31 was the announcement of the intention of leaving the place of the Supper, but the
actual departure is not until 18:1.

The **Kidron Valley** is literally the "Wadi of Cedars," a traditional
name for the gentle ravine east of the main city of Jerusalem. It is a
creek bed running north to south, separating the temple mount
from the Mount of Olives. This is a well-known site in the Bible,
receiving a number of mentions in the Old Testament (e.g., 2 Sam
15:23; Jer 31:40). After crossing the stream they enter an **olive
grove.** Although not named by John, this is the Garden of Gethsemane,[4] a
frequent meeting place for Jesus and his disciples (18:2). John identifies this as a κῆπος (*kēpos*), a "garden" (despite the well-intended NIV
translation of "grove"). The original reader of John would see this

---

[3]See the discussion of Foster, *Studies*. Foster is convinced that John
14:31 is "decisive" in indicating the upper room is vacated at that point
and makes this point several times. See especially his discussion on
p. 1229.

[4]The name "Gethsemane" means "olive press," a partial confirmation of
John's location with that of the Synoptics (see Matt 26:36; Mark 14:32).

word again in 19:41. In this way John brackets the Passion Narrative. It begins and ends in a garden.[5]

18:2-3. Judas arrives, leading a mob made up of two groups. One group is a **detachment of soldiers**. The Greek word for this group is σπεῖρα (*speira*). This is the word for a "cohort" of soldiers. A cohort in the Roman military system would be ¹/₁₀ of a legion, or about 600 men. This presents two problems for the interpreter. First, does this mean that the Romans were partners in the plot to arrest and execute Jesus? Are we intended to understand an unspoken collaboration between Pilate and the high priests? Some have argued that this is a Jewish military unit, or that these were Roman troops under the control of the high priests. Both of these conjectures are possible but unlikely (particularly the second). John seems determined that the reader understands this as a troop of Romans, acting under a Roman officer. This is shown by the delineation of the two groups and by the identification of the cohort's "commander" in verse 12 as a χιλίαρχος (*chiliarchos*, literally "ruler of 1,000"), the normal title for the commander of a Roman cohort of troops. So the answer to this question is, yes, the Romans were part of the plot even though we don't have all the details.

A second interpretive problem is in trying to understand how many people are actually in this Judas-led mob. Is this a full cohort of 600 soldiers? Many have seen this as implausible and found ways of making this number smaller, "part of a cohort." Yet there is no real justification for this, and the picture John paints is all the more dramatic if we see this as a group of 600+ armed men. The Roman way was not to fight battles with evenly matched forces, but to crush enemies with overwhelmingly superior numbers when possible. Even if they expect to find a few dozen men with Jesus, this apparent overkill is not out of character for the first-century Romans.[6]

The other group with Judas is made up of **officials from the chief priests and Pharisees**. This is not a bunch of clipboard-carrying bureaucrats, but rather a security force under the control of the

---

[5]Francis J. Moloney, *The Gospel of John*, Sacra Pagina 4 (Collegeville: Liturgical Press, 1998), p. 482.

[6]See the discussion of this in Raymond E. Brown, *The Death of the Messiah: From Gethsemane to the Grave* (New York: Doubleday, 1994), 1:248-249.

Sanhedrin, thus the NRSV's translation, "police." This is a group we have seen before in John (see 7:32,45-46). John vividly describes both groups as being equipped with **torches, lanterns, and weapons**.

18:4-6. There is no hiding in the crowd for Jesus. He is in control of the situation, equipped with both foreknowledge and composure. In John's version there is no kiss of betrayal, although the proximity of Judas is acknowledged (he is **standing there with them**). Jesus comes out to meet the throng and initiates the conversation. In response to Jesus' challenge to reveal their "person of interest," they answer, **"Jesus of Nazareth"** (cf. 19:19). More literally this answer is "Jesus the Nazarene."[7] While "Nazarene" can mean "one from Nazareth," it was also used as an early term for Christians as a sect of the Jews (see Acts 24:5). The Hebrew root behind this word is נצר (*naṣar*), meaning "to observe." Thus "Jesus the Nazarene" may not be identification by hometown so much as a title meaning "Jesus the Observant One."[8] Whether or not John's Greek-speaking readers would have known this is uncertain, however. It is likely that they (much like modern English speakers) would recognize "Jesus the Nazarene" as a traditional title for Jesus without knowing all the background meaning of "Nazarene."

Jesus answers back, **"I am he."** This is another *ego eimi* statement, literally, "I am." This is more than Jesus saying, "I'm your man." He is making a powerful statement of his divinity, his "I amness" nature as the Son of God (see comments under 8:58). The power of this claim is shown by John's observation that the arresting party **drew back and fell to the ground** when it is spoken (cf. Rev 1:17). The authority here is not in the cohort of troops, but in the powerful presence of Jesus.

18:7-9. The sequence of question, reply, and counterreply is repeated almost word for word, emphasizing the determination of Jesus to submit to the arrest. He has no thought of escape, but only concern for his disciples. Strategically this makes sense. In the plan of God the disciples were the crucial torch carriers of the Gospel. If they

---

[7]John distinguishes between being from the town of Nazareth (1:45,46) and being a "Nazarene" (18:5,7; 19:19).

[8]The meaning of the place name "Nazareth" is "watchtower" (place to observe). See the comments of Lindars, *The Gospel of John*, pp. 540-541.

had died at the same time as Jesus, the prepared force of evangelists would be demolished before its task began. John identifies this as the predetermined plan of God when he speaks of it as a fulfillment of prophecy. This is not a fulfillment of the Old Testament, however; it is a fulfillment of the prophetic words of Jesus (6:39; 10:28; 17:12).

18:10-11. Not everything proceeds according to design, however. While the mob allows Jesus to be in control, the impulsive Peter has his own plan: they must fight their way out! Peter is armed with a sword. This is a μάχαιρα (*machaira*), a short sword, about 20 inches long.[9] It is often stated that this was a very short sword, not much more than a dagger or knife. This seems unlikely from a practical standpoint, however. How would the slashing of a little dagger result in slicing off an ear? A dagger would be used to stab, not slash.

Before Jesus stops him, Peter gets in one good swipe and cuts off the ear of **Malchus**, a slave of the **high priest** (presumably Annas). John does not record the restoration of this ear (this detail is only at Luke 22:51). In John's account this rash act endangers Peter later that night (v. 26).

Jesus' confrontation of Peter is not aimed at the obvious wrongness of his violence, but at the potential it has for disrupting his plan. Peter seems determined to disprove Jesus' prophecy about his lack of loyalty (13:37-38). But Jesus must not allow Peter's behavior to stop him from drinking **the cup the Father has given** him (= his death).

2. Jesus' Trial before Annas (18:12-14)

[12]**Then the detachment of soldiers with its commander and the Jewish officials arrested Jesus. They bound him** [13]**and brought him first to Annas, who was the father-in-law of Caiaphas, the high priest that year.** [14]**Caiaphas was the one who had advised the Jews that it would be good if one man died for the people.**

---

[9]The word *machaira* is admittedly ambiguous in the first century context, but the standard military sword of the day was 17-21 inches long. See Stephens, *The New Testament World in Pictures*, p. 40.

18:12. The distinction between the cohort and the other **officials** is even more pronounced at this point. The officials/police are **Jewish**, implying the cohort and its **commander** are not Jewish. Yet they manage to do a team-arrest. How did this work? Did a Roman soldier grab the left arm and a Jewish policeman grab the right arm? We are not told, but quickly Jesus is **bound,** meaning his hands were tied behind his back.

18:13-14. Jesus is initially marched to the house of **Annas**, who is introduced here for the first time in John. John identifies **Annas** as the **father-in-law of Caiaphas**, the legitimate **high priest that year**. But John's language seems to indicate that he considers Annas to be high priest also. Peter's simultaneous entrance into the courtyard of the high priest is intended to be understood as the courtyard of the house of Annas (v. 15). The first "high priest" to question Jesus is obviously Annas (v. 19), who sends him to Caiaphas afterward (v. 24).

The historical reality is that Annas and Caiaphas were both high priests. Luke 3:2 speaks of the "high priesthood of Annas and Caiaphas." Annas had served as the high priest from AD 6-15, but had been deposed by the Roman governor, Gratus. A few years later Annas managed to arrange the appointment of Caiaphas, his son-in-law (high priest AD 18-36), thus ensuring a continuing influence over the office. Even beyond this family connection, however, a living former high priest must have maintained considerable influence, just as Americans still address former Chief Executives as "Mr. President."[10]

The author reminds us that we have met Caiaphas before. In an earlier picture of the Sanhedrin, Caiaphas was the one who gave the unintentional prophecy about the value of a single man dying for the nation (11:50), an ironic statement that John does not want his readers to forget.

---

[10]The most exhaustive discussion of the relationship between Annas and Caiaphas is to be found in Brown, *Death of the Messiah*, 1:404-411. Brown speaks to the remarkable influence of Annas by noting that "in the fifty years after his deposition five of his sons became high priests, as well as a son-in-law and a grandson" (1:408).

3. Peter's First Denial of Jesus (18:15-18)

[15]Simon Peter and another disciple were following Jesus. Because this disciple was known to the high priest, he went with Jesus into the high priest's courtyard, [16]but Peter had to wait outside at the door. The other disciple, who was known to the high priest, came back, spoke to the girl on duty there and brought Peter in.

[17]"You are not one of his disciples, are you?" the girl at the door asked Peter.

He replied, "I am not."

[18]It was cold, and the servants and officials stood around a fire they had made to keep warm. Peter also was standing with them, warming himself.

All four of the Gospels include the denials of Peter,[11] but only John divides these denials into two parts. This adds to the drama of this chapter, and gives a better sense of these events occurring at the same time that Jesus is being grilled by the high priest.

18:15-16. The disciple with Peter is the author, John.[12] An astounding detail not included elsewhere is that John **was known to the high priest**. This allows him both free access to the high priest's compound, and even the influence to get his friend Peter admitted also. This indicates that security is tight, and makes the privilege of John even more remarkable.

The nature of John's relationship to the high priest has been the subject of considerable speculation among scholars for many years. On the one hand it seems incredible that a Galilean fisherman would be an intimate with one of the wealthiest and most powerful men in Palestine. But, on the other hand, there is evidence that Zebedee, John's father, had a considerable fishing business (see Mark 1:19-20). If John is the unnamed disciple of 1:35ff, there is the suggestion that he was financially capable of leaving home and

---

[11]The other accounts of Peter's denials are found in Matthew 26:69-75; Mark 14:66-72; Luke 22:56-62.

[12]See comments on the identity of the "beloved disciple" in the Introduction.

following first John the Baptist and then Jesus himself. Such a person may have been a frequent visitor to Jerusalem, and if his prosperous family had made substantial gifts to the temple, it is not impossible that the young John had worked his way into the friendship circles of the high priest's family.[13]

18:17-18. Peter does not have to wait long for an opportunity to deny Jesus. The young servant girl in charge of the door/gate to the courtyard challenges Peter immediately: **"You are not** [another] **one of his disciples, are you?"**[14] The question implies that she is aware of another disciple who has been in and out of the high priest's compound. This is not John, who has gone unchallenged and seems to have hidden any connection to Jesus. We may only speculate that the "other disciple" was Judas, whom she must have seen coming and going. If this is what we are intended to perceive, her question may have the force of "Are you another one of the disciples of Jesus who is a part of the plot against him?" This setting makes it easy for Peter to answer, **"I am not."** The language of denial is striking, nearly the opposite of Jesus' affirmation, "I am he." Furthermore, just as John has Jesus answer the arresting soldiers, "I am he," twice (18:5,8), so too he records, "I am not," two times on the lips of Peter (18:17,25).

The author adds the further detail of Peter's joining a group warming themselves by a fire (indicating Peter never gets past the outdoor courtyard). Such foolhardy boldness! Peter is apparently confident that his loud denial has successfully obscured his identity, and that he is now safe.

---

[13]For the best recent justification of this position see Carson, *The Gospel According to John*, p. 582. Lindars, *The Gospel of John*, p. 548, mentions a tradition that John's family supplied Sea of Galilee fish for the high priest's household. He attributes this to the second century *Gospel of the Hebrews*, but offers no reference. I have been unable to discover such information among any known fragments of this book (it is not extant as a whole).

[14]There was a change in the NIV translation of this question in the later editions. The earlier editions read, "Surely you are not another of this man's disciples?" The 1984 revision changed this to "You are not one of his disciples, are you?" This unexplained revision loses the "another" and the insulting tone of "this man's" in the girl's question. Grammatically this "another" is justified by the nonconnective καί (*kai*) in the Greek text.

4. Jesus Interrogated before Annas (18:19-24)

[19]Meanwhile, the high priest questioned Jesus about his disciples and his teaching.

[20]"I have spoken openly to the world," Jesus replied. "I always taught in synagogues or at the temple, where all the Jews come together. I said nothing in secret. [21]Why question me? Ask those who heard me. Surely they know what I said."

[22]When Jesus said this, one of the officials nearby struck him in the face. "Is this the way you answer the high priest?" he demanded.

[23]"If I said something wrong," Jesus replied, "testify as to what is wrong. But if I spoke the truth, why did you strike me?" [24]Then Annas sent him, still bound, to Caiaphas the high priest.[a]

[a]24 Or (Now Annas had sent him, still bound, to Caiaphas the high priest.)

Now back to the main action. While John does not indicate by name which "high priest" is involved in the questioning of this section, it is clear that we are to understand it to be Annas. Annas gets the first shot at Jesus, then he is sent to Caiaphas (v. 23).

18:19-21. The specific questions of Annas are not recorded, only the general categories of **disciples** and **teaching**. The author presents Annas as fishing for something, perhaps a misstatement that could be used as a charge against Jesus. That Annas's questions are not motivated by a genuine concern to understand is shown by the response of Jesus. Clearly exasperated, Jesus refuses to be grilled in this way. His justification is that his teachings are a matter of public record. He has taught **openly to the world,** not **in secret.** There might have been private conversations (e.g., Nicodemus in chapter 3) or nonpublic fellowship times (e.g., the disciples in chapters 13–17), but there is no secret plot, nothing to hide. The implication is that even if Jesus patiently submits to answering these questions, Annas will learn nothing he does not know already.

18:22-24. The highly charged atmosphere of this scene now erupts with an act of violence. Jesus is rewarded for his straightforward yet impertinent defiance of Annas with a blow. This is probably an open-handed slap to the face, administered by one of the temple policemen.[15] We should remember that Jesus still has his hands tied behind his back, and poses no physical threat to anyone. He rightly demands justification for this insulting (and painful!) smack, and this unanswerable demand brings the interview before Annas to a close. He is transferred to Caiaphas, who perhaps lives in another wing of the same compound.

The NIV translation, **if I spoke the truth**, is misleading in this context. The Greek text uses two adverbs which are antonyms, κακῶς (*kakōs*, "wrongly") and καλῶς (*kalōs*, "rightly"). Jesus is saying, "If I spoke inappropriately, tell me what was wrong. But if I spoke appropriately, why did you hit me?" "Truth" is a very important theme in the Gospel of John, and for the NIV to wrongly imply that it is part of this conversation is careless and unjustified. This inquiry is far from a quest for truth, although that topic will come up in Jesus' interview with Pilate (vv. 37-38).

5. Peter's Second and Third Denials of Jesus (18:25-27)

[25]**As Simon Peter stood warming himself, he was asked, "You are not one of his disciples, are you?"**

He denied it, saying, "I am not."

[26]**One of the high priest's servants, a relative of the man whose ear Peter had cut off, challenged him, "Didn't I see you with him in the olive grove?"** [27]**Again Peter denied it, and at that moment a rooster began to crow.**

18:25. The author returns to Peter, who has two denials to go in order to fulfill Jesus' prophecy about him (13:38). We should not see any time lapse between verses 18 and 25. As soon as Peter joins the group around the fire, he is challenged again. The question is posed in language nearly identical to that of the slave girl (v. 17), and Peter's response is exactly the same, **"I am not."**

18:26. But now a third person questions Peter, and this time there is potential danger. This person is a relative of Malchus, the

---

[15]One is reminded of the similar treatment of Paul in his appearance before the high priest Ananias in Acts 23:1-5.

man who lost an ear to Peter's sword in the garden (v. 10), and presumably could be motivated by revenge. The man's question indicates that he was with the arresting horde, and despite the darkness and inevitable confusion, Peter seems familiar to him. Perhaps he would not even have paid any attention to Peter if he had not overheard the first two questions, but now he takes a closer look, and confronts Peter himself.

18:27. The third denial is barely out of Peter's mouth before the rooster crows. Crowing roosters are a sign of approaching dawn. Jesus' prophecy at the Last Supper was "before the rooster crows you will disown me three times!" (13:38). The force of the prophecy was that "loyal Peter" would deny his relationship to Jesus multiple times before the next sunrise. The crowing cock serves as his physical reminder. John presents this starkly, without comment, leaving the reader to imagine the emotional distress Peter must have felt (cf. Luke 22:62, "And he went outside and wept bitterly."). Perhaps Peter, not understanding everything that was happening, would see his actions as the fulfillment of another prophecy of Jesus, "one of you is going to betray me" (13:21, see comments on 13:36-38).

6. Jesus' Trial before Pilate (18:28–19:16)

Pilate Doubtful of the Prosecution (18:28-32)

[28]Then the Jews led Jesus from Caiaphas to the palace of the Roman governor. By now it was early morning, and to avoid ceremonial uncleanness the Jews did not enter the palace; they wanted to be able to eat the Passover. [29]So Pilate came out to them and asked, "What charges are you bringing against this man?"

[30]"If he were not a criminal," they replied, "we would not have handed him over to you."

[31]Pilate said, "Take him yourselves and judge him by your own law."

"But we have no right to execute anyone," the Jews objected. [32]This happened so that the words Jesus had spoken indicating the kind of death he was going to die would be fulfilled.

18:28. John includes no record of the trial of Jesus before Caiaphas or the Sanhedrin (the closest we get is the earlier meeting recorded in 11:45-53). Instead, he is transferred from Caiaphas directly to the Roman governor, Pilate. The location is the **palace of the Roman governor** (NIV), in Greek the πραιτώριον (*praitōrion*). In Latin this would be the Praetorium, Pilate's "headquarters" (NRSV), but there is some question as to exactly where this was. Pilate's normal residence would have been at Caesarea Maritime, on the pleasant Mediterranean coast. The place where he set up headquarters while in Jerusalem would have become the "Praetorium" upon his occupancy. But where was this? Two possibilities exist, the Fortress Antonia and the old Palace of Herod.[16] The Fortress Antonia was a massive and ancient stronghold situated on the northwest corner of the temple precincts. It dated back to the Maccabean period, the second century BC. It was used to house the Roman troops brought to Jerusalem at festival time. The Herodian Palace was built by Herod the Great and sat a little less than a half mile directly west of the temple. It, too, was a fortress, but had recently been made into a luxurious dwelling by the extravagant Herod. Most current scholars favor the Palace as the site of Pilate's Praetorium, but the Fortress Antonia cannot be ruled out completely. Antonia is the more traditional site, and pilgrims to Jerusalem today who trace the Via Dolorosa ("way of sorrows") will begin at the ancient location of Antonia.

Wherever this Praetorium is, the Jewish leaders refuse to enter it. This is because they would become "ceremonially unclean," i.e., have contact with Gentiles. Such obvious violation of the purity laws would have excluded them from the Passover celebrations of that day (Friday),[17] exclusion these leaders want to avoid. This reinforces a subtheme of John: that the Jewish leaders wanted to take care of the elimination of Jesus quickly and as quietly as possible,

---

[16]For detailed discussion on the site of Pilate's Praetorium, see Brown, *Death of Jesus*, 1:705-710.

[17]As already mentioned in the comments under 13:1, some scholars have trouble reconciling this account with the Passover mentioned in the Synoptic Gospels. They believe that John must be talking about Thursday morning in 18:28, and the Passover meal would come after sundown that evening. Yet the Synoptics clearly understand the Last Supper as a

and with their public involvement kept to a minimum. This causes something of a logistics nightmare for Pilate, who is forced to run in and out of the Praetorium in order alternately to interrogate Jesus and speak with the Jewish leaders.

18:29. Pilate is Pontius Pilate, the Roman governor of the province of Judea from AD 26-36. Both Josephus and Philo (first-century Jewish authors) record incidents concerning Pilate that portray him as a brutal, arrogant ruler. He kept order in Judea by the power of his Roman legionnaires rather than tact and diplomacy.

Pilate comes out to meet the delegation, indicating the clout that this group had. Pilate's later words to Jesus indicate that the high priests themselves were present (v. 35). This is done quickly despite the "early morning" hour (v. 28). Roman officials in the ancient world were known to be very early risers who liked to finish all business for the day by late morning, so this scenario is not at all unlikely.

Pilate begins the meeting by asking for the **charges** against Jesus. The Greek term here is κατηγορία (*katēgoria*, from which we get the English word "category"), meaning "formal accusation." If we understand Roman complicity in the plot against Jesus (see comments under 18:2-3), it is likely that Pilate is somewhat informed already. But this does not mean that the condemnation of Jesus is a foregone conclusion. Pilate may have allowed his troops to be used to arrest a potential revolutionary, but he is determined to judge the guilt or innocence of Jesus himself. The author paints a picture of Pilate and the Jewish leaders as enemies who have become reluctant allies against a common enemy. Pilate's dislike for the Jews, however, will not allow them to use him as a pawn in their own political chess game.

18:30-32. The idea of Pilate's earlier collusion seems to gain further confirmation here. The Jewish leaders seem surprised that Pilate is asking them for a formal accusation against Jesus. The generally acrimonious nature of the relationship is seen in their sarcastic response to Pilate. **"If he were not a criminal,"** they whine, "we

---

Passover meal. We must assume that John is speaking of continuing Passover celebrations in verse 28, for the actual one-day Passover was followed by the Feast of Unleavened Bread. For further information see Carson, *The Gospel According to John*, pp. 589-590.

wouldn't be here, would we?" But this is no answer to Pilate's question, so they are advised to judge Jesus themselves. Pilate obviously knows that this is not an option for them, or they would not have dragged Jesus to the Praetorium in the first place. His response is, in effect, "If you are going to be rude, you'll get no help from me."

The next response of the Jews gets right to the heart of the matter, **"We have no right to execute anyone."** This statement seems to go against the fact that the Jews of this period *did* execute people (e.g., Stephen in Acts 7). There is a lively dispute among scholars as to whether or not execution was a legal option withheld from the Jews of Judea by their Roman overlords.[18] We might note, however, that such a statement would surely have pleased the arrogant Pilate, even if the Jewish leaders had their fingers crossed as they said it. The proceedings of the Sanhedrin recorded in the Synoptic Gospels are in no way a model of integrity and honesty, and there is no reason to assume they are telling the truth in this claim. We would also note that in John's account the Jewish leaders never voice a formal accusation, yet Pilate seems to know the charge is that Jesus claims to be a "king" (v. 33). Jesus even confronts Pilate as to the source of this accusation (v. 34). Perhaps what the author wants us to understand is that they are saying, "We have no right to execute anyone *for illegally claiming to be a king*, and you know it!" This was a political crime that needed to be judged by the political masters of Judea, the Romans. Therefore, it is as if they are saying, "Pilate, we need you to execute him."

18:32. John, however, sees a prophetic and theological purpose behind all of this. Execution by the Romans would be crucifixion (whereas the Jewish method would likely have been stoning). The cross fulfills Jesus' words concerning the necessity of his being "lifted up" so that he might draw all men and women to himself (see 3:14-15; 8:28; and especially 12:32-33). Jesus' foreknowledge of his death by a Gentile court is a consistent theme in the Synoptic Gospels (e.g., Mark 10:32-34).

---

[18]See the extensive discussion of this matter in Barrett, *The Gospel According to St. John*, pp. 533-535.

Pilate Examines Jesus (18:33-38a)

³³Pilate then went back inside the palace, summoned Jesus and asked him, "Are you the king of the Jews?"

³⁴"Is that your own idea," Jesus asked, "or did others talk to you about me?"

³⁵"Am I a Jew?" Pilate replied. "It was your people and your chief priests who handed you over to me. What is it you have done?"

³⁶Jesus said, "My kingdom is not of this world. If it were, my servants would fight to prevent my arrest by the Jews. But now my kingdom is from another place."

³⁷"You are a king, then!" said Pilate.

Jesus answered, "You are right in saying I am a king. In fact, for this reason I was born, and for this I came into the world, to testify to the truth. Everyone on the side of truth listens to me."

³⁸"What is truth?" Pilate asked.

18:33. The action now moves to an inner court of the Praetorium for a private interview between Pilate and Jesus. Pilate cuts to chase and asks the key question, **"Are you the king of the Jews?"** This question interests him, for the Romans did not permit the Jews of Judea to have a "king" at this point in history. One claiming to be king could be guilty of inciting revolution against the Roman government, the crime of sedition.[19] Furthermore, for Pilate to ignore such a potential threat would have been negligence on his part, and he would have received a reprimand or much worse from his own superiors.

18:34. Jesus answers Pilate with an accusing question of his own. He broaches the crucial issue of the basis for this charge. No one has said anything about a king. Where has Pilate received his information? In effect Jesus is saying, "Who put you up to this?"

---

[19]See the article by J.B. Green, "Death of Jesus," in *The Dictionary of Jesus and the Gospels*, pp. 146-163. Of particular help in the question of the charge against Jesus is Green's section within the article, "3. Why Was Jesus Crucified?"

This assumes that we, the readers, are intended by the author to see some level of earlier collusion between Pilate and the Jewish leaders. As I have maintained in discussion throughout this chapter, this is a likely scenario. A conspiracy theory would see that earlier communication between Pilate and the Jewish leaders had forged an alliance between these two antagonists. The execution of Jesus would, for the high priests, eliminate an irritating yet popular critic and, for the Roman governor, remove a potential leader of revolution. It should be admitted, however, that there were other potential sources from which Pilate may have gained this information. He doubtlessly had some sort of spy network in place in his province, and may have received information earlier of the desire of some in Galilee to make Jesus a king (cf. 6:15). Or, he may have heard that this year's procession of pilgrims for Passover had taken on a different character with shouts of "Blessed is the King of Israel" being directed at Jesus (12:13).

18:35. Pilate's response is somewhat puzzling. **"Am I a Jew?"** he snarls. This is both an insult to the Jewish Jesus and an expression of cultural arrogance. Is Pilate a Jew? Of course not, and the very idea is unthinkable. Pilate is a Roman, and viewed his Jewish subjects as superstitious, stubborn, and uncultured. But while he may not admit to understanding the Jewish mind in this, he knows that a demand for execution by the high priests is a serious matter. He wants to learn more, and so gives Jesus an opportunity to tell his side. **"What is it you have done** *that is so terrible that they want you dead?"*

18:36-37. Jesus now returns to Pilate's original question, "Are you the king of the Jews?" because this is a good way to explain why the Jewish leaders are out to get him. He has no desire to be an earthly, political ruler (if so, the Jewish leaders might have given him silent support). He has no political agenda and is not on a mission of revolution to achieve Jewish independence from Rome. Jesus cites a piece of evidence: his followers have not taken up arms to resist authority.

Yet the answer to Pilate's question, "Are you the king of the Jews?" is "Yes!" Jesus is a king, but not a political king. His **kingdom is not of this world**. It **is from another place**. This is what makes him a threat to the Jewish leaders. He has no intention of leading a Maccabean-style revolt against Rome and is therefore no threat to Pilate. His mission is to lead a spiritual revolt against sin and the current Jewish system. His goal is spiritual salvation and eternal life for his followers, not political independence and freedom from tyranny. Jesus' followers are to be united by faith in him, not hate for Rome.

Jesus ends his statement by pointing again to the spiritual reality of his mission. He stands for **truth**, and attracts followers who seek truth. This is a supreme bit of irony. Supposedly Pilate should be seeking the truth before he agrees to execute Jesus, and Jesus claims that his main offense to the Jewish leaders has been that he is a truth-teller. Is this a less-than subtle way to remind Pilate of his official responsibilities?

The reader knows that "truth" is an important way to characterize Jesus. From the beginning John has presented Jesus as bringing God's gracious truth in contrast to the legalism of the Jews (1:14, 17). He has preached freedom by truth (8:32), spiritual freedom. He has claimed to embody truth himself (14:6).

18:38a. Therefore, when Pilate shouts his question, **"What is truth?"** the reader should know the answer. The truth is that Jesus is the Son of God. He has come into the human world to sacrifice his life in order that those believing in him might be given spiritual salvation. Pilate's question acts as a checkpoint for the reader to evaluate the author's presentation of Jesus. What is truth? The real question is "Who is truth?" and the answer is Jesus, the glorious Son of God.

In the narrative, however, Pilate has no thought of serving the readers in this way. He roars, "What is truth?" and gives Jesus no chance to respond. In effect he is saying, "Truth? If all you are about is a spiritual or philosophical quest for truth, you pose no threat to the Roman government! I have been tricked into agreeing to your execution under false accusations."

Barabbas (18:38b-40)

With this he went out again to the Jews and said, "I find no basis for a charge against him. ³⁹But it is your custom for me to release to you one prisoner at the time of the Passover. Do you want me to release 'the king of the Jews'?"

[40]They shouted back, "No, not him! Give us Barabbas!" Now Barabbas had taken part in a rebellion.

18:38b-39. On his way back out to talk with the Jewish leaders, Pilate concocts a little scheme that will allow everyone to save face. He does not think Jesus is guilty of anything deserving Roman execution and has detected that the Jewish leaders are manipulating him for their own purposes. So he announces, **"I find no basis for a charge against him."** In other words, Pilate is unwilling to have any sort of trial, because the preliminary inquiry has failed to show Jesus to be a revolutionary. But rather than force the issue, Pilate offers a way out. He wants to release Jesus according to a Passover custom. If this is done, the Jews can walk away thinking that Jesus is guilty but pardoned. Pilate can avoid entangling himself in a messy affair. And Jesus can escape with his life.

The custom of granting amnesty to a prisoner on Passover is not well understood or attested outside the New Testament. It is mentioned in all four of the Gospels, however, and must be seen as a traditional albeit unusual custom of that day.[20] It has been given the title *privilegium paschale* (Passover privilege) by scholars. While this seems very strange to Americans, people in many parts of the world are familiar with political imprisonment without trial. The release of such a prisoner serves to placate the population, while usually posing little threat to the state.

18:40. John does not tell us that Pilate has given them a choice, but the Jews in the crowd have an alternate candidate for release: Barabbas. Barabbas is described as one who has **taken part in a rebellion**. This NIV translation may be historically correct, but certainly includes a high level of interpretation. The Greek word used to describe Barabbas is λῃστής (*lēstēs*) and refers to a robber or thief (see John 10:1,8). It may have the connotation of a "bandit" (NRSV), in the sense of a freedom-fighter living in the wilderness and stealing from the government (*à la* Pancho Villa or Robin Hood), but this is not a necessary implication for this word. It is true that Mark describes Barabbas as a murderer and a revolutionary (Mark 15:7)

---

[20]See Matt 27:15; Mark 15:6; Luke 23:24. For defense of the historicity of this custom see B. Corley, "Trial of Jesus," *The Dictionary of Jesus and the Gospels*, p. 849.

as does Luke (Luke 23:19), but that should not dictate the translation here. John gives Barabbas no revolutionary aura, but portrays him as a common criminal.

Pilate's first attempt at compromise has failed, but he will come back with another plan to avoid giving the order for execution in chapter 19.

JOHN 19

The Flogging of Jesus and Delivering Over of Him to the Jews by Pilate (19:1-16)

¹Then Pilate took Jesus and had him flogged. ²The soldiers twisted together a crown of thorns and put it on his head. They clothed him in a purple robe ³and went up to him again and again, saying, "Hail, king of the Jews!" And they struck him in the face.

⁴Once more Pilate came out and said to the Jews, "Look, I am bringing him out to you to let you know that I find no basis for a charge against him." ⁵When Jesus came out wearing the crown of thorns and the purple robe, Pilate said to them, "Here is the man!"

⁶As soon as the chief priests and their officials saw him, they shouted, "Crucify! Crucify!"

But Pilate answered, "You take him and crucify him. As for me, I find no basis for a charge against him."

⁷The Jews insisted, "We have a law, and according to that law he must die, because he claimed to be the Son of God."

⁸When Pilate heard this, he was even more afraid, ⁹and he went back inside the palace. "Where do you come from?" he asked Jesus, but Jesus gave him no answer. ¹⁰"Do you refuse to speak to me?" Pilate said. "Don't you realize I have power either to free you or to crucify you?"

¹¹Jesus answered, "You would have no power over me if it were not given to you from above. Therefore the one who handed me over to you is guilty of a greater sin."

¹²From then on, Pilate tried to set Jesus free, but the Jews kept shouting, "If you let this man go, you are no friend of Caesar. Anyone who claims to be a king opposes Caesar."

¹³**When Pilate heard this, he brought Jesus out and sat down on the judge's seat at a place known as the Stone Pavement (which in Aramaic is Gabbatha).** ¹⁴**It was the day of Preparation of Passover Week, about the sixth hour.**

"**Here is your king," Pilate said to the Jews.**

¹⁵**But they shouted, "Take him away! Take him away! Crucify him!"**

"**Shall I crucify your king?" Pilate asked.**

"**We have no king but Caesar," the chief priests answered.**

¹⁶**Finally Pilate handed him over to them to be crucified. So the soldiers took charge of Jesus.**

Although there is nothing like a formal trial in this section (although Pilate does occupy the "judge's seat" in 19:13), it continues with some of the same dynamics of the last chapter. The reader knows that Jesus' death is coming, but there is a delay. John pictures the cowardly but stubborn Pilate pitted against the fanatically driven Jewish leaders, with the quiet but defiant Jesus caught in the middle. The underlying acrimonious relationship between Pilate and the Jewish leaders is near the breaking point. John adds to the intensity and drama by using sharp, choppy dialog to move the story along, a stark contrast to the extended monologues of the Farewell Discourses. From a legal standpoint, John's account emphasizes the innocence of Jesus of any sort of crime (see 18:23,38; 19:4,6,12).

19:1-3. Rather than give in to the demands of the Jewish leaders, Pilate continues to seek some type of compromise that is short of executing Jesus. Since the Barabbas ploy failed, Pilate now has him **flogged**. John gives no explanation for the flogging, and we are left to assume that it is a brutal expression of Pilate's frustration. The actions of the soldiers are to make Jesus a mocking parody of a king, probably intended to insult the Jews as much as to torment Jesus. It is not stated that Pilate has suggested this jeering farce, but he does use it to insult the Jews further (19:5,14).

Flogging (KJV, "scourged") was a regular preparation for Roman crucifixion, but could be a punishment by itself. It was practiced by the Jews of the first century as a part of extreme synagogue discipline (see Matt 10:17; 23:34). Flogging would be done by stripping the victim naked, and then tying him to a post, backside out. The flogger used a short whip with many thongs, called a *"flagrum."* These thongs were knotted with sharp pieces of bone or iron. The whipper or *"lictor"* stood at the side of the victim and struck him with sweeping horizontal strokes. This was done from each side, sometimes by two different lictors. Blows were struck on the back, the buttocks, and legs; the thongs wrapping around to abuse the front of the body also. The flagrum would cut through the skin and well into the deeper muscles, leaving "quivering ribbons of bleeding flesh."[1] While Jewish law limited flogging to 40 strokes (Deut 25:3), there is no reason the Roman soldiers would feel bound by this limit, so the number of blows to Jesus is unknown. The horrible severity of flogging was such that Peter could later comment of Jesus that by his "stripes" (KJV) we are healed (1 Pet 2:24). That Jesus is able to survive this torture and continue to converse intelligibly with Pilate is a testimony to a strong constitution and iron willpower.

The Roman soldiers charged with the flogging go far beyond the minimum duty. They also weave a small wreath out of thorny vines or branches and jam it on his head as a cruel and mocking **crown**. Exactly which plant these thorns come from is unspecified.[2] The Greek term for **thorns** used here is ἄκανθα (*akantha*), which may be related to the plant name *acacia*. There are several varieties of acacia shrubs native to Israel, some with 1–2″ long thorns, but this Greek word is not specific enough to be sure that John has the acacia plant in mind. It should be noted, however, that it is somewhat unlikely that there were any wild thorn bushes within the Praetorium compound. This means that one of the Roman soldiers hatched the idea of a barbarous crown, and sent a servant or underling out to find some thorn branches. Therefore, we may conclude that the flogging torture of Jesus was done in a leisurely manner rather than quickly.

---

[1]This description is from the remarkable article by William D. Edwards, Wesley J. Gabel, and Floyd E. Hosmer, "On the Physical Death of Jesus Christ," *JAMA* (March 21, 1986): 1455-1463 (quotation is from 1457). This is a detailed description of the medical aspects of Jesus' flogging and crucifixion written by a theologian and two medical experts, and includes a number of excellent and informative diagrams.

[2]It is estimated that there are more than 70 different thorny plants native to Israel.

The sadistic crown of thorns is accompanied by a **purple robe**, another way of lampooning the Jews and their "king." John does not tell us the source of the robe, although Luke seems to say that it came from Herod Antipas (Luke 23:11).[3] The tormenters even act out false obeisance to Jesus, chanting, **"Hail, king of the Jews."** The final insult of the soldiers is to beat the defenseless Jesus with slaps or punches to the face (about the only part of his body that did not have lacerations). Such slaps were a sign of utter contempt.

19:4-5. Now Pilate displays Jesus to the mob, but a shattered Jesus dressed as a bogus king. He announces Jesus with the fateful words, **"Here is the man"** (Latin: *"Ecce homo"*). It is a striking picture of the frail humanity of Jesus, dressed like a clown, beaten badly, and bleeding profusely. Pilate's words have the force of "here is your man, and see, I can do anything I like with him."

It is difficult to tell if Pilate is trying to appease the Jews or infuriate them. He appears to have a desire to occupy the high moral ground of an advocate for Jesus' innocence, but the sick game he is playing with Jesus as the game piece seems calculated to enrage the Jewish leaders even more. To suggest that this beaten, crushed man is their king is a jolting reminder of their national impotence in the face of Roman might.

19:6. Now, for the first time, the method of execution is shouted: Roman crucifixion (for comments on crucifixion see below, 19:17-18). Even though Jesus may have been gone from sight for an hour or more, the **chief priests** (Annas and Caiaphas, perhaps leading Sadducees) and their **officials** (the temple police) are still there. Pilate persists in toying with them. He flaunts the innocence of Jesus again, and challenges them, "Go crucify him yourselves." Even this go-ahead-and-do-it approval is an obvious taunt, for they have already admitted their lack of power to execute, and the Jewish way of execution was not crucifixion anyway.

19:7. Pilate's theatrics have not dampened the determination of the Jewish leaders in the slightest. Now a new charge is verbalized. Jesus must die, not because he has claimed to be a political king (and therefore a threat to Rome), but because he has claimed to be

---

[3]The interrogation of Jesus by Herod Antipas is not included in John's account. It is found only in the Gospel of Luke (Luke 23:6-12).

the **Son of God**. Pilate has forced the true motive from the Jewish leaders. Yes, it is true that Jesus is not a genuine menace to the government, but he has violated an important religious taboo, and for that he must die. The irony for the reader is very thick at this point. Jesus is dying for his claim to be the Son of God, and proving that claim is the central reason for the existence of the book of John (1:34,49; 11:27; cf. 20:31).

The real complaint of the Jewish leaders, then, is that Jesus has committed blasphemy. He has encroached upon the sacred territory of God in a way that cannot be permitted.[4] The probable "law" they are referring to is Leviticus 24:16. The high priests are actually justified in their pursuit except for one thing: they have never fairly considered that this charge might be true, that *Jesus is the Son of God*. As the author has commented earlier, this is not entirely a matter of logical decision. They have the hard heart, and this obduracy will not allow them to believe. Their hard, unbelieving hearts are being used by God to cause the death of Jesus and therefore enact the plan for saving the world (12:37-41).

19:8-10. The religious note has been sounded and now the superstitious Pilate retreats again, this time in fear. The Romans had a grudging respect for the religion of the Jews, partly because of its great antiquity. Pilate now realizes that he may have gotten himself into something he had not fully understood. If, as I have argued in the discussion of chapter 18, Pilate had collaborated with the Jewish leaders in the arrest of Jesus, it was as a political expediency, not a religious matter.

In the privacy of an inner room of the Praetorium, Pilate asks Jesus a surprisingly perceptive question, **"Where do you come from?"** The reader should be able to quickly supply an answer to this question, for it is a theological key to understanding Jesus and his purpose. The believer knows that Jesus "came from God" (16:27) and is "going back" to God (16:28). A sign of the faith of the disciples was their recognition that Jesus "came from God"

---

[4]Throughout John there are references to the longstanding perception among Jesus' Jewish opponents that his claim to be God's Son was blasphemous. This perceived blasphemy was an early cause for the leaders to seek his death (5:18; 10:33). See the discussion of Brown, *Death of the Messiah*, 1:829.

(16:30). But this is not the time or place for such information. For Jesus the hour of his death has come, and he makes no such claims to Pilate. Therefore, the fearful yet exasperated Pilate resorts to threats, and reminds Jesus, **"I have the power either to free you or to crucify you."**

19:11. Pilate's arrogant assertion of authority does get a response from Jesus. These are Jesus' last recorded words in the Fourth Gospel until he is hanging from the cross. Despite his weakened condition, he gives Pilate a small reminder of how authority works. All human authority is derivative in nature, not absolute. Pilate rules in Palestine, but is accountable to higher Roman authorities. He would have been answerable to the Roman legate in Antioch, and to the Emperor and the Senate in Rome. Ultimately, however, human authority comes **from above**, i.e., from God (cf. 3:31).

Jesus' words here have the sense of exonerating Pilate to some degree. Jesus is saying, "You are a pawn in this, not a player." The one with true culpability is the **one who handed** [Jesus] **over** to Pilate. It is difficult to know if this is a generalization for the violent mob outside, or if Jesus has an individual in mind.[5] If an individual, a choice must be made between the traitor, Judas, and the one who actually brings Jesus to Pilate, Caiaphas. In this context it seems likely that Jesus has the high priestly group in mind. Pilate acts from arrogance and expediency, the Jewish leaders act from unbelief and jealousy. Therefore, they are **guilty of a greater sin**. Literally this reads, "they have greater sin," but in this context sin = guilt.

19:12. Pilate's latest conversation with Jesus terrifies him to the point that he continues to seek a way to have Jesus released,[6] but every attempt is shouted down. Talk of Jesus as a blasphemer has now disappeared, and the political charges have reappeared. The latest outcry has the taint of blackmail, that the Jewish leaders might have reason to question Pilate's loyalty to the Roman State.

---

[5] See Lindars, *The Gospel of John*, p. 569. Lindars believes that this section has the effect of taking the responsibility for Jesus' death away from the Romans, and placing it upon the Jewish people in general.

[6] Another factor contributing to Pilate's terror, but not mentioned in John, was the dream of Pilate's wife that warned her of Jesus' innocence (Matt 27:19). The highly superstitious Pilate probably put great stock in such a thing, and interpreted it as a divine message.

To allow a potential revolutionary to escape would make Pilate **no friend of Caesar**. These are potentially career-ruining accusations for Pilate, for the reigning Caesar, Tiberius, was an old military general with no tolerance for disloyalty.

19:13-15. Preliminaries are over, and there is no easy way out for Pilate. Now he is forced to convene court and assume his role as the high judge of Palestine. Pilate does this by sitting in the **judge's seat**. This is the βῆμα (*bēma*), the traditional elevated bench of judgment used for public pronouncements in the Roman system.[7] When Pilate occupies the *bēma*, his verdicts have binding legal force. The author includes the detail that this is at a place called the **Stone Pavement**, probably a well-known feature of ancient Jerusalem. John also records the Aramaic name for this place, **Gabbatha**, although the meaning of this term is disputed. This is likely a semipublic area of the Praetorium precinct, somewhat akin to the steps of a state capitol building or the courtyard of a city hall.

When things are in place for the official judgment, Pilate begins by giving the Jewish leaders one last chance to relent. **"Here is your king!"** he sneers, implying, "Does this look like a dangerous rebel leader to you?" But the shouts continue, demanding that Jesus be condemned and crucified. Pilate takes a final shot at his adversaries by sarcastically asking, **"Shall I crucify your king?"** This is a no-win question for the Jewish leaders. To answer "Yes" makes them acknowledge Jesus as some type of king, which they have steadfastly refused to do. To answer "No" allows Pilate to release Jesus, and forces them to back down from their demand for his death. So rather than answer "Yes" or "No," the high priests themselves give a remarkable response, **"We have no king but Caesar."** For a first century Jew this statement is utterly outrageous, so outrageous that some have seen it as a polemical fabrication of the author. It would be like a patriotic American declaring, "Yes, I think we ought to let the United Nations control our tax money and our armed forces." Yet the splendid outrageousness of the statement is a strong argument in favor of its authenticity.

---

[7]The *bēma* of Pilate is also mentioned by Matthew (27:19). The *bēma* shows up in judicial settings in the book of Acts: Galio at Corinth (18:12-17) and Festus in Caesarea (25:6). *Bēma* is also used of the eschatological judgment seat of both God (Rom 14:10) and of Christ (2 Cor 5:10).

The Jewish population was among the most troublesome of all the peoples of the Roman Empire, mainly because of its general refusal to submit fully to Roman rule. These anti-Roman and nationalistic attitudes were to boil over twice in the next 100 years, resulting in the destruction of Jerusalem in AD 70, and the utter annihilation of Palestinian Judaism after the Bar Kochba revolt of AD 132-135. To say, "We have no king but Caesar" was to relinquish any future hope of an independent Jewish state, and to deny a theological foundation of the Jewish people: the sovereign Kingship of God himself. The people of Israel saw the LORD their God as the ultimate, eternal "King" (Ps 10:16; 98:6). He was the "King" over the gods of other nations (Ps 95:3), and the "King" over all the earth (Ps 47:7), even the "Great King" (Mal 1:14). Just as one could describe the LORD as "my God," it was also possible to remember Him as "my King" (e.g., Ps 68:24). How bitter these words must have tasted on the lips of the high priests!

The author also gives a time-frame reference. It is about the **sixth hour** (about noon by our reckoning) on the **day of Preparation of Passover Week**. Exactly what John means by this day has been hotly disputed. A literal translation of this phrase is "it was the preparation of Passover." I believe it is Friday, the preparation day for the Sabbath of Passover week.[8]

19:16. Pilate's bluster ends without a whimper. When the Caesar card is played for the second time, he can no longer oppose the Jewish leaders, so he gives the order for Jesus **to be crucified**. We are left with this impression of Pilate: a man who knows right from wrong, yet who allows his own self-interest to dictate his actions.

---

[8]The NIV has combined a considerable amount of interpretation to the text by translating the word πάσχα (*pascha*) as "**Passover Week**." This implies the day is Friday, the usual day of "preparation" for the Saturday Sabbath. The force of the NIV's interpretation is that this is "Friday of Passover Week." While this may be what John intends (and I believe he does), it is possible to interpret this as "Preparation for the Passover," i.e., Thursday. This is the translation of the NRSV and others, but this is every bit as guilty as the NIV of overtranslation. The NIV has attempted to interpret this text as referring to Friday in order to harmonize it with the Synoptic accounts. The NRSV has concluded it is Thursday and allowed the apparent contradiction to stand. Actually the text is ambiguous and cannot answer the day of the week by itself. It is from other considerations that we should conclude that this is Friday (see comments on 13:1).

7. The Crucifixion of Jesus (19:17-30)

[17]Carrying his own cross, he went out to the place of the Skull (which in Aramaic is called Golgotha). [18]Here they crucified him, and with him two others — one on each side and Jesus in the middle.

[19]Pilate had a notice prepared and fastened to the cross. It read: JESUS OF NAZARETH, THE KING OF THE JEWS. [20]Many of the Jews read this sign, for the place where Jesus was crucified was near the city, and the sign was written in Aramaic, Latin and Greek. [21]The chief priests of the Jews protested to Pilate, "Do not write 'The King of the Jews,' but that this man claimed to be king of the Jews."

[22]Pilate answered, "What I have written, I have written."

[23]When the soldiers crucified Jesus, they took his clothes, dividing them into four shares, one for each of them, with the undergarment remaining. This garment was seamless, woven in one piece from top to bottom.

[24]"Let's not tear it," they said to one another. "Let's decide by lot who will get it."

This happened that the scripture might be fulfilled which said,
"They divided my garments among them
and cast lots for my clothing."[a]
So this is what the soldiers did.

[25]Near the cross of Jesus stood his mother, his mother's sister, Mary the wife of Clopas, and Mary Magdalene. [26]When Jesus saw his mother there, and the disciple whom he loved standing nearby, he said to his mother, "Dear woman, here is your son," [27]and to the disciple, "Here is your mother." From that time on, this disciple took her into his home.

[28]Later, knowing that all was now completed, and so that the Scripture would be fulfilled, Jesus said, "I am thirsty." [29]A jar of wine vinegar was there, so they soaked a sponge in it, put the sponge on a stalk of the hyssop plant, and lifted it to Jesus' lips. [30]When he had received the drink, Jesus said, "It is finished." With that, he bowed his head and gave up his spirit.

[a]*24* Psalm 22:18

When it comes to the crucifixion, there are many points of contact between John's account and that of the Synoptic Gospels, but John has some significant additions. This unique material includes the controversy over the "title" attached to Jesus' cross, a much fuller explanation of the soldiers' casting lots for Jesus' tunic, the touching story of Jesus' entrusting the care of his mother to the "beloved disciple," and the details about Jesus' corpse not having the legs broken, but being pierced in the side.[9]

19:17-18. Although ancient crucifixion practices varied from place to place, the usual Roman method of this time required the victim to carry his **cross** out to the site of execution, as recorded by John. This probably refers to the heavy cross-beam or *patibulum*, weighing as much as 100-125 pounds.[10] The upright post (called the *stipes*) to which the *patibulum* would attach was permanently planted at the site of execution. All four Gospel accounts record the name of this place as **the Skull** (κρανίον, *kranion*), or **Golgotha** (the Hebrew/Aramaic word meaning "skull"). The Latin version of this place name is *Calvariae*, from which we get the traditional name, "Calvary." The exact location of Golgotha is uncertain today, but the best evidence points to the traditional hill now covered by the Church of the Holy Sepulchre in the Old City of Jerusalem. This church building dates back to the fifth century, and is built on a location that was outside the city walls in Jesus' time (see 19:20, cf. Heb 13:12).

Here Jesus is **crucified**, meaning he is affixed to the *patibulum* and it is lifted in place to the *stipes*. John does not mention the method of fastening here (none of the Gospels do). The tradition that Jesus was nailed to the cross is dependent upon words of

---

[9]There are many excellent studies on the physical aspects of Jesus' death by crucifixion. See the numerous medical journal references in the *JAMA* article by Edwards, Gabel, and Hosmer cited above. More information on a number of the details in this section may be found in this study. See also the excellent articles by another medical doctor, Garland Bare, "A Doctor Looks at Crucifixion," *The Lookout* (April 4, 1982): 2-3, 6. and "A Doctor Looks at the Burial and the Resurrection," *The Lookout* (April 11, 1982): 2-3, 9. For an in-depth monograph on this section see John Paul Heil, *Blood and Water: The Death and Resurrection of Jesus in John 18-21*, CBQMS 27 (Washington: Catholic Biblical Association of America, 1995).

[10]John makes no mention of the forced assistance given by Simon of Cyrene in carrying the cross, but then the procession to the cross lasts but a few words in the Fourth Gospel.

Thomas in 20:25 and early Christian tradition (cf. Luke 24:40). For example, the second or third century "Gospel of Peter" describes the removal of Jesus from the cross, including this statement, "And then they pulled the nails from the Lord's hands and set him on the ground."[11] John mentions the two other men being crucified without comment, except to say that they flanked Jesus, who occupies the middle *stipes*.

19:19-22. John's version of the "*titulus*" or **sign** (Greek: τίτλος, *titlos*) attached to the cross includes a continuation of the wrangling between Pilate and the Jewish leaders.[12] The high priests object to the wording, which is a continuation of Pilate's insulting behavior toward them. This time, however, Pilate will not be bullied, and the sign remains unchanged: **JESUS OF NAZARETH, THE KING OF THE JEWS**. The *titulus* was a legal instrument. Mark describes it as a "written notice of the charge against him" (Mark 15:26). This confirms that Jesus was not crucified for blasphemy, but for sedition, even though Pilate found the charge ludicrous. John notes that the notice is trilingual, in Aramaic (the spoken language of Jewish Palestine), in Latin (the official language of the Roman Empire), and Greek (the common language of trade and literature).

19:23-24. By custom the execution detail was entitled to any clothes or possessions left by the crucified victims. John's mention of **four shares** indicates there were four soldiers. They are able to divide Jesus' outer garments evenly, but pause before tearing his **undergarment** or "tunic" into four pieces. This is a valuable piece of merchandise, **woven in one piece from top to bottom**. To tear it would result in little more than rags, so they elect to cast lots for it. This would have been done by tossing dice or something like dice.

John's purpose in adding this detail is not to conform to an age-old stereotype of soldiers, though. He sees it as a fulfillment of prophecy, specifically Psalm 22:18. For John the fulfillment of prophecy is a confirmation of the divine plan of God at work. Even a small detail like this is important, for it shows the contempt with which Jesus was treated. To have one's clothes divided by dice

---

[11]Gospel of Peter 6:1. For the text of the Gospel of Peter see Robert J. Miller, ed., *The Complete Gospels* (Sonoma, CA: Polebridge Press, 1994).

[12]All the Synoptic Gospels mention this *titulus*; see Matthew 27:37; Mark 15:26; Luke 23:38.

tosses shows that one is in dire straits, a helpless victim of the strong and brutal. This contempt for God's anointed is not accidental, but an element of the plan of God for human redemption. Jesus does not die a "noble death" by drinking poison, nor a "glorious death" by falling in the heat of battle. He dies a degrading death without honor or mercy.

19:25-27. In contrast to the boisterous soldiers, John portrays another group standing nearby. This groups consists of at least five individuals: Mary the mother of Jesus (who has not appeared as a character in the narrative since chapter 2), Mary's unnamed sister (Jesus' aunt), Mary the wife of Clopas,[13] Mary Magdalene, and the beloved disciple (probably John himself). Mary Magdalene appears for the first time in John as if the readers already know who she is, and she will play a crucial role in the resurrection narrative of the next chapter.[14]

In a terribly poignant and touching scene, Jesus performs the final duties of the oldest son while hanging from the cross. He entrusts the beloved disciple (John) with the care of his mother. This man was suffering the excruciating result of his obedient submission to God, and "bearing the sins of the world" within his soul. Yet he does not cease to be a son who loves and cares for his mother to the best of his ability. This may have been intended as a temporary measure, until John could deliver Mary to Jesus' younger brothers, but tradition has seen this as the beginning of a long-standing relationship between John and Mary. John says it this way, **from that time on, this disciple took her into his house.**

19:28-30. This section pictures Jesus in his last minutes of physical life. John's key words here are the Greek verb τελέω (*teleō*), and its near synonym, the cognate verb τελείοω (*teleioō*). Both of these verbs have the sense of "to complete" or "to finish." The idea of future completion was mentioned by Jesus very early in the book. In 4:34 he informed his disciples that his "food" was "to do the will of him who sent me and to finish [*teleioō*] the work." In the high

---

[13]It is possible that the husband of this Mary is the disciple called "Cleopas" by Luke in the Emmaus Road incident (Luke 24:18). This is an intriguing connection, but the names are only similar, not identical, and this can be no more than an unprovable theory.

[14]Westcott, *The Gospel According to St. John,* 2:313.

priestly prayer Jesus verbalized that he glorifies the Father by "completing [*teleioō*] the work" given to him (17:4). Now the author/narrator tells the reader that Jesus understands all of this work to be **completed** or "finished" (*teleō*). This means that the Father's plan for human salvation has run its course, and its strategy has been successful. The perfect sacrifice has been offered to atone for human sins. Only one relatively minor item remains, a last Scripture to be **fulfilled** (*teleioō*) before his death. When this is done, Jesus announces to all the world, **"It is finished"** (*tetelestai*, from *teleō*), meaning "it is completed," or "it is brought to an end." The work he had been assigned in God's redemptive plan has been finished. His work being done, Jesus drops his head and gives up his spirit. To "give up one's spirit" or "breathe one's last breath" (cf. Luke 23:46) reflects the ancient way of saying, "he died." Ancients believed that the human spirit left the body with the last exhalation of breath.

The final Scripture fulfillment before death involves Jesus' quenching his thirst with a bit of **wine vinegar**. Although John does not specify the exact Old Testament passage he has in mind, we are probably to understand Psalm 69:21, "They . . . gave me vinegar for my thirst." Why this choice of beverage (probably better translated "vinegary wine")? Was this a last act of cruelty by the notoriously heartless soldiers? This is possible, but more likely the **jar** of vinegary wine was handy to quench the thirst of the soldiers on guard, and they are simply acting out of duty or even compassion or respect.[15] This was not wine drugged with myrrh offered to Jesus before the crucifixion to dull his pain (Mark 15:23). Jesus' call for something to drink was a normal response to what was an understandably great thirst.

8. Piercing Jesus' Side (19:31-37)

[31]Now it was the day of Preparation, and the next day was to be a special Sabbath. Because the Jews did not want the bodies left on the crosses during the Sabbath, they asked Pilate to have

---

[15]For reasons to understand ὄξος (*oxos*, "vinegary wine") as a preferred thirst quencher for Roman military personnel see Brown, *Death of the Messiah*, 2:1063.

the legs broken and the bodies taken down. ³²The soldiers therefore came and broke the legs of the first man who had been crucified with Jesus, and then those of the other. ³³But when they came to Jesus and found that he was already dead, they did not break his legs. ³⁴Instead, one of the soldiers pierced Jesus' side with a spear, bringing a sudden flow of blood and water. ³⁵The man who saw it has given testimony, and his testimony is true. He knows that he tells the truth, and he testifies so that you also may believe. ³⁶These things happened so that the scripture would be fulfilled: "Not one of his bones will be broken,"ᵃ ³⁷and, as another scripture says, "They will look on the one they have pierced."ᵇ

ᵃ*36* Exodus 12:46; Num. 9:12; Psalm 34:20   ᵇ*37* Zech. 12:10

19:31-33. John's language again identifies this day as the **day of Preparation** for the Sabbath, i.e., Friday. For religious reasons the Jewish leaders petition Pilate to have the crucifixion victims' bodies removed before this holy day. This means that the process of death by crucifixion needed to be accelerated, for a person could often hang on the cross for several days before dying. Pilate agrees, probably out of a willingness to get the distasteful episode behind him as quickly as possible. The method of quickening death is to break the legs of those on the crosses, probably using heavy clubs. This would have been terribly painful, and the trauma it brought to the body would have quickly exhausted any remaining strength or will to live. In Jesus' case, however, there is no need to break legs because he is already dead. The soldiers have no interest in needless desecration of a corpse.

The relatively quick death of Jesus (he may have been on the cross as little as 3 hours) is somewhat surprising to the soldiers, but should not be so to us. Jesus has already suffered enormous physical abuse in the flogging, and the terrible spiritual agony of betrayal and the bearing of human sins. As Paul writes, "God made him who had no sin to be sin for us, so that in him we might become the righteousness of God" (2 Cor 5:21).

19:34. Before leaving Jesus' body, however, the soldiers perform a simple test to confirm death. They slip a spear point through his ribs and into his inner chest cavity. The resulting flow of **blood and water** is sufficient evidence for them to verify that he is dead. The exact physical explanation for the water and blood has been debated over the centuries. If the heart is pierced, the blood is readily understood, but where does "water" come from? One should keep in mind that word order in the Greek language has a different value than it does in English. We tend to think sequentially, they thought more often in degrees of importance. Therefore, for John to write "blood and water" does not mean "blood first, then water." It is more likely that he means "lots of blood and some water." We may assume, then, the spear first pierces the *pericardial sac* around the heart, which releases a clear, water-like fluid. Then the spear pierces the heart itself, with a flow of red blood.[16]

19:35-37. There are two reasons that the author relates the gory details of the punctured corpse. First, he uses it to give the account eyewitness credibility. John is challenging the reader to reject any explanation of Jesus' resurrection that would say that Jesus did not really die. Some gnostic teachers of the late first century may already have been denying Jesus' death because of their denial of his true humanity. For some of these false teachers, Jesus was a divine figure who only "seemed" to be human in order to act out the drama of salvation. Such an immortal person was not capable of dying, so the death was an illusion. Elsewhere John warns against those who do not "acknowledge that Jesus Christ has come in the flesh" (1 John 4:2). The doctrine of Christ's full humanity must not be compromised. The author of Hebrews understood the importance of this for his own theological presentation. If Christ had not been human, he could not have died, and it is his death that destroys "him who holds the power of death — that is, the devil — and free[s] those who all their lives were held in slavery by their fear of death" (Hebrews 2:14-15). Without the death of Jesus there is no atonement. Without a human Jesus there is no death. John's eyewitness testimony leaves no room for doubt about the actual death of Jesus at the hands of professional Roman executioners.[17]

---

[16]See discussion in Edwards, Gabel, and Hosmer, "Physical Death," *JAMA*: 1463.

[17]While John probably does not have this in mind, his eyewitness account is also an effective argument against the so-called "Swoon Theory" of the resurrection. This theory originated in the early nineteenth century, and hypothesized that Jesus did not really die on the cross; he merely

A second reason for including the side-piercing incident is that it fulfills Scripture. John is able to see two sorts of Scripture fulfillment in this. The avoidance of broken legs allows Jesus to serve as a perfect sacrificial victim. The Passover lamb was to have no broken bones (Exod 12:46; Num 9:12). Furthermore, Scripture is also fulfilled in the piercing itself. John finds this language applied to the Davidic Messiah in Zechariah 12:10, and applies it to Jesus. This "piercing" is an eternal reminder of the rejection of Jesus by his own people, and reappears as a factor in the description of the eschatological Jesus of the Second Coming (Revelation 1:7). This future reckoning is implied in John's choice of the phrase, "They *will* look on the one they have pierced" = "They will be accountable to the one they rejected."

9. Jesus' Burial (19:38-42)

[38]Later, Joseph of Arimathea asked Pilate for the body of Jesus. Now Joseph was a disciple of Jesus, but secretly because he feared the Jews. With Pilate's permission, he came and took the body away. [39]He was accompanied by Nicodemus, the man who earlier had visited Jesus at night. Nicodemus brought a mixture of myrrh and aloes, about seventy-five pounds.[a] [40]Taking Jesus' body, the two of them wrapped it, with the spices, in strips of linen. This was in accordance with Jewish burial customs. [41]At the place where Jesus was crucified, there was a garden, and in the garden a new tomb, in which no one had ever been laid. [42]Because it was the Jewish day of Preparation and since the tomb was nearby, they laid Jesus there.

[a]*39* Greek *a hundred litrai* (about 34 kilograms)

---

fainted. After a few hours in the cool tomb (where he was mistakenly placed since he was assumed to be dead) he revived, escaped, and appeared to his disciples. This theory is so ridiculous that it barely deserves comment, but John's account of "blood and water" coming from Jesus' pierced side is a quick way to discount the Swoon Theory. People do not suffer the horrible abuse of scourging and a punctured heart, and then revive a few hours later without any medical treatment.

John's account of the burial of Jesus is in basic harmony with that of the Synoptic Gospels, but includes a number of additional details.

19:38. Joseph of Arimathea is known to all four Gospel authors.[18] In John he is presented as a secret disciple of Jesus and a man of considerable influence and wealth. His influence is shown in his access to Pilate for permission to take the body of Jesus. His wealth is shown by his ability to commandeer quickly a nearby tomb for the burial. What John means by portraying him as a "secret disciple" is less clear. Does this mean that Joseph participated in the activities of Jesus and his disciples when they were in Jerusalem, but clandestinely lest his association become known? Or does he mean something more like that Joseph was a "secret admirer" of Jesus, a "fan from afar"? This would make him one who had heard Jesus teach publicly and agreed with him, but had never had direct contact. The second scenario is more likely, because Joseph is contrasted with Nicodemus who *did* set up a nighttime meeting with Jesus in order to have personal contact (John 3:1ff).

19:39-40. Joseph's partner in the retrieval and burial of Jesus' body is Nicodemus, who has already appeared twice in the narrative (3:1ff.; 7:50-51). Nicodemus is a member of the Sanhedrin (7:50), as is Joseph (Mark 15:23), so we may be sure that the plot against Jesus was not unanimously endorsed by the leading Jews (see Luke 23:51). The spicy mixture they apply to the body is literally given as "100 pounds," but this is referring to the Roman pound of 12 ounces. Therefore the NIV is correct in saying **seventy-five pounds**, assuming our modern 16-ounce pounds.

---

[18]See Matthew 27:57; Mark 15:53; and Luke 23:50-51. The exact location of Arimethea is uncertain. It has traditionally been identified with the birthplace of Samuel, "Ramah" (see 1 Sam 1:19), but this is based upon little more than a marginal similarity between the two names. Later European legends found a romantic role for Joseph, who supposedly made his way to Gaul and then to Great Britain in the AD 60s. There he is reputed to have established a Christian outpost at Glastonbury. Also connected with Joseph in later legends is the preservation of the so-called "Holy Grail," the cup Jesus used at the Last Supper. This has sometimes given him a role in the Arthurian cycle of legends so popular in Britain and America.

The Jews of this period did not practice any type of embalming or mummification of corpses. The usual method of burial would be to wash the body thoroughly (quite a task for the bloody Jesus), to rub it with oil, and to wrap it tightly with a linen shroud that would hold spices within its folds. The amount of spices used would have been very expensive, probably worth thousands of dollars. The ability of Nicodemus to produce such amounts on short notice speaks to both his resourcefulness and his wealth.

19:41-42. As mentioned above (18:1), John's Passion Narrative begins and ends in a garden. The ending garden is nearby Golgotha and contains a **new tomb**. John presents this as a matter of convenience, that **the tomb was nearby**, without giving any details as to why it was available. The Synoptic Gospels describe this as Joseph's own tomb, newly carved out of a hillside (see Matt 27:60). We should understand that this is nothing like a modern grave plot in a cemetery. This was intended to be a family tomb for the Joseph clan, and to be used for many generations. For Joseph to give it up to Jesus was an act of great extravagance and powerful respect.

The actions of Joseph and Nicodemus are extraordinary in several respects. First, they are making public their allegiance to Jesus, whereas before Joseph had maintained secrecy "because he feared the Jews" (v. 38). This is a bold and potentially dangerous move. After all, Jesus has just been killed. What is to stop the Jewish leaders from rounding up his disciples for execution next? Second, this is not the usual treatment for the corpse of a crucifixion victim. Part of the reason for crucifixion was to keep the corpse on public display for some time after death as a deterrent to the general public. Such corpses would be dishonored by general rotting and by the pecking of birds and the gnawing of wild animals. Joseph and Nicodemus refuse to allow this. They use what political power they have to secure the body of Jesus and to give it a decent and honorable burial. Third, and perhaps most extraordinary of all for these prominent Pharisees, their handling of a corpse would defile them and make them ceremonially unclean (Num 19:11). Thus, they were sacrificing their opportunity to participate in the coming Sabbath activities, and perhaps even celebrations of the following week for the Feast of Unleavened Bread.

JOHN 20

C. THE RESURRECTION OF JESUS (20:1–21:25)

If chapters 18–19 of the Fourth Gospel are called the Passion Narrative, chapters 20–21 may be called the Resurrection Narrative. The sequence of events for John's Resurrection Narrative is roughly the same as that of the Synoptic Gospels: events at the tomb on Sunday morning, events in meetings of the disciples in Jerusalem, and then events back in Galilee. But beyond this rough outline, the actual events recorded by John are nearly unknown from the Synoptic accounts.[1] Only in John do we find the personal encounter between Jesus and Mary at the tomb, the preliminary, symbolic endowment of the Holy Spirit upon the disciples, the incident of Thomas's doubting, and the triple "Do you love me?" testing of Peter.

The scenes in this final section are brief and fast moving. John introduces the settings quickly, and his "dramatic personnel" enter the scenes suddenly and without flourish. John's resurrection appearances may be divided into two categories: those in Jerusalem (chapter 20) and those in Galilee (chapter 21).

1. Peter and John at the Empty Tomb (20:1-9)

[1]Early on the first day of the week, while it was still dark, Mary Magdalene went to the tomb and saw that the stone had been removed from the entrance. [2]So she came running to Simon Peter

---

[1]There have been numerous ways of harmonizing all the resurrection appearances of Jesus. For a straightforward and plausible scheme see Murray J Harris, *3 Crucial Questions about Jesus* (Grand Rapids: Baker, 1994), pp. 107-109.

and the other disciple, the one Jesus loved, and said, "They have taken the Lord out of the tomb, and we don't know where they have put him!"

³So Peter and the other disciple started for the tomb. ⁴Both were running, but the other disciple outran Peter and reached the tomb first. ⁵He bent over and looked in at the strips of linen lying there but did not go in. ⁶Then Simon Peter, who was behind him, arrived and went into the tomb. He saw the strips of linen lying there, ⁷as well as the burial cloth that had been around Jesus' head. The cloth was folded up by itself, separate from the linen. ⁸Finally the other disciple, who had reached the tomb first, also went inside. He saw and believed. ⁹(They still did not understand from Scripture that Jesus had to rise from the dead.)

20:1-2. Mary Magdalene has been introduced to the readers of John rather abruptly as one of the people who maintained a vigil at the cross (19:25). As mentioned above, she is presented as if the readers are already acquainted with her, yet there is no explanatory or background information given about her. We must assume that she was well known in the early Christian community, either through the accounts of the Synoptic Gospels, through other traditions, or a combination of both.[2] Mary is pictured here as a model of devotion to Jesus. She is one of the last ones at the cross, and the first one at the tomb on **the first day of the week** (= Sunday). Later in this chapter she is the first actual witness to the resurrected Jesus.

Magdalene means "woman from Magdala," a small city on the west side of the Sea of Galilee. Luke records Mary as an early disciple

---

[2]There has been a great deal of interest in the study of Mary Magdalene in recent years, largely through the efforts of feminist biblical scholars. Sometimes this has been combined with an interest in early Gnostic Christian literature, which portrays the women in the early church as having a much wider role than allowed for in the orthodox tradition. A prime example of this is the *Gospel of Mary*, a second or third century work found among the Nag Hammadi collection discovered in Egypt in 1945. This intriguing little book presents Mary as one of the leaders of the postresurrection apostolic community, a vocal person who is able to lecture the others, including Peter. For text of the *Gospel of Mary* see Miller, *The Complete Gospels*, pp. 361-366.

of Jesus (Luke 8:2), and indicates that she helped support the community of disciples in a financial way. While there is an old and
early tradition that Mary was a prostitute, there is no support for
this in the New Testament itself.

In John's account Mary goes to the tomb of Jesus very early on
Sunday morning, but we are not told why.[3] It is **still dark**, before
sunrise, perhaps 4 a.m. or so. For John, darkness is associated with
unbelief, and certainly Mary does not come away from this initial
experience believing that Jesus has been raised from the dead.[4]
When she arrives, she finds that the tomb is open (**the stone had
been removed**) and apparently abandoned. This causes Mary to
run in a panic to where **Peter and the other disciple** (= John) are
staying, and report to them. Her initial report says nothing about a
resurrection, but merely that the body is missing. Mary assumes
that someone has **taken** (stolen) the body, and apparently fears that
it might be desecrated. Her panic is not caused by an encounter
with the supernatural (yet!), but by her continuing respect for Jesus
even after his death.

20:3-4. Peter and John do not wait for details, but race to the
tomb. It truly is a race, for John **reached the tomb first**. This probably indicates that he was younger than Peter. We can well imagine
these two men causing quite a stir by running wildly through the
streets of the city just as people were beginning their day.

20:5. In what we are intended to see as an eyewitness account,
John relates that he **bent over** to peek into the open tomb. The
verb translated **bent over** is παρακύπτω (*parakyptō*), meaning literally to "stoop alongside," and is to be distinguished from "stooping
down" (κατακύπτω, *katakyptō*; see John 8:8). Here it means something like, "lean down and in." John is careful to say that he "leans
in" without entering the tomb (his feet remain outside). It also
implies that he must duck his head because the entrance is less
than head height. It is the same verb used to describe Mary's

---

[3]Cf. Luke 23:55–24:11. In this account Mary visits the tomb along with
several other women. They bring spices and perfumes for the delayed
preparation of Jesus' corpse. This indicates that either they were unaware
that Joseph of Arimathea and Nicodemus had already done this, or they
did not think the two men did an adequate job.

[4]See Moloney, *John*, p. 518.

looking into the tomb in verse 10. This may be out of respect, but more likely it is a position of safety to allow for a quick retreat if there is danger within the open tomb. (Remember, it is still barely light. Would you have gone in?) John sees the **strips of linen** used to wrap the body, but no body, confirming Mary's story that the corpse was missing.

The word translated **strips of linen** is ὀθόνια (*othonia*), a plural form of ὀθόνιον (*othonion*). This is a relatively rare word, and its meaning is not entirely certain today. Some have seen a contradiction here between John and the Synoptic Gospel accounts. All three of the Synoptic authors describe Jesus' burial garb as a σινδών (*sindōn*),[5] a single linen cloth, whereas John's plural, *othonia* seems to imply multiple cloths wrapped around the body. There is no real contradiction, however, as Luke's account demonstrates. Luke uses both words. When Jesus is first removed from the cross, Luke has him wrapped in a *sindōn* (singular), but when Luke's Peter looks into the empty tomb he sees the *othonia* (plural). From this evidence we should probably understand *othonia* to be a generic plural meaning "grave clothes."[6]

20:6-7. Before John has much time to think about this, Peter arrives and charges into the tomb. Either he is more reckless than John is, or unafraid because there is no apparent danger. Peter also sees the linen burial wraps, but goes in further to see the **burial cloth.**[7] This is the cloth that was wrapped around the face of the

---

[5]Matthew 27:59; Mark 15:46; and Luke 23:53. The only other occurrence of *sindon* is in Mark's unique story of the young man wrapped in a linen sheet (*sindon*) who leaves it behind in the Garden of Gethsemane and escapes naked (Mark 14:51-52).

[6]This *sindōn/othonia* is what is believed by some to be the famous Shroud of Turin. The authenticity of the Shroud is highly debated, and even scientific investigation has not satisfactorily answered all the questions concerning its date and origin. Whether it is the actual burial cloth of Jesus or not, it does show what an ancient burial cloth may have looked like. It is a single linen sheet, approximately 14.5'×3.5' and contains the front and back images of a man about 6' tall who has been flogged and crucified. The man has long hair and a beard. His image on the Shroud is like a photographic negative, leading many to believe that it was "flashed" upon the cloth at the instant of Jesus' resurrection.

[7]This "burial cloth" is the Greek word σουδάριον (*soudarion*). This is the same word used for the cloth that wrapped the dead Lazarus's face in

body, perhaps to keep the jaw closed.[8] This has been folded neatly and laid at a place separately from the other grave clothes. The author may include this description to help dispel later claims that the body had been stolen. Body snatchers would probably not have unwrapped the corpse, and would certainly not have taken the time to fold any of the burial garb if they had unwrapped it.

20:8-9. John, the **other disciple**, finally enters the tomb himself. His response is recorded in simple but beautiful language, **he saw and believed**. Yet he sees nothing more than an empty tomb and grave clothes in various states of tidiness. So what does he believe? Before we answer this question, we should note that the statement, "he saw and believed," anticipates the later meeting with Thomas in which Jesus pronounces, "blessed are those who have not seen and yet believed" (v. 29). This is true faith for John; faith based on reliable testimony, not eyewitness experience. This is the type of faith the author hopes to bring to the readers (v. 31). In addition, the candid admission of verse 9 points to the fact that at this stage neither Peter, nor John, nor anyone else understood the empty tomb as pointing to a resurrected Jesus. Before the event, no one but Jesus knew that he would die and, within a few hours, life would return to his body so that he could encounter his disciples physically.

The author's editorial comment in verse 9 indicates the confusion of the early community. What happened was not what they expected. The Jewish expectation of Messiah included nothing about untimely death, and even less about resurrection of the Messiah. When John says **they . . . did not understand from Scripture**, he is referring to their incorrect messianic expectations. It was through later study of the Old Testament that the early church began to see that Jesus' life, death, and resurrection conformed to the prophetic intention of Scripture.[9]

John 11:44. It has been associated with a relic known as the "Sudarium of Oviedo," an ancient linen cloth measuring about 32"×21". This cloth is in the Cathedral of Oviedo in Spain, and its history in Spain can be traced back to the beginning of the seventh century.

[8]See under John 11:44, note 14.

[9]See Acts 2:25-32, where Peter expounds upon Psalm 16 as a prediction of Jesus' resurrection.

2. Jesus' Appearance to Mary (20:10-18)

[10]Then the disciples went back to their homes, [11]but Mary stood outside the tomb crying. As she wept, she bent over to look into the tomb [12]and saw two angels in white, seated where Jesus' body had been, one at the head and the other at the foot.

[13]They asked her, "Woman, why are you crying?"

"They have taken my Lord away," she said, "and I don't know where they have put him." [14]At this, she turned around and saw Jesus standing there, but she did not realize that it was Jesus.

[15]"Woman," he said, "why are you crying? Who is it you are looking for?"

Thinking he was the gardener, she said, "Sir, if you have carried him away, tell me where you have put him, and I will get him."

[16]Jesus said to her, "Mary."

She turned toward him and cried out in Aramaic, "Rabboni!" (which means Teacher).

[17]Jesus said, "Do not hold on to me, for I have not yet returned to the Father. Go instead to my brothers and tell them, 'I am returning to my Father and your Father, to my God and your God.'"

[18]Mary Magdalene went to the disciples with the news: "I have seen the Lord!" And she told them that he had said these things to her.

20:10-12. A new scene is presented in this section. The setting is still the garden tomb, but the personnel have changed. Peter and John exit, and we learn that Mary Magdalene has now arrived back at the tomb, presumably having tagged along at some distance behind the two men. Either the men do not notice Mary, or their confusion over the empty tomb has made them oblivious to her highly agitated state, for the author presents them as leaving without a word of encouragement or comfort.

Mary is weeping but not paralyzed. She, too, peeks into the tomb and sees something that Peter and John did not: **two angels in white**. It is likely that the identification of these beings as **angels** comes upon later reflection by Mary, for she still does not seem to understand that anything supernatural or miraculous has happened. For the reader, the dramatic tension builds. When will she realize?

20:13. The angels ask her a significant question, a question of concern, **"Why are you crying?"** This is the question we wish Peter and John had asked. The answer is obvious to Mary. Mary weeps because the great crush of events has overwhelmed her. Her Master has been disgraced and executed as a common criminal. Now the final insult has come: his body has apparently been stolen. She does not understand the ironic intent of the angelic question. They mean, "Dear sweet Mary, you don't need to cry any more."

Peter and John have offered no solution to the missing body, so she boldly challenges these two. "The body is missing," she says. "Someone has taken it, maybe you. I don't want trouble. I just want to know where Jesus' body is."

20:14. The dramatic pressure builds even further. Before the angels have a chance to answer, a new player enters the scene and grabs Mary's attention. This is Jesus, but a hidden Jesus for Mary. She does **not realize that it** [is] **Jesus.**

20:15. Jesus asks the same question as the angels did, **"Why are you crying?"** Then he adds another question, **"Who is it you are looking for?"** The reader will know that this second question has already been asked twice by Jesus at his arrest (18:4,7). As the arresting mob found the Jesus they sought, so too will Mary. Mary mistakes Jesus for the caretaker of the garden (κηπουρός, *kēpouros*, a **gardener**). This indicates that there is nothing remarkable about Jesus' appearance at this time. He is probably dressed in ordinary clothes (maybe even clothes borrowed from the caretaker's shack) and with a hat or hood hiding his face. Also contributing to Mary's failure to recognize Jesus is her teary vision as well as the general lack of light in this early morning setting. Mary's answer reveals her intention completely. She is not just concerned to learn the location of the missing body, she wants to restore it to the tomb.

20:16. The tension is almost unbearable for us now. Will she miss Jesus, or will she know? There is much more at stake here than Mary's ability to recognize a dear friend, because in learning that it is Jesus she will also learn that Jesus has risen from the dead.

Jesus makes himself known in a mild, gentle manner. He merely calls her name in a personal, revealing way, **"Mary."** No more questions. No scolding. No explanations. "O dear Mary, I didn't desert you!" As Jesus said earlier, the shepherd "calls his own sheep by name and leads them out" (10:3). He leads Mary out of her "slough of despond," with the comforting reality of his presence.

Mary's response is also just a single word, **"Rabboni!"** "Rabboni" (or "Rabbouni," NRSV) is an honorific Aramaic[10] title meaning "My teacher." The precise distinction between "Rabbouni" and the more common "Rabbi" is difficult to see, although some have suggested that "Rabbouni" shows greater respect and is therefore more suitable for use by a woman.[11] This may be the case, but these subtle distinctions would be as lost on John's original readers as they are on us today. More likely is that John is concerned to preserve the actual word used by Mary, having ascertained it from her through personal interview.

20:17. At first glance it is difficult to understand Jesus' next statement to Mary, **"Do not hold on to me, for I have not yet returned to the Father."**[12] It is even more confusing in the KJV, "Touch me not; for I am not yet ascended to my Father." This has sometimes been interpreted as if Jesus is telling Mary to keep her hands off of him because the touch of a human would pollute him. He must first make a quick trip to heaven for God's approval, and then he will return to appear to the gathered disciples. In old interpretations this was often tied to Jesus' descent into hell while dead, where he battles Satan, preaches to the dead, or does other things. None of this is necessary or justified.[13] A closer look at the grammar of this verse will bear this out.

---

[10]The text actually speaks of this as being "in Hebrew," although the NIV translators have interpreted it to be the linguistically similar Aramaic. The form "Rabbouni" is not decisive enough to rule out Hebrew as the original language of the statement, but the form is more likely Aramaic.

[11]See Lindars, *The Gospel of John,* p. 606.

[12]There are a number of old manuscripts and versions that add a phrase at the end of verse 16, "and she ran forward to touch him." This is a later addition to the text preparing the reader for the rather abrupt statement of Jesus in verse 17. It is rightly rejected as inauthentic both because of its harmonizing nature and because of its lack of support in the best manuscripts. See Metzger, *Textual Commentary,* p. 255.

[13]The theory that Christ descended into hell during the period of his death is a very early tradition, and even occurs in the second century Apostles' Creed. This theory has no clear support in the New Testament, although certain passages have been interpreted this way (e.g., Rom 10:7; Eph 4:9).

The phrase translated "Do not hold on to me" translates a Greek phrase consisting of an imperative verb (ἅπτου, *haptou*) with a negative (μή, *mē*). We refer to this imperative + negative construction as a prohibition. It is significant here that the imperative verb, *haptou*, is in the present tense. In a prohibition the present tense is used to indicate that ongoing action must cease. What this means is that Jesus is not saying, "Don't touch me," but "Stop touching me" = "Let go of me!" Jesus' reason for this is that he has "not yet returned to the Father," i.e., he will be with them on earth for awhile, so Mary does not need to attempt to hold him. This is a temporary situation, however, for he will eventually return to the Father in heaven.

This points out another weakness in the NIV translation of this verse. The verb that is translated "returned" and "returning" is ἀνα–βαίνω (*anabainō*), which means, literally, to "go up" or "ascend." While "return" is a possible translation, it misses an important connotation of this verb in John. John often uses *anabainō* to refer to the journey to heaven (see 1:51; 3:13; 6:62). In verse 17 the use of this verb reflects the ancient worldview that heaven was in the sky, and that a journey to heaven was a journey upward. This paragraph is John's final explanation of the ascension of Jesus. Just as he had Jesus explain the Lord's Supper in chapter 6 rather than at the Last Supper in chapter 13, in a similar manner the author has Jesus explain the ascension while still at the garden tomb rather than at the very end of the narrative. Jesus does not just return to his Father, but to **my Father and your Father, to my God and your God**. In his ascension he is a forerunner of what believers will also experience. He is the "firstfruits of those who have fallen asleep" (1 Cor 15:20). Remember that he promised his disciples, "I am going there to prepare a place for you" (14:2). He makes a way for us.

20:18. Mary becomes the first to tell others of the resurrected Jesus. This is quite significant for John. He repeats her name fully, **Mary Magdalene**, to emphasize her identity. She reports to the **disciples** (the group Jesus intended by his designation "brothers" in verse 17), and her report reflects more than just a human encounter. Her words are **I have seen the Lord,** and they remind us of the words of Isaiah, "I saw the Lord, seated on the throne" (Isa 6:1).[14] This is the

---

[14]See also 1 Kings 22:19; Amos 9:1; cf. Psalm 16:8 and its quotation in Acts 2:25.

first of three confessions of Jesus as "Lord" in this chapter (vv. 18,25, 28; on the significance of the use of "Lord" see comments under verse 28). Mary reports everything, but John does not comment as to whether or not her testimony is accepted (cf. Luke 24:22-24).

3. Jesus' Appearance to the Disciples with Thomas Absent (20:19-23)

¹⁹On the evening of that first day of the week, when the disciples were together, with the doors locked for fear of the Jews, Jesus came and stood among them and said, "Peace be with you!" ²⁰After he said this, he showed them his hands and side. The disciples were overjoyed when they saw the Lord.

²¹Again Jesus said, "Peace be with you! As the Father has sent me, I am sending you." ²²And with that he breathed on them and said, "Receive the Holy Spirit. ²³If you forgive anyone his sins, they are forgiven; if you do not forgive them, they are not forgiven."

20:19-20. A quick scene change: later that day (Sunday), still in Jerusalem. Now the disciples have congregated again in a safe house. The **doors** are **locked for fear of the Jews.**[15] This may indicate an actual manhunt going on for Jesus' disciples, but more likely it is a justifiable sense of paranoia from a group whose leader has just been arrested and executed without legal cause. The locked doors serve a dual purpose in the narrative. They quickly portray an atmosphere of fear among the disciples, and serve to make the sudden entrance of Jesus a supernatural act.

Jesus' unexplained appearance is followed by his words, **"Peace be with you."** "Peace" is the traditional Jewish greeting שׁלם (*shalom*), meaning, "I wish you personal peace and well-being" (see comments at 14:27). This is followed by a display of the wounds on

---

[15]Even relatively modest homes had a way to bar the door, although these mechanisms were crude by modern standards. The simplest would be no more than a bar on brackets or a bolt that slid through heavy rings secured to the door and the doorframe. See Keener, *Background Commentary*, p. 317.

Jesus' hands and side, the still-present effects of the crucifixion. Although in a resurrection body, this is still the human Jesus.

The disciples have now had the experience of Mary Magdalene. They can say, "I saw the Lord!" (cf. v. 25; see comments on "Lord" at verse 28). This brings them great happiness; they are **overjoyed**. The presence of Jesus has changed the atmosphere from anxiety to gladness, from fear to joy.

20:21-23. Jesus has not come just to exchange pleasantries, however. He performs three separate but related tasks with his disciples. First, he gives them a commission. **"As the Father has sent me, I am sending you."** The word translated "sent" is the verb ἀποστέλλω (*apostellō*). *Apostellō* has the connotation of "sending with responsibility and authority." This is the verb Jesus uses to describe the manner in which he was "sent" by the Father. He was given a task and he was granted authority. The word translated "sending" is the Greek verb πέμπω (*pempō*). This is the word used to describe Jesus' sending of the disciples. Before we assume that there is a radical difference between these two verbs, we should notice the structure of this sentence. A wooden, literal translation of it would be *"Just as* the Father commissioned me, *even so* I am sending you" (italics added). In other words, there is no substantial difference between Jesus' sending of the disciples, and the Father's commissioning of him. How is he sending the disciples, then? He is sending them in an *apostellō* manner; i.e., he is commissioning them as Apostles with responsibility and authority. Jesus is sending them to continue his mission of bringing salvation to the world (see 3:17; 17:18; cf. 6:57).

Second, Jesus endows the new apostles with the resources they will need to function effectively. He gives them the **Holy Spirit**. In this gift they not only have the comfort of the heavenly Advocate in their lives, the true peace of God; they also have the convicting power of the Holy Spirit for their ministry. In 16:8-11 Jesus outlined three aspects of the Holy Spirit's power of conviction. The Holy Spirit convicts the world of its sinful unbelief, of the certainty of its condemnation, and of the righteous vindication of Jesus. How will this ministry of the Holy Spirit be accomplished? In part, at least, through the preaching and teaching of the Apostles and their converts.

A great deal has been written about whether or not this is John's version of the Day of Pentecost. Does John intend us to see this as a full, supernatural endowment of the Holy Spirit as portrayed by Luke in Acts 2? The short answer to this is "No"; it is a type of symbolic foreshadowing. Jesus has already taught that the Holy Spirit will not arrive until he departs (16:7). Furthermore, there is no radical change in the disciples at this point. They are still back in the locked room in the next scene.[16]

Jesus has given the apostles a task (bring salvation to the world). He has given them the resource to assist in the task (Holy Spirit). Now, third, he gives them authority; and it is a terrible authority. *They have responsibility in regard to the forgiveness of sins and the withholding of forgiveness!* At first glance it seems that Jesus has given them too much. The authority and ability to forgive sins rests with God alone (cf. Mark 2:7). But a closer reading shows that God has not lost authority over forgiveness. It is a two-stage process: If you [disciples] forgive, they are forgiven [by God].

We cannot separate authority in regard to forgiveness from the first two items. The apostles must preach the good news of Jesus' atoning sacrifice, "the Lamb who takes away the sins of the world" (1:29). The Holy Spirit must convict the unbeliever of sin. True forgiveness is granted to the truly repentant believer. To those who believe and repent, the preacher may promise forgiveness and know that God will agree. But for the unbelievers there is no such promise, and God will also agree.

4. Jesus' Appearance to His Disciples with Thomas Present (20:24-29)

[24]Now Thomas (called Didymus), one of the Twelve, was not with the disciples when Jesus came. [25]So the other disciples told him, "We have seen the Lord!"

But he said to them, "Unless I see the nail marks in his hands and put my finger where the nails were, and put my hand into his side, I will not believe it."

---

[16]For the long answer see Carson, *The Gospel According to John*, pp. 649-655.

²⁶**A week later his disciples were in the house again, and Thomas was with them. Though the doors were locked, Jesus came and stood among them and said, "Peace be with you!"** ²⁷**Then he said to Thomas, "Put your finger here; see my hands. Reach out your hand and put it into my side. Stop doubting and believe."**

²⁸**Thomas said to him, "My Lord and my God!"**

²⁹**Then Jesus told him, "Because you have seen me, you have believed; blessed are those who have not seen and yet have believed."**

20:24-25. At this point we learn that not all of the disciples were present for Jesus' Sunday evening appearance. **Thomas** was not there, although we are not told why. Some time in the week following he is with the other disciples and they repeat Mary's confession to him, **"We have seen the Lord!"** This is the second great confession of Jesus as Lord, anticipating the even greater confession of Thomas himself in verse 28.

Thomas isn't buying it, however. We have already been introduced to Thomas as a passionately loyal man (11:16). He withholds belief until he can personally experience the crucified and risen Jesus. In what seems to be an overreaction, Thomas insistently boasts that he must poke his finger through the nail holes in Jesus' hands, and stick his fist in the spear hole in Jesus' side. This is the type of boast a man will make when he never expects an occasion to follow through on his words. On the other hand, it reveals a Thomas who is deeply hurt by the death of Jesus. He is confused, and is guarding against any type of trickery that might hurt him even more.

20:26. After this brief interlude with Thomas, the scene reverts to the locked house. This time everybody is there, including Thomas. As in verse 19 the locked doors are no barrier for the resurrection body of Jesus. He is able to come and stand in the middle of the disciples without any problem. Jesus again repeats the greeting, **"Peace be with you."**

20:27. Having quickly taken care of these preliminaries, however, Jesus turns immediately to Thomas. Jesus knows exactly what Thomas has been boasting, presumably through Godlike omniscience. He challenges Thomas with the worst words a big talker can hear: What's stopping you? Go ahead and do it!

While Jesus' offer to let Thomas probe his scars was doubtlessly sincere, his message to Thomas comes in the second sentence: **"Stop doubting and believe."** This NIV translation is adequate, but misses the symmetry and force of the original Greek text. Jesus employs two antonym adjectives here, "unfaithful" (ἄπιστος, *apistos*) and "faithful" (πιστός, *pistos*). The statement begins with a prohibition (imperative + negative, see comments on verse 17), and ends with an implied command. A more literal translation would read, "Thomas, do not be *unfaithful,* but be *faithful."* It is an issue of faith or unfaith, a theme throughout the Fourth Gospel that has now come to a head in one of the disciples. Thomas must choose. Will he be a believer or an unbeliever?

20:28. Thomas dares not touch Jesus' wounds. He has just been overwhelmed with evidence that demands faith: a Jesus with a crucified and risen body, and who knows his inner thoughts. And so he blurts out what is the third and greatest confession of this chapter, **"My Lord and my God!"** Theologically, this is the highest confession of Jesus' divinity in all the New Testament, and, therefore, its implications will be considered carefully.

The Greek term for "Lord" is κύριος (*kyrios*). The word occurs 52 times in John with a number of connotations. We should note that the author of the Fourth Gospel is careful in how he uses the term. On the most basic level it is used 34 times as a polite title of address with no necessary theological entailments. This is something like our word "Sir." It is used this way frequently in John when different people address Jesus. This usage is also seen in Mary's respectful reference to the body of Jesus as "the Lord" (20:2,13).[17] A second way *kyrios* is used by John is in quotations from the Old Testament. In these four instances *kyrios* refers to God, and is the standard Greek equivalent for the Hebrew name for God, YHWH or Jehovah.[18] A third way *kyrios* is used in John is in the Farewell Discourses. In this way Jesus often (five times) makes reference to himself as "lord" in the sense of "master" or

---

[17]These 34 are John 4:11,15,19,49; 5:7; 6:34,68; 8:11; 9:36,38; 11:3,12,21, 27,32,34,39; 12:21; 13:6,9,25,36,37; 14:5,8,22; 20:2,13,15; 21:15,16,17,20,21.

[18]The 4 times *kyrios* occurs in an Old Testament quotation are John 1:23; 12:13,38 (2×).

"teacher" to his disciples/students. Sometimes this takes on the language of the master/slave relationship (e.g., 15:20).[19] A fourth way John uses *kyrios* is in editorial references to Jesus where the author speaks as the narrator. In these places we see that a very normal and comfortable way for the Apostle John to refer to Jesus was as "the Lord." This occurs five times, and is closely related to the next way.[20] A fifth way *kyrios* is used in John is as a divine designation for Jesus, Jesus as God. In these four instances *kyrios* will appear with an article, "the Lord," and will be a verbal statement of one of the characters in the story.[21] These are the most theologically significant instances of *kyrios* and all occur in the last two chapters of John. They show the gradual understanding of the disciples as to the divinity of Jesus. After the resurrection they may say emphatically, "Jesus is the Lord" (cf. Rom 10:9). He becomes more than the Rabbi Jesus of history; he is the Risen Lord of faith.

The statement of Thomas in verse 28 is not only a member of this final category, it is the most important member, and therefore the most significant use of *kyrios* in the entire book. Furthermore, it is among a very small number of places in the New Testament where Jesus is clearly referred to as "God" (θεός, *theos*).[22] Thomas, the one accused of unbelief, makes a radical shift to become a mouthpiece for the highest possible confession of faith in Jesus. In some ways this is the climax of the book of John.

20:29. We, the readers, quiver with the finality of Thomas's statement. How could we go any higher in our understanding of Jesus? Yet the Risen Lord does not bask in this mighty confession. Instead he pricks Thomas's bubble a bit and brings him back to earth. "Of course you believe," says Jesus. "You have witnessed enough to convince any sane and reasonable person that I am the Son of God risen from the dead, and the necessary object of faith. But many will be called upon to believe without such overwhelming

---

[19]The 5 times *kyrios* is used by Jesus in the Farewell Discourses are John 13:13,14,16; 15:15,20.

[20]The 5 times *kyrios* is used by the author as narrator are John 6:23; 11:2; 20:20; 21:7,12.

[21]The 4 times *kyrios* occurs in some type of confessional statement about Jesus are John 20:18, 25, 28; 21:7.

[22]Some of the clearest of these include Titus 2:13 and 2 Peter 1:1.

personal experiences." True faith is beyond personal experience. It is the evaluation and acceptance of the testimony about Jesus. We have no right to expect our own visitation by the Risen Lord to draw us to faith. Jesus has given to the church the task of bringing people to faith through the faithfully preached message of salvation and the convicting power of the Holy Spirit.

5. The Purpose of This Gospel (20:30-31)

[30]Jesus did many other miraculous signs in the presence of his disciples, which are not recorded in this book. [31]But these are written that you may[a] believe that Jesus is the Christ, the Son of God, and that by believing you may have life in his name.

[a]31 Some manuscripts *may continue to*

20:30. The author confides that he has not exhausted his supply of miracle stories about Jesus, perhaps a nod to the fact that his material is so very different from that of the Synoptic authors. He has chosen which **miraculous signs** to include very carefully in order to build the reader to a correct understanding of Jesus.

20:31. This correct understanding is the position of faith, life-giving faith. To bring others to faith is why John went to the huge effort of writing this book, an enormous and splendid accomplishment for anyone in the ancient world. John is saying, "I have given you more than enough. Now it's up to you to believe."

If we pay a little more attention to which Greek words in this sentence have articles and which do not, we would come up with this translation, "These things have been written so that you may believe that the Christ, the Son of God is Jesus." It isn't so much that John wants to convince us that this man named Jesus was really the messianic Son of God. His reasoning is more Jewish-oriented at this point. The Jews expected God to send a Messiah. John is saying, "Pay attention! That Messiah you have been expecting? He came, and his name was Jesus, and he was truly the Son of God." And that message is still applicable to unbelieving Jews and non-Jews today.

JOHN 21

C. THE RESURRECTION OF JESUS (20:1–21:25) CONTINUED

The resurrection appearances in chapter 20 take place in Jerusalem, those in chapter 21 in Galilee. This follows the pattern of the Synoptic Gospel accounts.[1] The actual material of this chapter is unique to John, although Luke includes a story similar to the miraculous catch of fish but in an entirely different context (Luke 5:1-11).

Some scholars have argued that chapter 21 is a later addition to the Fourth Gospel, primarily because 20:30-31 is such a fitting climax to the book. In these cases chapter 21 will be treated as an afterthought, or as a supplement added by later editors. There is, however, no manuscript evidence or tradition that the Fourth Gospel ever existed without chapter 21. Not allowing the author to make additional comments after the conclusion of 20:30-31 is an inappropriate application of modern standards to an ancient writing. This also misses what seems to me to be the intended presentation scheme of John. He clearly states his purpose of bringing the reader to faith at the end of chapter 20, but chapter 21 serves to issue the final challenge to faith, "Follow me!" For this reason, we conclude that it is an intended part of the original composition of the Apostle John.

---

[1]See, for example, Matthew 28:10, where the resurrected Jesus directs the disciples to meet him in Galilee, and Matthew 28:16, where they go there. Mark 16:7 also mentions a return to Galilee, although without further detail. Admittedly, Luke's account does not mention a return to Galilee, instead keeping the action in the vicinity of Jerusalem. However, in Luke's second volume, the book of Acts, he does mention that the resurrection appearances lasted for 40 days (Acts 1:3), leaving ample time for a journey to Galilee and back to Jerusalem.

6. Jesus' Appearance to Seven Disciples and
the Great Haul of Fish (21:1-14)

[1]Afterward Jesus appeared again to his disciples, by the Sea of Tiberias.[a] It happened this way: [2]Simon Peter, Thomas (called Didymus), Nathanael from Cana in Galilee, the sons of Zebedee, and two other disciples were together. [3]"I'm going out to fish," Simon Peter told them, and they said, "We'll go with you." So they went out and got into the boat, but that night they caught nothing.

[4]Early in the morning, Jesus stood on the shore, but the disciples did not realize that it was Jesus.

[5]He called out to them, "Friends, haven't you any fish?"

"No," they answered.

[6]He said, "Throw your net on the right side of the boat and you will find some." When they did, they were unable to haul the net in because of the large number of fish.

[7]Then the disciple whom Jesus loved said to Peter, "It is the Lord!" As soon as Simon Peter heard him say, "It is the Lord," he wrapped his outer garment around him (for he had taken it off) and jumped into the water. [8]The other disciples followed in the boat, towing the net full of fish, for they were not far from shore, about a hundred yards.[b] [9]When they landed, they saw a fire of burning coals there with fish on it, and some bread.

[10]Jesus said to them, "Bring some of the fish you have just caught."

[11]Simon Peter climbed aboard and dragged the net ashore. It was full of large fish, 153, but even with so many the net was not torn. [12]Jesus said to them, "Come and have breakfast." None of the disciples dared ask him, "Who are you?" They knew it was the Lord. [13]Jesus came, took the bread and gave it to them, and did the same with the fish. [14]This was now the third time Jesus appeared to his disciples after he was raised from the dead.

[a]1 That is, Sea of Galilee   [b]8 Greek *about two hundred cubits* (about 90 meters)

21:1. In John's account we are not told why the disciples return to Galilee. It seems quite a natural thing to do, since they are all

Galileans.[2] John sets the scene by placing the group on the shore of the **Sea of Tiberias** (the Sea of Galilee, see 6:1).

The word translated **appeared** is a significant theological term. It is the Greek verb φανερόω (*phaneroō*) and means to "reveal" or "show." It is often used in a context of divine revelation (see comments at 17:6). In this verse John is saying, "Jesus revealed himself." This is language usually reserved for God and marks the high Christology John maintains, particularly after the resurrection. The verb *phaneroō* is used in a similar way again in 21:14 to serve as an *inclusio* and bracket this section.

21:2. The cast of characters numbers seven: Peter, Thomas, Nathanael (not mentioned since 1:49), the sons of Zebedee (James and John), and two other disciples. These other two may be Andrew (Peter's fisherman brother) and Philip (Nathanael's good friend). This is merely speculation on our part, but makes even more sense if we remember that Philip and Andrew are linked elsewhere in John (see 6:7-9; 12:22).[3] The listing of these seven is a good way for John, the author, to be included as an eyewitness without drawing attention to himself.

21:3-4. Perhaps after the disciples have a round of "What do you want to do?" "I don't know, what do you want to do?" the restless Peter announces that he will do something familiar and reliable: go fishing. This is not the casting of line and hook from the shore, but boat fishing with a net. A boat is found and the seven go out onto the lake. Fishing on the Sea of Galilee was often done at night (see Luke 5:5), perhaps because it was usually a more successful time, but more likely because the fresh fish would then be ready for sale in the early morning. The fishing expedition may have supplied a diversion and companionship, but little else because no fish

---

[2]The one possible non-Galilean among the 12 was Judas Iscariot. He has vanished from John's narrative, although his disappearance is unexplained in the Fourth Gospel.

[3]The very end of the second century *Gospel of Peter* seems to begin this same story of fishing after the resurrection, but the text breaks off abruptly while the narrator is still introducing the cast of characters (the ending of the book having been lost). This introduction mentions Andrew and Levi (Matthew), leading some to conclude that they may have been the two unidentified disciples of John 21:2.

are caught. At first light the fishers see a person watching them from the shore. It is Jesus, but a hidden Jesus (cf. 20:14).

21:5-6. The boat is near enough to the shore that the man on the shore is able to converse with the boat crew (v. 8 indicates 100 yards). The Greek word he uses to address them is παιδία (*paidia*, a plural form of παιδίον, *paidion*). The NIV misses the meaning of this word rather widely by translating it as **friends**. *Paidion* is a diminutive of the word παῖς (*pais*), which is used for a minor household member, usually a child but sometimes a slave. The diminutive *paidion*, then, means "little child."[4] Jesus' call to the boat has the sense of "Hey kids! Did you catch anything?"

The fishermen admit their failure without embellishment. They are directed to cast the net one more time, this time to starboard (**the right side**). This is the opposite side from where they had been casting, and probably the side of the boat facing away from shore. Ancient fishing on this lake was not done with huge drag nets used by modern fishing boats to scoop up every living thing even hundreds of feet deep. Their nets were relatively small and useful only in comparatively shallow water. Standard practice would have been to cast the net between the boat and the shore. But when they follow the "stranger's" directions, the catch of fish is so enormous and heavy that it cannot be landed in the boat.

21:7-8. John, the author mildly disguised as the beloved disciple, quickly puts this all together. He interprets the size of the catch as more than fisherman's good fortune; it is miraculous. The man on the shore who directed this miracle can be none other than Jesus. He quickly relays this conclusion to the more slow thinking Peter, **"It is the Lord."**[5] This is a confession of faith, "It is the Risen Lord!" The one who multiplied fish and bread in chapter 6 is still working miracles for the disciples.

---

[4]*Paidion* as a word used to address one's disciples apparently was favored by John himself in his later years. He uses it in 1 John 2:18 to address all the readers of that book (translated by the NIV as "dear children"). Brown's suggestion that the plural *paidia* be translated "lads" here is relatively accurate but sounds hopelessly British for American ears (Brown, *John*, 2:1074).

[5]For analysis of John's use of the term "Lord" (*kyrios*) in this context, see the discussion above at 20:28.

Peter, the career fisherman, is so startled by Jesus' presence that he forgets what is undoubtedly one of the greatest catches of fish he has ever seen. He cinches up his clothes and dives into the water in order to swim to the Lord. This would be something like a real estate agent hopping in her car and driving away the minute before closing the sale on a million dollar house. John adds several eyewitness details to give authenticity to the narrative. He says that Peter is "naked" (KJV, NRSV). The Greek word used to describe Peter's state of dress is γυμνός (gymnos), which literally means "naked," but not necessarily "completely naked." It could be used to describe someone who was inadequately clothed.[6] The NASB translation, "stripped for work," gives an accurate version of John's intended meaning here.

The author also gives a good word picture of the process of getting the marvelous catch to the shore. The narrator's perspective remains in the boat, again pointing to the eyewitness author.[7] Despite Peter's desertion, the remaining six fishermen maintain the presence of mind to tow the net to the shore. In this way they avoid breaking their net or swamping the boat.

21:9-13. When they arrive on shore, Jesus again proves to be in control of the situation. A fire is ready for cooking, having burned down to **coals**. Already upon the fire are some ὀψάριον (opsarion), probably fish fillets (see notes at 6:9). Fish fillets can be quickly cooked if laid directly on a bed of coals, skin side down. Combined with the bread (ἄρτος, artos) Jesus has provided, we have the same two ingredients found at the multiplication of loaves in chapter 6, with the author even using the same terms. The parallel between these two incidents becomes even more marked in verse 13, where Jesus takes the bread and the fish fillets and distributes them (cf. 6:11). But this time something new is added. The disciples are able to provide an abundance of fish through their own miraculous catch.

Obviously Jesus has provided a hot breakfast for these men who have worked all night, but there is more going on in this story. It

---

[6]See 2 Corinthians 11:27 where Paul uses the cognate word γυμνότης (gymnotēs) to describe a condition of inadequate clothing which causes him to suffer from cold weather. He is obviously not referring to complete nakedness.

[7]Carson, *The Gospel According to John*, p. 671.

has the sense of "passing the baton" to the disciples. Before they were dependent upon Jesus to multiply fish. Now, through the miraculous grace of God, they multiply the fish themselves. The expansion of the ministry of Jesus will be dependent upon them, although empowered by God. In his ministry Jesus multiplied believers. Through the apostles' future ministry, believers will continue to be multiplied. This story provides another way of saying, "As the Father has sent me, I am sending you" (20:21).

There are a couple of eyewitness details in this section that deserve special notice. First, John carefully records the number of **large fish** in the net as 153. These are Sea of Galilee fish, perhaps the perch-like *tilapia* that inhabit this freshwater lake today. Tilapia easily grow to 2 lbs. in weight, so John's description may imply fish that are 3-5 pounds. If so, one can understand why the net was so heavy, perhaps 500-700 lbs. of fish. This would have been a small fortune for these fishermen, for whom a few dozen fish would have been a good catch.

Is there any significance to the number 153? Christian authors have found symbolic meaning in this number for centuries. Cyril of Alexandria, writing in the fifth century, imagined that 100 represented the Gentiles saved, 50 the remnant of the Jews saved (2:1 ratio), and 3 was the Trinity. Augustine, also writing in the fifth century, supposed that 153 represented the law and grace. This was because the sum of all the numbers between 1 and 17 is 153 (1+2+3+... 17=153). The number 17 could be broken down to 10 (Ten Commandments = Law) and to 7 (the number for grace). Jerome, another fifth century writer, claimed that 153 was the number of known species of fish (in his day), so the story symbolized that someday persons from all nations would come to Christ. While these explanations are imaginative and entertaining, it is more likely that John includes this detail because he was there. Someone took the time to count the exact number of fish, and the remarkable number was burned in his memory forever. This is a great fish story that involves an exact number, not the hands spread to indicate the size of a whopper and spreading further as the years go by.

Another detail that should be noted is the continuing inability of the disciples to recognize Jesus by sight. In verse 12 the author indicates that they all **knew it was the Lord**, yet there is still a lingering question of identity. Some still feel an impulse to ask, **"Who are you?"** This may be intended to tell the readers that Jesus' appearance is somehow different, although we are not given a hint as to what the difference might be.

21:14. The author finishes this section by summarizing what has happened since the resurrection. The miraculous catch of fish and breakfast fellowship are the third time the Risen Lord has appeared to a group of disciples, and it will be the last time in the Fourth Gospel. This is the only time after the resurrection that John refers to Jesus' having been **raised from the dead** (but see 2:22). On the expression **Jesus appeared,** see comments on 21:1.

7. Jesus' Admonition to Peter about Peter (21:15-19)

[15]**When they had finished eating, Jesus said to Simon Peter, "Simon son of John, do you truly love me more than these?"**

"Yes, Lord," he said, "you know that I love you."

Jesus said, "Feed my lambs."

[16]**Again Jesus said, "Simon son of John, do you truly love me?"**

He answered, "Yes, Lord, you know that I love you."

Jesus said, "Take care of my sheep."

[17]**The third time he said to him, "Simon son of John, do you love me?"**

Peter was hurt because Jesus asked him the third time, "Do you love me?" He said, "Lord, you know all things; you know that I love you."

Jesus said, "Feed my sheep. [18]**I tell you the truth, when you were younger you dressed yourself and went where you wanted; but when you are old you will stretch out your hands, and someone else will dress you and lead you where you do not want to go."** [19]**Jesus said this to indicate the kind of death by which Peter would glorify God. Then he said to him, "Follow me!"**

21:15-17. This section is one of the most well known and frequently preached sections in John. Before plunging in to it, a few preliminary observations are in order.

A great deal has been made over the difference between the two words used for "love" in this passage. The verbs are ἀγαπάω (*agapaō*) and φιλέω (*phileō*). Many times we have been told that *agapaō* is reserved for a superior, Godlike love, whereas *phileō* is a lesser, friendship love. *Agapaō* is supposed to mean "I love you unreservedly," whereas *phileō* merely means, "I like you a lot." Those who are tempted to build a sermon on this distinction would do well to read the comments of D.A. Carson in his little book, *Exegetical Fallacies*.[8] Carson makes the point that "there is nothing intrinsic to the verb ἀγαπάω or the noun ἀγάπη to prove its real meaning or hidden meaning refers to some special kind of love."[9]

Jesus' conversation with Peter in verses 15-17 uses these two verbs in this way:

Round #1. Jesus: "Do you love (*agapaō*) me? Peter: "Yes I love (*phileō*) you."

Round #2. Jesus: "Do you love (*agapaō*) me? Peter: "Yes I love (*phileō*) you."

Round #3. Jesus: "Do you love (*phileō*) me? Peter: "Yes I love (*phileō*) you."

Those observing this shift and assuming it to be significant interpret this passage in a manner similar to this: Twice Jesus asks Peter if he loves him unreservedly. Twice Peter answers that he likes Jesus a lot. The third time Jesus asks Peter if he even likes him. Peter is upset, and repeats that he really, really, really does like Jesus. This interpretation assumes that the repeated questioning of Peter is an attempt by Jesus to get him to deliver the correct response, "Lord, I love (*agapaō*) you." Peter's responses reveal either a high degree of insensitivity or a candid admission of a lack of genuine love for Jesus.

This interpretation should be rejected on at least three counts. First, if Peter's responses are inadequate, this inadequacy would be news to both Peter and the author. Peter is completely unaware of any slight in his answers, so much so that the third question

---

[8]D.A. Carson, *Exegetical Fallacies* (Grand Rapids: Baker, 1984). See particularly pp. 30, 51-54.

[9]Carson, *Fallacies*, p. 30. One of Carson's primary examples is that John 3:35 uses *agapaō* to indicate the love the Father has for the Son, whereas John 5:20 has the same idea using the verb *phileō*.

wounds him deeply, and the author fails to offer any explanation. Second, the author is apparently oblivious to the variation in meaning between these two verbs. This is shown when in verse 17 he summarizes all three questions of Jesus as being "Do you love (*phileō*) me?" Third, this interpretation fails to propose any reason for the threefold questioning of Jesus. If the intent of Jesus is to get Peter to say, "Yes I love (*agapaō*) you" (in effect to get Peter to capitulate to him), Jesus has failed without comment.[10]

If this is not a stylistic gem playing upon the shades of meaning between two Greek verbs, then what is going on here? We can better answer this question if we return the passage to its context within John.

After breakfast is over, Jesus and Peter apparently go for a walk in semi-privacy (see v. 20, where the beloved disciple is "following"). There has been no such intimate moment between Jesus and Peter since the resurrection, and Jesus has an important piece of business to take care of: the triple denials of Peter during Jesus' interrogation at the high priest's house (18:15-18,25-28). Peter is eager to make things right with Jesus, as shown by his dive from the boat and swim to shore (v. 7). Although at first Peter does not understand what Jesus is doing, Jesus now gives him three opportunities to confess his love. This is a trying time for Peter, for by the third question he must have understood the connection to his three denials. This is why the author makes the point that **Peter was hurt because Jesus asked him the third time**. *Three times! He knows I denied him not once, but **three times!***

Having that out of the way, Jesus proceeds to what he must give Peter. He gives Peter two things in this passage. First, he gives him a work: to be the shepherd of Christ's sheep, to feed Christ's lambs. This is a charge that Peter accepts and follows for the rest of his life, if we are to judge by 1 Peter 5:1-2. Here the aged Peter charges his "fellow elders" to follow his example and be shepherds of God's

---

[10]An extremely thorough analysis of the potential difference between these two verbs is to be found in Hendriksen, *Exposition*, 2:494-500. In the end, however, Hendriksen decides that while the difference is slight, it is important. The flaw in Hendriksen's argument, however, is that he is more concerned with historical precedents for these verbs than the actual context in John.

flock![11] Peter's task (and the task of a church elder/pastor) is more
than just *saving the lost*. It includes *nurturing the saved*. Peter's life is
a testimony that he loved Jesus and his sheep **more than these**
things, presumably more than nets, boats, and the other familiar
tools of fishing.

21:18-19. A second thing Jesus "gives" to Peter in this passage is
another prophecy of his future (cf. 13:38). As Dr. Bryant preached,
"He gave him a cross." Tradition dating back to the end of the first
century (Clement of Rome) places Peter's death in Rome during
the persecutions of Nero (AD 64-68). Origen, writing at the beginning of the third century, reports the tradition that "Peter was crucified at Rome with his head downwards, as he himself had desired
to suffer."[12] John, writing at a time when Peter's death at Rome was
15 years or more in the past and probably known to his readers,
understands that Jesus' words are prophetic of Peter's future. He
will die and **glorify God**. This is pictured by Jesus' description of
Peter's future. Jesus tells Peter that in his old age, **"You will stretch
out your hands** [on a cross]." This will be accompanied by his state
of captivity and humiliation.

Jesus has one last thing to say to Peter, **"Follow me."** This sets the
tone for the final section of the book. It also acts as *inclusio* bracketing. Jesus' ministry begins with a call to Philip to "Follow me" (1:43).
It ends with a renewed call to Peter, "Follow me" (21:19, 22).

8. Jesus' Admonition to Peter about John (21:20-23)

**[20]Peter turned and saw that the disciple whom Jesus loved was
following them. (This was the one who had leaned back against
Jesus at the supper and had said, "Lord, who is going to betray
you?") [21]When Peter saw him, he asked, "Lord, what about him?"**

---

[11]Although verses 15-17 have occasionally been used by Roman Catholic
apologists to establish the primacy of Peter and therefore primacy of the
bishop of Rome (the pope), there is no indication in the text that John has
any intention of using this story for this purpose.

[12]Origen's comment is recorded by Eusebius, *Church History*, 2.1.
Eusebius is usually reliable and compiled this history during the first half
of the fourth century.

22Jesus answered, "If I want him to remain alive until I return, what is that to you? You must follow me." 23Because of this, the rumor spread among the brothers that this disciple would not die. But Jesus did not say that he would not die; he only said, "If I want him to remain alive until I return, what is that to you?"

21:20-22. Peter will not allow it to end this simply, though. He turns and sees John **following**, perhaps eavesdropping. John identifies himself as the one who asked Jesus, **"Lord, who is going to betray you?"** We should remember that in the narrative, Peter may have seen himself as the betrayer (see comments at 13:36-38 and 18:27). It is likely that John may have been a witness to, or at least known about, the three denials. So rather than accept Jesus' prophecy and challenge, Peter asks, "What about him?" Peter must learn that one's relationship to Christ is not defined by pointing to other people. Jesus' response, in effect, is "Mind your own business! Your call is to follow me." Following Jesus must be an individual decision.

Dietrich Bonhoeffer, the twentieth-century Christian martyr, understood this well. In his book, *The Cost of Discipleship*, Bonhoeffer said:

> The cross is laid on every Christian. The first Christ-suffering which every man must experience is the call to abandon the attachments of this world. It is that dying of the old man which is the result of his encounter with Christ. As we embark upon discipleship we surrender ourselves to Christ in union with his death — we give over our lives to death . . . . Suffering, then, is the badge of true discipleship. The disciple is not above his master.

Bonhoeffer followed the call to the end. He was executed by the Nazis in Flossenburg prison, April 9, 1945, just hours before its liberation by the Allied forces. He did what he could to be a pastor for believers, even while in prison. He followed Jesus even at the cost of his own life.

By now it must be clear to the readers that Jesus is talking to them, too. **"Follow me!"** John's Jesus commands. No excuses, no delays. Don't try to postpone your decision by judging other

Christians. Jesus' call is for you, "Follow me!" This is the call to faith that constitutes the primary purpose of the book (20:31).

21:23. After Peter's final lesson is completed, the author speaks to correct a mistaken legend that was circulating in the early church during his lifetime. Apparently the story had been perpetuated that Jesus promised John that he would be alive at Christ's Second Coming. But a close reading shows that this is not what Jesus said at all. He is merely using John as a foil for Peter's objection. Even if Peter dies on a cross and John is still alive at the Second Coming, it makes no difference. Peter must still heed the command, "Follow me."

There are two possible reasons the author felt it necessary to comment on the rumor of John's supposedly supernatural longevity. First, it is possible that some had interpreted this statement to Peter as a promise of immortality for John, that he would never die. It is probable that John did live to be a very old man by ancient standards, well into his 80s. But he well knew that he was not immortal and wanted to verify that with his readers. A second possibility is that these last few verses were added after his death. Suppose for a minute that first-century Christians believed John was promised he would live until the Second Coming of Christ. This is no problem as long as he is alive, but a big problem when he dies. Many would be disappointed and even lose faith. It would have been important, therefore, to correct this false teaching.

9. Testimony to the Truthfulness of the Contents of the Fourth Gospel (21:24)

²⁴This is the disciple who testifies to these things and who wrote them down. We know that his testimony is true.

21:24. The book ends appropriately with a personal note from the author. He is the beloved disciple, and the book rests upon his eyewitness testimony. A further note comes from the editorial committee or "Johannine community" which may have had a hand in bringing this book to its final form. They add a simple endorsement, **We know that his testimony is true.**

10. The Selective Nature of the Contents of the Fourth Gospel (21:25)

[25]Jesus did many other things as well. If every one of them were written down, I suppose that even the whole world would not have room for the books that would be written.

The book ends on a striking note of hyperbole. The author wants the reader to know that only a small sample of the marvelous deeds of Jesus has been recorded. He has already given his criteria for selection, "these [miraculous signs] are written that you may believe" (20:31). He ends with an expression of human inadequacy. We can never know or appreciate Christ enough. The splendor of Christ surpasses and eludes our senses and abilities or capacities. The Gospel of John ends with Christ's triumphs, his power, and his grace.